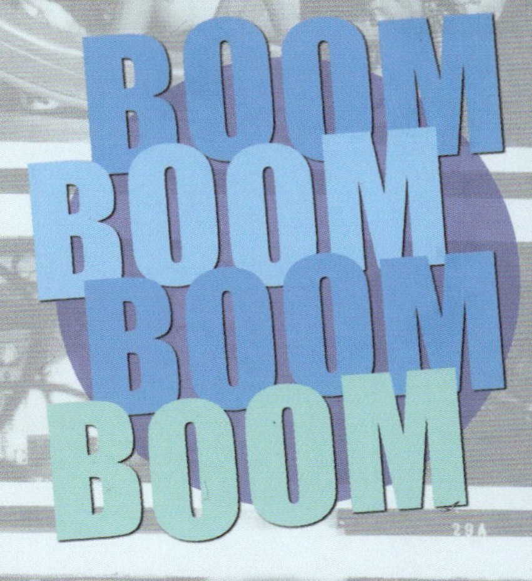

THE AMERICAN RHYTHM & BLUES PHOTOGRAPHS OF

BRIAN SMITH

ENGLAND 1962 - 1966

SIMON ROBINSON

EASYONTHEEYEBOOKS

CONTENTS

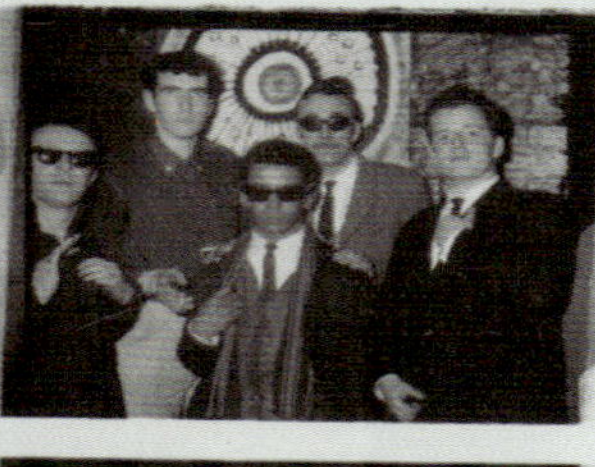

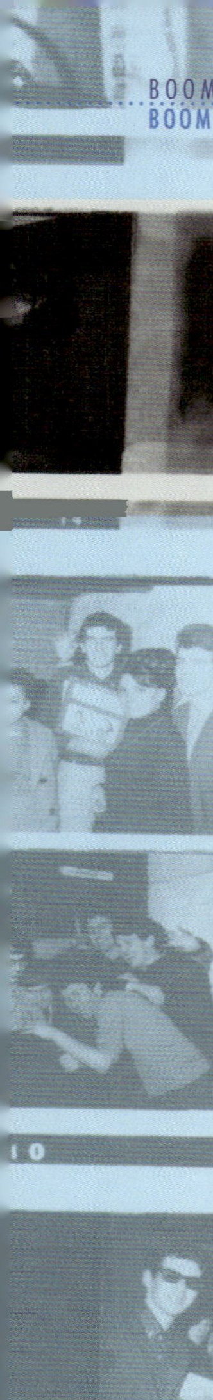

Front cover: Johnny Guitar Watson, April 1965 at the Twisted Wheel Club. Inset left to right: Screaming Jay Hawkins and Brian Smith; Little Richard; Buddy Guy.

This page right: Chuck Berry (details page 33).

Above: negative contact sheet with Brian Smith on the right, Roger Eagle back left, inside The Twisted Wheel Club.

Previous page: A business card for Dave Waggett, Art Editor at R & B Scene Magazine, adapted to show Brian Smith's credentials. He used to show these at the door or when applying to hall managers for permission to interview musicians and take photographs.

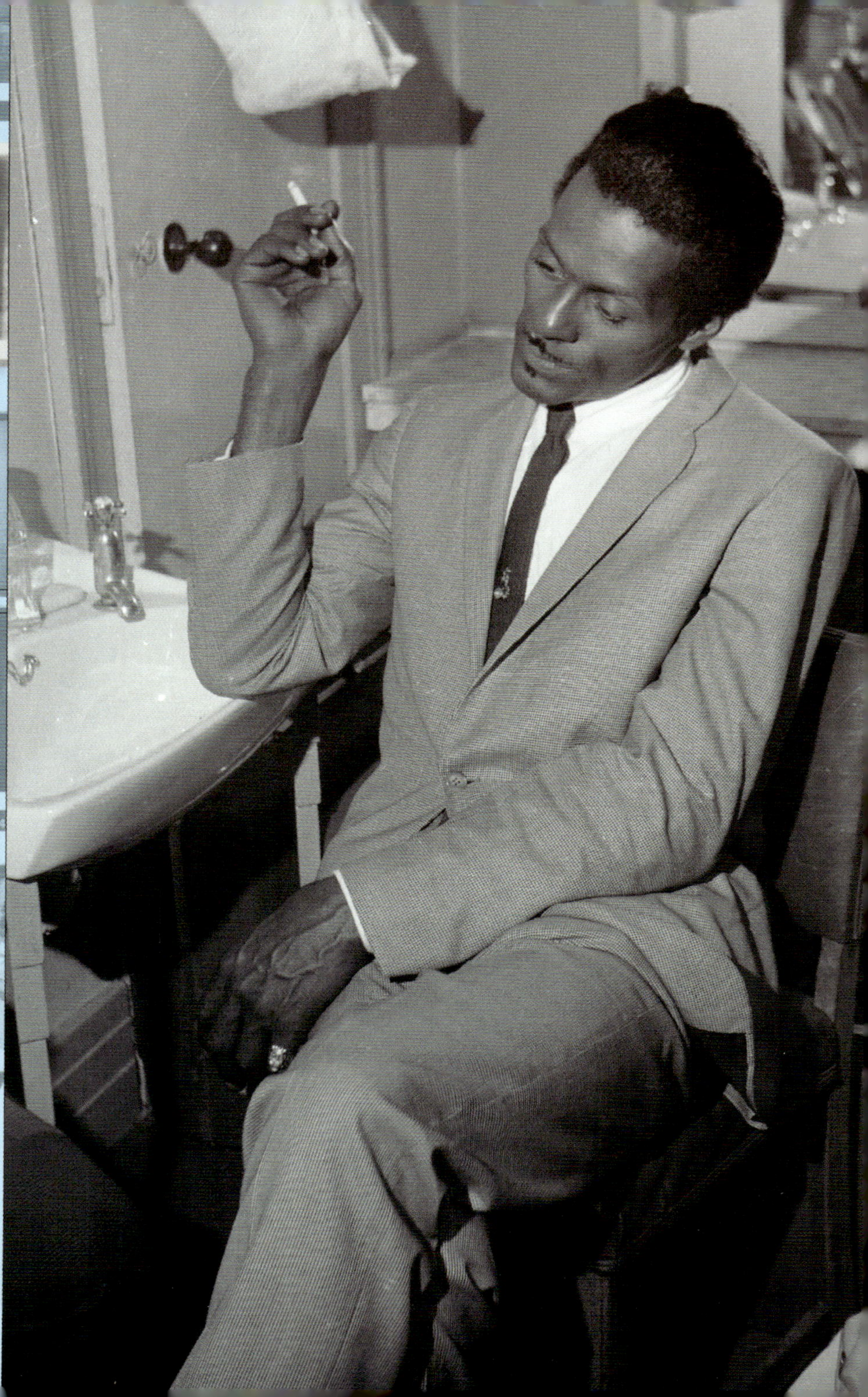

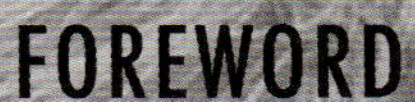

FOREWORD

"Boom, boom, boom, boom, I'm gonna shoot you right down."

If you're immediately thinking 'John Lee Hooker', go to the top of the class – or rather to page 69 of this remarkable book, where you can see JLH onstage at Manchester's Free Trade Hall during his first visit to Britain in 1962 and backstage at the same city's Twisted Wheel club a couple of years later. It's one of the fascinating aspects of this book that, as arresting as the performance photographs are (sometimes almost incredibly close to the action – check out Little Walter and Little Richard) the backstage, offstage and rehearsal shots take us to another, more intimate, place entirely. It's the difference between a timeline and in-depth investigation.

Apart from some quite glitzy photographs of Muddy Waters, Howling Wolf and Jimmy Reed, and certainly one very well-used one of John Lee Hooker, there's not a lot here that any of the artists (or their managers or agents) would pick out for use as promotional material – but they tell us so much. I would recommend that you don't 'flip' through this volume as if it were this month's issue of a magazine, but dwell on each image as you come to it. What is the great Chicago blues drummer Fred Below saying to Robert Pete Williams? What is Chuck Berry's expression telling us in that picture of him at a post-gig Chinese restaurant with the guys from R & B Scene and his fan club? What is coming to bring their music to Europe like for people who've spent little or no time out of America in their lives? Muddy, Wolf and Memphis Slim all had previous experience of Europe, but for many of these artists, these were uncharted waters.

I think it's fair to point out that this book is celebrating more than the photography of Brian Smith. His work also puts the spotlight on two venues in particular, the aforementioned Manchester Free Trade Hall and the Twisted Wheel, and two events, or rather strings of events: the American Folk Blues Festivals, and the musical output of Granada Television – especially programmes directed by Johnnie Hamp. Brian's talents manoeuvred him into all of these situations and more, and turning these pages brings constant reminders of how strong and vibrant the music scene was in Manchester in those times.

My own personal experience of some of these great stars of the blues began with Memphis Slim, whom I interviewed for Oxford Opinion magazine. That was published on the 3rd of June 1961; I was reintroduced to him by Humphrey Lyttelton backstage at the first AFBF tour a year later, and then I didn't see him again until a live recording I played on for him in 1986.

T-Bone Walker I met at the Marquee Club's recording studio in London; we later had a very pleasant evening at the actress and singer Queenie Watts' house in Essex, and he was kind enough to invite me to his home in Los Angeles – which I took advantage of when The Manfreds were in the US. For me, it was definitely one of the highlights of that tour.

The great Otis Spann and Matt "Guitar" Murphy came down to the Marquee to sit in with us on what must have been a day off from that year's (1963) AFBF. I cherished that! But the only one I wrote a tribute song about was Sonny Boy Williamson. His lifestyle and his dress sense were a matter of opinion, but he could be a poetic songwriter, and his harmonica playing was sublime. Brian's camera caught all aspects of his personality – and of so many more of the multifarious cast of characters we can feast our eyes on in this riveting book.

Thank you, Brian!

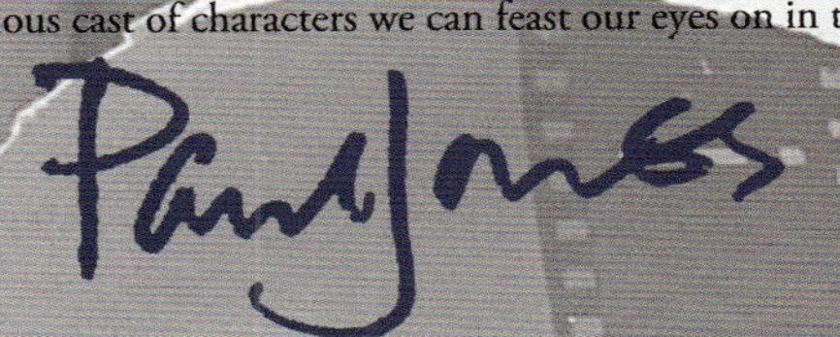

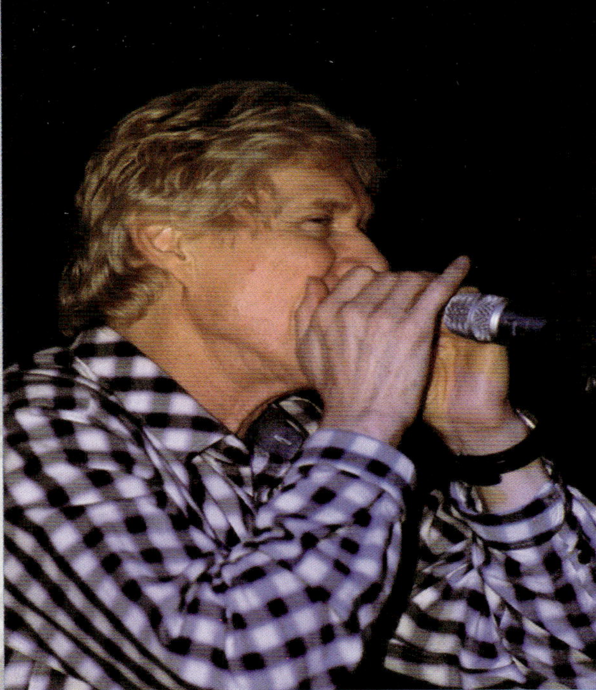

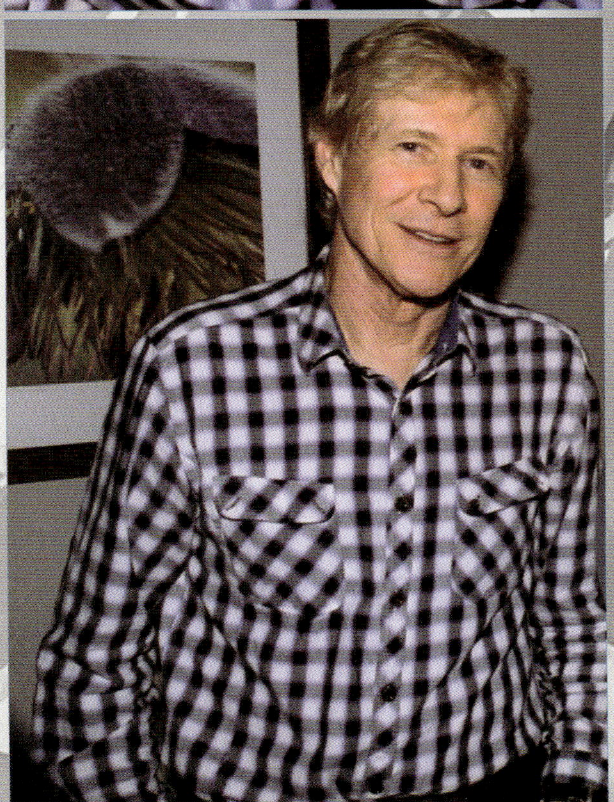

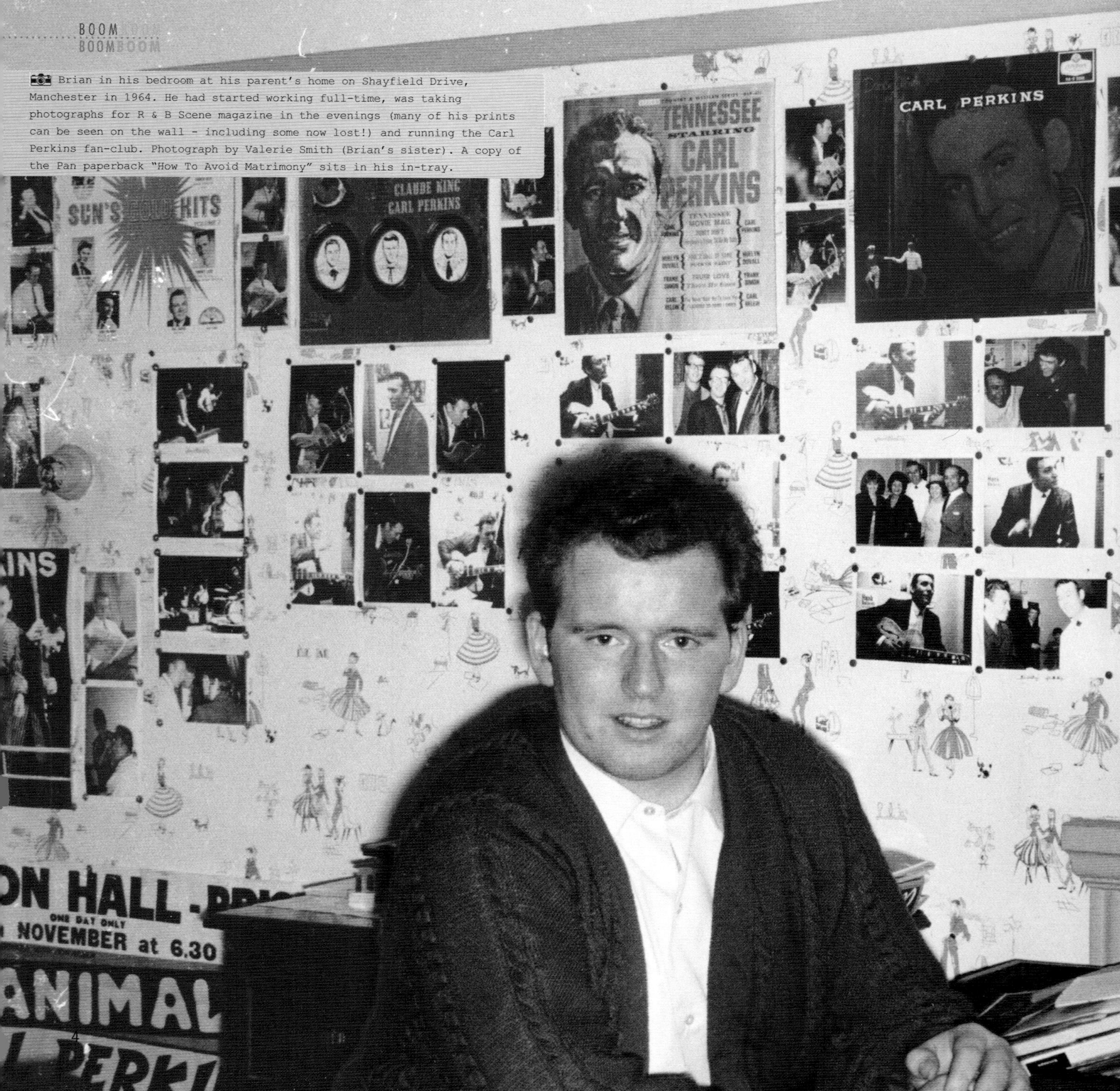

Brian in his bedroom at his parent's home on Shayfield Drive, Manchester in 1964. He had started working full-time, was taking photographs for R & B Scene magazine in the evenings (many of his prints can be seen on the wall - including some now lost!) and running the Carl Perkins fan-club. Photograph by Valerie Smith (Brian's sister). A copy of the Pan paperback "How To Avoid Matrimony" sits in his in-tray.

4

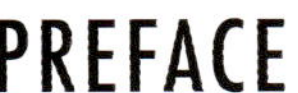

PREFACE

Where once it was a case of trying not to stand behind someone tall at a music concert, today most gig goers have to peer through a sea of mobile phone screens to catch a glimpse of what is happening on stage. At one recent rock show I was baffled to see three people stood next to each other all filming the show on their phones. Never mind one of them doing it and then sharing, they seemed oblivious of the fact that just feet away a professional crew were documenting it for a DVD. I've even seen fans filming the on-screen displays... This seemingly insatiable urge to document one's path through life seems to have become a universal phenomenon over the last decade, made possible by mobile phone technology and the seductive lure of social media. The speech balloon to a Private Eye cartoon of a chap capturing a concert on his phone summed it up: *"I'll experience the reality later...."*

How then did music fans manage before the world went digital? Did everyone drag a Kodak Box Brownie along to concerts in the Fifties? Were rock shows awash with half-frame Olympus cameras in the Sixties? The answer is most assuredly not. Apart from official photographers from the music papers or press agencies, rare enough at concerts outside London, for most popular music shows the vast majority of audience members were content to enjoy the atmosphere and the performance. And at jazz or blues shows in particular it was simply not polite to disturb your fellow concert goers by popping off flash bulbs every few minutes.

Which is why people like Brian Smith are special. Brian was one of that oft mentioned first generation of teenagers, hitting his teens in the 1950s. And like many of his generation popular music was a big part of life; album sleeves and posters adorned his bedroom wall, while pocket money went on 10" 78s and LPs. Live concerts then grabbed him, and with his mates he would try to get a few sleeves autographed at the stage door. But he took his camera with him and in doing so, unwittingly began documenting the music scene in Manchester at a pivotal moment in U.K. pop history. He became involved with

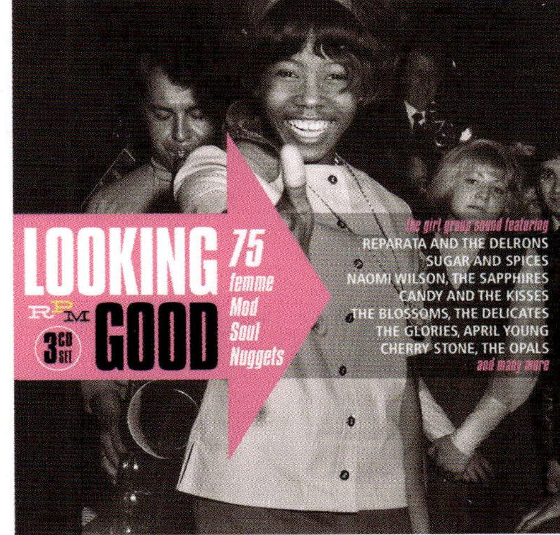

One of Brian's photographs of Millie used by RPM Records for a Mod Soul CD. Below: Brian with Georgie Fame at Buxton Opera House 2002 (photo Mike Sanchez).

perhaps Manchester's most legendary music venue, The Twisted Wheel Club, and also one of the first music magazines devoted to rhythm and blues, Manchester's R & B Scene. The photograph opposite shows Brian in his bedroom at the time, snapped by his sister, a wall almost totally covered in posters, flyers, sleeves and photographs, including some of his own.

Brian never made much money from his photography (except once, perhaps ironically

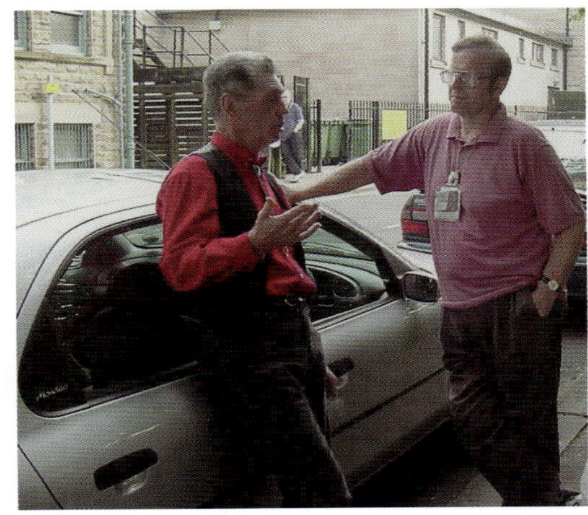

PREFACE

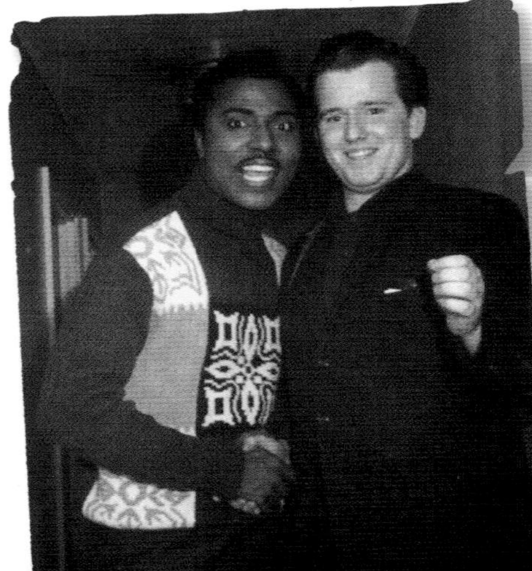

given the artists' reputation, for a Chuck Berry print!), content to see his hobby as a means to help him and his mates meet some of their musical heroes. Brian's picture taking only spanned a few years, and when he got engaged and family responsibilities arrived, he literally hung up his camera and got on with working life.

It was only in the late Seventies with pioneering labels beginning to reissue early blues material, a market given added impetus by the compact disc revolution a decade later, that people started to track Brian down. His archive was not always treated with the respect it deserved, negatives and prints on loan would sometimes be lost and even when digital scanning became possible the local photo processors didn't really know what they were handling.

Nevertheless Brian's collection of images was at last being seen as of historical value. It was in preparing some CD reissues that music consultant Mark Stratford, through his work for another pioneering reissue label Connoisseur Records (and then co-

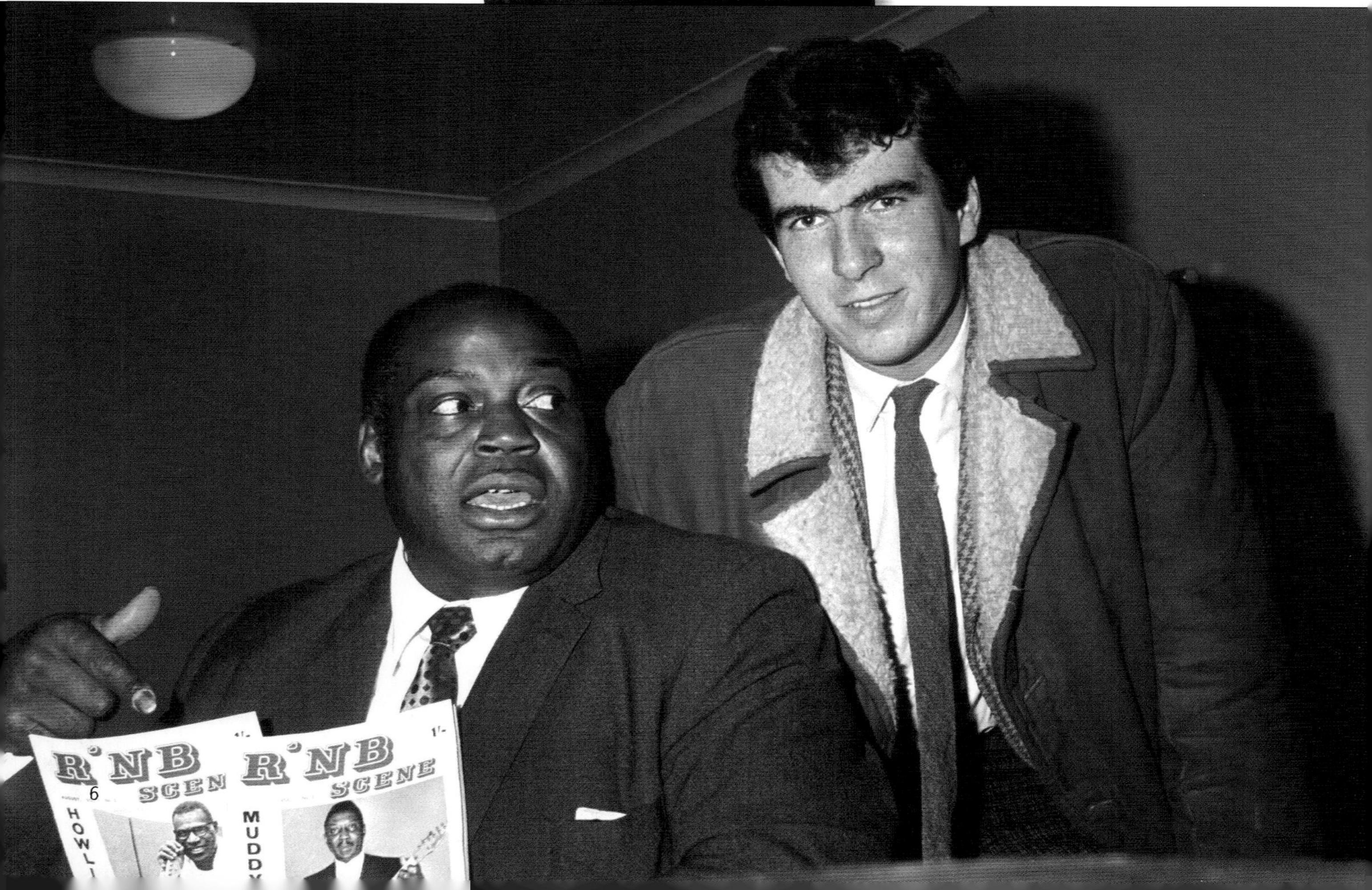

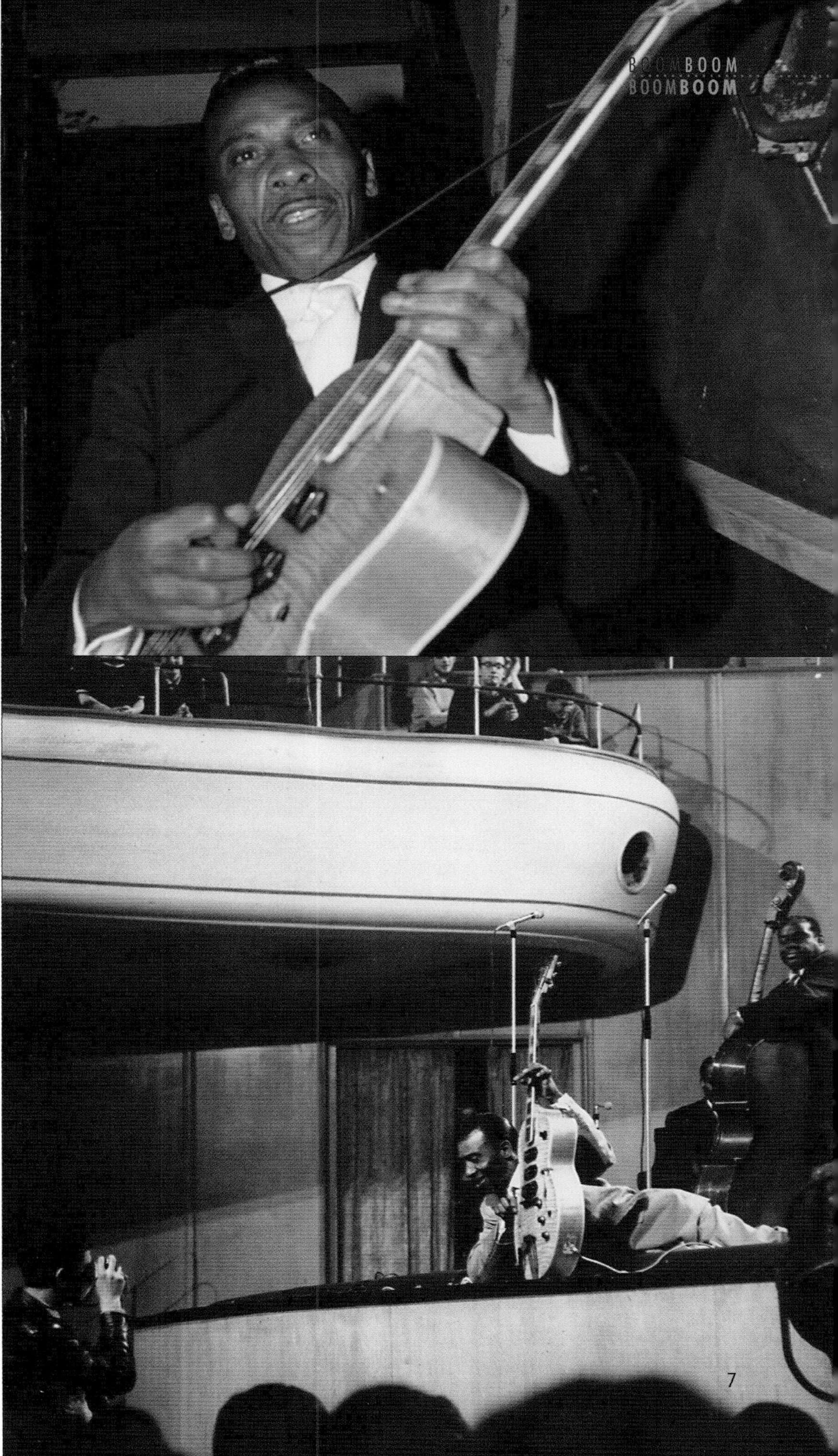

Right: T-Bone Walker at The Twisted Wheel, 1964. Below: One of Brian's first concert images, at the Manchester American Folk and Blues festival in 1962. *"I went along as I'd heard T-bone Walker played like Chuck Berry – I didn't realise it was the other way around!"*

founder with myself and rock historian Roger Dopson of the long-running RPM reissue label), came across Brian's material for the first time. He expressed surprise that nobody had ever tried to publish a proper book of the photographs and brought the idea to me.

As someone with a passionate interest in archive photography (and who as a teenager in the Seventies also tried to take pictures at concerts, so could appreciate exactly what Brian had gone through to get these images), just a brief look at some of the material confirmed that this was a project well worth attempting. Delving into the collection, working initially with Brian's existing scans and prints, it wasn't until a couple of meetings down the line that I thought to ask Brian if he had any negatives left. The next time I arrived at his house, he had filled two fraying supermarket bags full of odds and ends, and I brought these back to the Easy On The Eye office to investigate.

Inevitably this extended the time frame of the book considerably. Once I had sorted out all the negatives, some still in strips, others as individual frames, and a few patched together with masking tape (for reasons which never became clear!), I decided to go back to square one and scan everything. Despite some damage and dirt marks from hasty film processing fifty plus years ago, using a professional Nikon 4000 negative scanner it was possible to both provide Brian with a hi-res back-up and ourselves with the best possible source material. In all around 400 negatives survived. Where there were gaps, we have worked from older scans and some original prints. The wear and tear on a print or negative to me is part of the history, so we resisted the temptation to run riot with quick fix digital 'dust and scratches' filters which up close are never that great anyway. Instead photographs have been digitally retouched by hand using mainly Photoshop repair tools only where damage detracted from the overall feel of the image. So not only is this the first ever collection of Brian's material but the photographs have never looked better.

Taking its title from the John Lee Hooker classic, the book also restores many of the images which have been ripped for the web often uncredited and in terrible quality. And it gives us a glimpse of what must surely be one of the most exclusive collection of selfies around!

Based as he was in Manchester, Brian had a huge choice of concerts but much of the selected material shows the visiting American Blues artists who most interested the young photographer, as well as some of the British musicians who also idolised them. In all well over seventy musicians are featured and most of the images come from the great local venues: the Free Trade Hall; The Odeon, ABC Apollo, The Southern Sporting Club (formerly The Corona), The Jigsaw Club (aka The Manchester Cavern), the Oasis, the Princess Theatre and of course the first Twisted Wheel Club. Brian and his friends did also venture further afield if a particular favourite was on tour and transport was available, the locations are noted in the book where identified.

It was also quite clear assembling the book that Brian had an instinctive eye for a photograph. Some are as good as anything a professional might have taken in the same situation and I'm sure that had Brian wanted to he could have taken up photography full-time. Many of the backstage photographs in particular, which became his stock in trade, where the situation was more relaxed and Brian could pick his moment, are really well composed. And as so few people were doing this at the time, the work is now of enormous interest to music fans and social historians.

While the book layout progressed I was able to quiz Brian about each and every shot and his recollections add a lot to the text and captions, and helped us to date as many as possible. I am very grateful for his patience in this regard.

The book balances the best of Brian's work of the period alongside a few shots which might not be technically perfect but capture the spirit of the times so well. Brian for example still winces about some double exposures, but to me these mistakes illustrate exactly what he was up against. Images had to be taken quickly, and often Brian only had time to take one or two of an artist in poor lighting, setting the focus manually (no SLR!), working with one of just three shutter speeds and worried the film might run out… Lesser people might have given up. Thank goodness Brian persevered and we can all now enjoy this remarkable body of work.   Sorry it took so long Brian!

Simon Robinson / Easy On The Eye Books

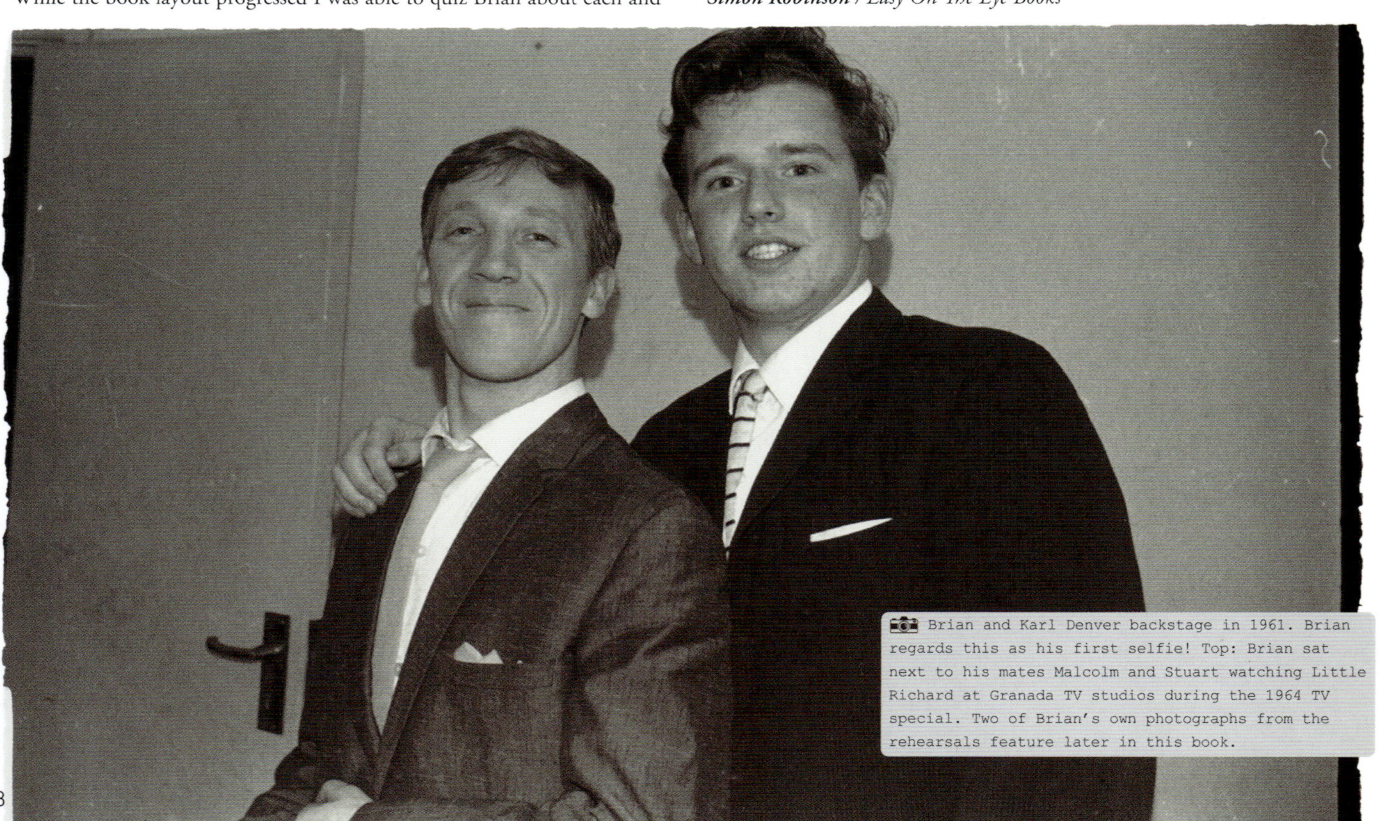

📷 Brian and Karl Denver backstage in 1961. Brian regards this as his first selfie! Top: Brian sat next to his mates Malcolm and Stuart watching Little Richard at Granada TV studios during the 1964 TV special. Two of Brian's own photographs from the rehearsals feature later in this book.

BRIAN'S STORY

Brian Smith is a Manchester lad through and through, born into the North of England's largest city in the middle of a World War, in June 1943. His parents were solid working class; Albert, a railway clerk and mum Irene, who worked as a garment machinist - the city was built on textiles. They had two children, Brian and Valerie. Manchester had long been building large swathes of new council houses to replace the Victorian slums and Albert and Irene moved into theirs on the Wythenshawe estate in 1937, living there for seventy years until their deaths (Irene in 2006 and Albert two years later).

An important industrial base and centre for war production, the city suffered from an intense aerial blitz in 1940, and continued to be bombed heavily throughout the war. Emerging from such destruction, Brian and his contemporaries experienced and enjoyed at first hand the growth of the popular music boom (and were some of those early teenagers agonised over in old news reports from the time). By the end of the Fifties, Manchester had become an important centre of popular music, thanks in part to its centre as a trading city with ship canal links to the Mersey, and rivalling Liverpool and London (a position it retained right through into the Punk era). Brian saw it happen, through big band, swing, skiffle, early rock and roll and into the blues and pop boom.

Although he had been taken by his father to his first variety show (headlined by Josh White, that's the programme on the right) when he was just eight, it was when one of the neighbourhood lads' older brother who, with his own jazz friends, took Brian and his mate along with them to a few of the early jazz shows at Manchester's Free Trade Hall around 1954 and 1955 that he got hooked. *"It was these concerts which introduced me to live music,"* Brian recalls. Bombed in the war, the Free Trade Hall interior was rebuilt to accommodate the Manchester Hallé Orchestra, but jazz and swing shows helped support the venue. Chris Barber was a regular, and always chose his guest acts with care, bringing along names like Sonny and Brownie, Rosetta and Big Bill Broonzy, some of which shows Brian was able to get to. They also hosted some of the regular pop package tours, although after violence and damage during (of all things) a Cliff Richard show, these were dropped for several years.

Lonnie Donegan was on one particular show with Chris and like other youngsters it was through skiffle that Brian began to learn about the blues. Donegan's influence at the time was considerable, reworking blues material for a new audience. Then in 1958 Barber was able to put Muddy Waters on the bill as his guest, and Brian heard the real thing for the first time as he remembers:

"Lonnie Donegan was a major milestone for me. Essentially I was a rock'n roller in the Fifties, although Donegan, Barber and Muddy were developing my other tastes alongside this. My first blues albums were Muddy At Newport and Howling Wolf which I bought in 1961, 62. I very much came to blues via Rock'n Roll and Donegan."

The Manchester Palace and the Hippodrome, home for years to variety bills, started to bring in pop and rock'n'roll acts while national promoters began to use big cinemas such as the Manchester Odeon for tours with acts like Bill Haley and The Platters as well as multi-artist packages put together by Larry Parnes and Arthur Howes. Brian saw Bill Haley at The Odeon on February 13th 1957; *"My first Rock'n Roll stage show! He may be viewed as a bit anachronistic now, but was definitely spine-tingling at the time."*

Brian suggests that 1957 was something of a pivotal year for rock and pop fans in Britain. *"I saw The Platters at Manchester Palace in April, Frankie Lymon the following week, Charlie Gracie in September (all topping variety bills). Then a Jazz and Skiffle bill at the Free Trade Hall, Freddie and The Bellboys at the same place, Lonnie Donegan, and home grown rockers like Tommy Steele and Terry Dene."*

So Brian and his school-mates weren't exactly short of choice. To feed his appetite, he would read Beat Magazine, which was mostly jazz but also had some rock and roll coverage. He added Hit Parade magazine to his reading list in the mid-Fifties and started taking the New Music Express and Disc, two of the growing number of UK weekly music papers, around 1958.

Aside from music, the Fifties also saw Brian become interested in photography. Many schools saw this as a skill worth supporting and Brian joined his senior school's photographic society in 1954, learning the basics on a Brownie 127 (a present from his Dad), Kodak's entry level amateur camera. His family hadn't owned a camera before; until 1960 his Dad just borrowed an Ensign box camera from his Aunt to take on holidays.

Brian did some printing to learn the basics and even got hold of a developing

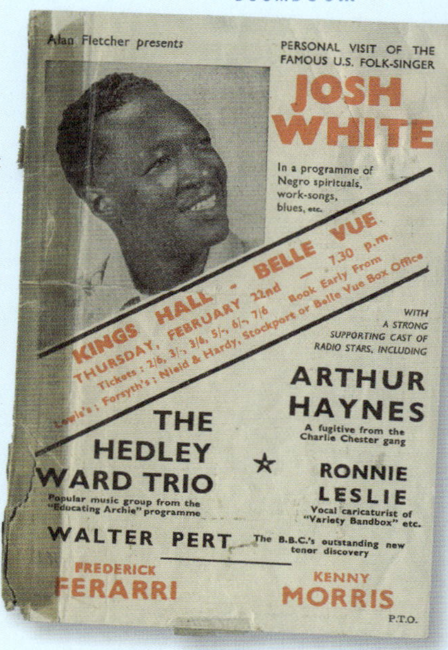

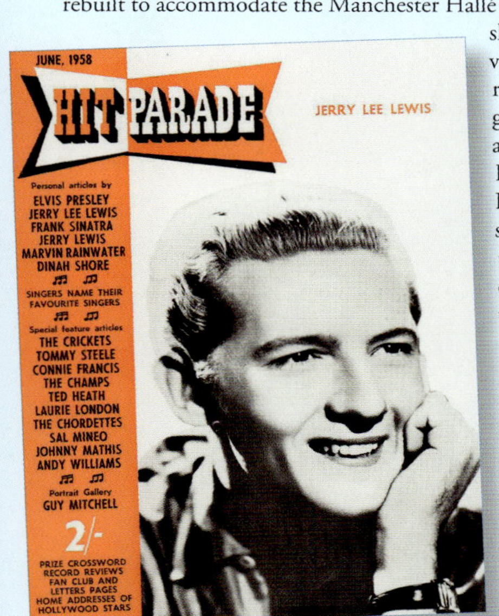

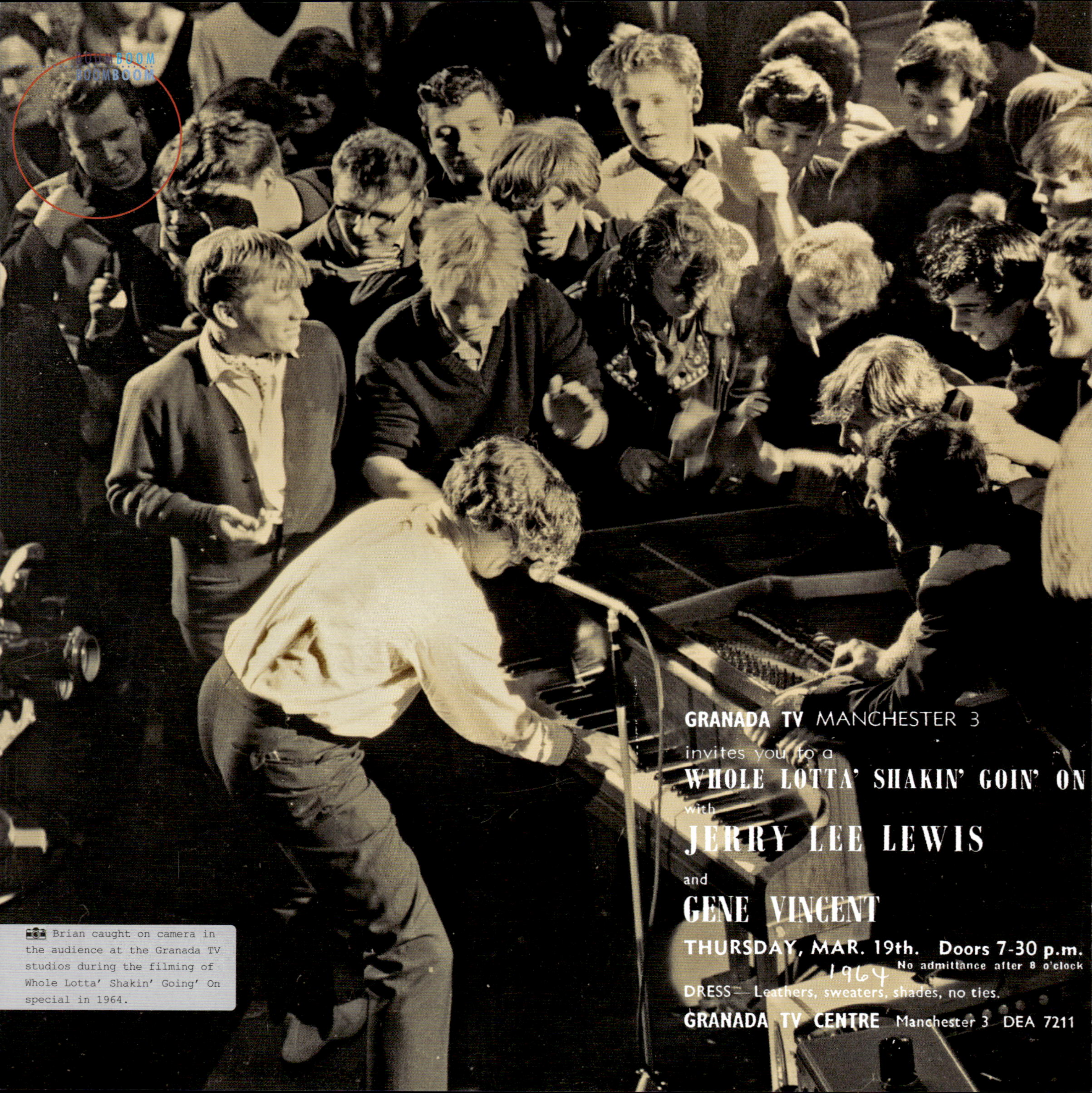

Brian caught on camera in the audience at the Granada TV studios during the filming of Whole Lotta' Shakin' Going' On special in 1964.

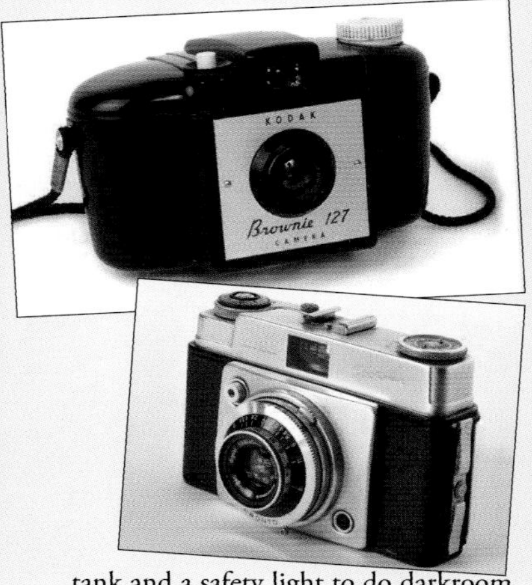

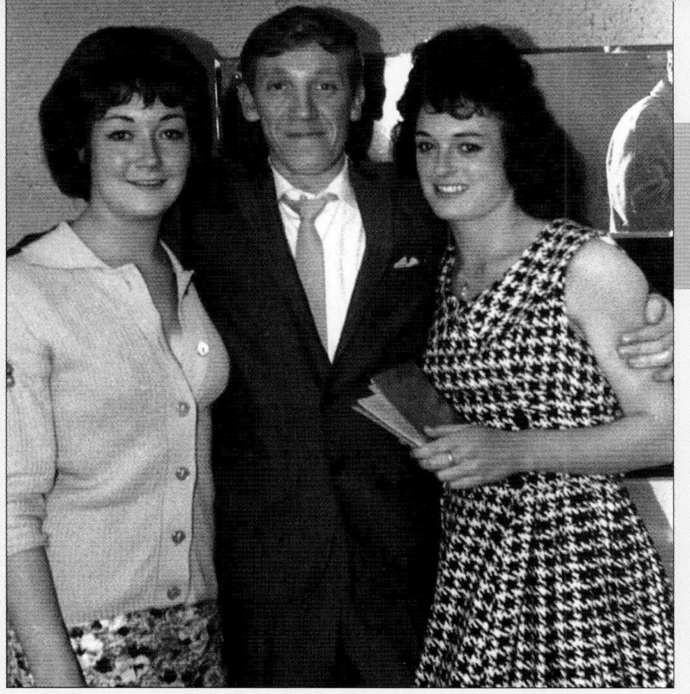

The two autograph hunters are Sheila (left) and Patsy, local Gorton sisters who frequented the Sporting Club. Sadly for fashion historians, Brian's shot of the pair and two more of their friends in matching leopard skin bikinis in Rhyl that summer have not survived.

tank and a safety light to do darkroom work at home but the chemicals and paper proved too expensive. He left school that year, kept on his summer holiday job at a grocers shop and then started in the local Manchester tax office in January 1961.

He persevered with the Brownie (top) then moved on to what he calls his first 'proper' camera, an Ilford Sportsman, again bought for him by his Dad, this time to mark his 18th birthday in June '61 (Brian's had the film advance lever as above, an 'extra').

The Sportsman had limitations, with just three shutter speeds (1/25, 1/60 and 1/200) but was synchronised for flash at any of the settings. It had an eye-level view-finder for composition only. Focus was set by working out the distance to your subject and turning the focus ring round the lens to the marker. He did try developing some 35mm film at home but it was easier to use the camera shop across the road from his office. They would develop and supply a contact strip (literally a long roll of paper with all the negatives contacted onto it), and he could order a set of small enprints cheaply at the same time as they were done on automatic processors. Anything larger would be more expensive.

With the Sportsman and a roll of Ilford black and white film (*"never been bettered"* is his opinion) costing around 6s 10d, Brian wondered for the first time about trying to take photographs at concerts. His plan was to get a decent shot or two, get them printed, then when the group were next in town he could take them to get signed.

However his first ever photo of a performer was taken at a BBC Manchester Studio performance by the Northern Dance Orchestra. *"They had singers as their weekly guests,"* Brian explains. *"They used* the Playhouse in Hulme as a live recording venue. We went because it was local and free, primarily for the music."*

Brian saw Karl Denver, Shane Fenton and others this way. The Springfields were then due at the Playhouse studios in 1961 and Brian decided to take his Sportsman along for the first time. Not thinking, he took a shot from his seat at the back of the auditorium, using a flash. Dusty Springfield hadn't been expecting this and it threw her performance, so much so that the producer had to ask for a retake of the song, to Brian's horror. *"The Producer came out and said 'would the gentleman who took the photograph please come and have a word with us afterwards?'. I was petrified! I thought I was going to have my camera confiscated so I just put it under my coat and snuck out! Later I thought if I had taken my bollocking I may even have got my photograph, and this did influence me to 'ask first' next time."*

The earliest of Brian's music photographs to survive is this one above of Karl Denver, taken in Autumn 1961. Denver enjoyed a run of yodelling pop hits in Britain from 1961 and with his trio was Manchester based so The Southern Sporting Club was a regular booking - it is said that the bar would be opened early for him when he was appearing! *"My mother worked at a factory in Sharston [Manchester] along with Jerry Cotterell's wife, who was Karl's bass player, so that got us lots of free tickets to things including a show at The Yew Tree on our estate. He had a residency there, and we visited regularly, even when I was still at school....he was pretty powerful for such a place, doing old blues and jazz stompers and later recorded a live LP there. So that was the first local person that we followed. It was one of several introductions to blues*

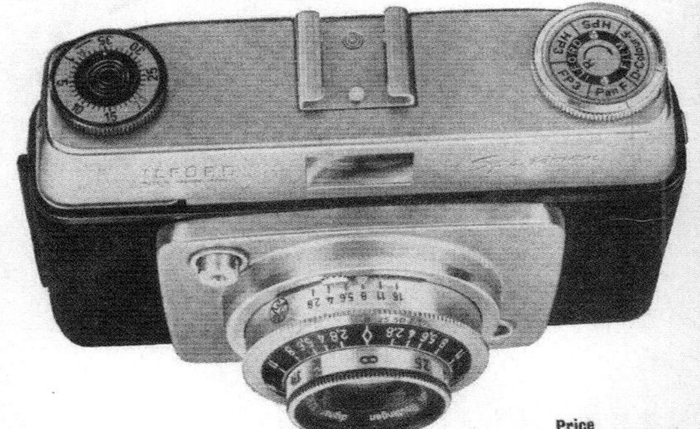

BRIAN'S STORY

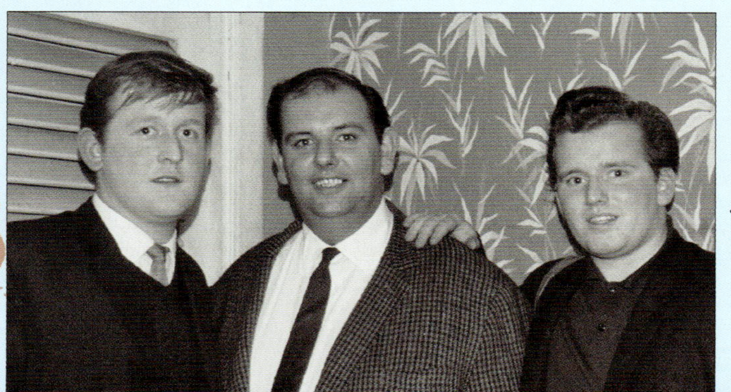

because he sang old Nellie Lutcher songs, and things like 'Weary Blues' and Jimmie Rodgers' 'Blue Yodels' and Leadbelly 'In The Pines'. So we became fans. He was exceedingly popular on the estate. Jack Good discovered him there and Decca tried to make a ballad singer out of him, and so he ploughed a more poppy furrow then," says Brian. Karl would later open the Twisted Wheel Club on January 27. 1963, a gig which Brian also went to.

Incidentally while The Southern Sporting Club conjures up images of rural golf, it was actually a run down cinema called The Corona and regularly hosted bands, even The Beatles played there. It became The Mayflower hosting many big Punk names, then a heavy rock venue called The Stoneground, prior to demolition in 1985. Who needs history?

Ohne more event which really helped put Manchester on the popular music map was the first American Folk Blues Festival package tour. Developed in Germany, promoted by Horst Lippmann and Fritz Rau, with a dozen or so shows in October 1962 it was going to bypass the UK but ABC TV agreed to film it for their Sunday *Tempo* arts show on ABC Weekend North (the footage is thought to be lost). The one off concert, promoted under the Jazz Unlimited banner, drew a great audience and showed Lipman and Rau that it was worth doing more here. So the AFBF event came to Britain again in the following year and on into the Seventies, with Manchester usually one of the venues. Brian was excited by the tour: *"It was promoter Paddy McKiernan who brought these sort of shows to the Free Trade Hall. Under the 'Jazz Unlimited' banner, he booked many of the Chris Barber gigs and other jazz shows there in the Fifties."* Brian remembers Paddy, who was based in nearby Stockport, as a nice bloke and one they pestered early on for photo access. *"He booked Howling Wolf and Louis Jordan the same year as the first Folk Blues Festival but both were cancelled through illness."* Paddy was happy to encourage Brian and his friend's interest and sometimes got them front row tickets, and even his first Howling Wolf album. *"He really deserves the credit for the first Manchester-only show."*

That it only visited Manchester was much to the annoyance of the London blues afficianadoes. Not wanting to miss out, The Rolling Stones made the journey up in a dormobile just to catch the event which featured T-Bone Walker, John Lee Hooker, Memphis Slim, Willie Dixon, Shakey Jake Harris and Helen Humes. Brian also took his camera along; the *"first photographs of any consequence that I took"* as Brian now puts it.

While he had almost got thrown out of the TV studio, at regular concerts, cameras were much less of an issue. There were very few fans doing this and none of the draconian anti-camera rules which became a feature of concerts in the Seventies. Brian tried to blend in and be discreet, but he and his mates were keen to take things a bit further and get some off-stage pictures. They tried hanging about the stage-doors but soon tired of getting cold doing that and just began asking to be allowed in.

As they were polite and did what they were told, door staff usually acquiesced. Brian even became known to some of the regular door staff as 'the fan with the camera.' Brian was also recognised by the Ancills, who ran the important import shop Record Rendezvous and Hime & Addison's music shop which handled concert tickets, ran the door at the Free Trade Hall and looked after FOH there.

Brian and his mates also got to know Brian Bint, the manager of Manchester Odeon, who also booked pop and blues gig. They then ventured across the Pennines to Sheffield City Hall and Brian says most of his early access to take photographs and meet musicians was at one of these three venues.

Having gained the trust of local staff it was also good sense to be polite to the promoters, who often accompanied the tours. Despite his formidable reputation they found Don Arden very accommodating. The two photographs on this page were taken on Brian's camera by his friend backstage after a Little Richard concert at Manchester Granada in November 1963. Brian is stood with Don Arden and his wife, and with Peter Grant and Brian's great friend Malcolm Race on the left. At the time Grant was working as Arden's road manager. Brian and Malcolm both became quite friendly with Grant early on, who introduced them to Don Arden as *"The greatest punters in the world!"* The pair were very proud of this, and even more so when Grant got Arden to *"give us a pass, on his*

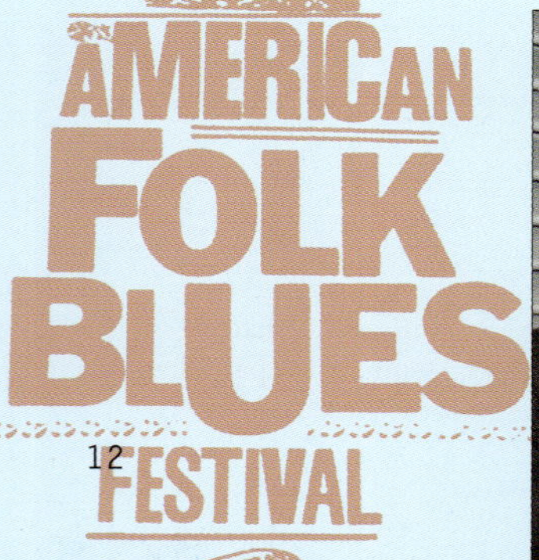

business card, to ALL his shows..." Looking back, Brian says: *"I think Peter Grant, Brian Bint and Barry Ancill got me into more concerts than all the rest put together!"*

Malcolm stayed in touch with Grant who decided to break from Arden and step out on his own as a promoter and manager (and soon took on Led Zeppelin). (He later offered Malcolm a job but Malcolm found it hard to make the move from Manchester to London, and had to turn it down.)

Once backstage to meet the musicians and chat, Brian would do his best to take a couple of photographs, and often take photos of each other with the musicians, such as this one (right): *"Gene Vincent and me, Sheffield City Hall"*, Brian explains. *"This was taken in May 1963 on one of our trips over."* After taking shots of each other with Vincent they had them printed for him to sign later on the tour. Later as a cash-strapped new parent Brian sold many of his signed photos and the negatives were also lost, so he had nothing to remind him of the meeting until it turned up inside a reissue CD booklet.

So from 1962 on there was quite a scene developing; decent tours to go to, big names from the UK and US and quite a lot happening locally - with bands like The Beatles starting to play one-nighters in and around Manchester.

Into this mix the r'n'b and blues scene was also starting to grow. There is an acknowledged irony that many black blues artists had begun to enjoy a cult following in Britain and Europe when they were still largely unknown or acknowledged back home. Through the distribution of records in specialist shops and the early concert performances helped by Barber and others, the scene burgeoned in Britain in the first half of the Sixties just as British bands, hugely influenced by the music, and having assimilated (sometimes acknowledged, sometimes not) many of the ideas, themes and songs, were now reworking the music and would soon be taking them back to America to massive acclaim.

With the start of some of the big Blues package tours, and spurred on by the excitement of mixing with famous musicians, Brian and his mates hit on a new idea to ease their access to meet bands and take pictures. They set themselves up as the Northern Society Of Popular Music, printing letterheads and business cards to impress local officials. The idea was initially spurred on by trying to get in to Sheffield City Hall on a less ad hoc basis. It was quite a long trek over (or under) the Pennines and they didn't fancy going all that way to be refused permission and felt something official looking would help. *"We went to a lot [of shows there] because they had every decent package show going and it was a good hall. It was easy to get about in there, Wilson Peck [the main music shop in Sheffield] handled all the ticketing. When we first went we used to just write and ask for a ticket. Then we dreamt up the Northern Society of Popular Music, which never really existed beyond a letterhead, but you wrote a nice letter to the Town*

Hall [who owned and ran the venue at arms length] saying 'could we take pictures' of somebody. We had to write to the town hall department in advance to get in, so we could turn up at the concert with their letter of authority."

This canny move worked in Sheffield and the "society" also came into use back in Manchester and further helped them gain official access to venues and dressing rooms, with road crew and staff seeing the NSPM cards and letting them through. Few bothering to ask what it was the NSPM actually did... *"One you had been allowed in, you had the run of the place, learned where all the dressing rooms were!"*

As Brian explained, Sheffield City

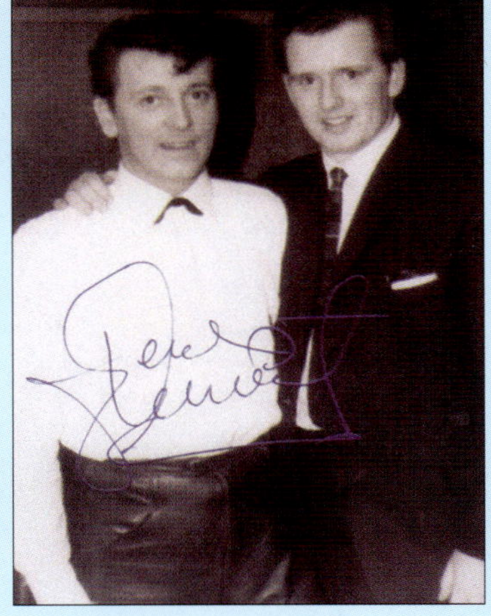

Hall hosted a lot of Rock'n'Roll shows and he would go over usually on the train with his friend Malcolm Race throughout the 1962 to 1965 period, catching the late night train back. Brian recalls one trip with 'big Malcom' (an *"inside leg man at C&A in Manchester!"*) straight from work . *"He was very tall and he'd have his lovely black suit on and on this occasion I hadn't got a letter from the council because we'd just gone on the spur of the minute. So we went through, we knew the way, and once you got in the dressing room you were OK for the night. But you just had to get there. We're half way down the corridor and two commissionaire fellers came round the corner. They liked to be officious, they enjoyed it. What do we do now? But as they approached Malcolm pulls his tape measure out of his coat pocket, gives me one end of it and he starts measuring bits of the wall and I'm suddenly writing it all down. This feller comes up and he's just about to have a go when Malcolm goes 'Excuse me sir, would you mind that piece there for me?' 'Oh yes, sir.' And he did this and I wrote down all these pointless dimensions of various things, just lengths of wall and then Malcolm says 'thank you, that's very helpful.' 'No anytime, anytime,' and they shuffled off ... and we were in!"*

Indeed the dressing room was large and open plan, designed originally for an orchestra. So for a package tour once you were in there you could meet everyone on the bill. The Beatles were coming up and as usual they wrote off to request permission to take photos on behalf of their society. They realised they were unlikely to get an OK for The Beatles, so cleverly asked instead to meet The Brook Brothers who were on the bill, and got approved. In the end they called the trip off as they had an invite to Malcolm's brother Tony's 21st birthday party instead

BRIAN'S STORY

(Tony was Brian's oldest schoolmate). But then Brian had seen the Beatles a number of times already, mostly at the out of town venues on the circuit set up by the Liverpool promoters, places like Northwich Memorial Hall and The Majestic in Crewe (where he also saw The Rolling Stones). And before anyone asks, his Beatles negatives, taken at the Oasis Club in Manchester, have long gone. *"I sold them in 1968 to help pay for my honeymoon. I did keep a set of prints for myself but these have also disappeared. There were no other photographers there, so if any pictures of The Beatles from The Oasis ever surface, it would be good to see them again."* They must be out there, drop us a line...

Brian sometimes cadged a ride on Tony Race's motorbike, and travelling like this they saw shows by Gene Vincent, Jerry Lee Lewis and even Brenda Lee. The photograph below shows Brian with Chuck Berry at the Bolton Odeon in May 1964, with his friend Roger Fairhurst. However, by far the majority of his trips to gigs outside Manchester were with his friend Neil Carter. Brian recalls ranging as far afield as Leeds, Birmingham, Halifax, Rochdale, Bolton, Nottingham, Newport, Blackpool, Sheffield and even London with Neil.

The second American Folk & Blues Festival took place in 1963, this time in Manchester's Granada TV Studio rather than a public venue, filmed for a show produced by Johnnie Hamp, who made many iconic popular music shows for Granada over this period.

Having already taken photographs at a few other Granada shows that year, including their famous *It's Little Richard* show (one is shown oppposite) and *Scene At 6.30*, Brian got to know the people at Granada, including Johnnie Hamp's secretary. As a result, she would ring Brian at work from time to time and ask him to find people to help fill the small TV studio for recordings at short notice. She would bike over a pile of tickets and Brian would hand these out to people at the Tax Office where he was worked. They then nipped down after work for the filming, which generally took place around tea time. Not being into light entertainment, Brian himself often didn't bother attending these events.

But he did take photos during the rehearsals for some of the *Scene At 6.30* shows when these had someone he regarded as musically interesting as a guest, such as Bo Diddley or Screaming Jay Hawkins. Sometimes he got invites to the lunch-time rehearsals too. The film would then be edited and broadcast usually later that day as part of *Scene At 6.30*, the North West's early evening local news programmes. A few of Brian's photographs from Granada have survived and appear in the book.

As well as the concerts Brian had also

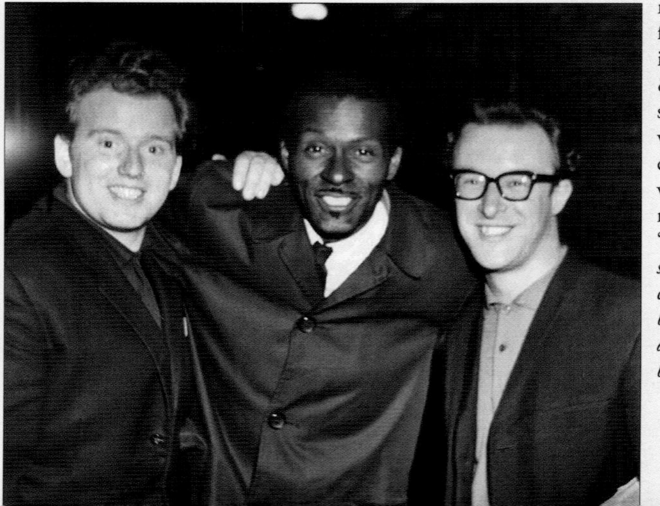

immersed himself in blues and r'n'b music, listening to as many records as he could over the next couple of years. Once he began taking his camera to shows, he set out to photograph his favourite stars and this included most of the big name American blues and rock'n'roll musicians who played locally. Many of them first came over as part of the big blues package tours, but seeing there was an enthusiastic crowd in Britain and many small clubs putting on live music promoters began to get them to return for solo tours.

Most of these blues and jazz clubs had restricted age policies, so people of Brian's age couldn't normally get in. *"We did get in to one to see The John Barry Seven very early on, but only because my friend Tony Race's mum had gone to school with John Barry's mum, and she sent us tickets!"* But once he was old enough this extended the choice of music considerably.

Brian could now get in to places like the Manchester Sports Guild (a jazz and folk club near the cathedral), the Jung Frau, the Clarendon Trad Jazz club, the Oasis (where an up and coming band called The Hollies are said to have taken their name from the Christmas decorations) and The Bodega (Brian remembers seeing Alexis Korner here in 1963 when his *Marquee* album was doing well).

A new venue had opened in January 1963 in what had been a basement cafe called The Left Wing Coffee House, already known to Brian: *"It was a grill at lunchtimes, and was one of the places we lunched from work. My office was only five minutes away from 1961 to 1970."* Sited on the corner of Brazennose Street and a narrow access road called Ridgefield (which also housed the Rockingham Club, Manchester's first gay club, in the basement opposite), the new tenants reopened the cafe which they renamed the Twisted Wheel with beat groups playing at the weekend. They ran the business from offices upstairs and looked after a couple of local groups too. The cafe then started playing records at lunchtimes and evenings during the rest of the week and a work colleague of Brian's, Jeff Mullin, became the first disc jockey there, so Brian and his mates were early regulars and he soon met other like-minded music fans, making several long-time friends. So it was that one day Brian was in his usual record shop haunt, Hime & Addison on John Dalton Street, a sheet music shop with a well stocked vinyl department in the basement, complete with listening booths. He was approached by Roger Eagle who noticed what Brian was listening to. *"I was buying this Chuck Berry EP or something, and suddenly this sheepskin coat on long legs darts across and basically said 'you like rhythm and blues do you? You know we've got rhythm and blues sessions down at the Twisted Wheel*

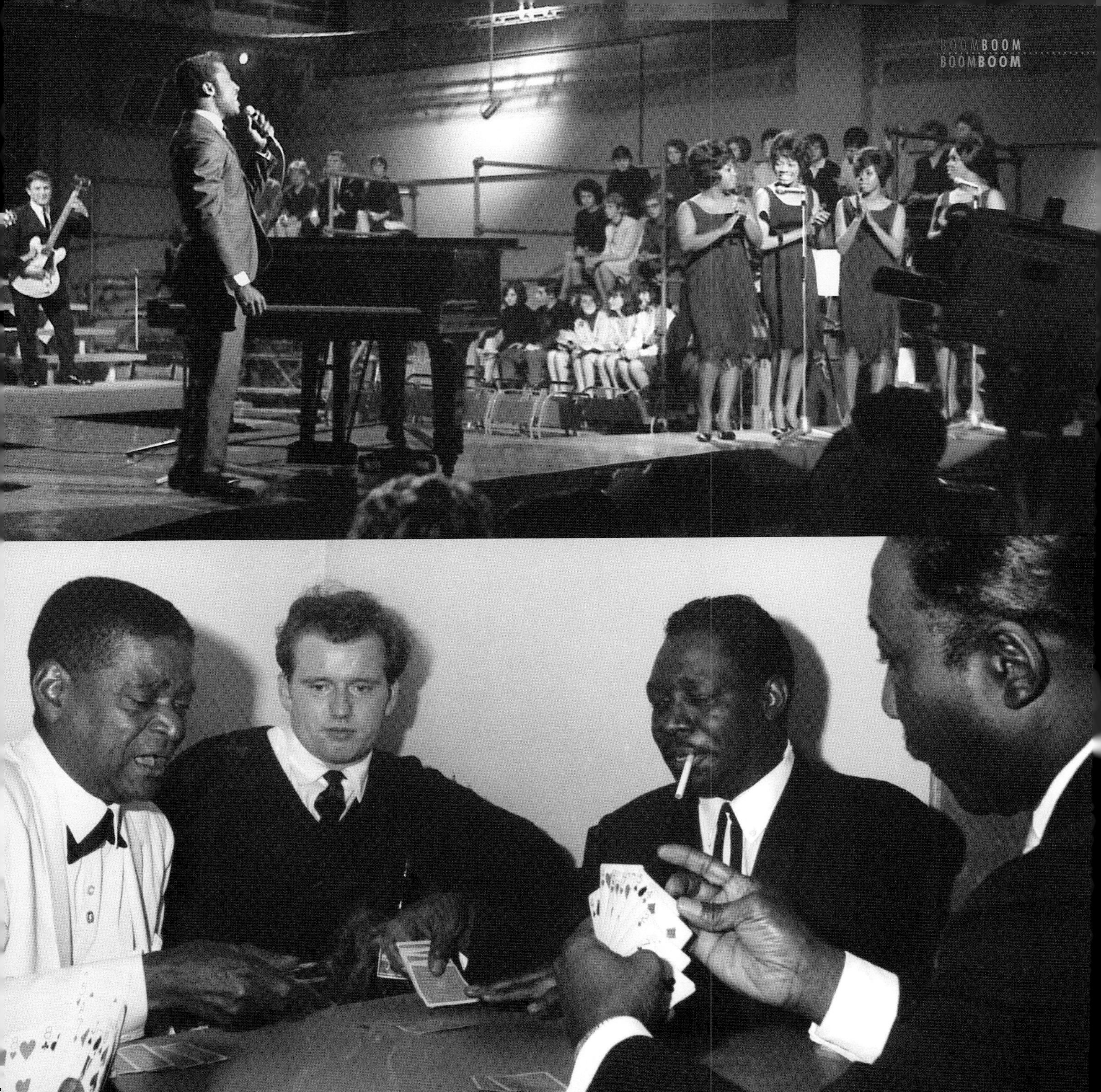
BOOM BOOM
BOOM BOOM

and you've got to come.' In conversation it emerged Brian already owned a rare Screaming Jay Hawkins 10" 78, and Roger, asked him (*"or 'ordered', as was Eagle's way!"* recalls Brian) round to his bed-sit that evening to play the record. It was September 1963 and Roger (who had moved up from Oxford to work in town a year before) had just become the new DJ at the Twisted Wheel after the owners spotted him sat with a coffee and a pile of newly purchased rhythm and blues records, and got chatting. They let him make his mark as a DJ and before long he began to push for some all night events, persuading the club owners, the Abadi brothers, to go with it. *"My meeting with Roger was just before the very first one,"* recollects Brian. *"I said 'well there's a chunk out of the Hawkins 78, you can't play it all.' He said 'never mind fetch it round, here's the address.' That is how most people met Roger. So I went round to this little pit he had in Chorlton and then on to the all-nighter, with Spencer Davis."*

A feature of clubs in London, while music licenses often ran to 2.00am at the weekend, this was the first time anybody had tried a proper all-nighter in the provinces. After an evening's music, people had to leave prior to the all-nighter which Roger planned to run on Saturday night from midnight until 7.00am Sunday morning. Seven hours of records and live music with himself as the DJ. That Roger could consider all-nighters was down to licensing laws. As the club was not selling alcohol, their hours were not subject to the same restrictions as pubs and licensed clubs. The Twisted Wheel's first such event on September 28. 1963, with Spencer Davis doing a solo acoustic set and The Graham Bond Quartet on the bill, went down well. Club goers took blankets to spread out on the floor to grab a little sleep when needed. Caffeine from strong coffee and Cola helped keep people going.

"I started going to The Wheel most weeks, and that's where I met lots of people like Neil Carter and Roger Fairhurst. They all did DJ nights of their own. Technically I did myself but only for sort of 15 minutes at a time when Roger went and stretched his legs! But it was far too tricky for me, it was hard enough just finding the discs... even when he said 'put

that on and then that on', and sometimes it was a side of an LP. But switching the turntables over and getting the records right was nerve wrecking enough for me. No patter, no introduction just changing the records over, that was enough! But it enabled me to say if I wrote to a record company for freebies that I was 'a Disc Jockey at local club'."

Once he became connected to the Twisted Wheel, Brian could also trek to clubs they had connections with, like the Esquire in Sheffield. Seeing him take photographs of the musicians, Roger and the regulars, Ivor Abadi suggested that Brian could take shots of the punters and print them up so he could pin them on the club wall. The idea was that people would come back the next week and see their photos on the wall and maybe buy a copy (Brian didn't keep these negatives, which would have been an amazing social history archive! I've told him off). As well as this, in return for photographing the bands Roger guaranteed Brian free entry to the Twisted Wheel. It sounded like a good deal; *"I could never have afforded to be there so much otherwise! I actually mostly sold photos of club goers to* stop *them appearing on the wall, because I'd photographed a girl who was supposed to be spending the night at her friends! If it got out that there was a picture of her at the Twisted Wheel... It had a reputation which was worse than it deserved, because it wasn't licensed and they were pretty hardline there. If anybody was seen to hand over anything suspicious, two large bouncers would get them out, rough them up a bit and take them round to the police station which was two streets away."*

Roger Eagle soon had the Twisted Wheel Club buzzing and as word spread it got busier, as he began to air discs not heard anywhere else in Manchester. People were already queuing to be part of that first all-nighter, and it looks as if Brian's photographs are some of the only images taken in the original Brazennose Street.

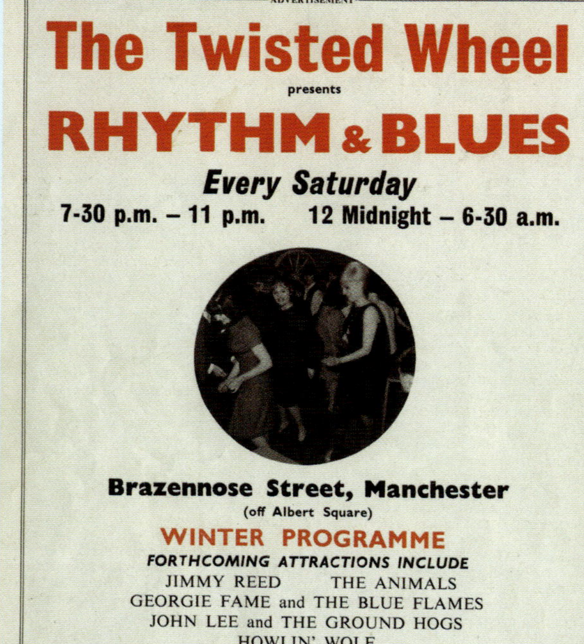

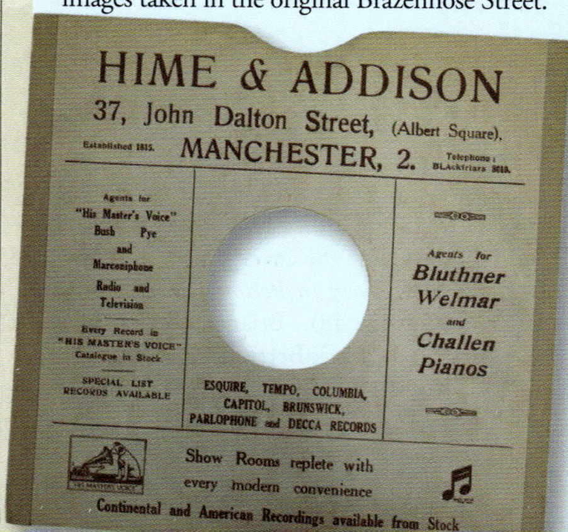

The TWISTED WHEEL

Brian had tickets for Cyril Davis, due to appear in January '64 at the Twisted Wheel. Quite a few of those who turned up didn't know Cyril had died 10 days before. The Cyril Davis R'n'B All Stars played anyway, with vocalist Long John Baldry, who brought along Rod Stewart as a featured singer. Brian remembers a blistering night, no planned set, just the band (Carlo Little and The Savages essentially) and singers blasting out r'n'b standards with Stewart taking his turn He even played guitar on some numbers. Frustratingly the club was so packed (Cyril had a good following and a hit) that it was impossible to get near enough to take photographs during the show. It was also a very emotional evening as many in the crowd hadn't heard of Cyril's death. Brian took just one shot of Stewart outside on this night. Today you would click away with a DSLR and not worry about anything (except the four figure cost of trading up the camera when the next leap in technology renders it obsolete).

Brian's sturdy Ilford Sportsman remained in use until mid-1964 and he recalls the Chuck Berry shows as being the last time he used it. He then purchased a Praktica 4F SLR 35mm camera with money he got for his 21st birthday. Produced between 1960 and 1964 in East Germany, this camera could in many ways hold it's own against West German and Japanese 35mm cameras but was more affordable. It gave him more options and flexibility at concerts.

Brian's photographs were rarely published at the time. Had he been London based, he might have gone on to develop a career as a rock and pop photographer, but even in a happening city like Manchester there was little opportunity to earn a living doing this at the time.

He did give Chuck Berry copies of a some of his shots from the 1964 show in Bolton which found their way into the *Chuck Berry Songbook*, a printed collection of sheet music with accompanying photos of Berry on his U.K. tour. It was the first time Brian got a fee, three Guineas (*"I had to push for it!"*) for any of his photographs, and the last time until the Eighties.

What Brian did not know was that another of the photographs made the cover of a Chuck Berry EP and an LP (*Chuck Berry In Person*) released only in Japan in 1964 (see page 48). Brian only spotted them forty years later in a Chuck Berry discography.

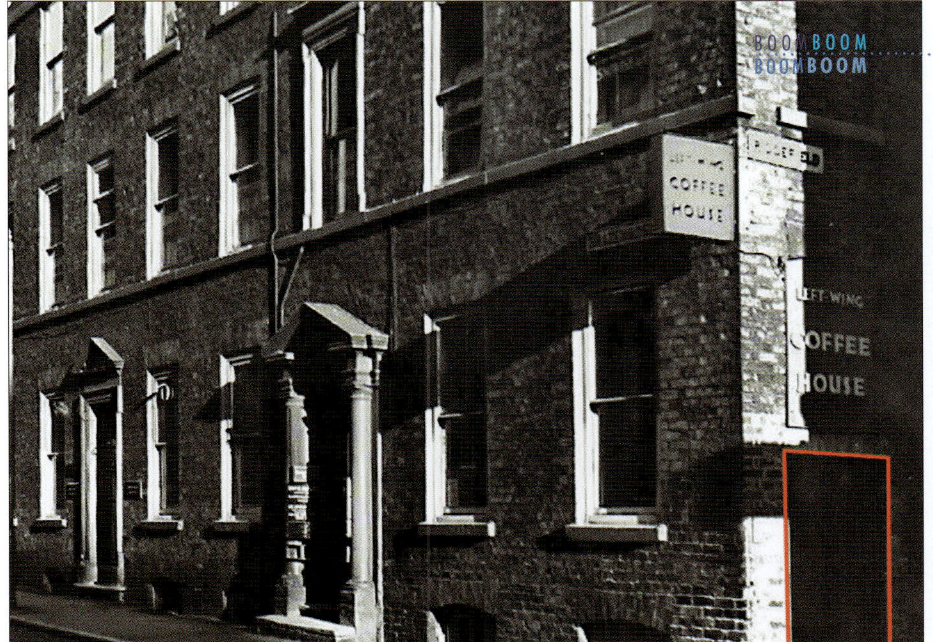

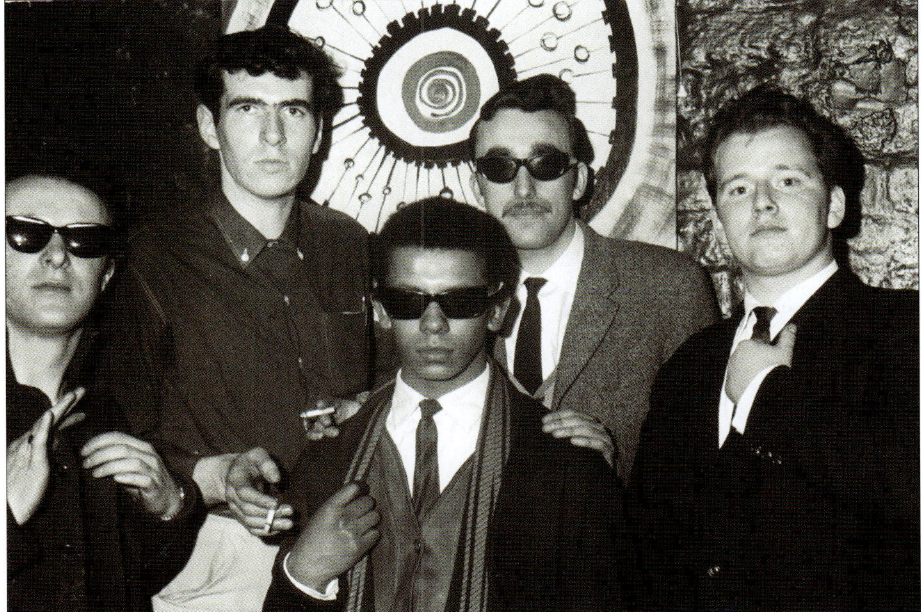

Top: The Left Wing Coffee House and basement entrance to what became the Twisted Wheel Club. Roger's offices were upstairs via the first portico doorway. The block was demolished in the Seventies. Fools. Above: Brian set this photo up inside the club; back l - r Roger Eagle, Dave Waggett, Brian and in front two of the club regulars, Roger Fairhurst and Tony Niles.

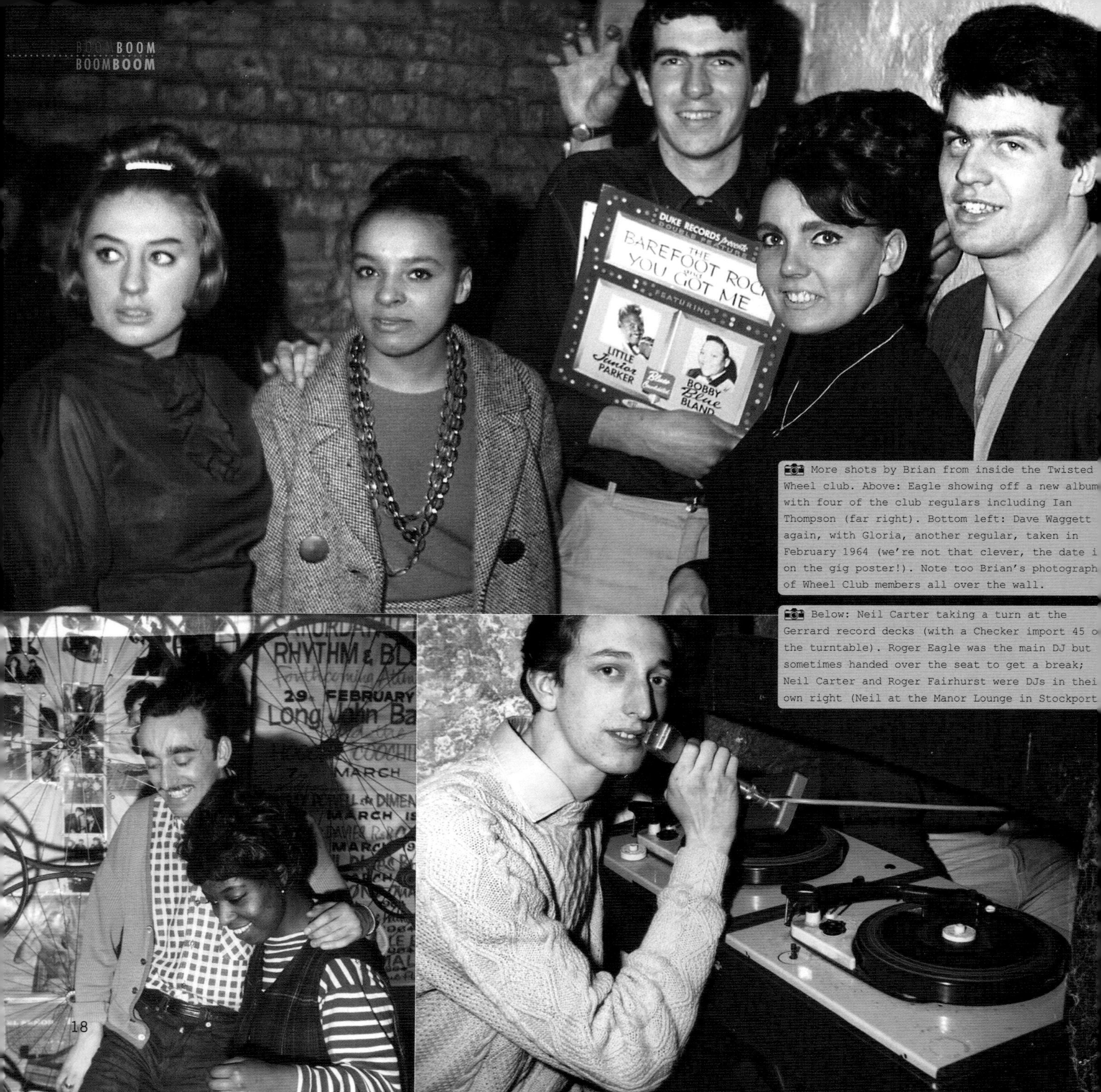

More shots by Brian from inside the Twisted Wheel club. Above: Eagle showing off a new album with four of the club regulars including Ian Thompson (far right). Bottom left: Dave Waggett again, with Gloria, another regular, taken in February 1964 (we're not that clever, the date i on the gig poster!). Note too Brian's photograph of Wheel Club members all over the wall.

Below: Neil Carter taking a turn at the Gerrard record decks (with a Checker import 45 o the turntable). Roger Eagle was the main DJ but sometimes handed over the seat to get a break; Neil Carter and Roger Fairhurst were DJs in thei own right (Neil at the Manor Lounge in Stockport

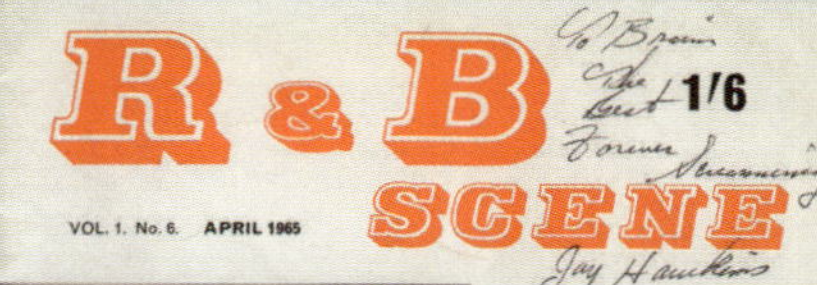

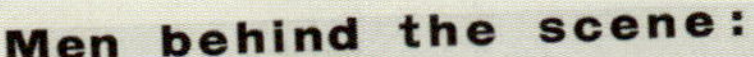

Men behind the scene:

No. 1   Mike Bocock

Mike Bocock, ex-president of the Chuck Berry Fan-Club, lives, sleeps, and eats, with the music of his idol. Indeed, first thing in the morning, when lesser mortals may be tuning in to a "welcome to another day" type radio programme, Mike is activating his Berry collection. Probably, first on will be the latest release, which, even if its several weeks old will still need further study. Next maybe a series of Chuck's instrumentals, followed by Mike's favourite "Sweet Little Sixteen." But whatever it is, it will be Berry.

Mike, a native of Bolton, must be the world's leading authority on Chuck Berry. It would take a brave man to dispute this fact. Not a week goes by without a communication from the American Chuck Berry Fan Club, and not an evening fades before he has answered a pile of mail concerning the man himself. (When

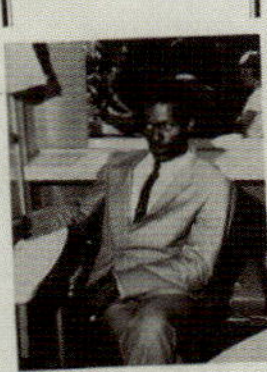

Chuck Berry

A dressing-room 'photo by Brian Smith

he was president of the fan club he only averaged one night out every three months.)

As a person, Mike is tallish, dark-haired, and wears glasses in times of danger. Although there is no doubt as to his favourite, he is not blind to the records of other artistes, and has a very respectable collection, especially of Muddy Waters, Bo Diddley, and Jimmy Reed. Aged twenty, with a girl-friend by the name of Janet, Mike hopes to visit Berry Park in Missouri later this year when it is completed. I hope that he will be in a position to write to R'N B SCENE and give us details of this exciting venture. For while Chuck is now once again hitting the headlines, Mike is quietly working away in the background, providing information and enthusiasm for one of the greatest rhythm and blues orientated artistes of all time. Long may he continue to do so.

15

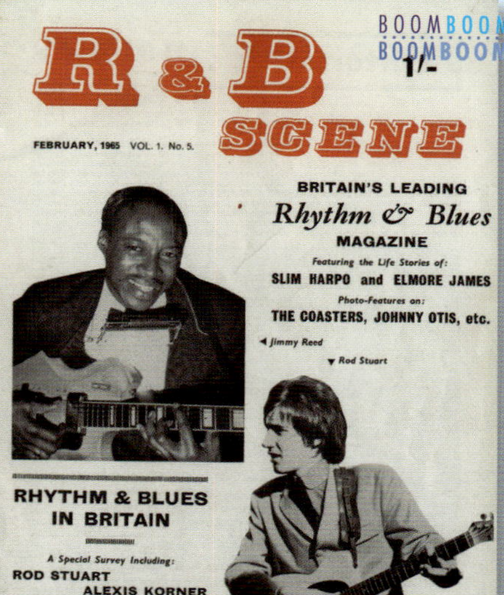

As if he wasn't busy enough, Roger Eagle launched **R & B Scene magazine** (the title changed three times! We will try and stick with this) early in 1964 and asked Brian if he could supply some of the photographs, which he was keen to do. It was edited by Roger from his flat in Chorlton-cum-Hardy, put together by himself, with Roger Fairhurst (assistant editor), artwork by Blackpool-based David Waggett and promotion by Neil Carter. Brian (who was once listed inside as R & B Scene's culinary expert!) had his first photos (of Sonny Boy Williamson) in Issue 2. There was no money to pay contributors, so Brian would eek out a 24 exposure black and white film across a number of shows, which is why he sometimes only took one or two photographs per artist, just making sure he had something for the magazine. He didn't have a darkroom, mostly using the local camera shops for processing and printing.

R & B Scene gave Brian a focus for his work and over the next fifteen months as their official cameraman, he took photographs with the magazine in mind.

The idea of the staff was to use the magazine to help promote the music of their favourite American R'n'b acts, British musicians (the first editorial sang the praises of Tony McPhee and Steve Winwood) and the local scene, including The Twisted Wheel, which usually had a full page advert on the back

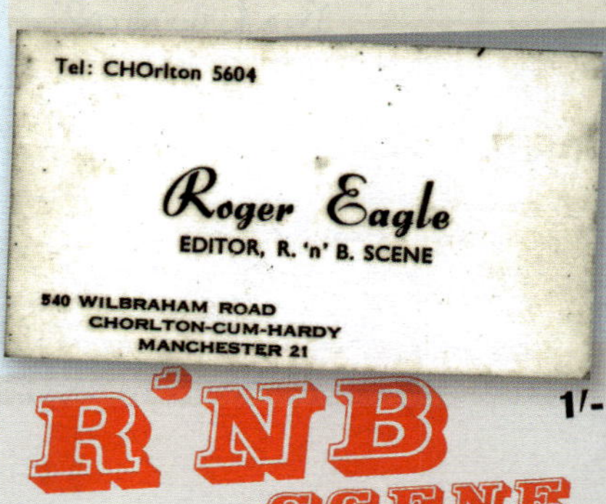

page. It sold (initially for 1/- [5p]) in the Wheel and other local venues and Roger Eagle recalled Brian Jones buying a copy off him once when he was in London. As well as articles and pictures, the magazine aimed to educate and inform readers, with suggestions for building a Rhythm and Blues record collection, reviews and a gossip column penned by Daddy Cool.

Roger persuaded Twisted Wheel owners the Abadis to fund the printing as publicity for the club, but they quickly pulled out due to the cost. It never made a profit and after this was only kept afloat thanks to Roger's mother, distinguished Oxford University Press editor Dorothy Eagle, who covered the cost of printing. Brian's photographs augmented publicity images from promoters and labels, and sometimes appeared on the cover (left and top left). Brian even made the front (top left) acting as Screaming Jay Hawkin's straight man, taken by Roger in London. Brian also offered prints for sale via the small ads.

The magazine was printed letterpress by Thomas Yates Ltd. in Rochdale on gloss paper and was more than a fanzine, but distribution was poor, they had no editorial or design experience and most of them had full time jobs. Nevertheless it was an important early pioneering UK music title, well written and enthusiastic. Seven issues were produced, the last dated July 1965. Now very collectable, copies fetch £30 or more at auction.

BRIAN'S STORY

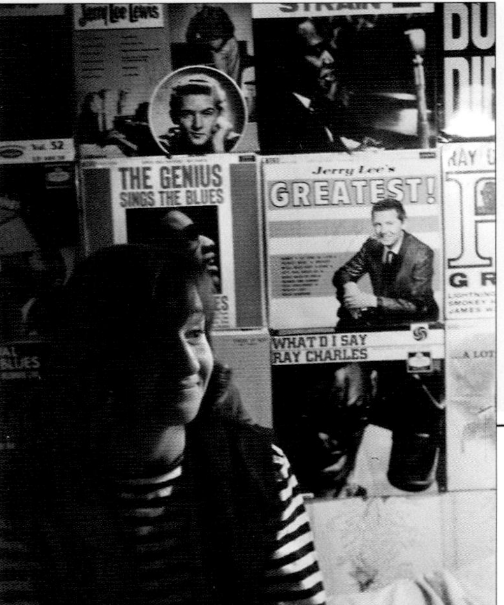

Brian and Carl Perkins at the Odeon May 22. 1964. plus adverts for the fan-club and Brian's photographs.

Brian and Dave Waggett were also busy and had started the short-lived Carl Perkins fan club together. As huge fans, they were chatting to Carl backstage and got the go-ahead there and then, with a nice signed letter of approval (which Brian discovered now hangs in the Hard Rock cafe in Memphis). They only did three newsletters and he feels the club *might* have lasted longer had not Carl also authorised two other UK fan-clubs on the same trip. Nevertheless he remained in touch; *"He was totally genuine, and always remembered me. The last time I saw him was just before he died, the Thunderbird Club down in Northampton. I hadn't seen him for a few years, he'd had cancer and he'd come back from it. We had a good old reminisce. On the way out I'd said my farewells and he came back out into the car park to get me, he wanted to get a picture I'd shown him with the [my] kids, to take home to show his wife – that was the measure of him, he never came across as the star at all."*

With all these activities and a growing record collection, Brian eyed his sister's bedroom with envy. *"I had the little box room, covered in LPs [Val can be seen in there below], and I'd been after her bigger bedroom for ages and been completely blanked! Then the Rolling Stones were on at The Manchester Palace. I just had a bright idea and said to her 'if I got you in would you swap bedrooms?' She said 'oh yeah, yeah, yeah!' and so that was it. We didn't have a phone, I went to the call box, phoned The Palace, spoke to the stage door keeper and said 'Is it all right if I come and take some pictures for the Northern Society for Popular Music? And he says 'Oh come down, just ask for Bert', so I did. I thought the place was going to be rammed with people, we went in there, there's nobody else. We were the only two in. The Stones were there, the only pictures I took with all five of them and Val looking petrified. And that's how I got [the bedroom]. She was true to her word, I'll say that for her!"*

Val (below left) must have been the envy of all her friends while the story does explain why in the picture in his room on page 4, the wallpaper is perhaps a bit girlier than one might have expected.

Although they never got to play there, The Rolling Stones were themselves fans of The Twisted Wheel as Brian remembers. *"They certainly did drop into more than one of the all-nighters at the Wheel."* The rest of the audience were respectful and left the group in peace, however at one all-nighter Roger Eagle, having seen them as they came in, pulled a sly trick on them. *"Without any announcements, he simply played every track on the first Stones LP, in the same order, but by the original artists. Nobody said anything and I doubt many punters realised, but a couple of the Stones did quietly smile. It was mutual respect really!"*

Under Roger's careful tutelage (he now had his own office upstairs) The Twisted Wheel went from strength to strength during 1964 with the all-nighters attracting kids from all over the North and a growing Mod faction as well, with scooters double parked the length of the street some evenings. It was extended in September '64 to provide more dancing space but still had to turn away thousands on some nights (the club membership list ran to 14,000 people). Indeed the dance scene and the live music did sometimes clash, at least one act had to ask for the music to be turned down during their set. The club also had a lot of clout now when it came to booking bands and helped Manchester to become the destination for bands after London with up to 200 clubs open in the city around this period.

The Abadi's knew they needed a bigger site though and The Twisted Wheel finally moved to bigger premises in late 1965. It was a bit of an end of an era for many of the regulars. Brian himself never took any photographs at the new Whitworth Street site. Roger Eagle moved too but became disenchanted as the music scene changed towards soul dance music. He found some of his tastes weren't those of the new crowd or the bosses, who began to interfere. Nevertheless his work *"undoubtedly paved the way for its later pre-eminent position as the birthplace of Northern Soul,"* in Brian's opinion, though he agrees Roger did lose interest. *"He eventually tired of the gradual move to repetitive dance records which became the focus of Northern Soul. He was a gospel spreader, and this music was only a small part of what he wanted to spread. Also they seemed more interested in dancing than in live music. He eventually moved on and began promoting concerts (and kept his*

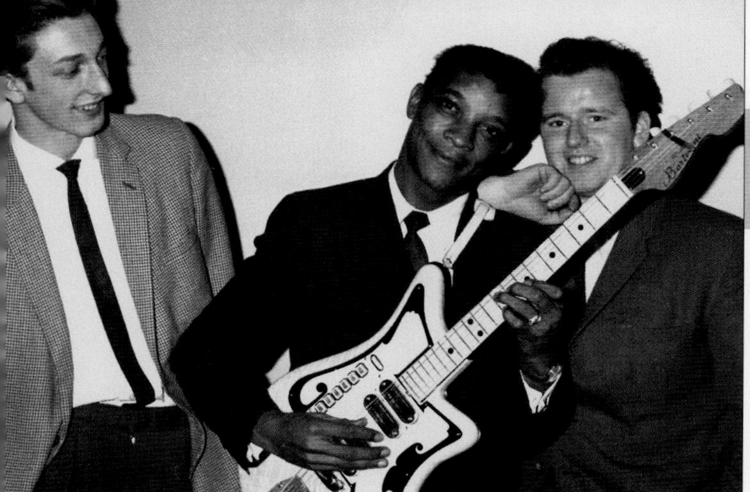

Left: Brian (right) and his friend Neil (left) with Hubert Sumlin at the Free Trade Hall, probably when guesting on a Chris Barber show in November 1964. Below: taken by Brian in part of the Twisted Wheel reserved for the musicians; behind T-Bone Walker his backing band are hard at work, while he grabs a cigarette and chats with Screaming Jay Hawkins (left).

mission to educate people to new music) for the rest of his life." Roger left in 1967 (The Wheel kept on until 1971) to pastures new including a little club in Liverpool called Erics. As for Brian, with the original club gone and R & B Scene magazine also folding in 1965 he began to ease up on photography and started saving to get married, which he did in 1968, to his *"long suffering wife"* (his description!) Shirley. They met at work and he recalls that after his first date in 1965, having seen her safely onto the bus home, Brian dashed off for the all-nighter at The Twisted Wheel to catch Larry Williams and Johnny Guitar Watson (taking the brilliant photo used on our cover).

Photographing Big Joe Turner in colour in 1966 was also the last American Folk & Blues Festival covered by Brian. He took some now famous shots of Chuck Berry at the Princess Club in 1967 and then photographed Bill Haley at the Carlton in Warrington, on May 3rd, 1968 (*"My friend Dave Clarke was the DJ there at the time"*). Taken on colour slide these were his final forays into music photography for many years. That Brian should close on Haley was quite fitting: *"I'd seen Haley and the lads on his first tour. He was a real gentleman too, when I met him at the Odeon in '64."*

Over the next few years Brian was kept busy with work and family life, he and Shirley went on to have four children. It wasn't until the 1980s and a revival of interest in blues music that Brian's images began to be sought out. American blues artists were also coming over to tour again. Brian began photographing some of these musicians once more when they came to the North West and got to know some of them well, often finding artists themselves keen to get a photo of their shows two decades before after Brian had shown them his old prints.

As time passed magazines like Blues Unlimited (which began just before R'n B Scene but was only a Roneo stencil fanzine), Sailor's Delight (which became Blues & Rhythm) and Juke Blues (which came out of the last days of Blues Unlimited) began printing retrospective articles and Brian was being asked for photographs. He supplied a lot of prints and as a result record companies, having seen them in the specialist magazines, started to ask for images for covers and booklets on CD reissues. Labels such as ACE and MCA, the owners of Chess, were on the phone, followed by writers and publishers preparing books on R'n'B and Blues artists, as well as documenting the history of venues like The Twisted Wheel. The photos even found their way into The Rock 'n' Roll Hall of Fame and then Martin Scorsese's documentary The Blues. Literally hundreds of records, books, TV programmes, museums, exhibitions and magazines have used Brian's shots over the last 30 years, not always with permission; there are well over fifty John Lee Hooker CD and download albums for sale on the web, all with the identical shot by Brian on the front, and all used without permission or any payment (some are shown later in the book, page 73).

The proudest moment for Brian during this time was when he discovered some of his photographs had been chosen by designers making the interpretive boards put up along the Mississippi Blues Trail (*"and for once I was credited!"*).

Brian retired from his day job in 2007 but from his new home base in Cheshire found himself busy "curating" his archive, and the idea for a book began to surface, spurred on by friends and music writers who urged him to "do something". After talks with RPM Record boss Mark Stratford, Easy On The Eye became involved and the result is this fascinating collection featuring much of his material from the monochrome days of the early sixties.

Untrained, and using quite basic cameras, Brian, "the fan with a camera", produced remarkable images with a real presence and quality and in so doing managed to capture a unique and relatively short lived scene in fascinating detail. Not only on-stage, but back in the dressing rooms, where he photographed these giants of the blues relaxing with a beer and a pack of cards, or posing for souvenir pictures with British fans, male and female, a remarkable cultural melting pot considering that many of the musicians themselves could not even travel on a bus next to whites in some States back home at that time. It shows how music could and can cross any boundaries.

To be there witnessing many of the famous blues musicians appearing here for the first time is enviable enough, but to be there with a camera recording the scene is something blues fans worldwide can be grateful for today.

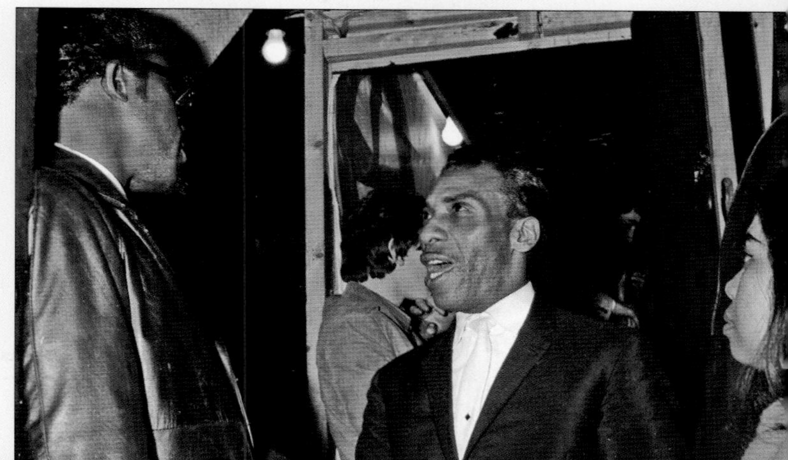

CHUCK BERRY

Brian saw Chuck Berry a number of times. Berry had a reputation for being difficult with management and promoters but then many tried to cut corners and conditions on the U.K. tours were not always what artists had been promised. Berry arrived on day one of a Don Arden promoted tour, was driven to his accommodation 'pit' in Bayswater, took one look and didn't even get out of the car, telling the driver to go on to the Hilton (where he stayed on most subsequent tours!).

Brian says Berry was always very good with him and his mates, though he did witness one occasion when friction loomed. He was with Berry and Carl Perkins. *"We went to one gig near the end of that first tour where all the bands went on strike, wouldn't go on stage, and Peter Grant who was then a roadie, an exceedingly nice and helpful chap, he kept coming to the pub and saying (to everyone) "C'mon you know the show's in ten minutes, and the money's on its way, there's a car coming", and Berry was the spokesman and he just says "no dough, no show" and went back to his mineral water. Then the money arrived, some sweating character who'd come hurtling up in a cab is suddenly handing bundles of cash out to Eric Burdon and The Nashville Teens and everybody else. Berry just counts his up, puts it in his briefcase, stands up and says "Gentlemen, I believe we have a show to do!" and just walks out the door."*

The live shots on the page opposite show the problem Brian faced trying to capture with a modest camera the musicians dashing around, but the slight motion blur does really give a feel of those early shows. Berry did 24 dates back to back, often two performances a night, with no days off (though the sets were much shorter on the package tours), and was backed by Kingsize Taylor & the Dominoes. The rest of the bill comprised The Nashville Teens, The Other Two, Carl Perkins, The Animals and The Dominoes. The Swinging Blue Jeans were booed off at London by the local rockers so had been dropped by the time Brian saw the tour.

Brian's mate Neil Carter gave Berry a lift in his car from the Bolton Odeon to the Chinese restaurant later (overleaf - Neil ended up ferrying Screamin' Jay, Little Walter and others around Manchester in his time).

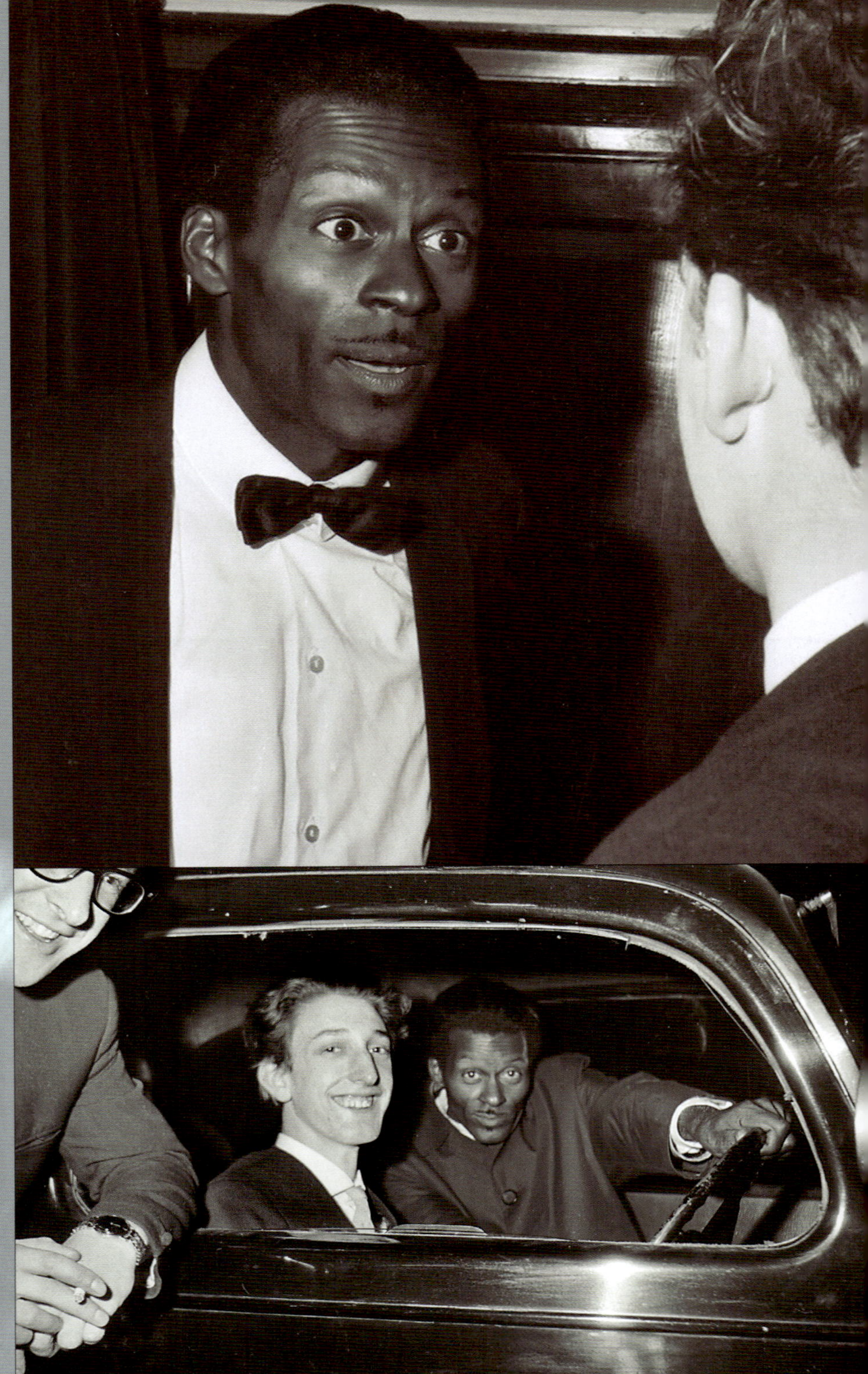

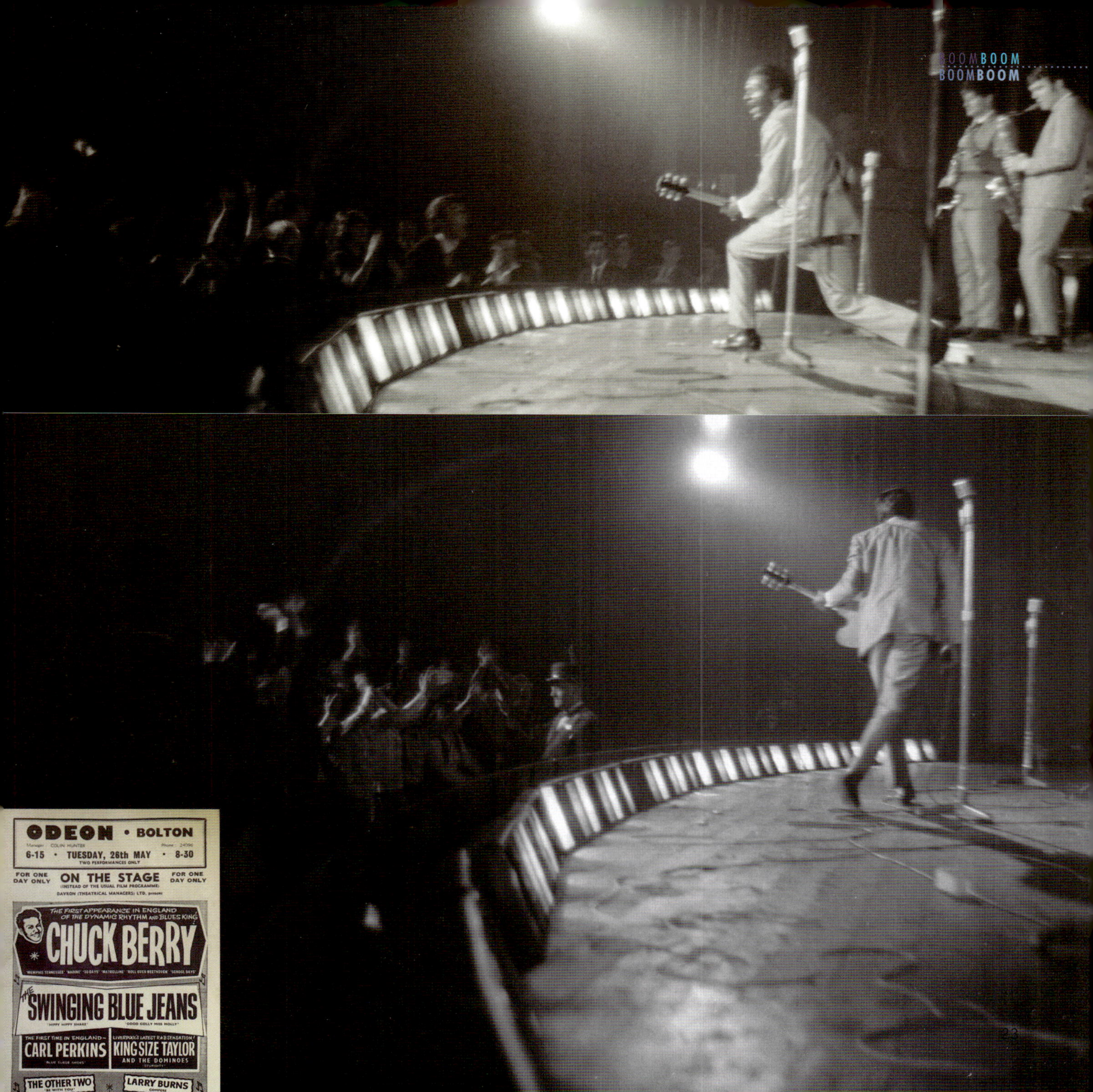
BOOMBOOM
BOOMBOOM
ODEON • BOLTON
Manager   COLIN HUNTER
Phone 24296
6-15 • TUESDAY, 26th MAY • 8-30
TWO PERFORMANCES ONLY
FOR ONE DAY ONLY
ON THE STAGE
(INSTEAD OF THE USUAL FILM PROGRAMME)
FOR ONE DAY ONLY
DAVRON (THEATRICAL MANAGERS) LTD. present
THE FIRST APPEARANCE IN ENGLAND OF THE DYNAMIC RHYTHM AND BLUES KING
CHUCK BERRY
"MEMPHIS TENNESSEE" "NADINE" "30 DAYS" "MAYBELLINE" "ROLL OVER BEETHOVEN" "SCHOOL DAYS"
THE SWINGING BLUE JEANS
"HIPPY HIPPY SHAKE"   "GOOD GOLLY MISS MOLLY"
THE FIRST TIME IN ENGLAND—
CARL PERKINS
"BLUE SUEDE SHOES"
LIVERPOOL'S LATEST R&B SENSATION!
KING SIZE TAYLOR
AND THE DOMINOES
"STUPIDITY"
THE OTHER TWO
"BE WITH YOU"
LARRY BURNS
COMPERE

 # CHUCK BERRY

Below: Chuck with fans at a Chinese restaurant in Bolton, May 26, 1964, after the shows at the Odeon. On the left are Neil Carter and Roger Fairhurst (behind), both R & B Scene magazine staffers. On the right are Mike Bocock (a local lad who ran a Chuck Berry Fan Club) and his girlfriend, then Paul Alford and closest to the camera Bob Richardson. Right and opposite page: Berry in the Birmingham Gaumont dressing room, 1965.
Far right : Don Arden's mother Sarah Levy (Sharon Osbourne's grandmother) with Berry. Don's relatives all lived in the Manchester area and came to many of the local shows he promoted.

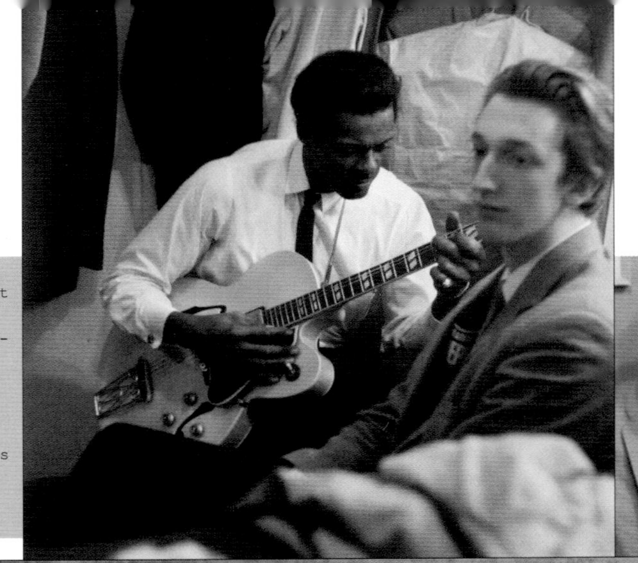

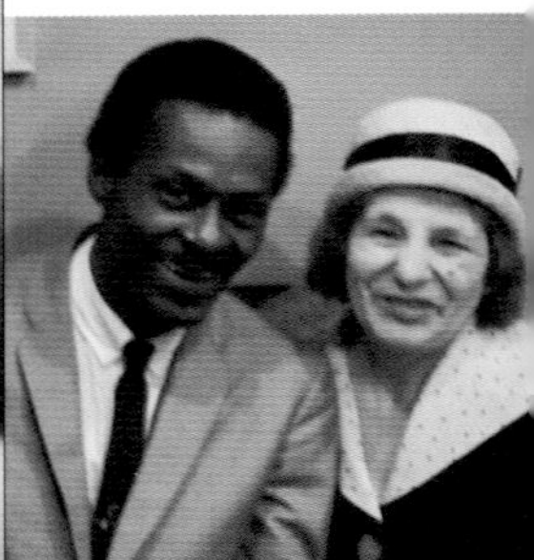

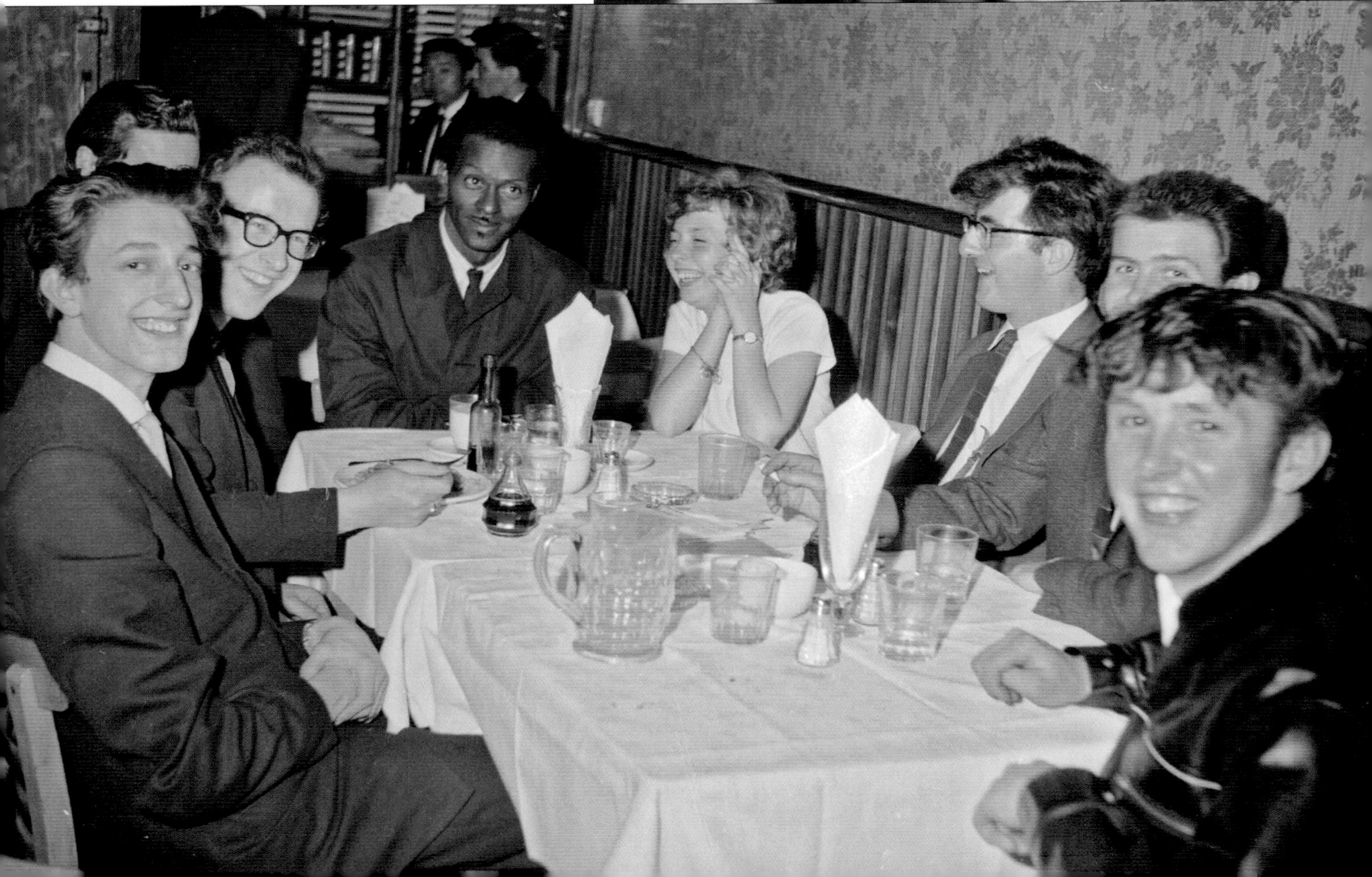

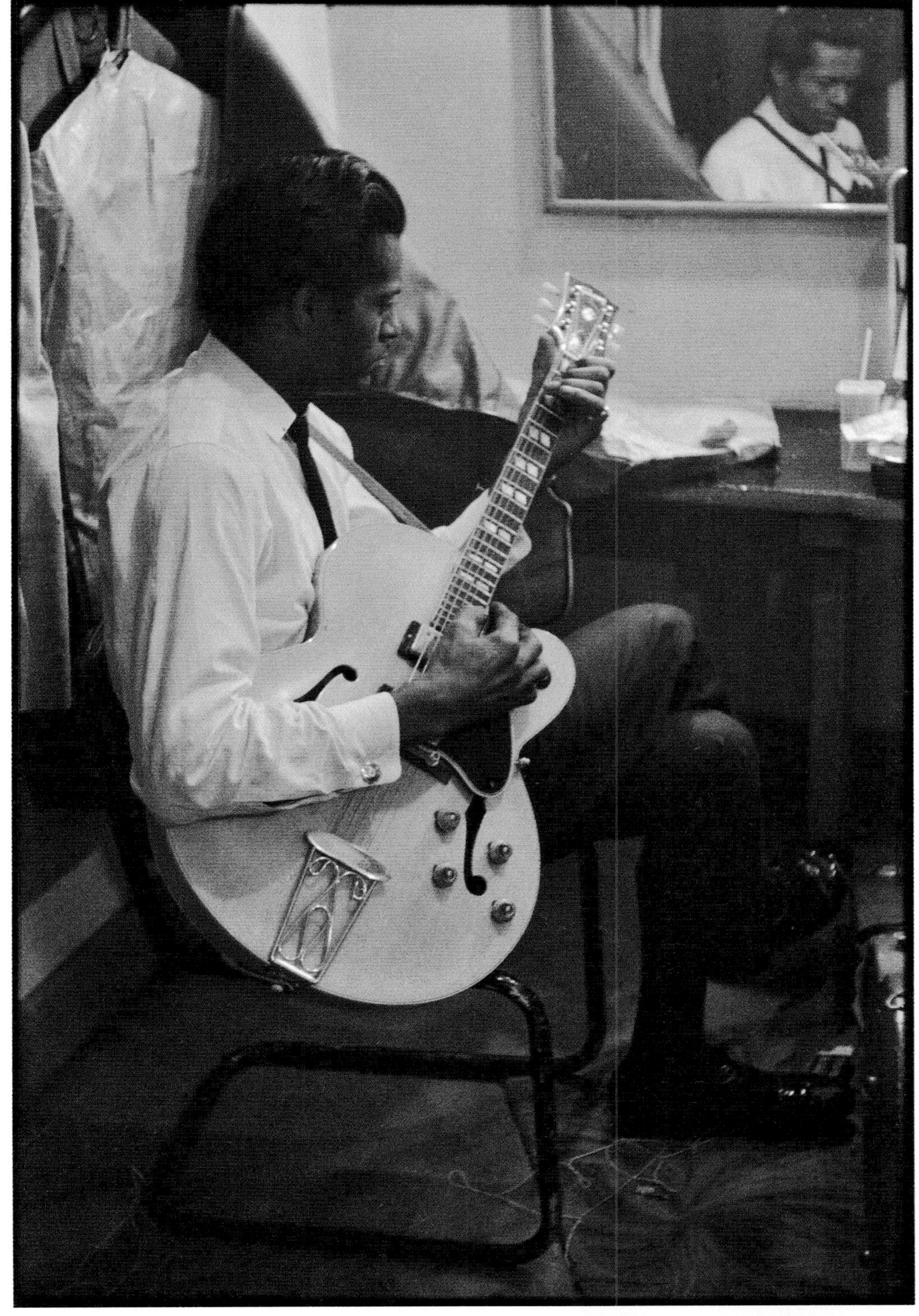

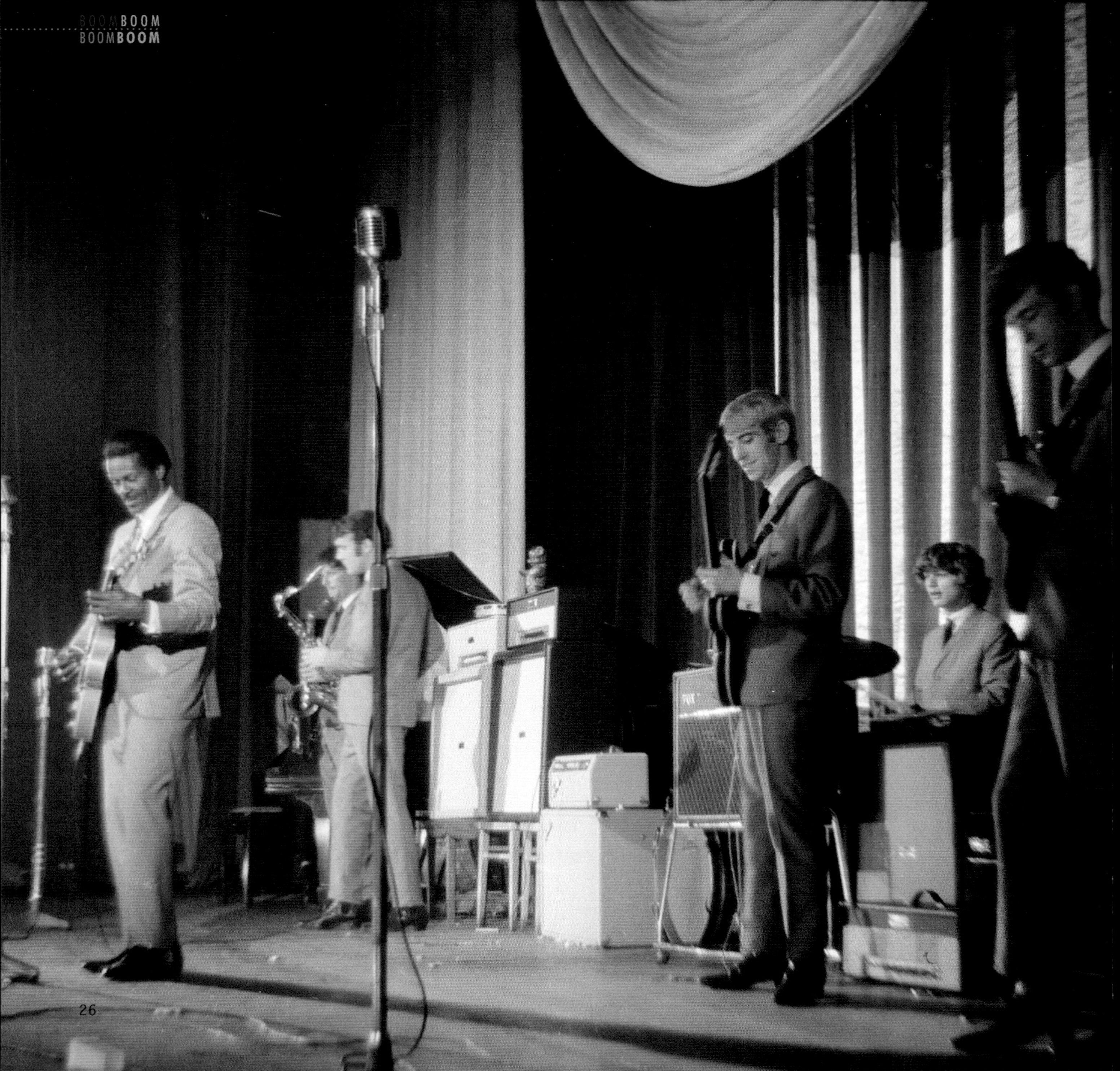

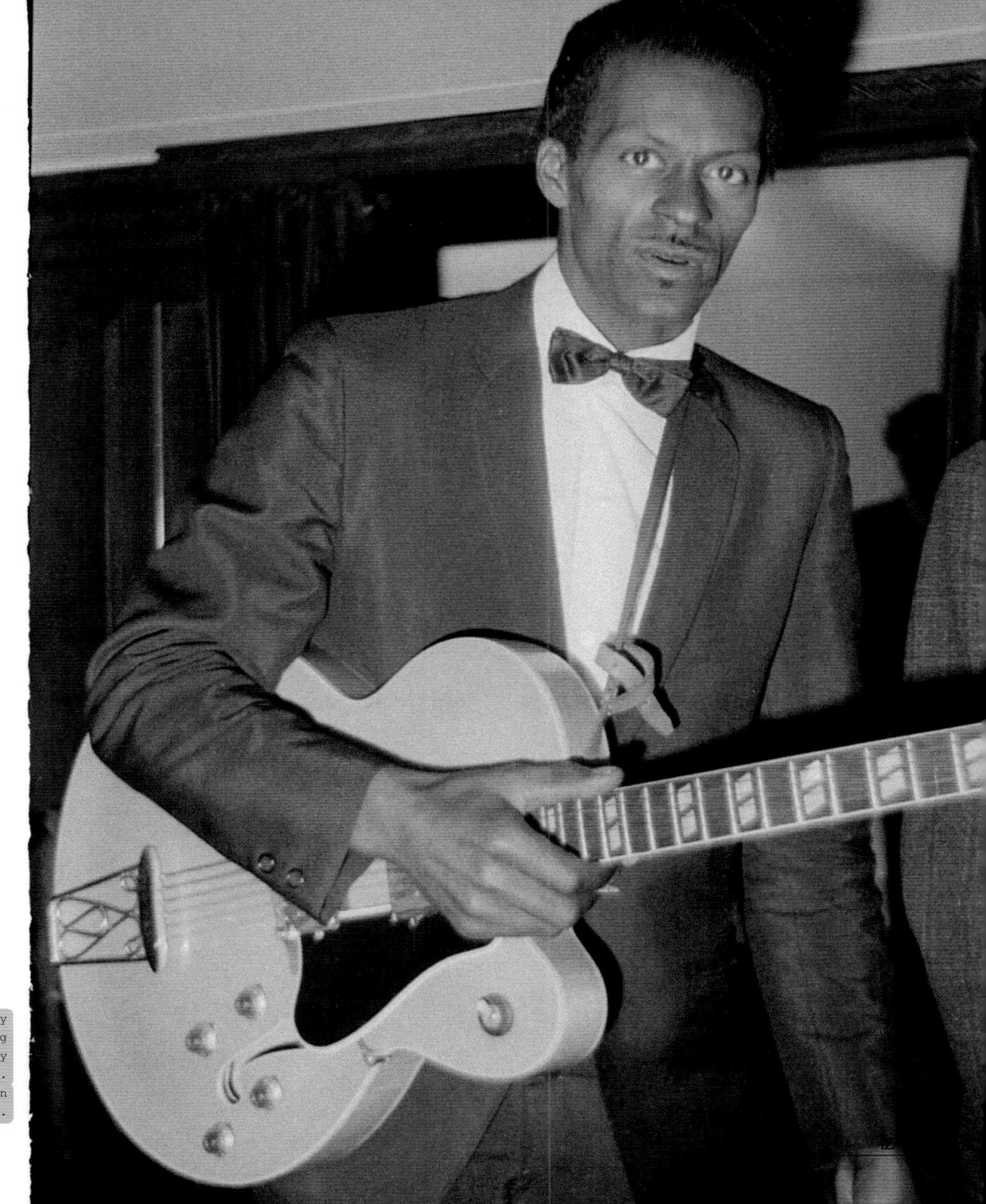

📷 Right: Berry backstage in the dressing room at Sheffield City Hall waiting to go on. Left: Concert at Bolton Odeon, May 1964.

Photographs on these two pages were taken at Sheffield City Hall, May 14th 1964. Promoted by Don Arden, and the first photographs of Berry Brian had taken, Berry was backed by Kingsize Taylor's Dominoes, with sax player Dave Woods. Brian met Berry later on the tour and gave him some prints as souvenirs. One of these turned up around 1965 on the cover of a rare Japanese E.P. and another from the same show appeared on a Japanese album (see below). Brian didn't find out about these until he saw them in a discography over forty years later!

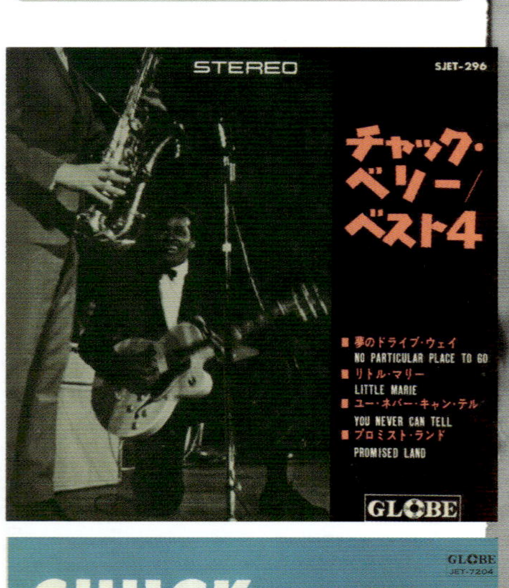

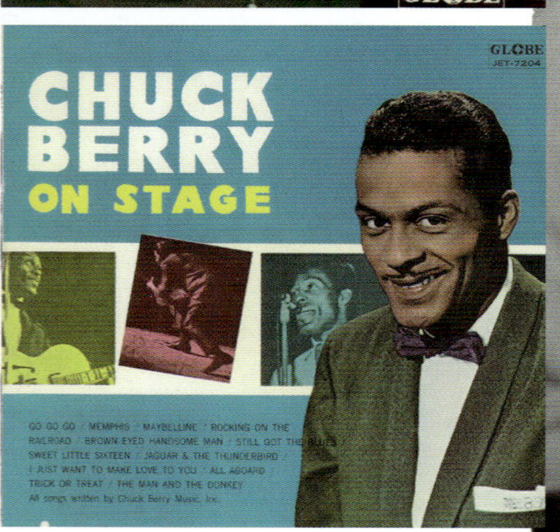

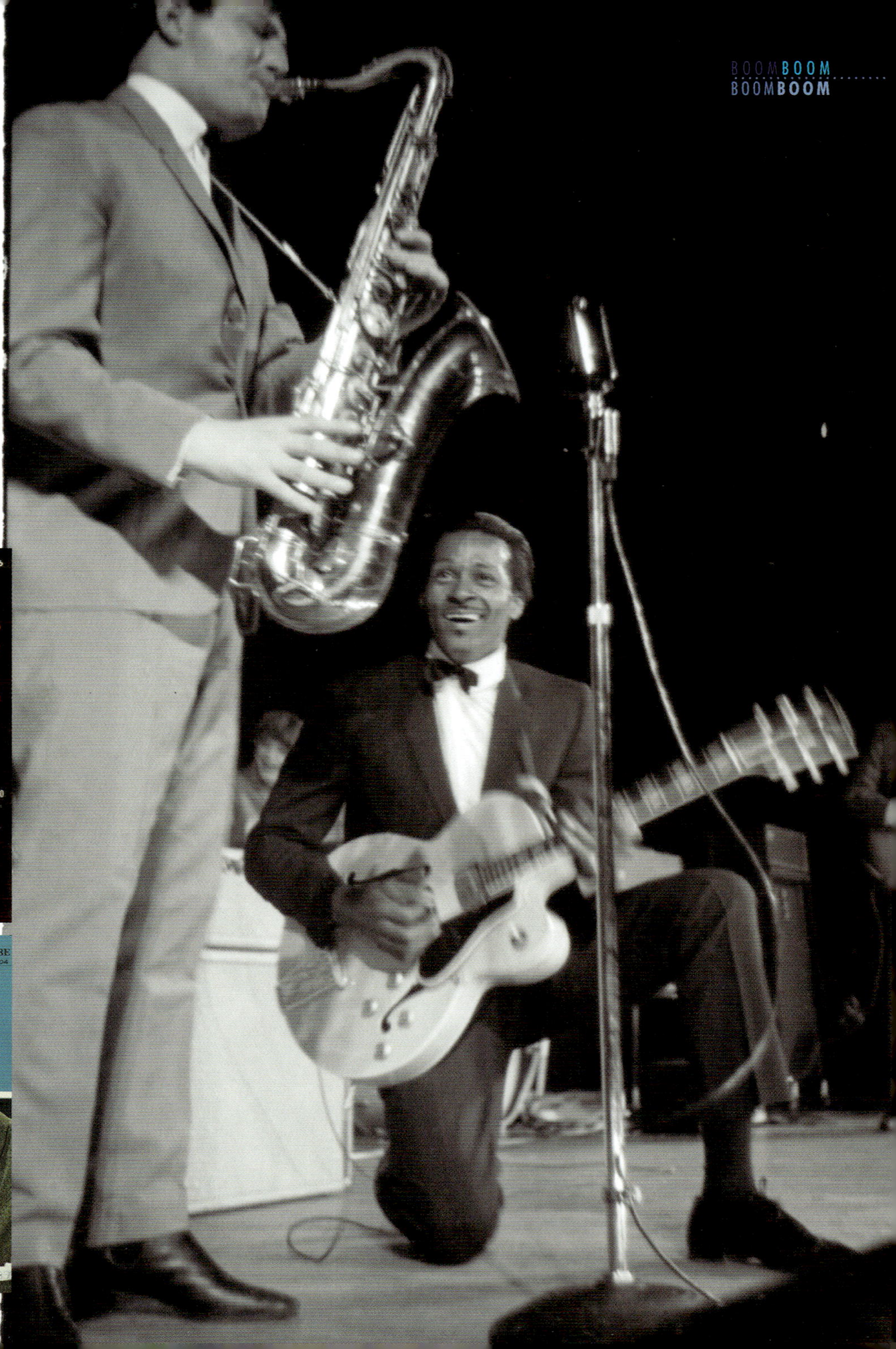

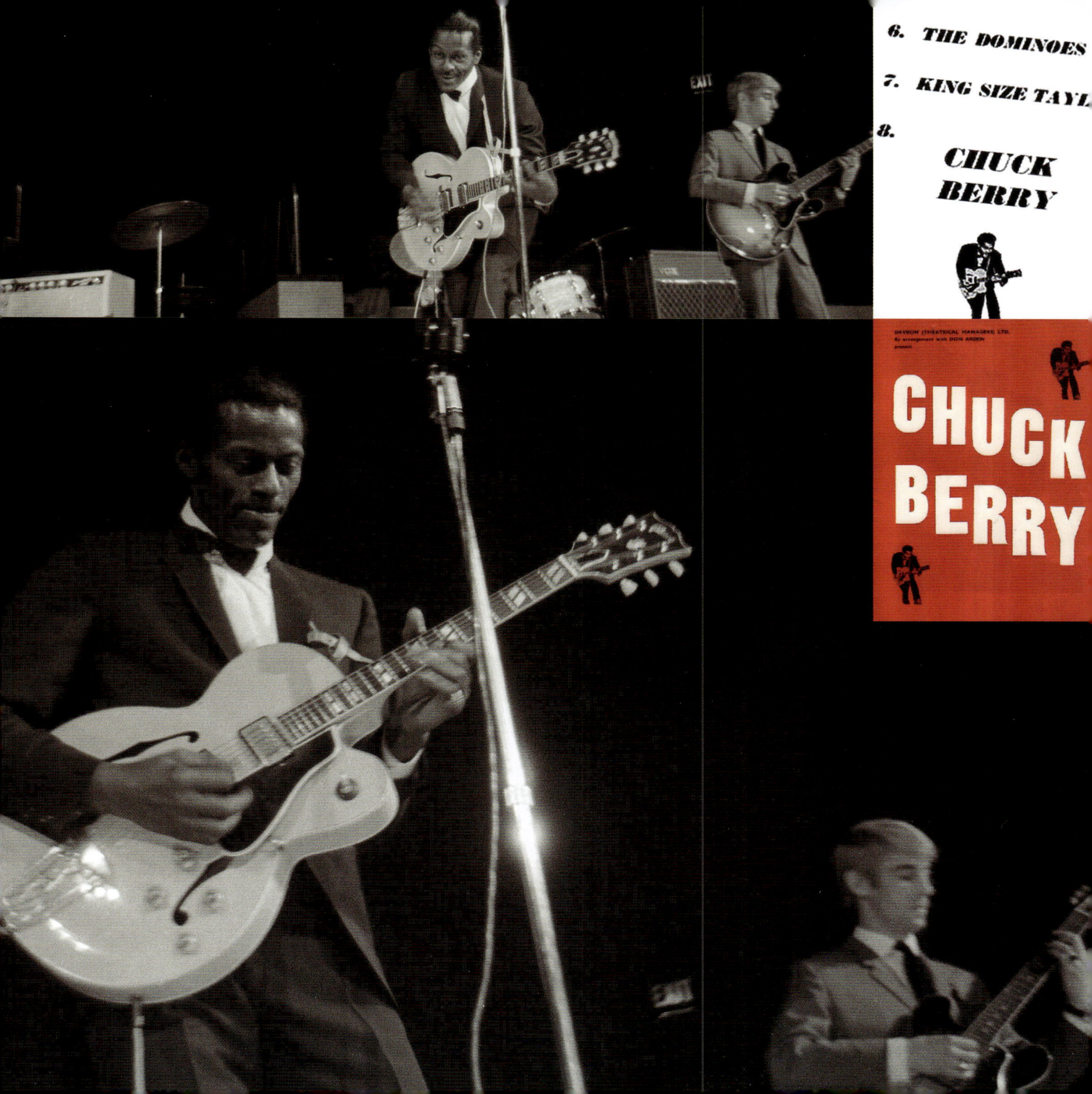
6. THE DOMINOES
7. KING SIZE TAYL
8. CHUCK BERRY
CHUCK BERRY

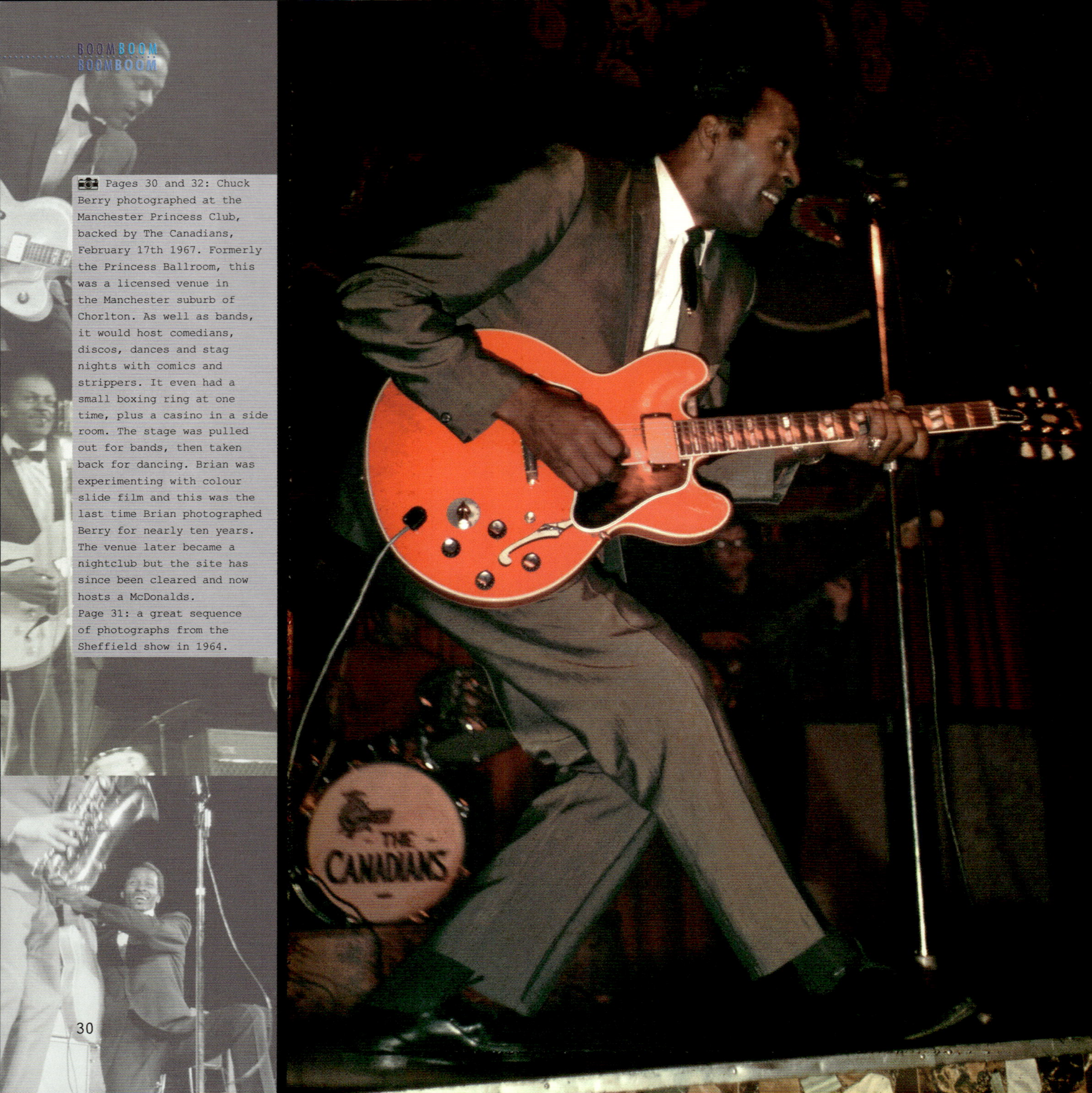

Pages 30 and 32: Chuck Berry photographed at the Manchester Princess Club, backed by The Canadians, February 17th 1967. Formerly the Princess Ballroom, this was a licensed venue in the Manchester suburb of Chorlton. As well as bands, it would host comedians, discos, dances and stag nights with comics and strippers. It even had a small boxing ring at one time, plus a casino in a side room. The stage was pulled out for bands, then taken back for dancing. Brian was experimenting with colour slide film and this was the last time Brian photographed Berry for nearly ten years. The venue later became a nightclub but the site has since been cleared and now hosts a McDonalds.

Page 31: a great sequence of photographs from the Sheffield show in 1964.

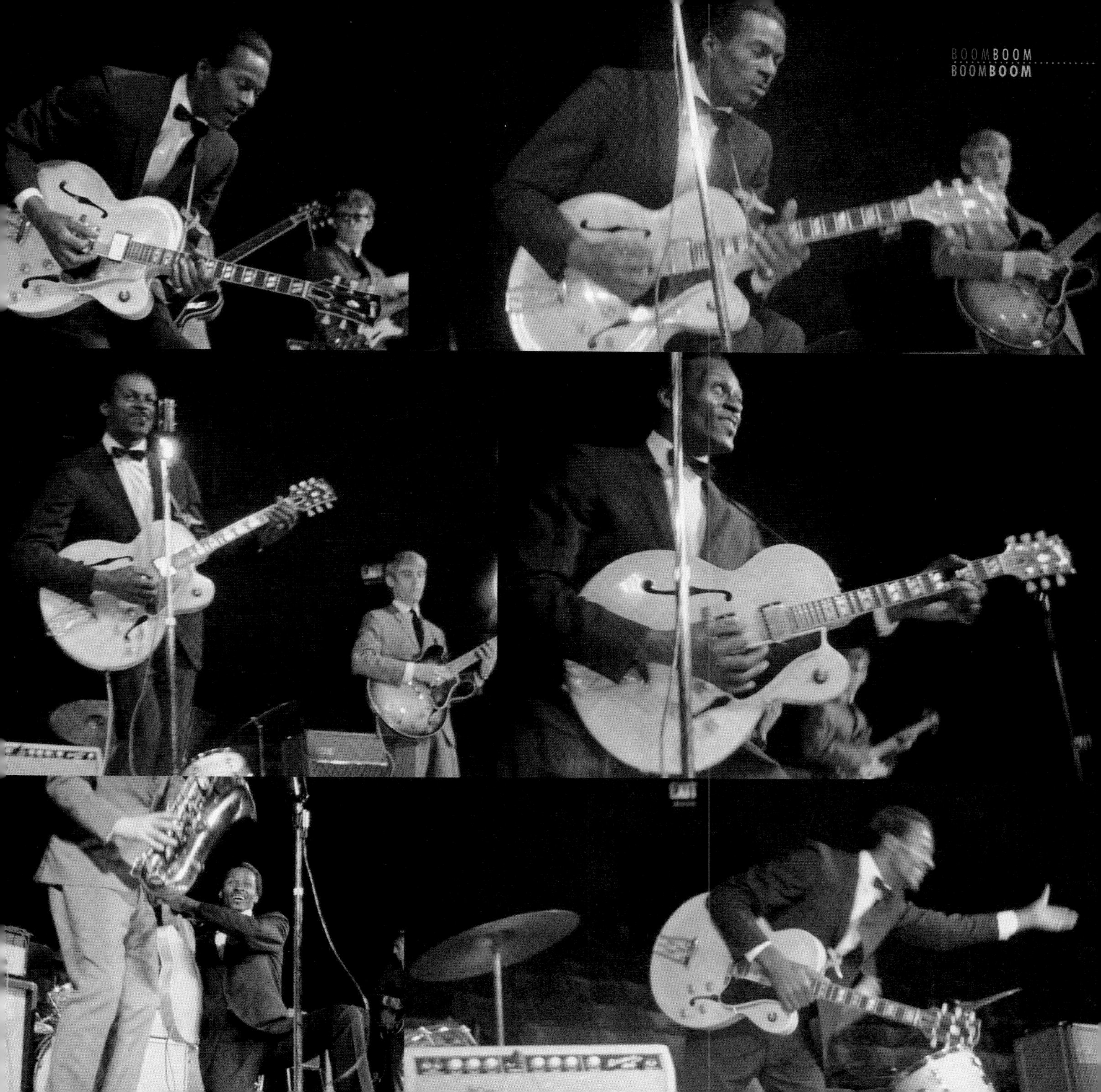
BOOMBOOM
BOOMBOOM

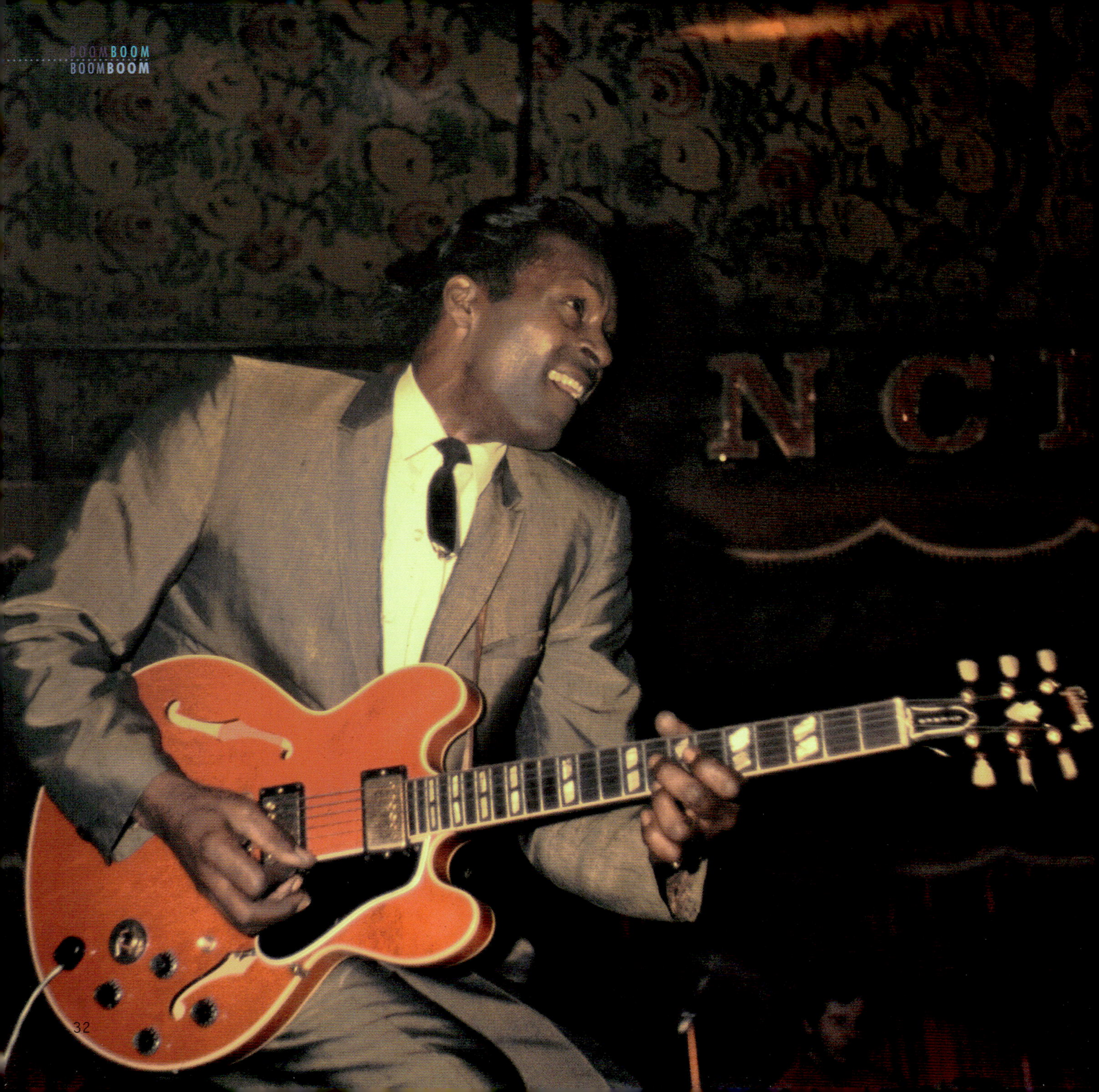

BOOMBOOM
BOOMBOOM

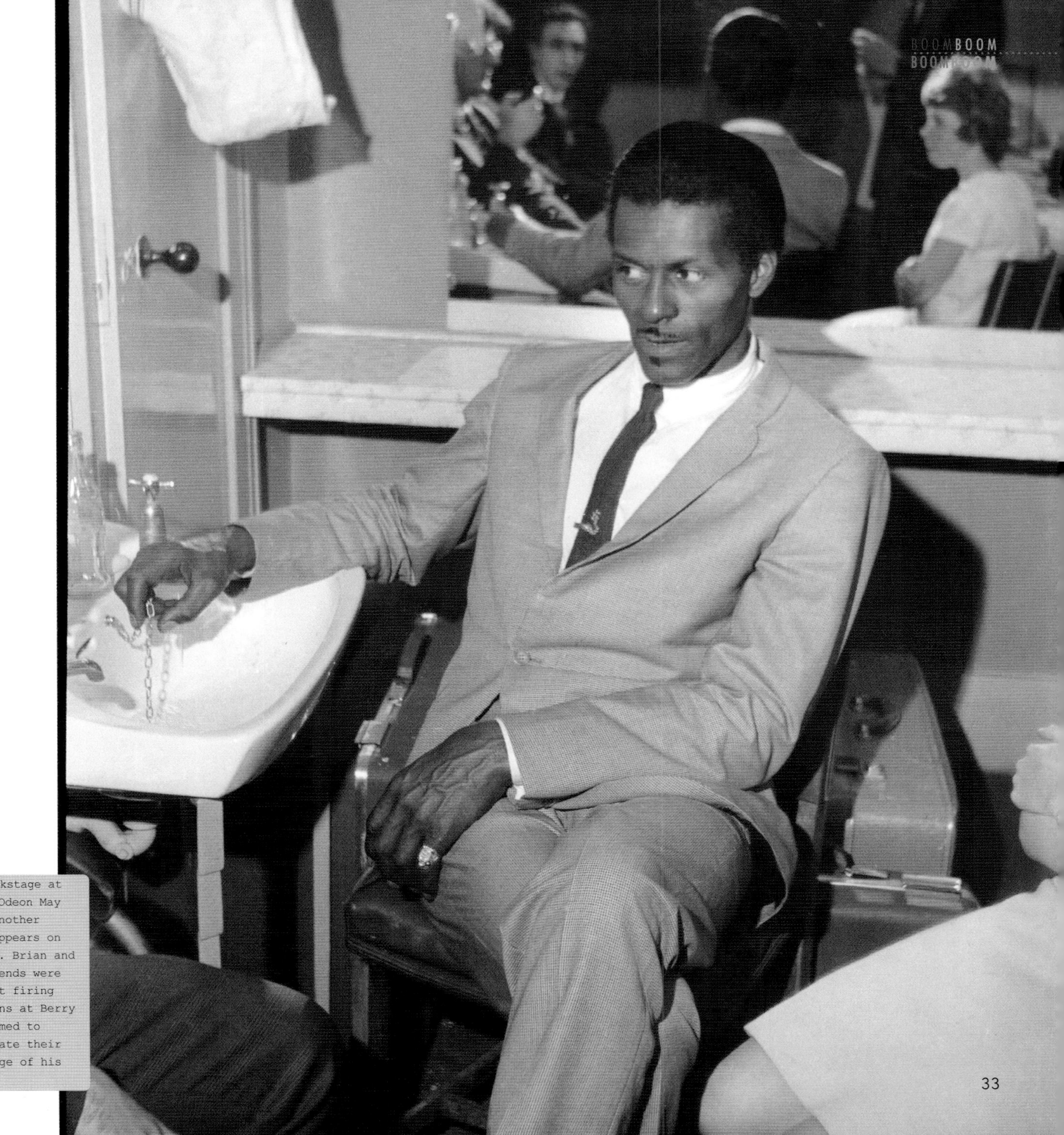

Backstage at Bolton Odeon May 1964 (another frame appears on page 2). Brian and his friends were just sat firing questions at Berry who seemed to appreciate their knowledge of his work.

BIG MAMA THORNTON and HELEN HUMES

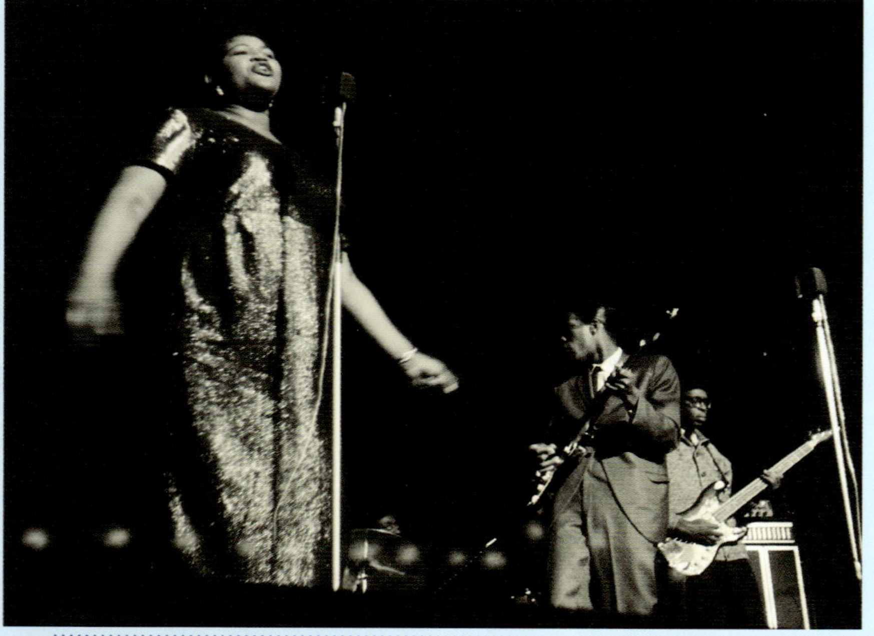

Brian admits to being a little intimidated at meeting Big Mama Thornton (opposite page) as he'd been chatting to John Lee Hooker some weeks before, who described her to him as *"A big woman. B..b.. built like a truck-driver!"* Big Mama was appearing as one of the acts on the 4th American Folk Blues Festival, which toured the U.K. during October 1965. Brian went to the Manchester Free Trade Hall show on the 15th. The billing was Big Mama Thornton, Lonesome Jimmy Lee, Eddie Boyd, Buddy Guy, Fred Below, J.B. Lenoir, Walter Shakey Horton, Roosevelt Sykes, Mississippi Fred McDowell and Doctor Ross. After chatting with her for a time backstage he dared to produce his camera. *"As she saw me about to take a pic, she seized my wrist in a vice-like grips and said, firmly 'Not with my head-rag on'! She grabbed her hat and planted it on her head and posed for this one photograph."* Though as Brian points out you can still see her head-scarf anyway. A memorable portrait but Brian quit while he was ahead, though he did take this distant shot (left) of her on-stage in a more glamorous gold lamé outfit, with Buddy Guy on guitar and Lonesome Jimmy Lee on bass.

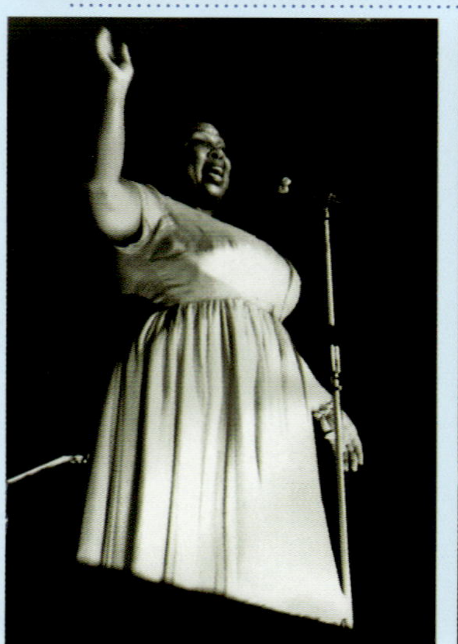

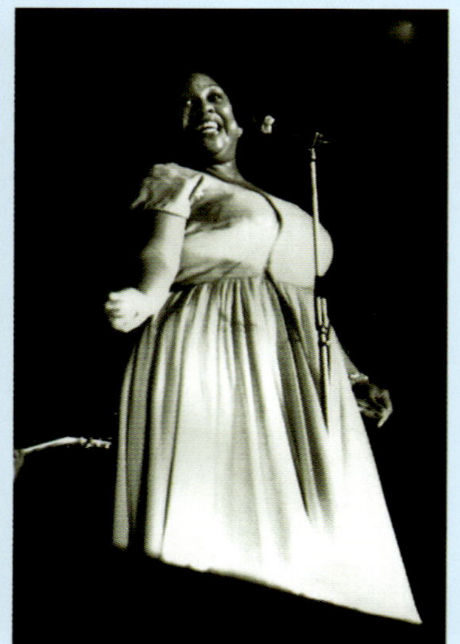

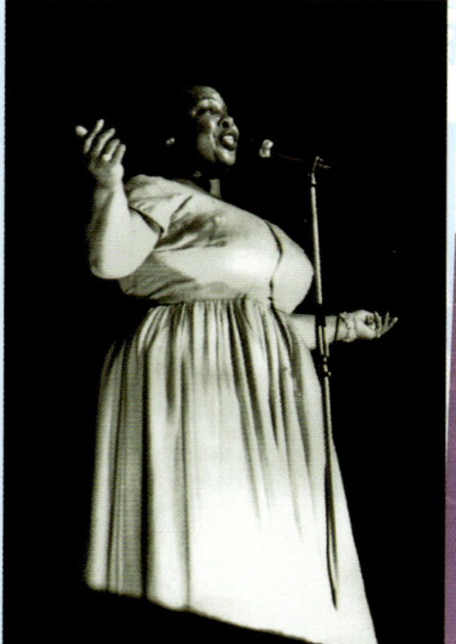

Brian describes Helen Humes (left) as one of the last great female jazz and blues shouters, seen here on the first AFBF tour at The Free Trade Hall, Manchester, Oct 31 1962. That's the tour programme below.

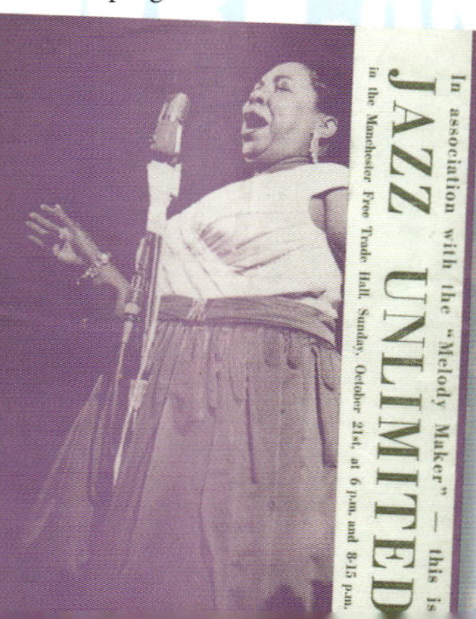

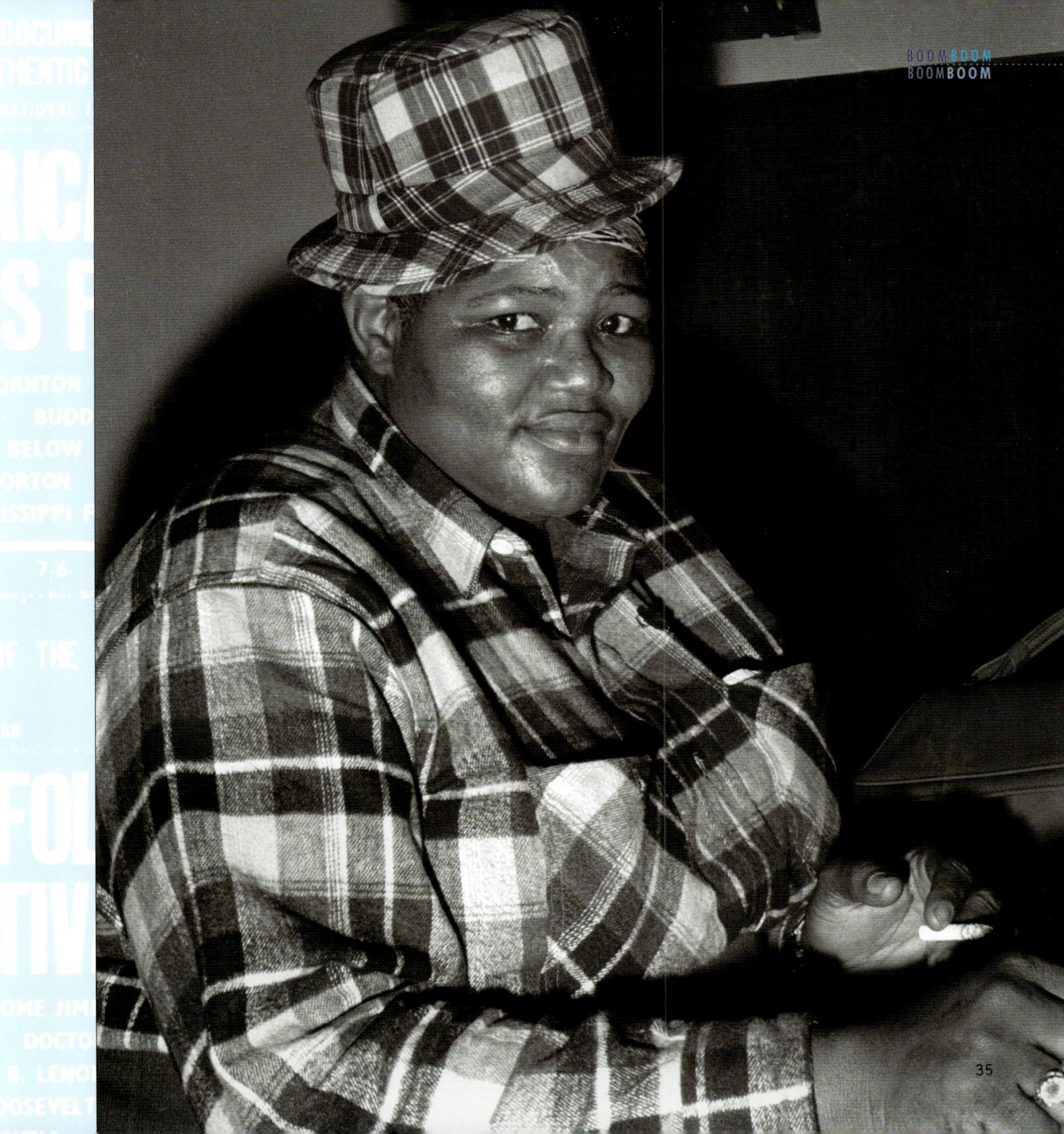

35

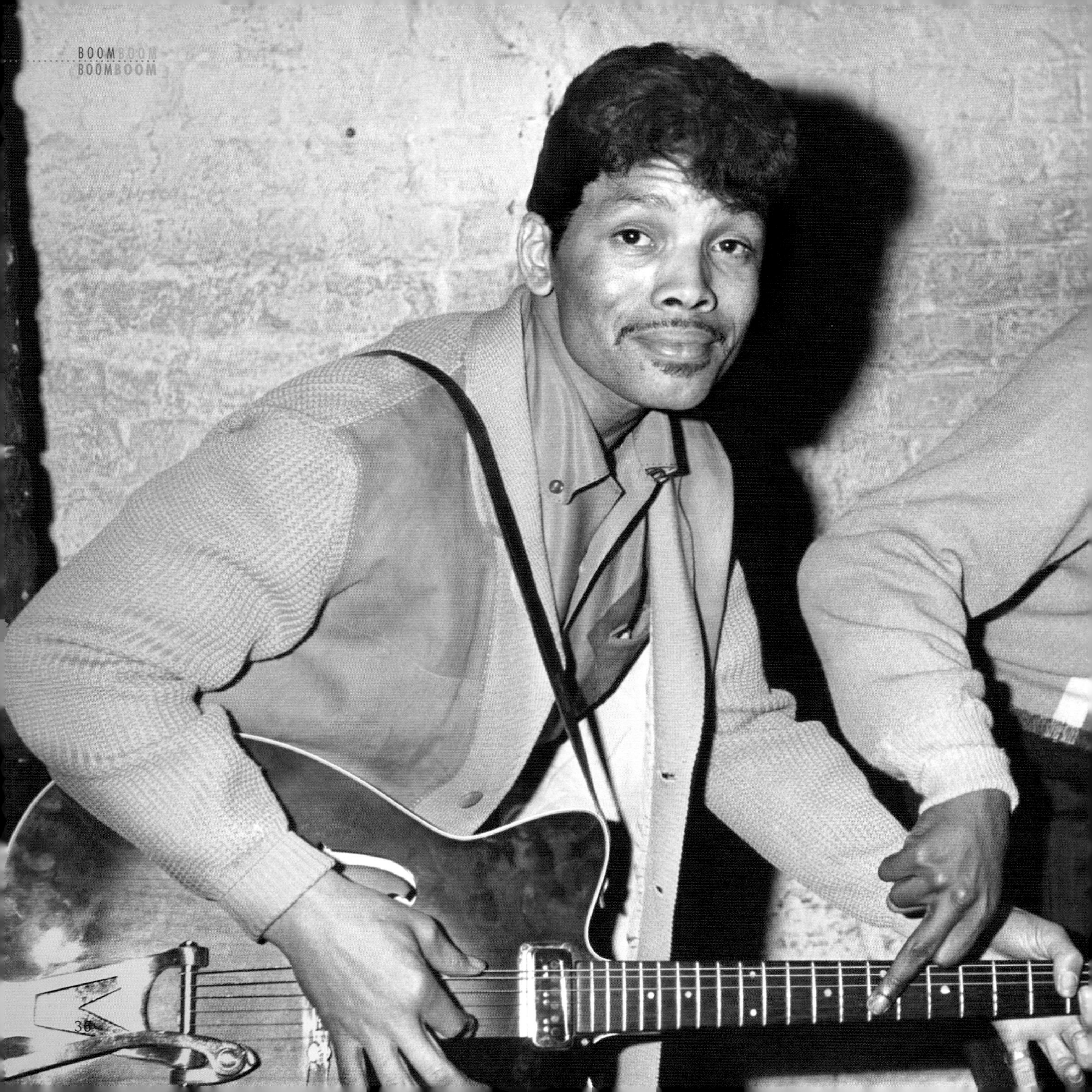

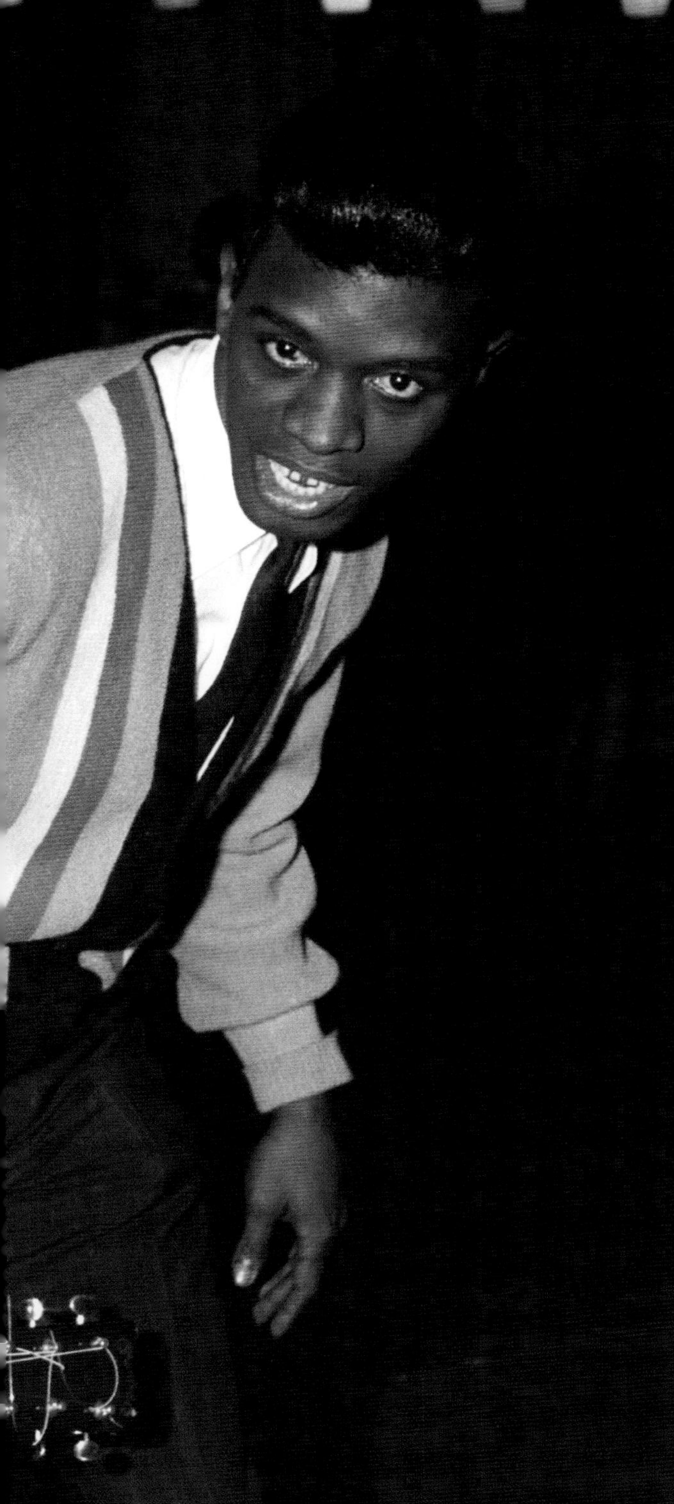

LARRY WILLIAMS and
JOHNNY 'GUITAR' WATSON

Most of these photographs were taken at a Twisted Wheel Club all-nighter on April 3rd 1965. Brian saw his new girlfriend onto a bus home after their first date (now a fifty years plus marriage!) then hot-footed it over to the Wheel. Larry Williams was booked to tour on what turned out to be his only visit to Britain. His own records had been much covered and, having just teamed up with Watson the pair came over together (one story suggests that Larry told promoters Johnny had been Elvis's guitarist to help sell the idea). They even cut a studio album for Decca (in a day) and a live album in the Marquee's back-room studio (introduced by Screaming Lord Sutch) while over here. The pair had played Manchester a week before at the Princess Club (and another at The Domino the same night) where Brian (who remembers the backing band as Hogsnort Rupert's Good Good Band, not a name you'd forget in a hurry!) took a few more shots (page opposite, left).

It was however The Stormville Shakers, who backed most of the tour. Singer, songwriter and producer Phillip Goodhand-Tait helped form The Stormsville Shakers in the late 1950s and wrote about touring with Larry and Johnny on his website: *"By 1965, original rock 'n' roll was unfashionable. Nevertheless Larry attracted a loyal following. Like many visiting Americans, due to Musicians Union reciprocal agreements in the UK and USA at the time, he was forced to work with any pick-up British band his UK agent or promoter provided. There was never any rehearsal time but in the Stormsville's case, that didn't matter. We were fans and knew his records well. It was normal practice for an Agent to book a visiting artist from the U.S. for a fixed fee for a few weeks and sub-let as many dates as possible to other promoters to make a profit. The more gigs, the more profit and so two shows-a-night was not unusual, sometimes three.*

"After a show together at The Plaza Ballroom, Guildford, the following night we were booked together again at the Twisted Wheel Club, Manchester. We met there early with our American friends, intending to rehearse but instead, we frittered away the hours in a nearby coffee bar. Larry signed my 45 rpm copy of She Said Yeah and Johnny Watson cracked us up complaining that English coffee was served in such small cups. He addressed the waiter with mock despair "What do ya call this, eye wash?" Johnny was the craziest band leader. Larry would normally begin a song with piano and then Johnny would lead us into it at break-neck speed. It was like clinging on to a fairground ride. He'd alternate solos with Larry's piano and occasionally turn to David or Tony for an impromptu sax solo. Johnny's guitar solos were dynamite. He was Chuck Berry and Jimi Hendrix rolled into one. The faster the ride, the more exciting it seemed."

The promoter approached them around midnight and asked if they could do a second set and Larry saw the chance for them to earn a little bonus. *"A debate began about money. My own problem was that the Stormsville Shakers were due to gig at the Witch Doctor Club in Hastings the next night. Without a motorway network, that journey involved a slow crawl through the night. Larry wasn't going to pass up extra reward and we parted, leaving him to work with a local band, while we drove south through the night."*

Roger Eagle was a big fan of Williams and would often play his single *Boney Moronie* a couple of times a night and helped arrange the Wheel booking. They already had a large blow up of a Larry Williams photo at the bottom of the stairs

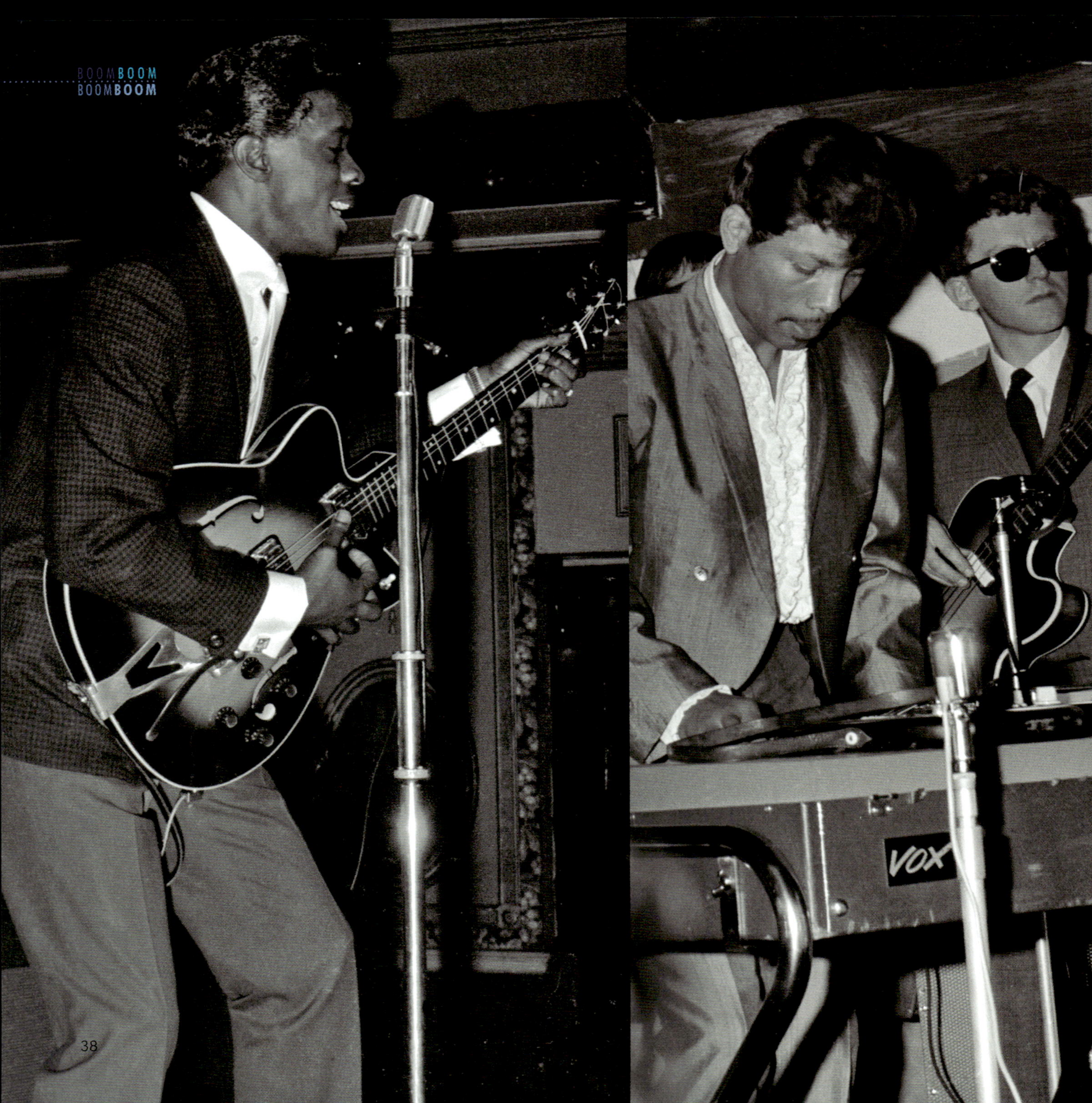
VOX

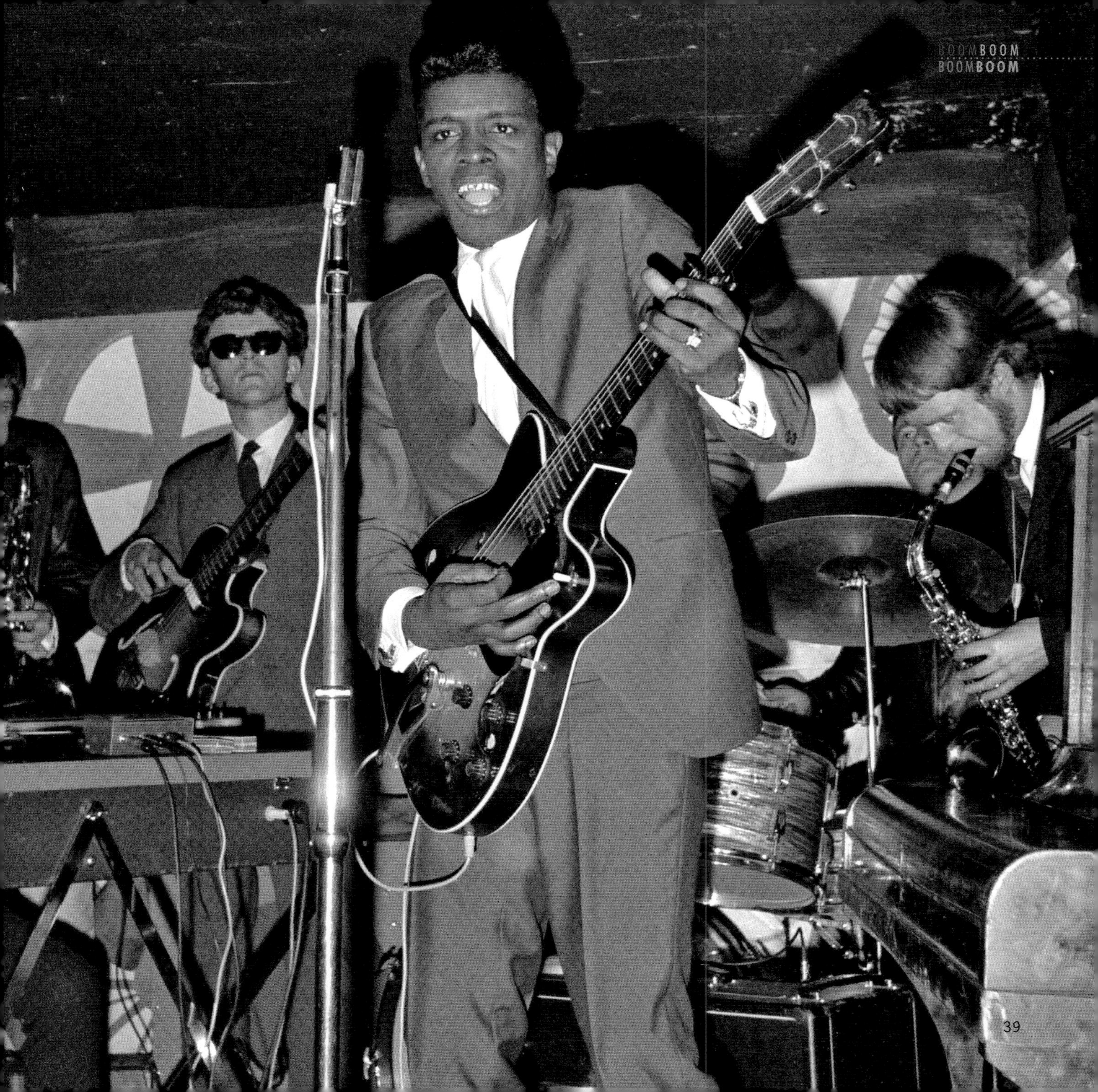

BOOMBOOM
BOOMBOOM

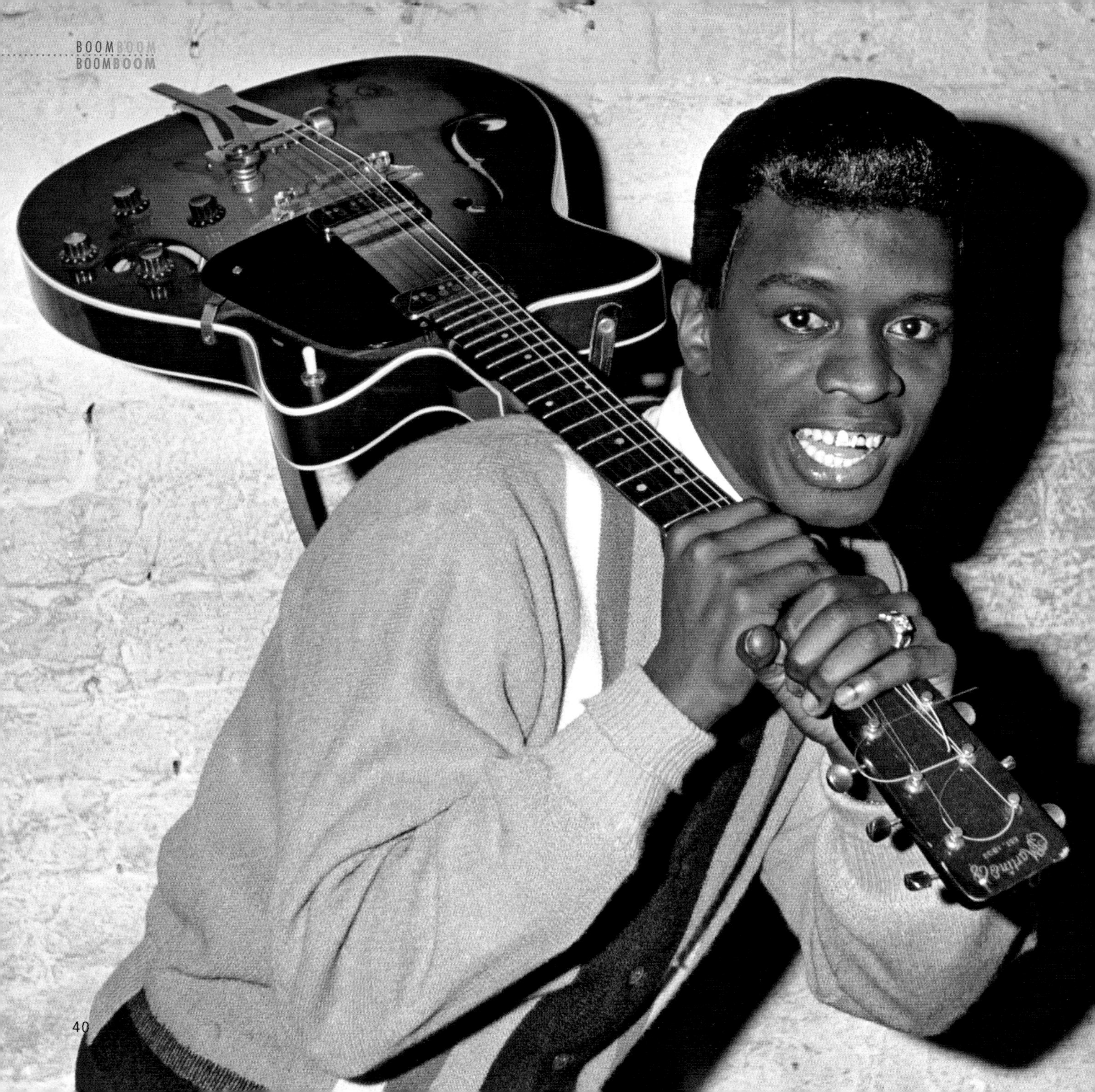

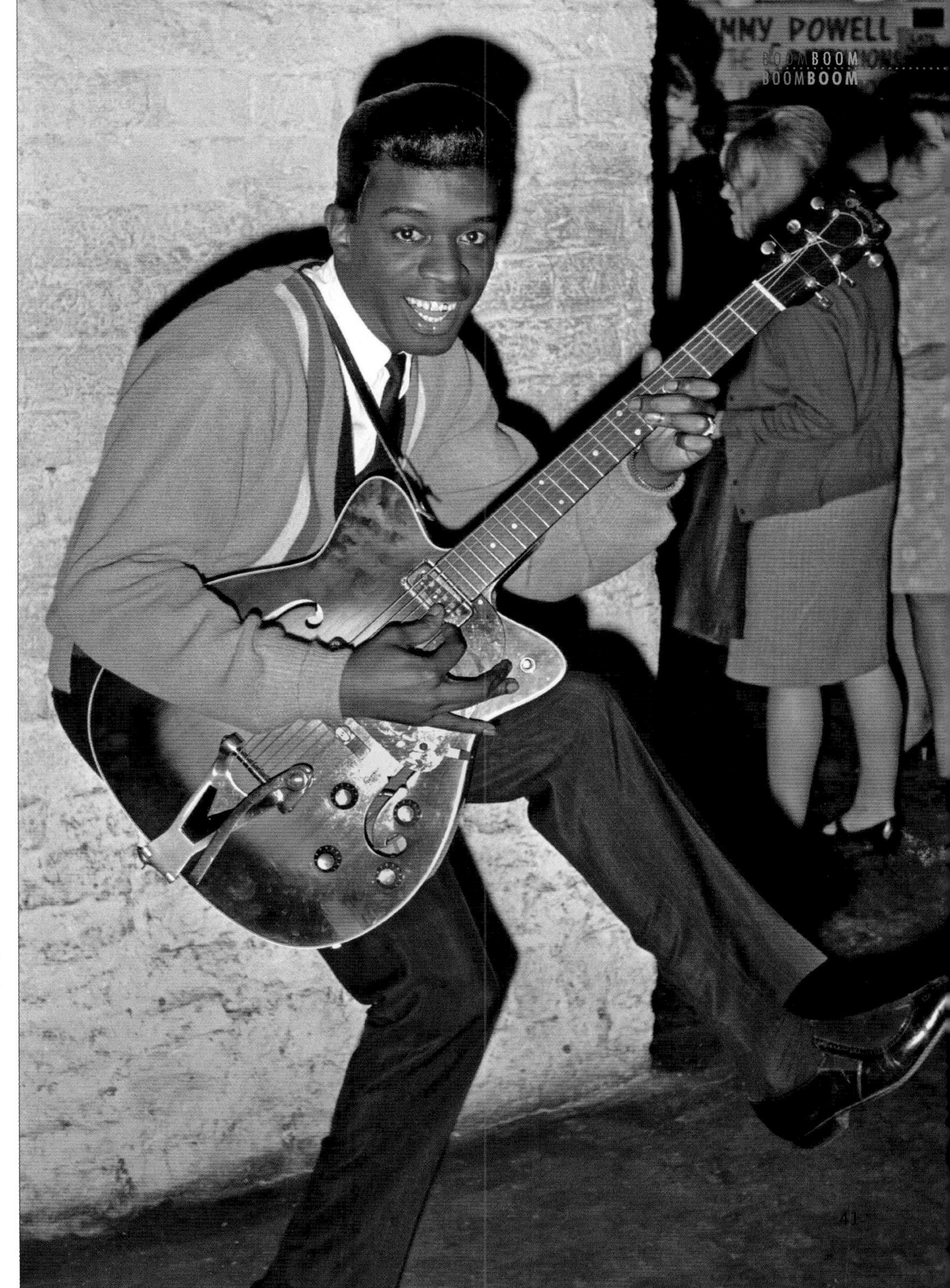

the club. The all-night bill also included The Hipster Image and The Fossils. When The Stormsville Shakers had to cry off, The Hipster Image replaced them for the second set. The band were managed by Kevin Donovan who ran a similar club to The Wheel over in Hanley, Stoke On Trent, called The Place. They checked over the set list and went for it, and they are the band we can see in the live photographs - their one and only Decca single now goes for around £900.

The backstage shots of Johnny 'Guitar' Watson are some of Brian's best - *"a few decent black and whites"* as Brian modestly refers to them! (Some of them appeared on an Ace Records CD *Untouchable*, where they were hand coloured to great effect.) What adds a special quality to the shots is the incidental detail of the club itself, usually cropped off but retained here, including the poster for next weeks Wheel all-nighter - Jimmy Powell and the 5 Dimensions, plus John Lee Hooker and The Groundhogs.

As for Johnny 'Guitar' Watson, The New York Times critic Peter Watrous wrote: *"There are few more lascivious sounds in popular music than the voice of Johnny (Guitar) Watson. When he sings 'Booty Ooty' or 'Hot Little Mama,' it isn't just come hither he's singing. It is something much more joyous, and completely unprintable."*

Flamboyant is the other word often used to describe his music, and his approach to rhythm and blues influenced performers such as Jimi Hendrix, Frank Zappa and Stevie Ray Vaughan amongst many.

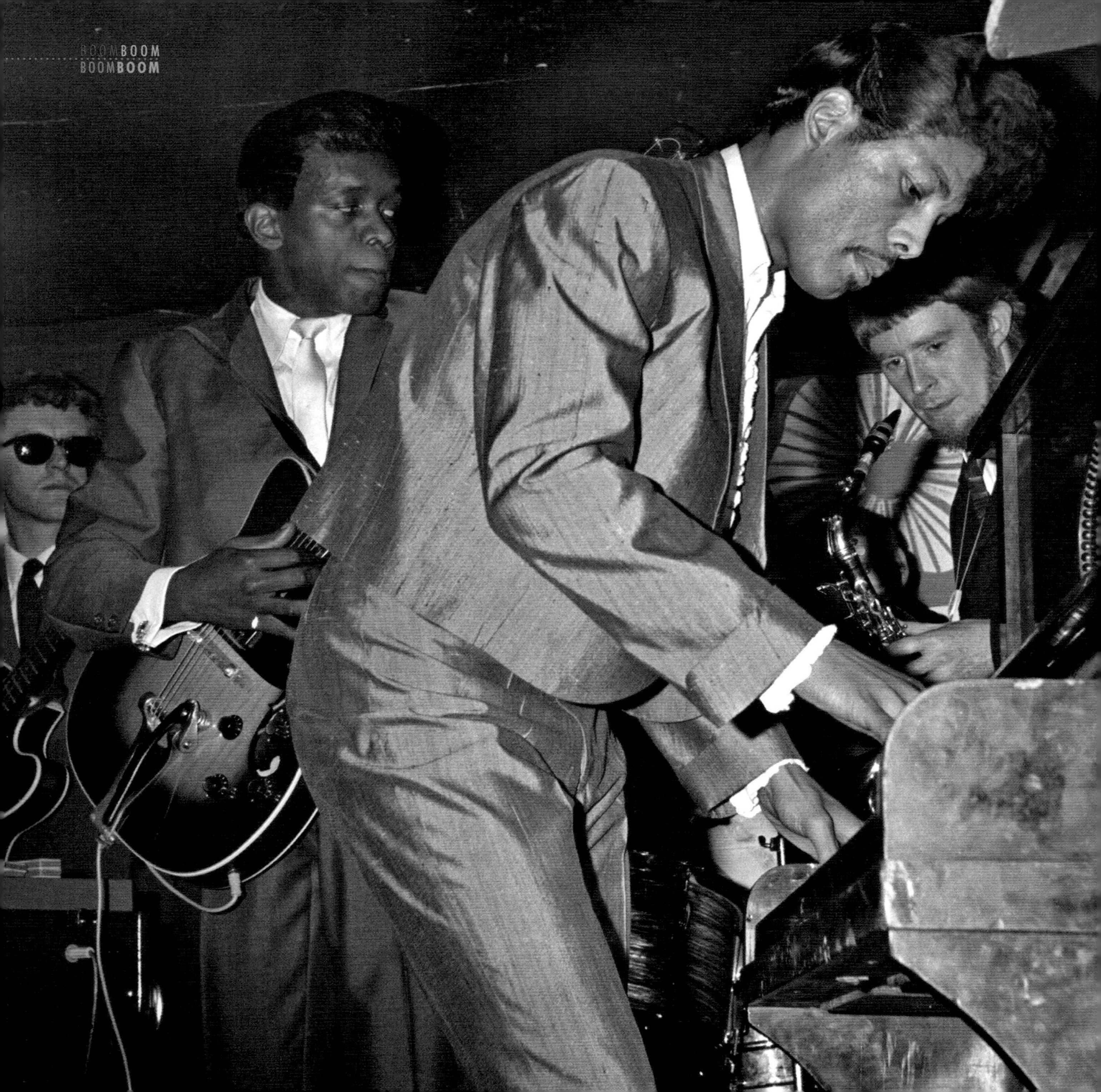
BOOM BOOM
BOOM BOOM

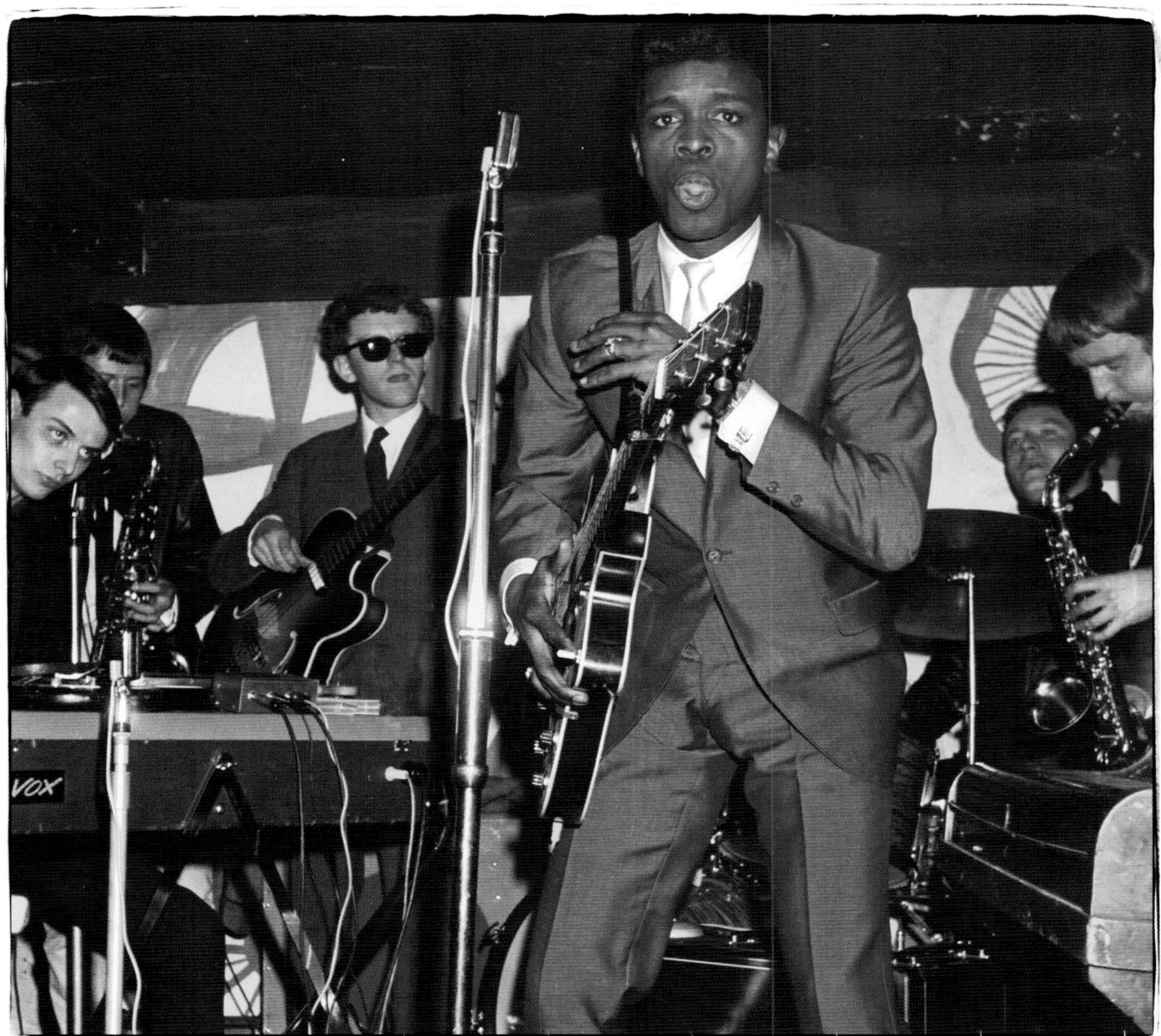

📷 Eric Leese put names to backing band The Hipster Image for us: *"On the far left is my head! I am playing my Vox organ but also played guitar. Behind me, just visible, is Colin Cooper on tenor Sax and vocals. Tony Dirkin in shades on Bass. To the right of Johnny on drums, is Keith Webb, then Frank Proudlove on sax and vocals. Colin went on to form Climax Blues Band, I joined the Mike Cotton Sounds when we split."*

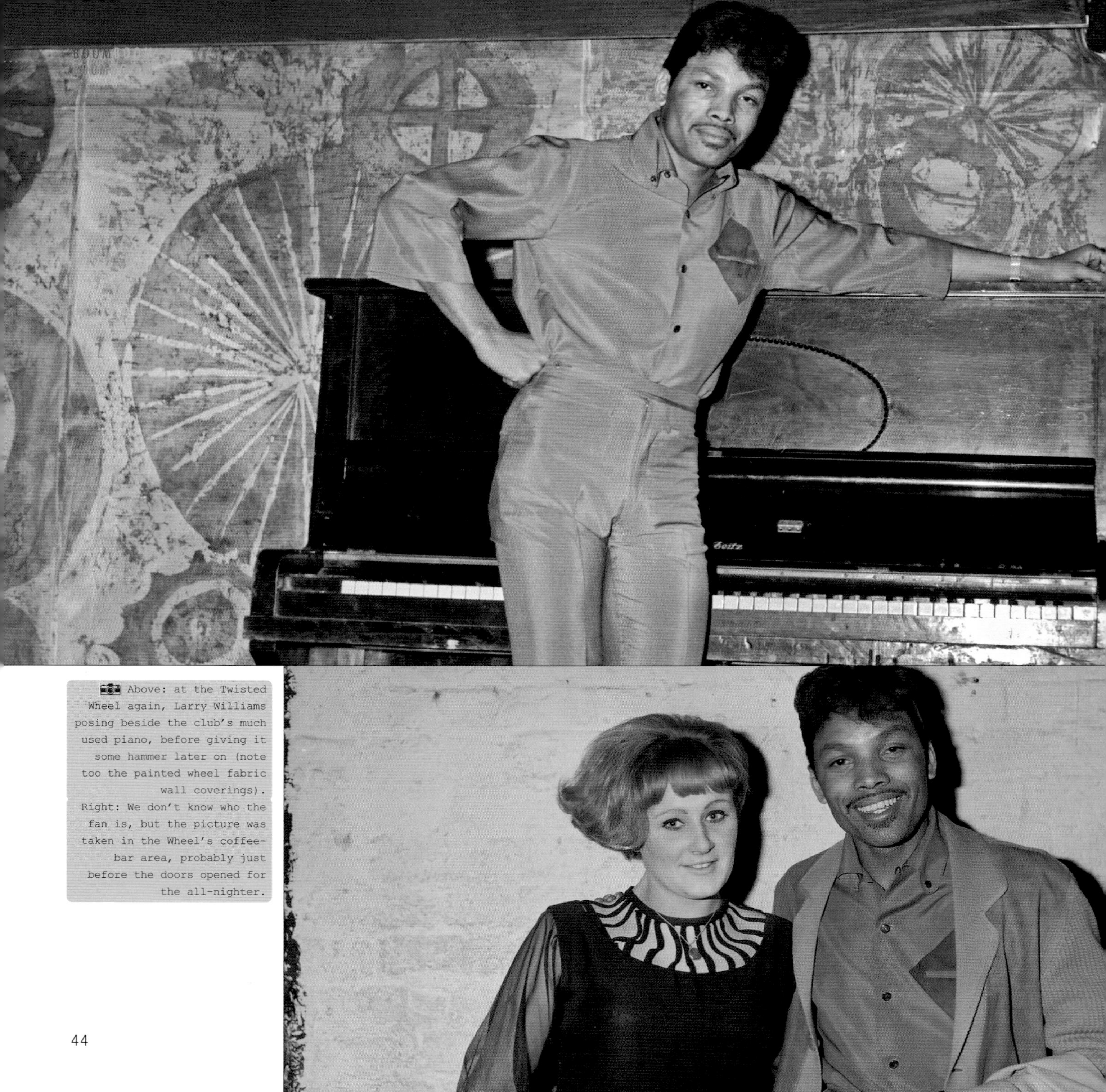

Above: at the Twisted
Wheel again, Larry Williams
posing beside the club's much
used piano, before giving it
some hammer later on (note
too the painted wheel fabric
wall coverings).
Right: We don't know who the
fan is, but the picture was
taken in the Wheel's coffee-
bar area, probably just
before the doors opened for
the all-nighter.

BUDDY GUY

Brian first photographed guitarist and singer Buddy Guy backstage (below) on the 1964 American Folk Blues Festival tour (flyer overleaf), between Eddie Boyd (left) and Fred Below (right). This show opened up opportunities for many of the blues artists to return for more bookings, hence Guy appearing at The Twisted Wheel Club on March 6th 1965, where Brian took the terrific live shots on the next four pages, which really capture both the energy of Guy's act and also the ambience of the club's cramped, low-ceilinged stage area. Roger Eagle was of the opinion at the time that Buddy was the best guitarist he had ever seen, and he was certainly doing tricks later copied by Jimi Hendrix. Buddy took time out between the evening show and the all-nighter at The Wheel to go for some dinner with Brian and friends, and he took the shot of Buddy there (left), against the diamond pattern wallpaper. *"It was the Al-Khayam Indian restaurant, in nearby Lloyd St*

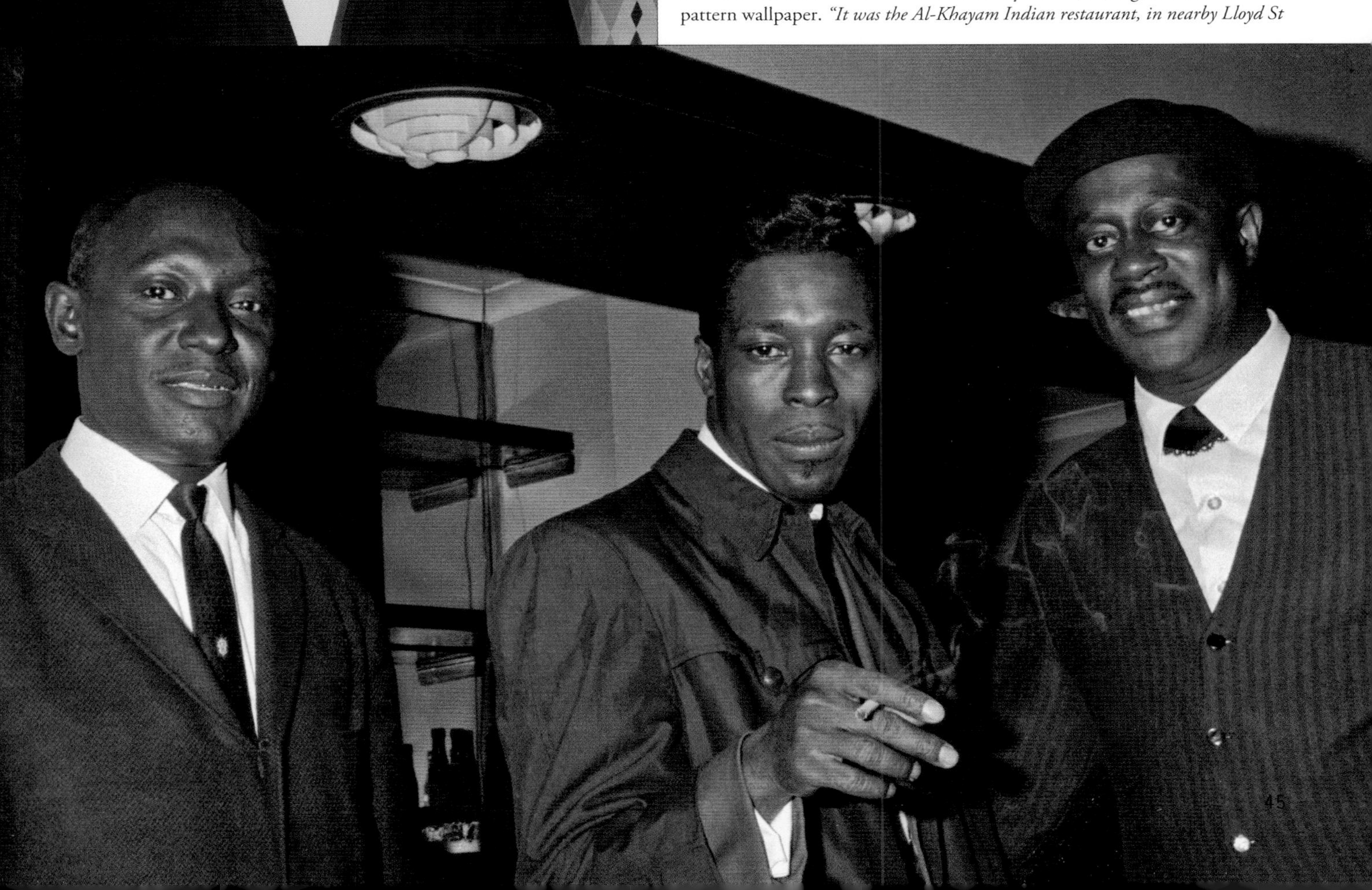

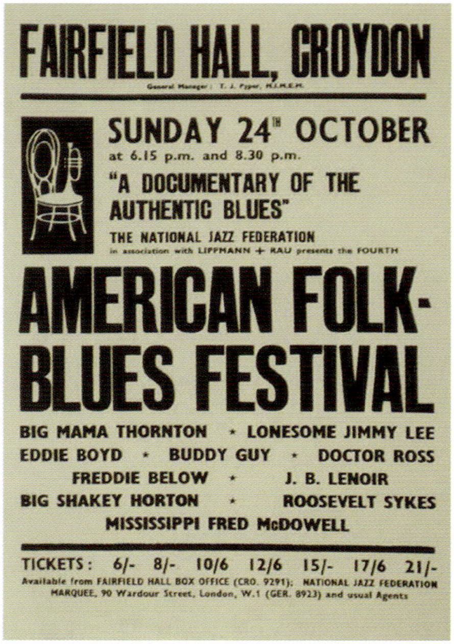

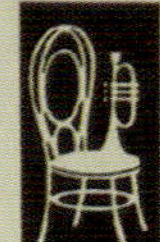

FAIRFIELD HALL, CROYDON

General Manager : T. J. Pyper, A.I.M.E.E.

SUNDAY 24TH OCTOBER

at 6.15 p.m. and 8.30 p.m.

"A DOCUMENTARY OF THE AUTHENTIC BLUES"

THE NATIONAL JAZZ FEDERATION
in association with LIPPMANN + RAU presents the FOURTH

AMERICAN FOLK-BLUES FESTIVAL

BIG MAMA THORNTON • LONESOME JIMMY LEE
EDDIE BOYD • BUDDY GUY • DOCTOR ROSS
FREDDIE BELOW • J. B. LENOIR
BIG SHAKEY HORTON • ROOSEVELT SYKES
MISSISSIPPI FRED McDOWELL

TICKETS : 6/- 8/- 10/6 12/6 15/- 17/6 21/-

Available from FAIRFIELD HALL BOX OFFICE (CRO. 9291); NATIONAL JAZZ FEDERATION
MARQUEE, 90 Wardour Street, London, W.1 (GER. 8923) and usual Agents

(actually above the Oasis Club) and we knew it well as it was a regular lunchtime eaterie for me and my workmates," recalls Brian.

For The Wheel concert's first set, Guy needed a backing band. The Soul Agents were supposed to play but couldn't find the venue having got lost en route, so another local outfit, Cops 'n' Robbers, stepped up to the plate. *"There was NO rehearsal whatever. Buddy came into the club which was already open and very busy and, after just a short discussion they went straight on. He kept time by foot-stomping and, most memorably for all those present, slamming his guitar-neck into the low ceiling above the stage!"* It's no wonder their bassist was keeping a close eye and following Guy's every move, as can be seen in some of the shots.

The Soul Agents eventually arrived and were able to back Guy's second performance. They also got to do their own set, and - as if the evening had not been memorable enough already - had Rod Stewart guest as well.

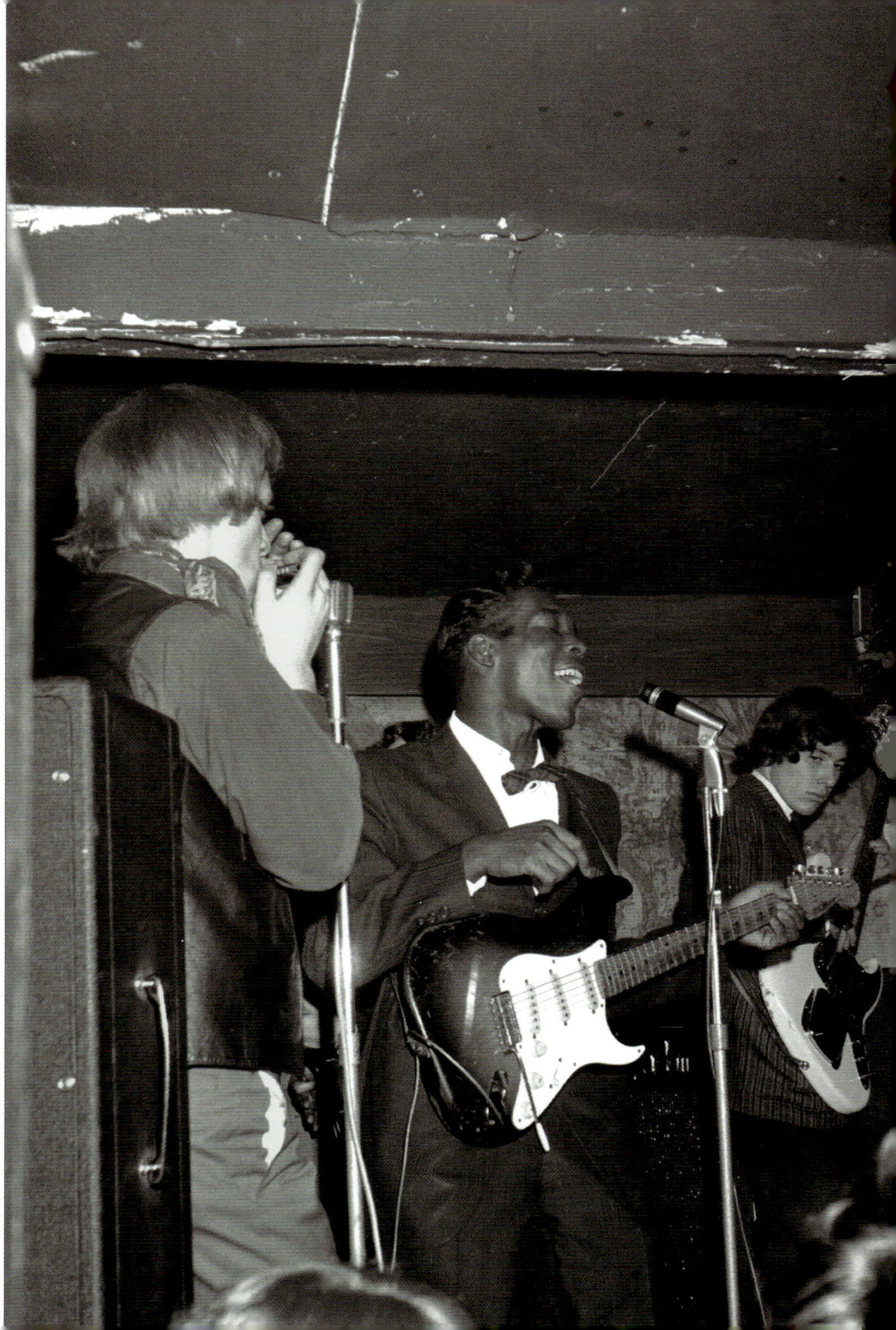

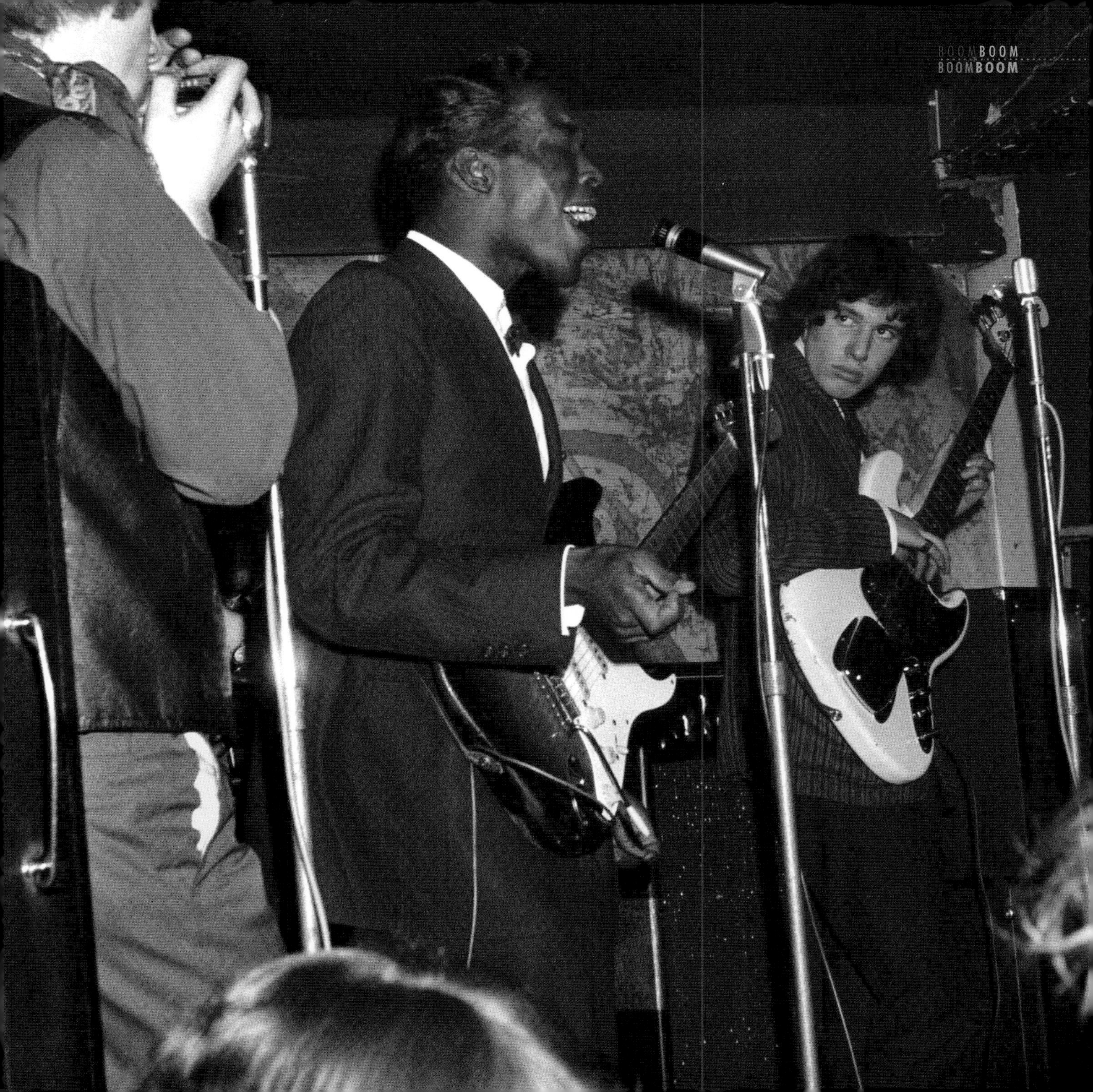

BOOMBOOM
BOOMBOOM

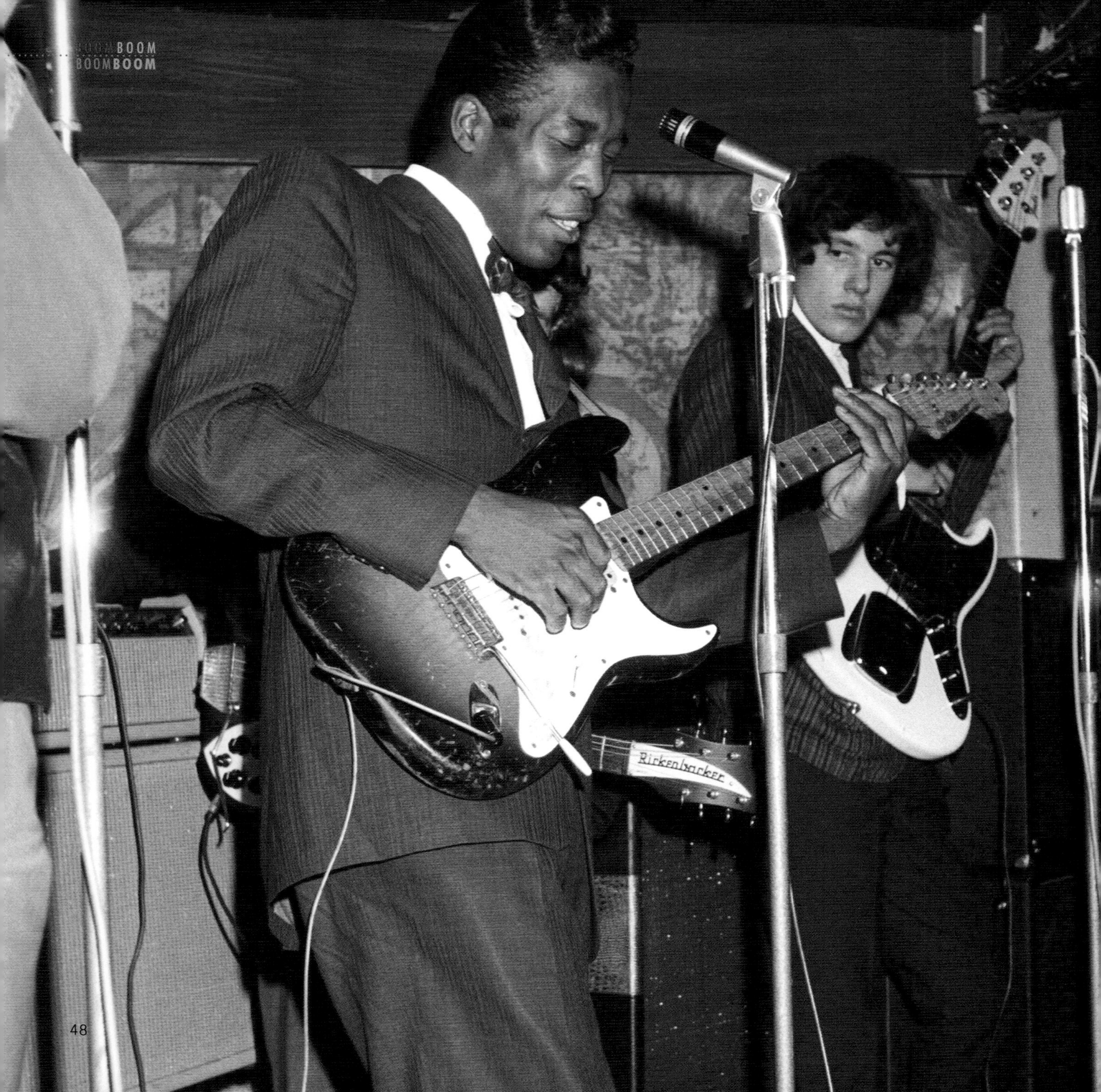

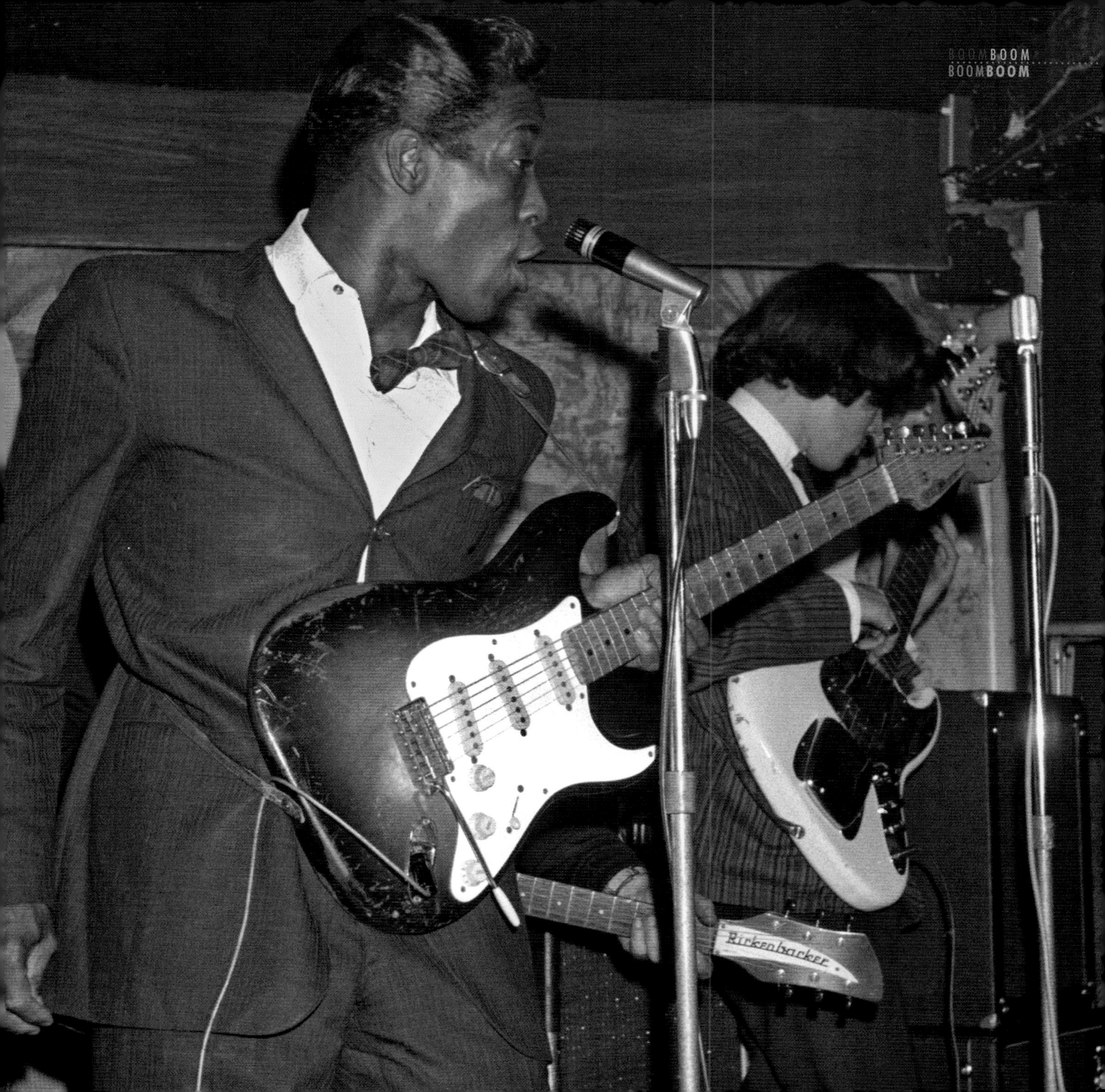

BOOMBOOM
BOOMBOOM
Rickenbacker

J. B. LENOIR

Brian saw J.B.Lenoir on the fourth American Folk Blues Festival tour at the Free Trade Hall in Manchester in 1965 (tickets 6/- to 15/-), promoted by the National Jazz Federation and organised, as before, by Lippmann and Rau.

An influential blues musician and songwriter in the post-War years, we think this was Lenoir's only European trip (sadly Lenoir died just two years later after a car crash back in America). As the organisers relied on Willie Dixon to help put the bills together, this may explain how Lenoir was picked, as Willie had been championing his work. Brian photographed most of the musicians on the bill backstage having secured access in advance by writing to the manager. This fabulous image just shows J.B. warming up before his spot. Brian and his friends were so busy backstage that apart from Jimmy Lee he didn't get much chance to see any of the acts during the on stage rehearsals. He was at the front for the show itself, but struggled to get many decent live shots with the slower speed 'flash' film he was using, although the image below shows Walter Horton, J.B. and Fred McDowell together on-stage.

By this time Brian Smith was on great terms with staff at the Free Trade Hall. Having covered the earlier AFBF and Blues & Gospel shows there for R & B Scene in 1964, he knew all the ropes, though it was uncertain if the magazine would be able to use his pictures. *"There was actually no manager at the Free Trade, it was a municipal facility and wonderfully informal. All front-of-house was handled by our local record shop staff, Hime & Addison and Barry's Record Rendezvous, whom we all knew well (and were advertisers in the mag!)."*

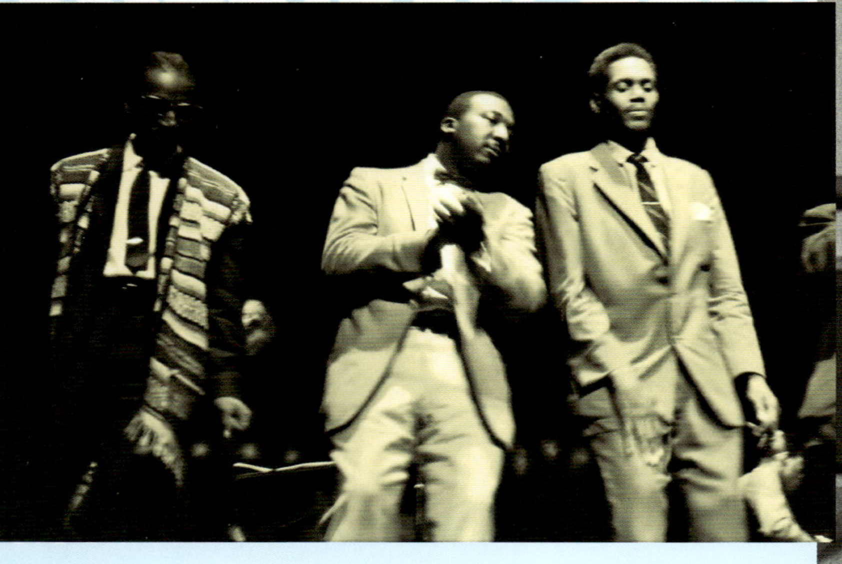

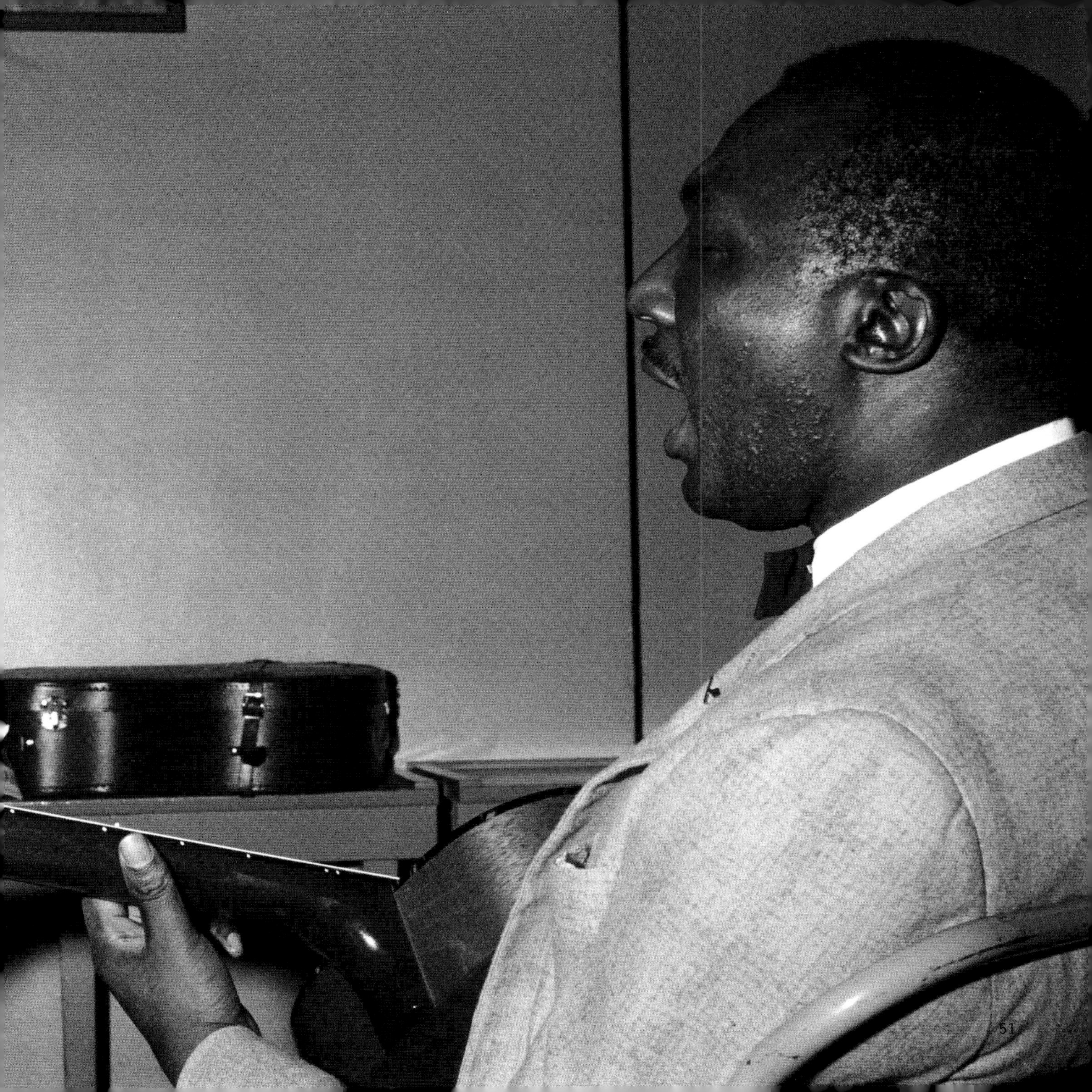

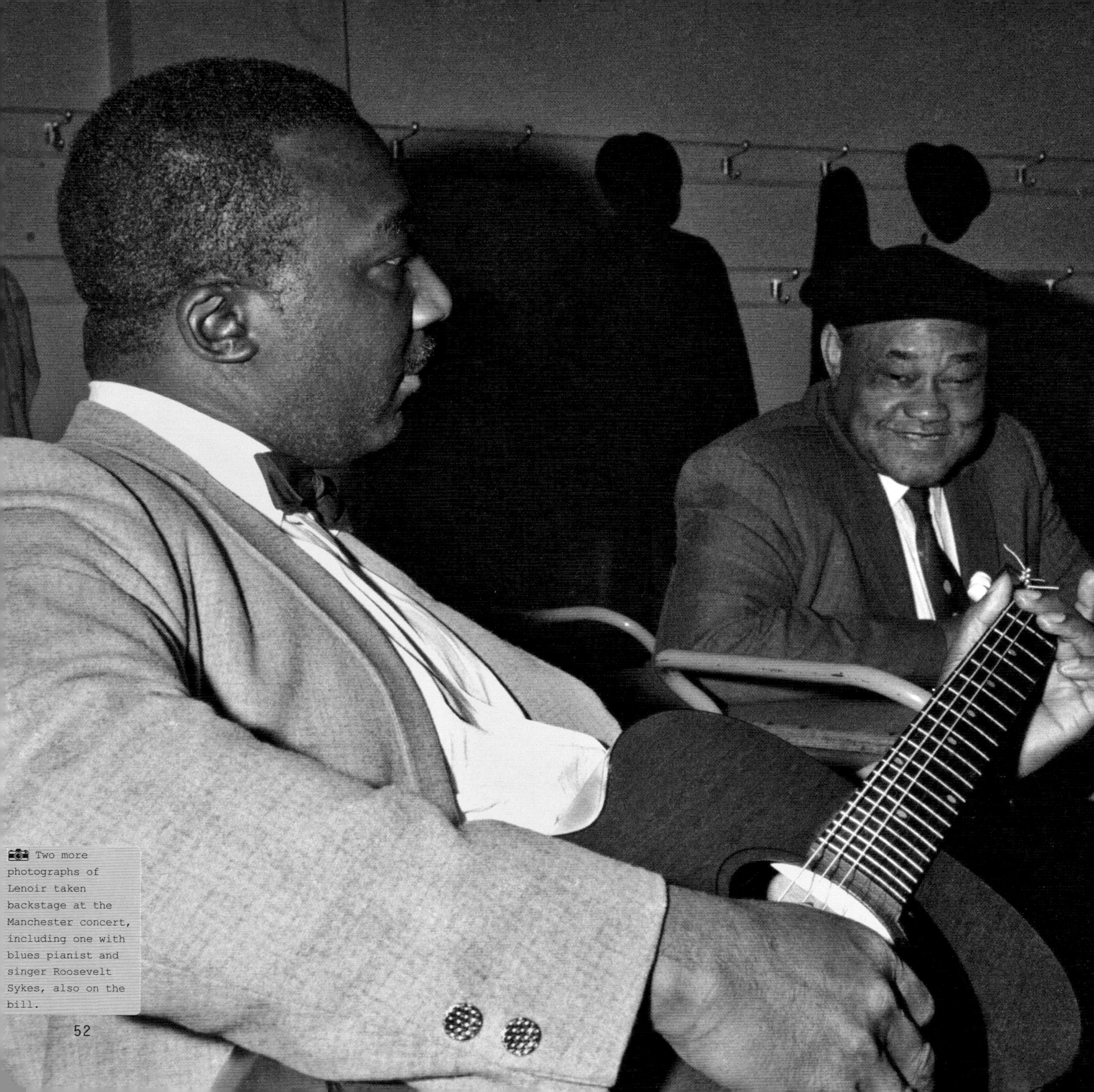

Two more photographs of Lenoir taken backstage at the Manchester concert, including one with blues pianist and singer Roosevelt Sykes, also on the bill.

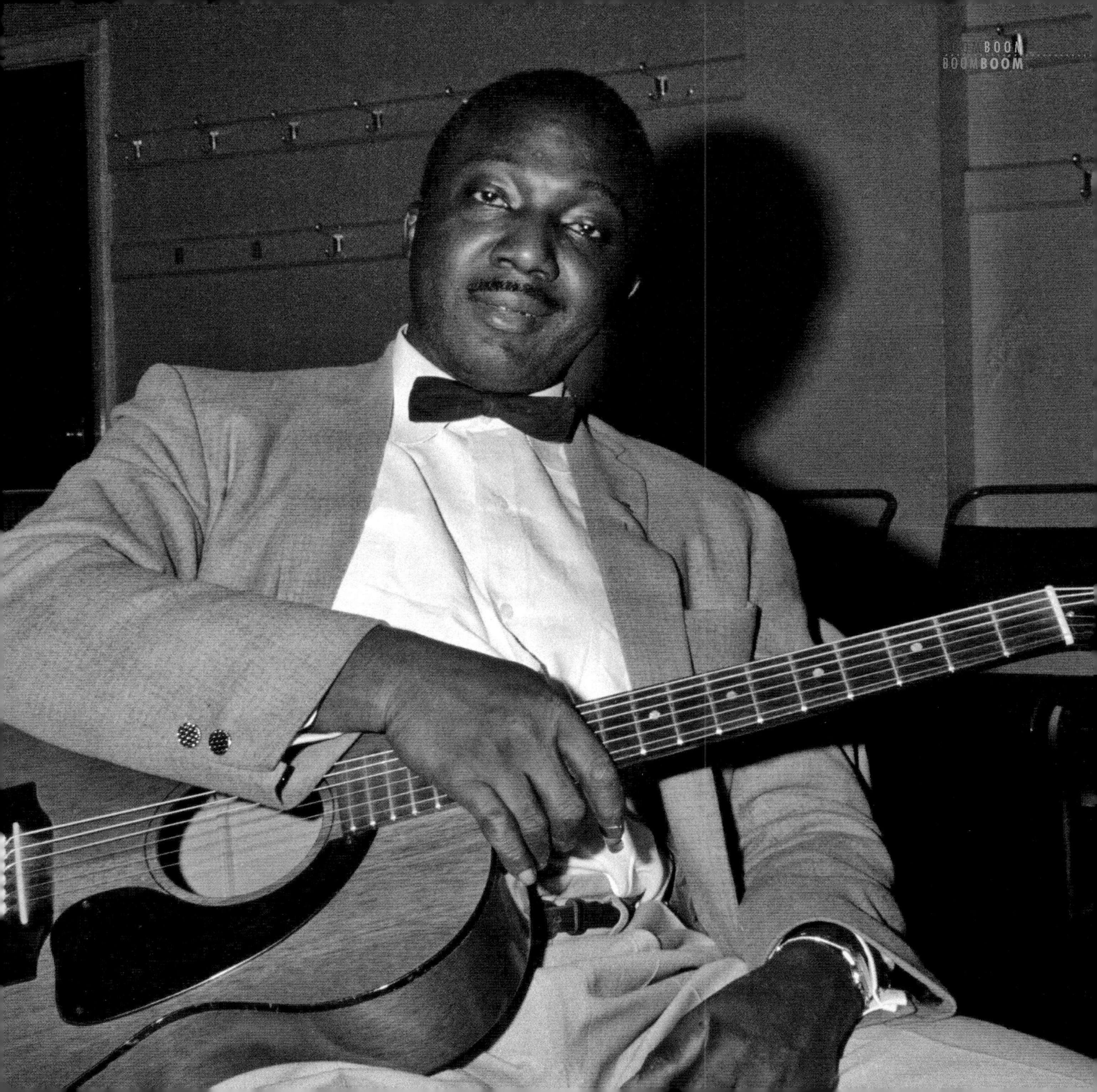
BOOM BOOM
BOOM BOOM

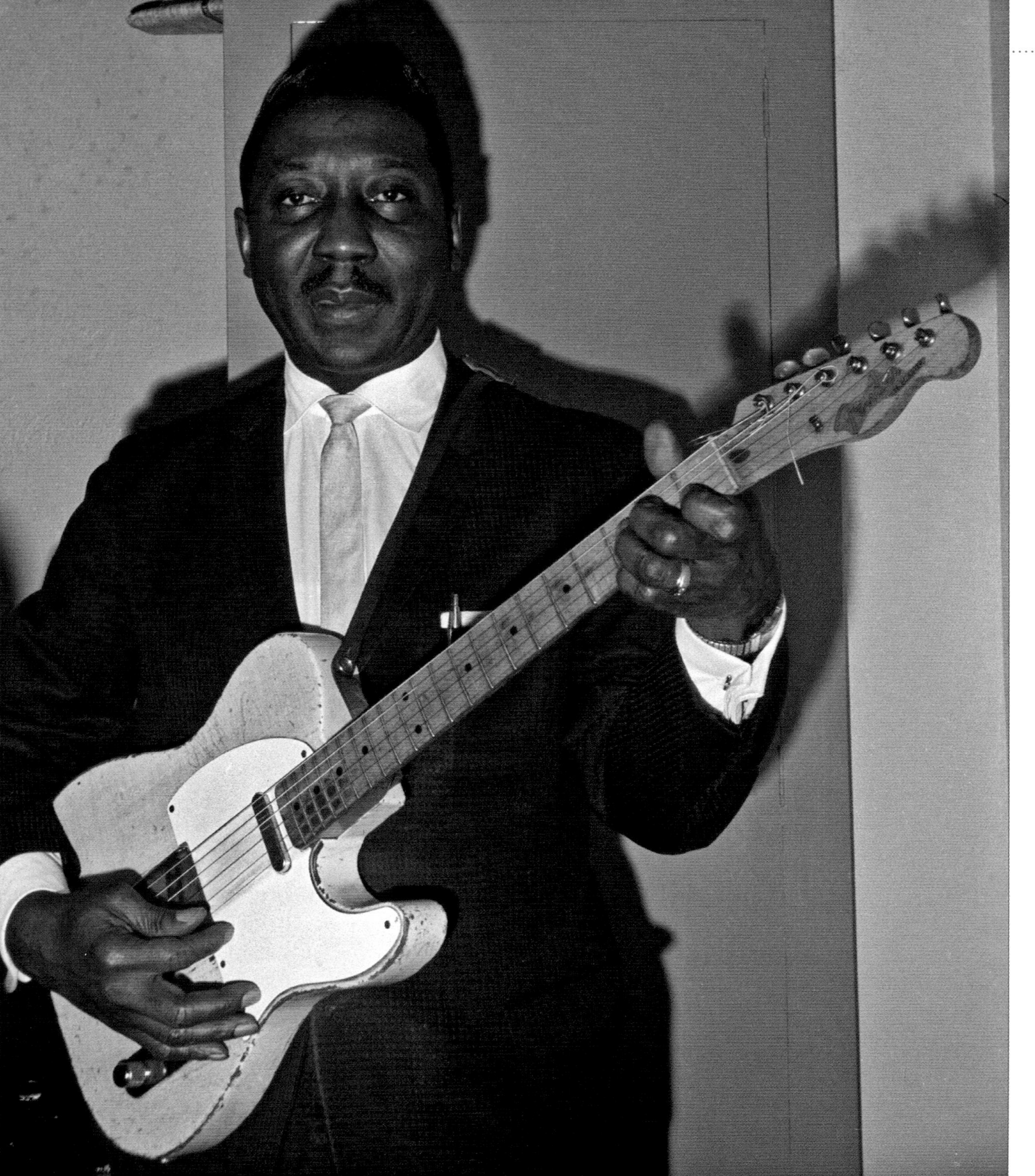

MUDDY WATERS and friends

Another package tour popular with blues fans at the time was the American Folk Blues and Gospel Caravan, put together in America and managed in the UK by promoter Harold Davison, running through April and May 1964. Based on the success of the American Folk Blues Festival it was *so* popular that six more shows had to be added. Once more this gave Brian and his mates an opportunity to meet (and him to take photographs of) several big names under one roof, once again backstage at Manchester Free Trade Hall. Brian even got Muddy Waters to pose for him with his battered Fender Telecaster (left). He took just the one frame, but it is a wonderful shot of the blues legend, and made up for the fact that as he wasn't able to take any live photographs of the guitarist.

Muddy and other musicians on the bill then passed the time as they often did with a good humoured game of cards (which they always carried with them). Brian took the opportunity to get several unique shots of them playing (with Roger Eagle top left left). Sat at formica topped tables, with the 'Jubilee Builds You Up' ash-trays and packets of Swan Vesta matches, they all seem very relaxed.

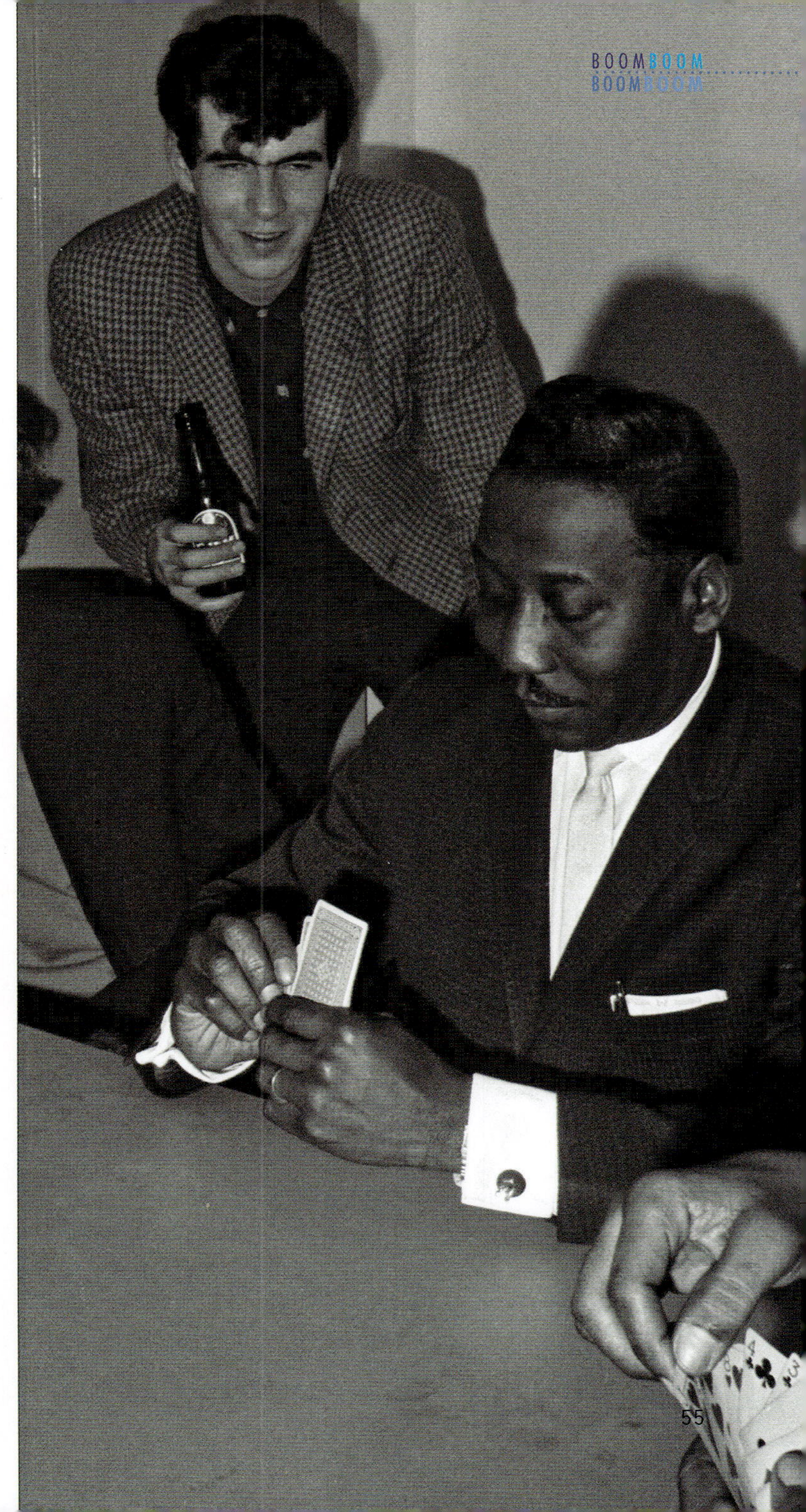

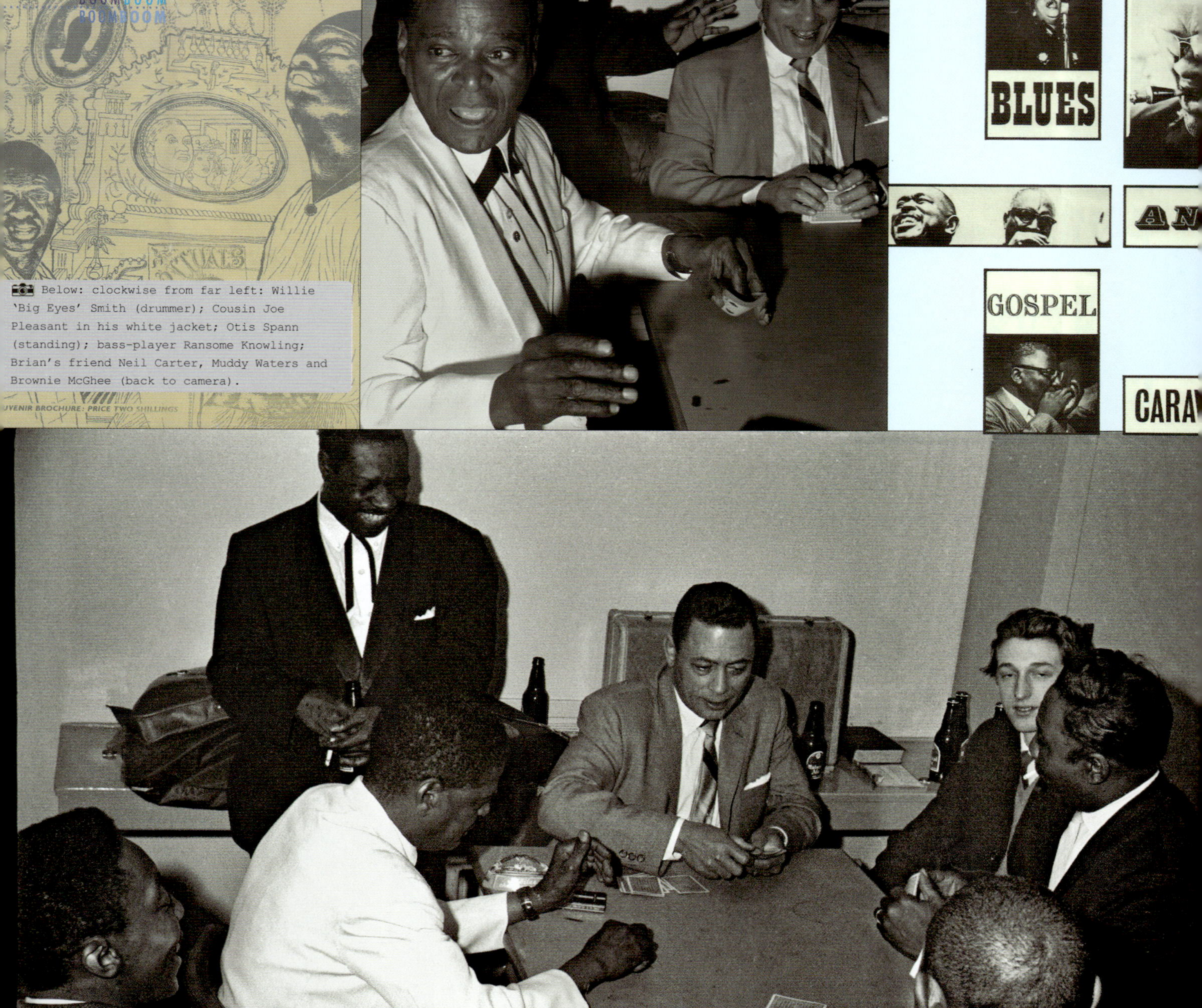

Below: clockwise from far left: Willie 'Big Eyes' Smith (drummer); Cousin Joe Pleasant in his white jacket; Otis Spann (standing); bass-player Ransome Knowling; Brian's friend Neil Carter, Muddy Waters and Brownie McGhee (back to camera).

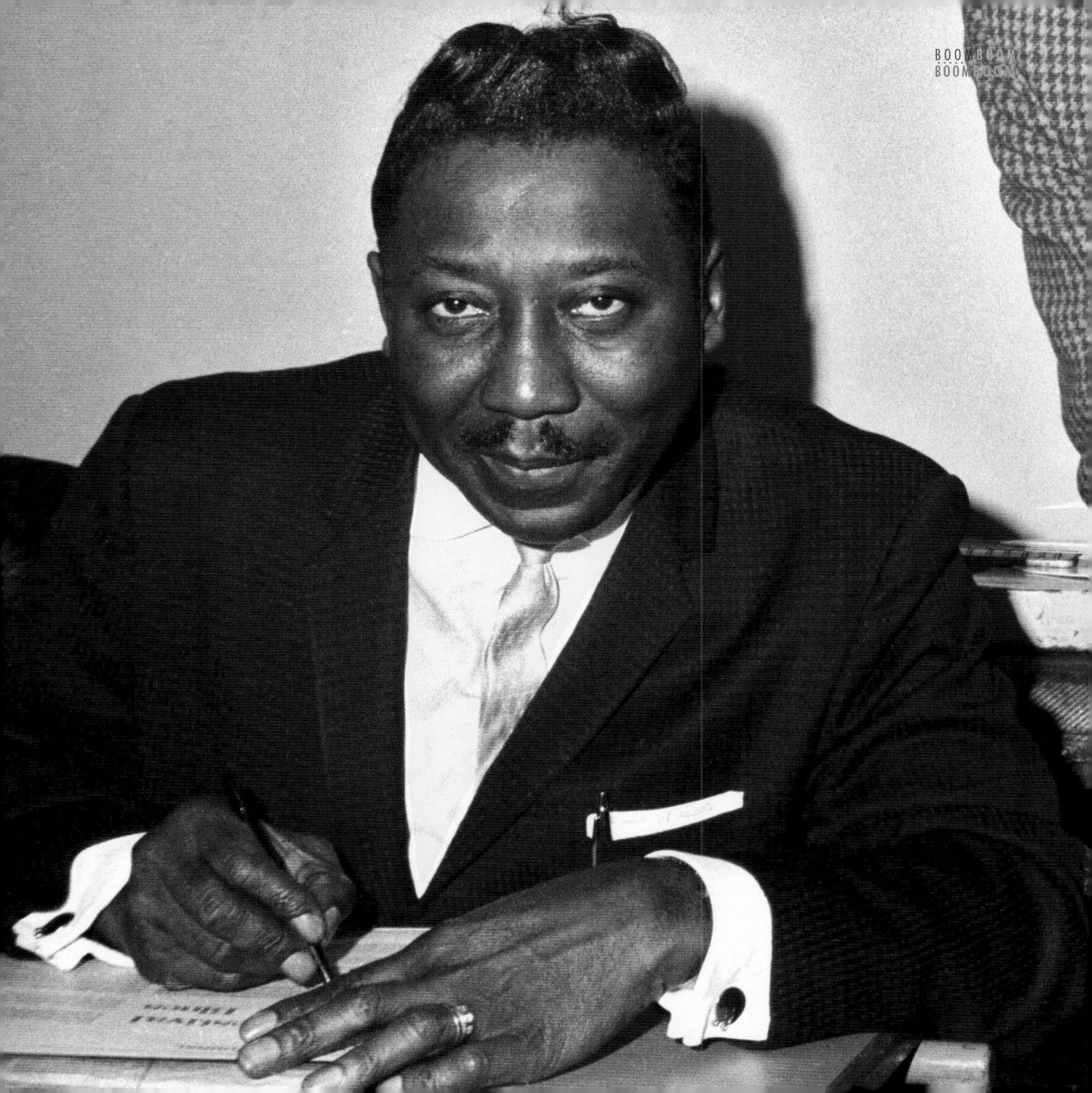

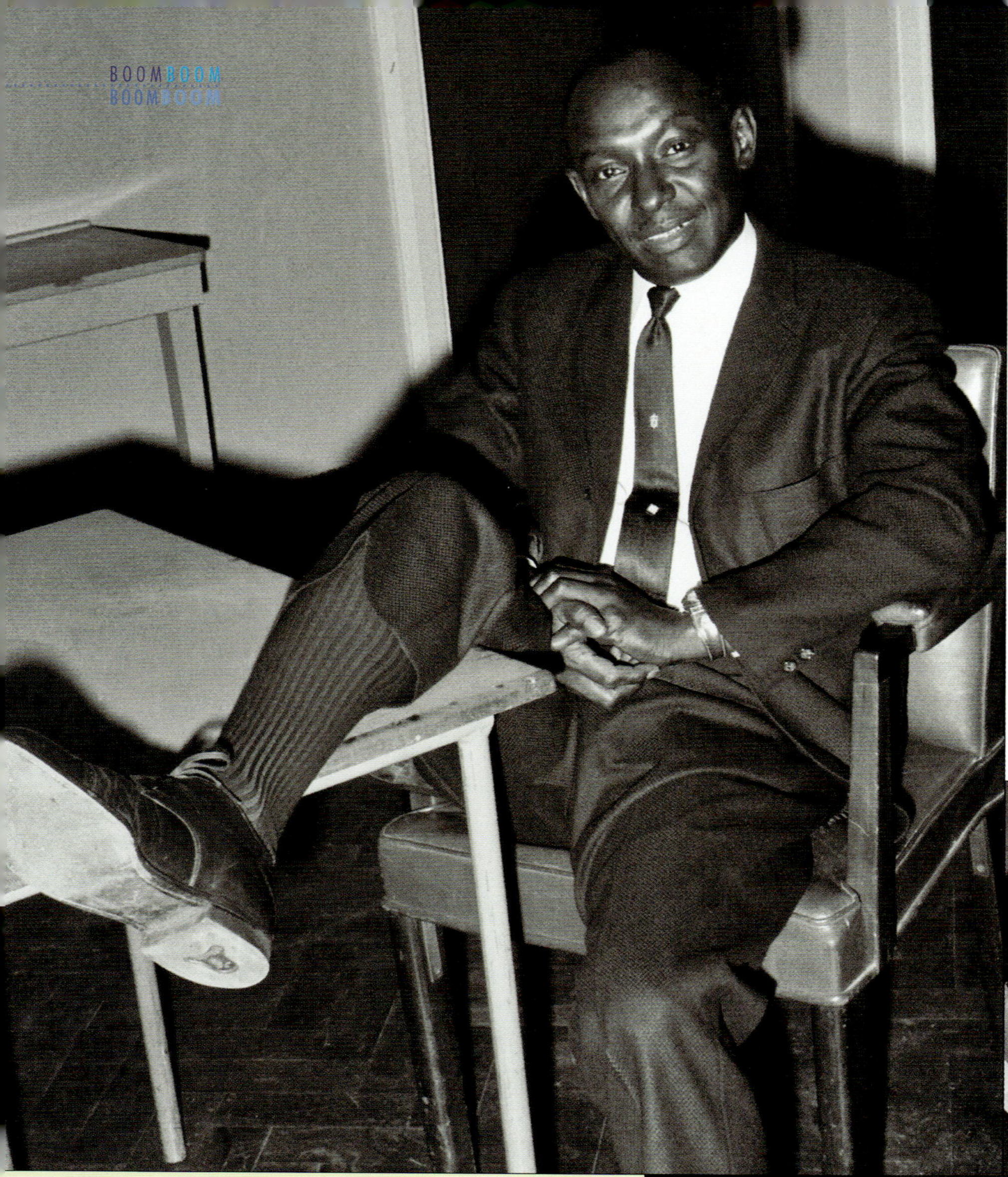

EDDIE BOYD

Also looking relaxed here is American blues pianist, singer and songwriter Eddie Boyd, photographed by Brian backstage, on tour with Buddy Guy's band in 1965 as part of the same American Folk Blues Festival at Manchester on October 15th (Brian paid 15/- for a stalls ticket at the second house). Brian had also gone along to watch the Blues & Gospel Train TV show being shot by Granada on a disused station the day before but it was too dark to take photos. Eddie Boyd soon moved to live in Europe, first in Belgium then settling in Finland in 1970, and recorded with some of the big British blues names.

Brian and his friends again took vinyl along to be signed while he snapped away. *"That's Rick Green on the left, the only pic I ever got of him, and Neil Carter, both of R & B Scene, and Dave Clarke - later a noted collector, reviewer and blues-cartoonist known as 'Latchford Slim'."*

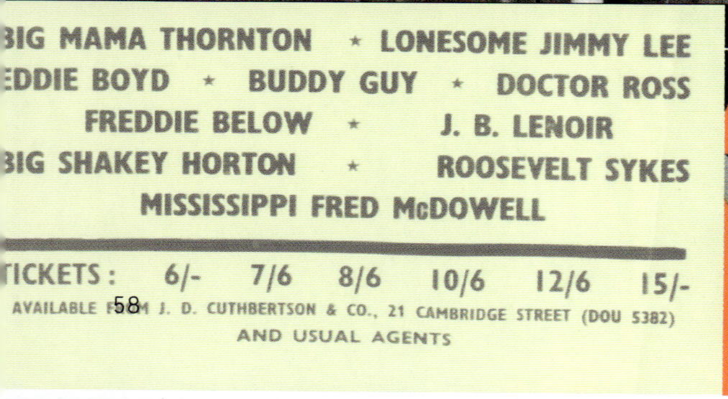

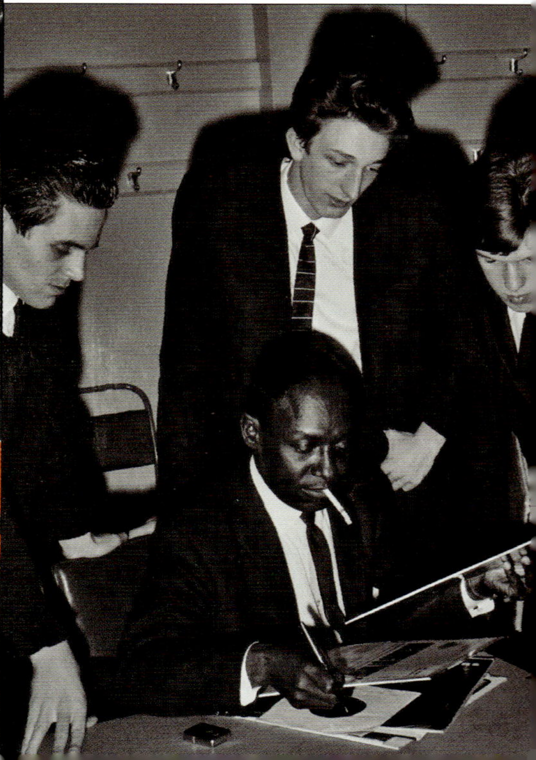

BIG MAMA THORNTON   ★   LONESOME JIMMY LEE
EDDIE BOYD   ★   BUDDY GUY   ★   DOCTOR ROSS
FREDDIE BELOW   ★   J. B. LENOIR
BIG SHAKEY HORTON   ★   ROOSEVELT SYKES
MISSISSIPPI FRED McDOWELL

TICKETS :   6/-   7/6   8/6   10/6   12/6   15/-
AVAILABLE FROM J. D. CUTHBERTSON & CO., 21 CAMBRIDGE STREET (DOU 5382)
AND USUAL AGENTS

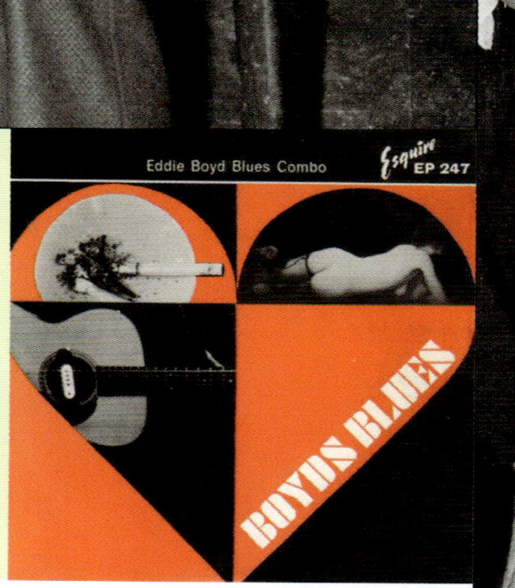

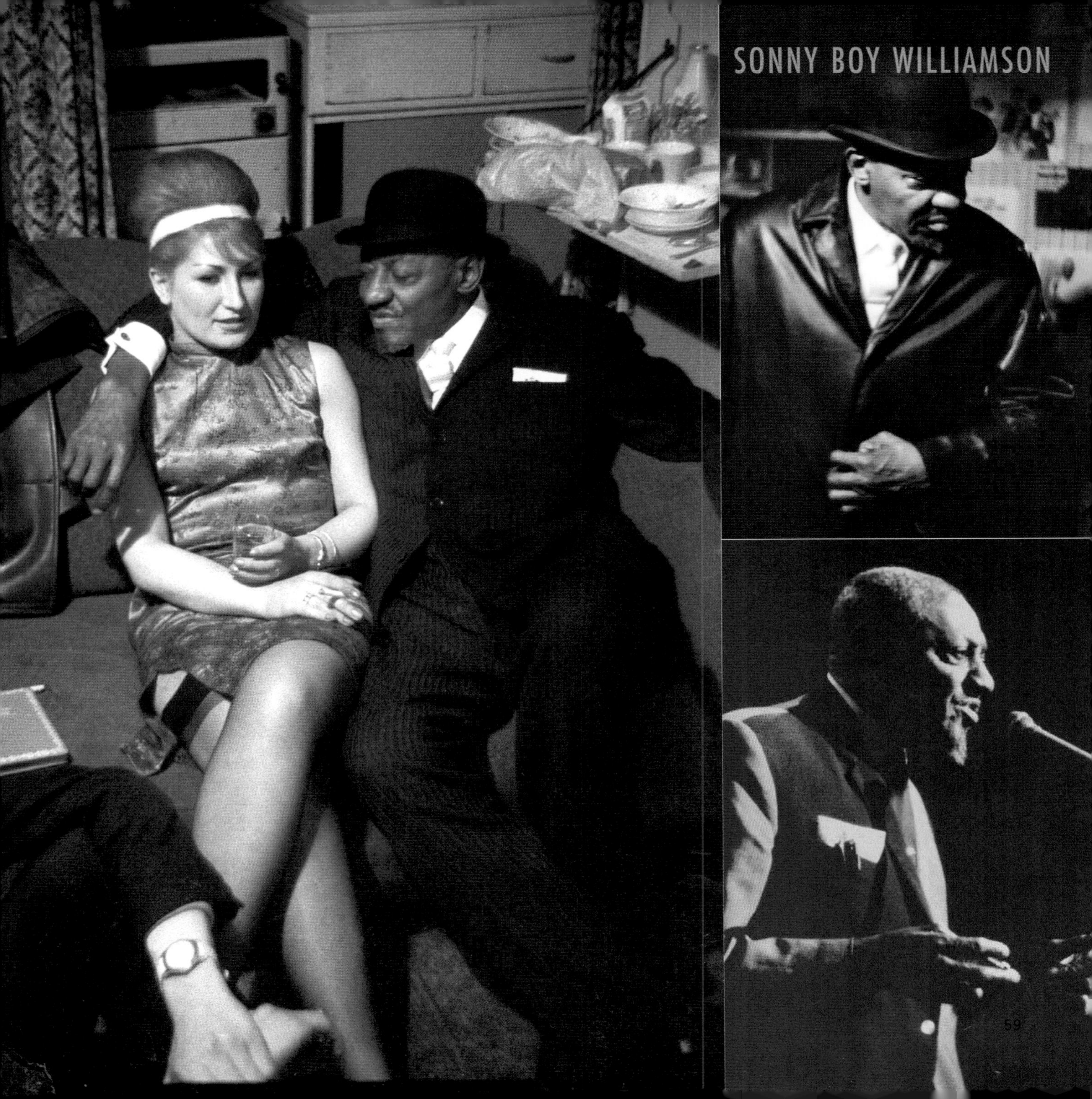
SONNY BOY WILLIAMSON

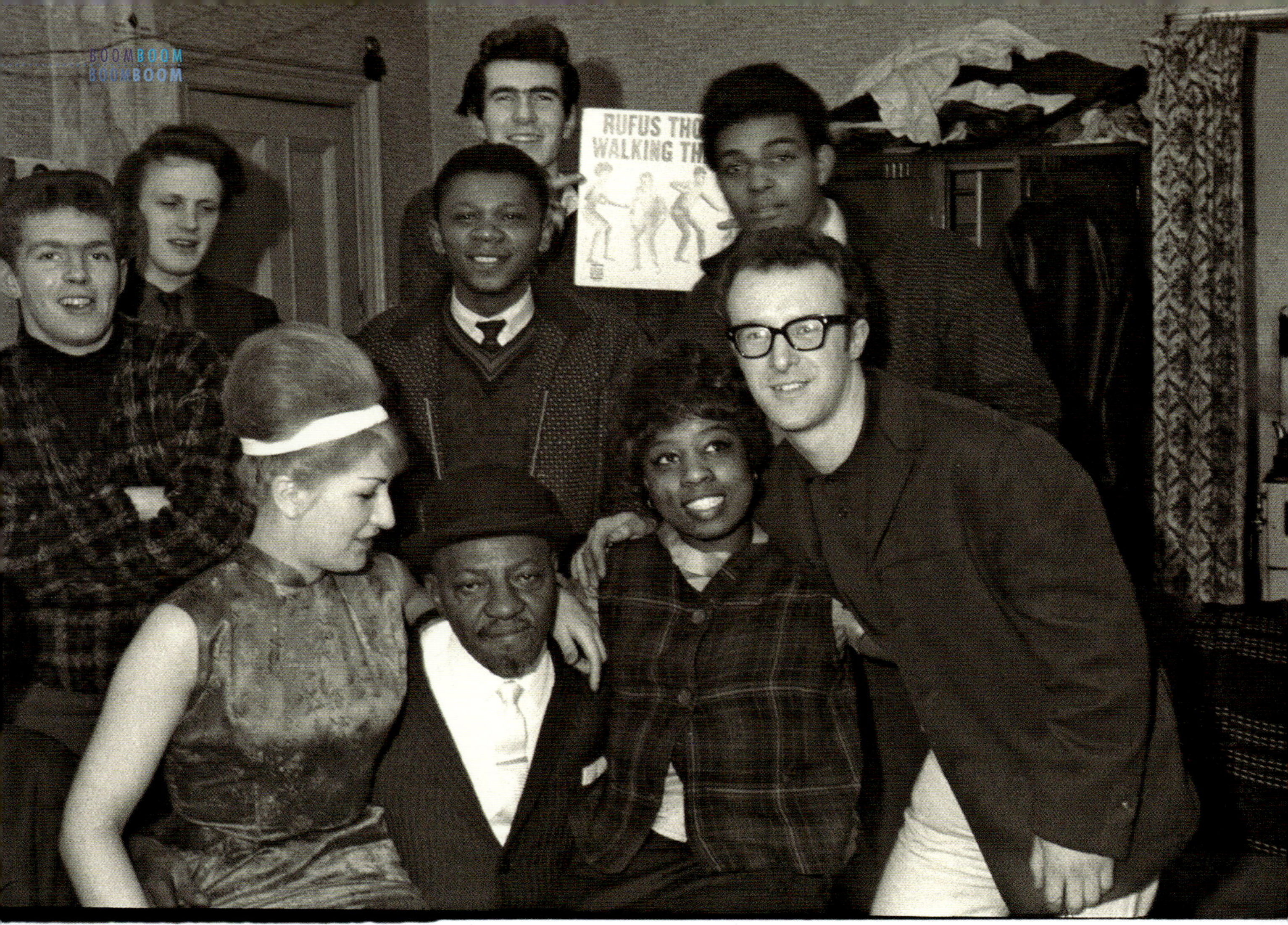

These images of the influential blues harmonica player, singer and songwriter Sonny Boy Williamson were taken by Brian in unusual circumstances. Williamson had been to Britain in 1963 on the second Blues festival package tour and returned at the end of 1963 for a dozen shows backed by The Yardbirds running through into early 1964 as Brian recalls: *"(Sonny) went down well cos he'd got this image of the bowler and the checkered suit and everything. He was on a club tour for Giorgio Gomelsky (I think) and was on at the Twisted Wheel on Sunday, Feb 16th 1964. Roger Eagle, who was the all-night DJ for the show, was given the job looking after Sonny Boy for 24 hours, and at the last minute he was also asked to put him up. Well, Roger lived in this little, real sort of crummy student type bedsit in Wilbraham Road in Chorlton*

[540; it's still there, I wonder if the current resident has any inkling of the history? Ed.], but he took him round, Sonny Boy and this lady, who is best described as a salaried travelling companion, she was from Liverpool."

The word passed around Roger's friends (*"half of us weren't even on the phone!"*) that Sonny Boy was passing the afternoon at Roger's flat if they wanted to come over and meet the great man. *"So we went round and spent what was left of the day chatting. Until a car came for him at the end of the afternoon, we had him to ourselves. I just had a handful of flash bulbs and a film that wasn't really very suitable (hence the grain), but what came out of it is these shots and a couple of them have become sort of iconic."* It is the almost incongruous nature of the very humble flat, the kettle on the antique cooker, and the unwashed dishes on the worktop, which adds to the bohemian look. Brian also took one of his regular portraits for the R & B Scene magazine (right): *"That one was the nearest to a standard technique I ever had, which is basically down on one knee and that was it. The shadow became a bit of a trademark and sometimes it worked, like there."*

The flat was much as music fans' flats have always been, album sleeves and posters on the walls. They spent the afternoon listening to tales of his life (*"some of them possibly true!"*) until at one stage Sonny Boy had a quiet word with Roger, who quickly shepherded everyone else out of the flat and joined them as they gathered in the lobby at the top of the stairs. The reason for the exodus soon became clear to them as Roger's rickety old bed began to make a racket. *"He was giving her one, and you can hear this bed creaking away, although not for a terribly long time!"*

Roger, Brian and the others were allowed back in and tried to act nonchalantly as Brian marvelled at the scene: *"She's sat there doing her nails, beehive in place, he's flopped back in the chair in his long-johns!"* He felt it was diplomatic to keep his camera in its case, but was in for a surprise. *"Roger called me over a bit concerned and told me he had a request from Sonny Boy: 'Ah wants you to take a picture of ma woman holding ma rod...'"* Roger and Brian made an excuse of some kind and what might have made a real exclusive for their blues magazine was not to be. As Brian says today, what the hell would Boots' photographic counter service have made of that?

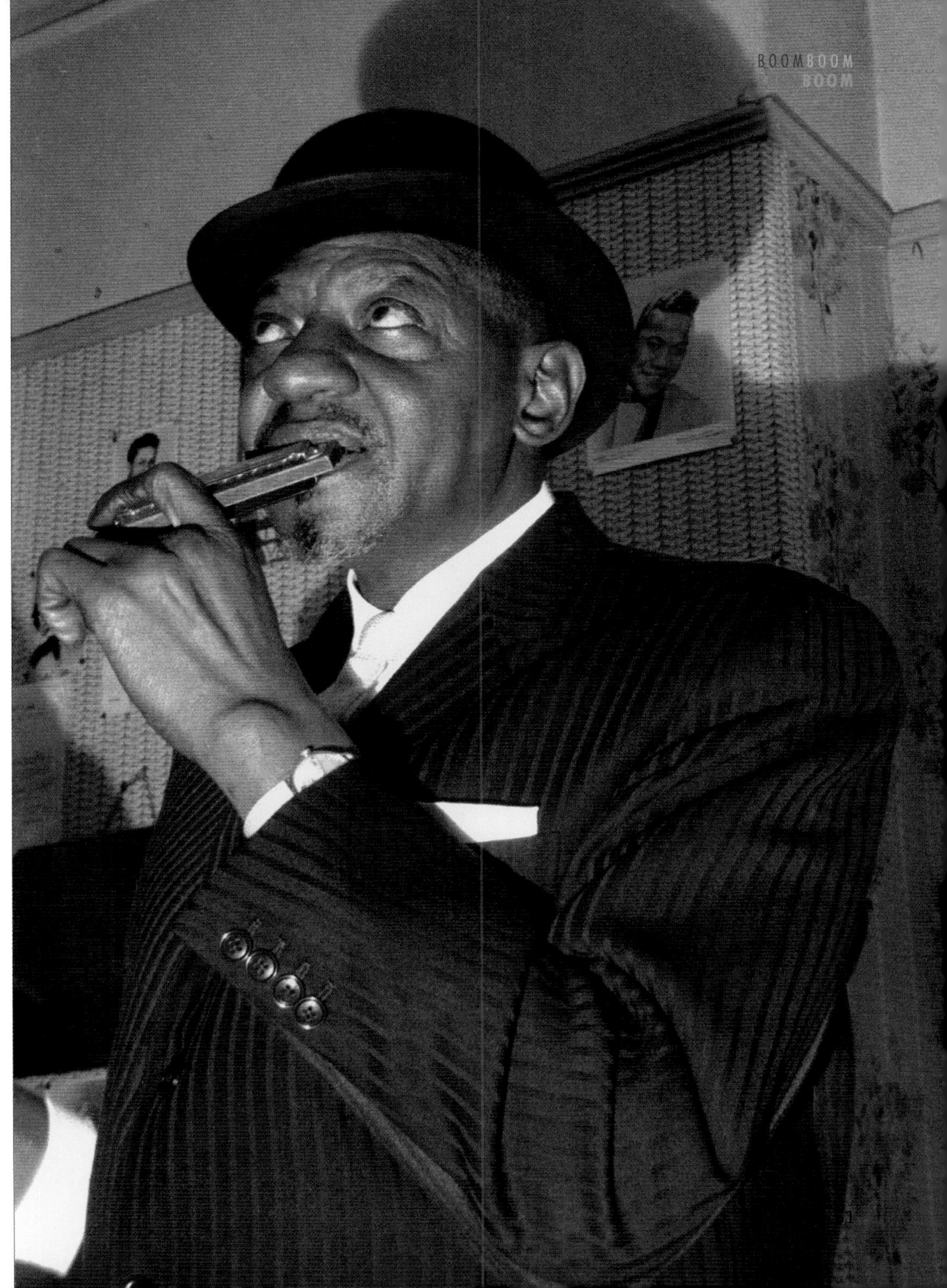

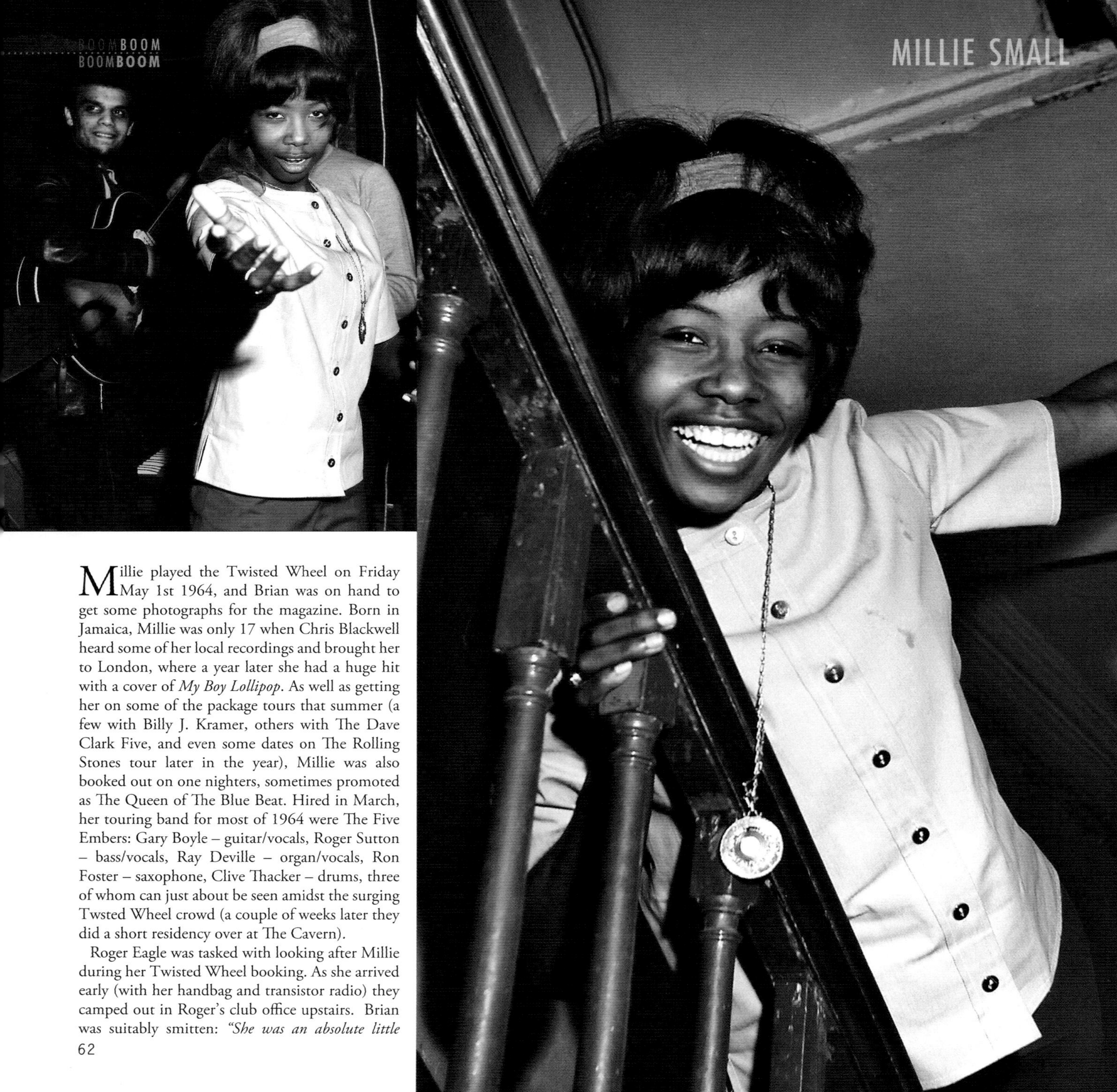

Millie played the Twisted Wheel on Friday May 1st 1964, and Brian was on hand to get some photographs for the magazine. Born in Jamaica, Millie was only 17 when Chris Blackwell heard some of her local recordings and brought her to London, where a year later she had a huge hit with a cover of *My Boy Lollipop*. As well as getting her on some of the package tours that summer (a few with Billy J. Kramer, others with The Dave Clark Five, and even some dates on The Rolling Stones tour later in the year), Millie was also booked out on one nighters, sometimes promoted as The Queen of The Blue Beat. Hired in March, her touring band for most of 1964 were The Five Embers: Gary Boyle – guitar/vocals, Roger Sutton – bass/vocals, Ray Deville – organ/vocals, Ron Foster – saxophone, Clive Thacker – drums, three of whom can just about be seen amidst the surging Twsted Wheel crowd (a couple of weeks later they did a short residency over at The Cavern).

Roger Eagle was tasked with looking after Millie during her Twisted Wheel booking. As she arrived early (with her handbag and transistor radio) they camped out in Roger's club office upstairs. Brian was suitably smitten: *"She was an absolute little*

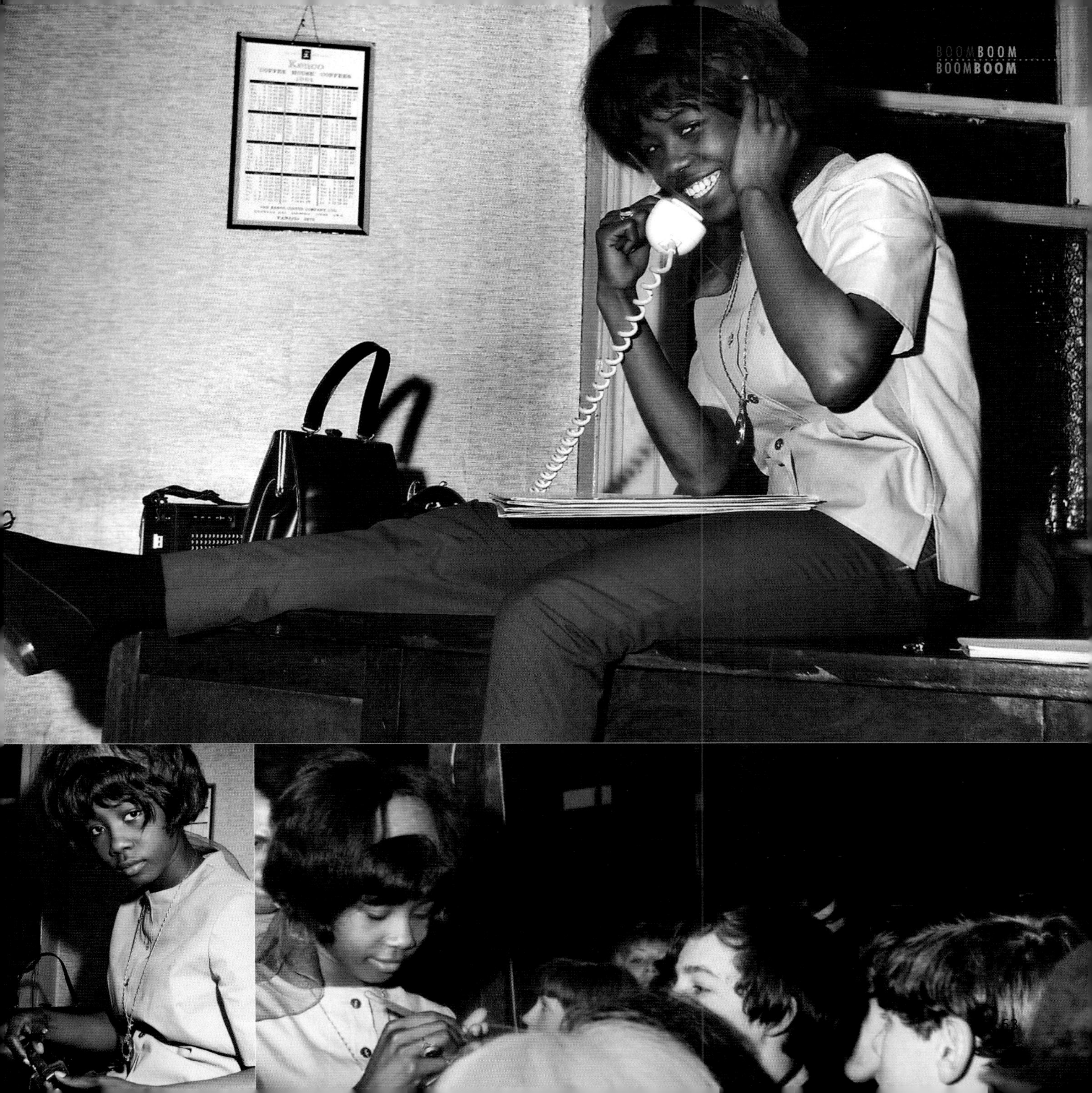
BOOM BOOM
BOOM BOOM

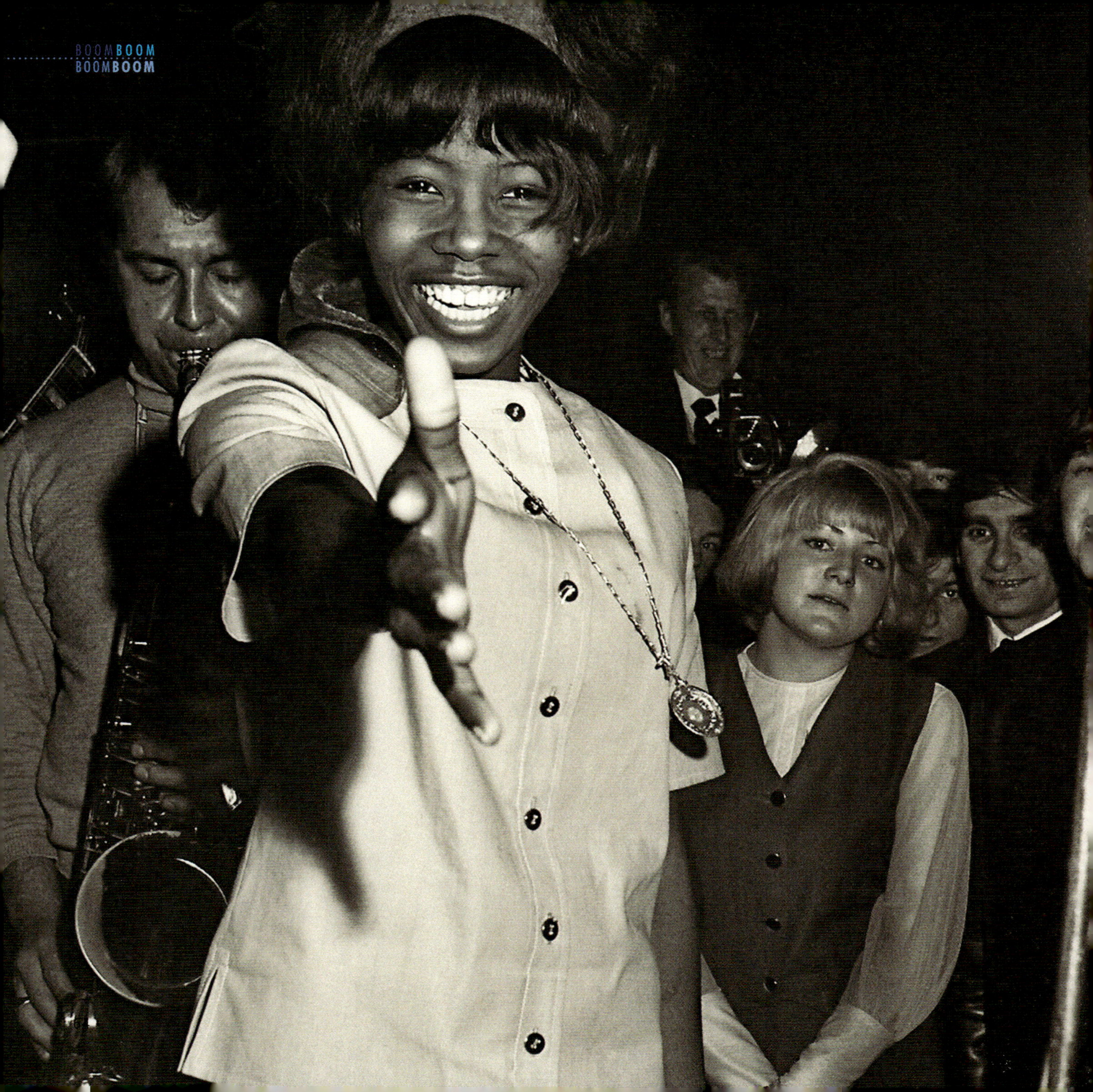
BOOMBOOM
BOOMBOOM

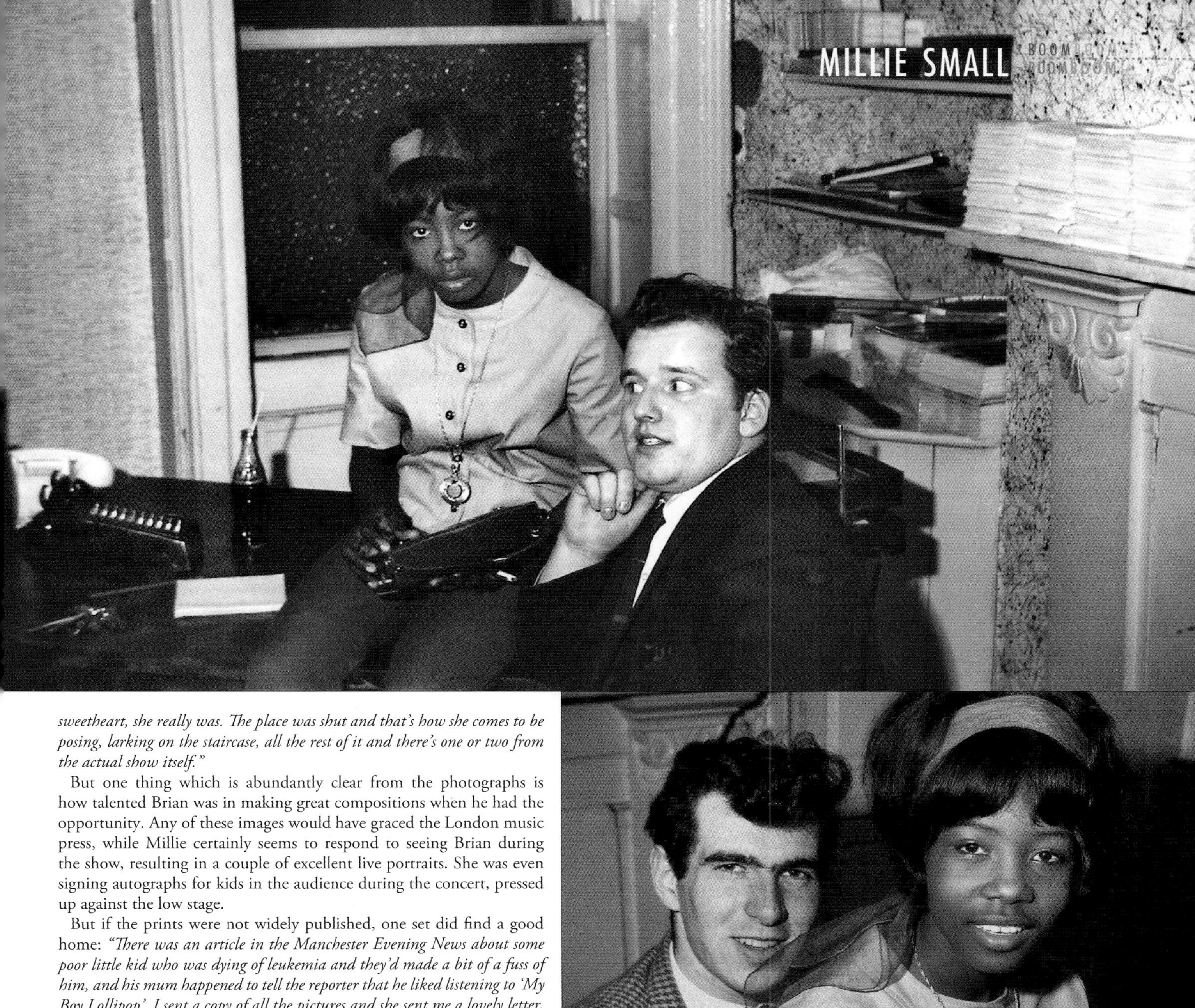

sweetheart, she really was. The place was shut and that's how she comes to be posing, larking on the staircase, all the rest of it and there's one or two from the actual show itself."

But one thing which is abundantly clear from the photographs is how talented Brian was in making great compositions when he had the opportunity. Any of these images would have graced the London music press, while Millie certainly seems to respond to seeing Brian during the show, resulting in a couple of excellent live portraits. She was even signing autographs for kids in the audience during the concert, pressed up against the low stage.

But if the prints were not widely published, one set did find a good home: *"There was an article in the Manchester Evening News about some poor little kid who was dying of leukemia and they'd made a bit of a fuss of him, and his mum happened to tell the reporter that he liked listening to 'My Boy Lollipop'. I sent a copy of all the pictures and she sent me a lovely letter, she said they were all hung round his little cubicle in hospital."*

We had to include the shot of Brian and Millie above - which Roger Eagle took as a souvenir (the piles of tickets and other Wheel ephemera are tantalising) - and this great one of Roger and Millie.

INEZ and CHARLIE FOXX

Although brother and sister duo Charlie and Inez Foxx had a smash hit in America with *Mockingbird* in 1963, their career lasted longer in Britain, long enough for them to be added to the big Rolling Stones package tour of Autumn 1964. They also did some smaller club shows, including the Twisted Wheel on July 8th, where Brian, short of time and film, he took just two shots of the duo, only one of which came out (and survives as a dusty print). *"I couldn't snap them on stage because as you've seen on some pictures it was just so packed!"*

Charlie and Inez returned to the UK regularly during the second half of the Sixties for soul nights and indeed played The Twisted Wheel again in 1969 as this flyer shows.

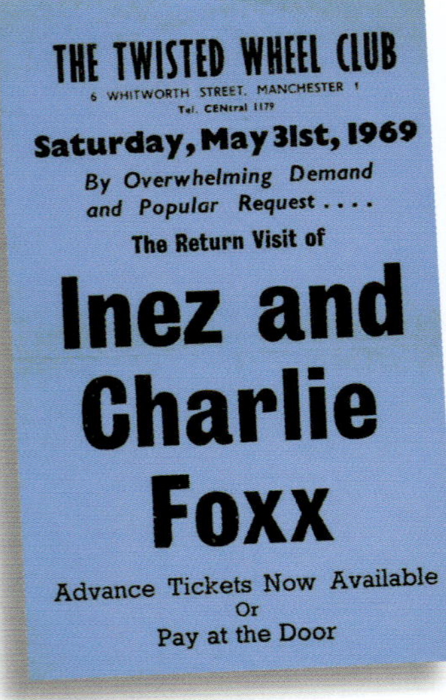

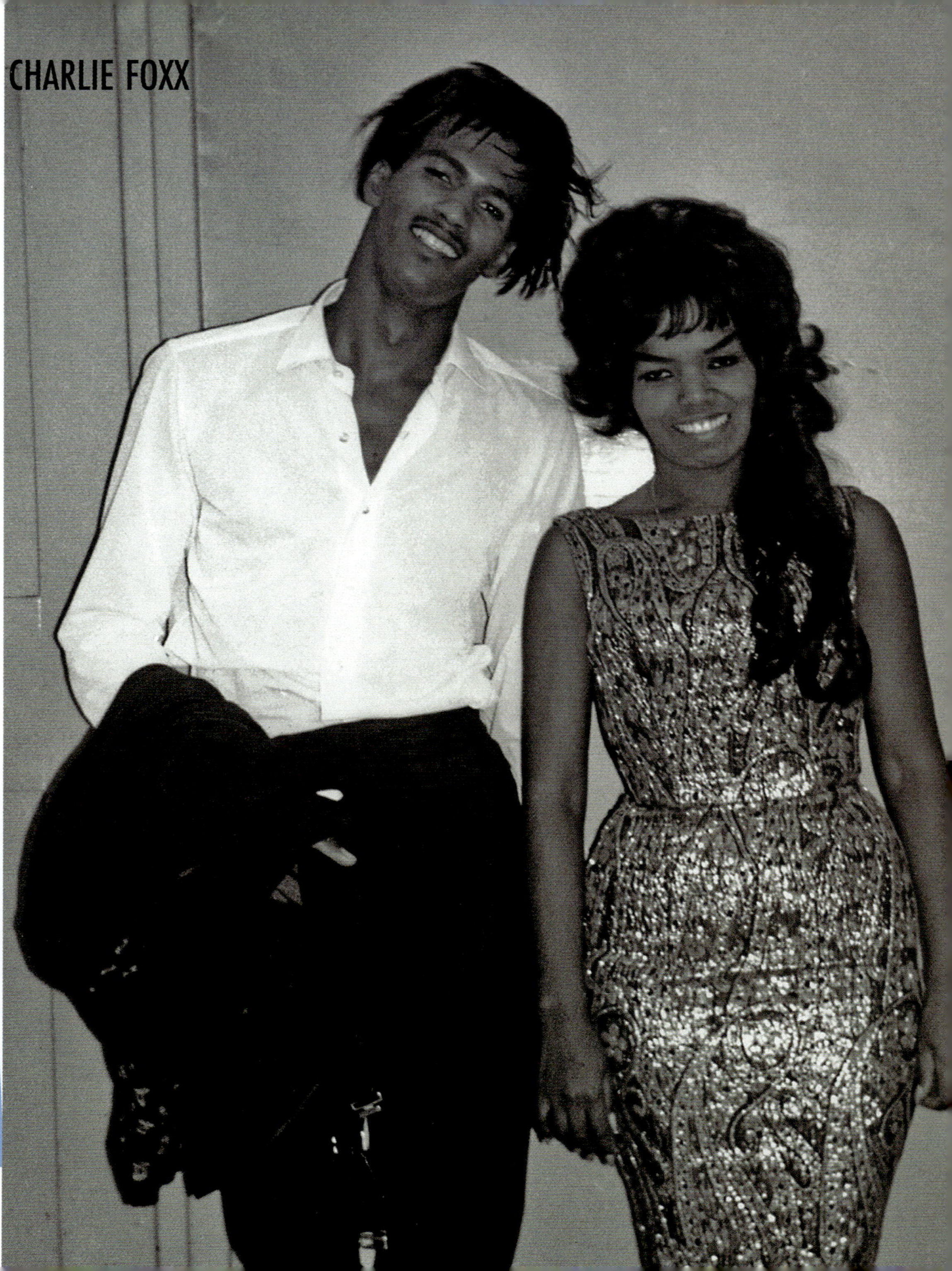

The RAELETS

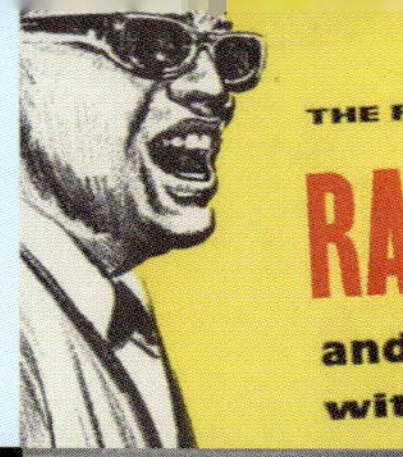

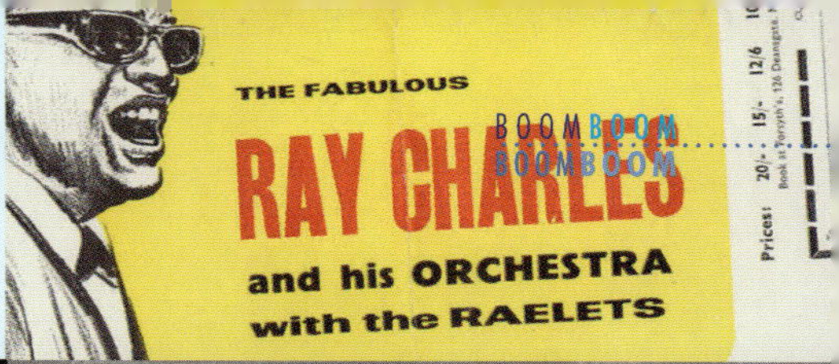

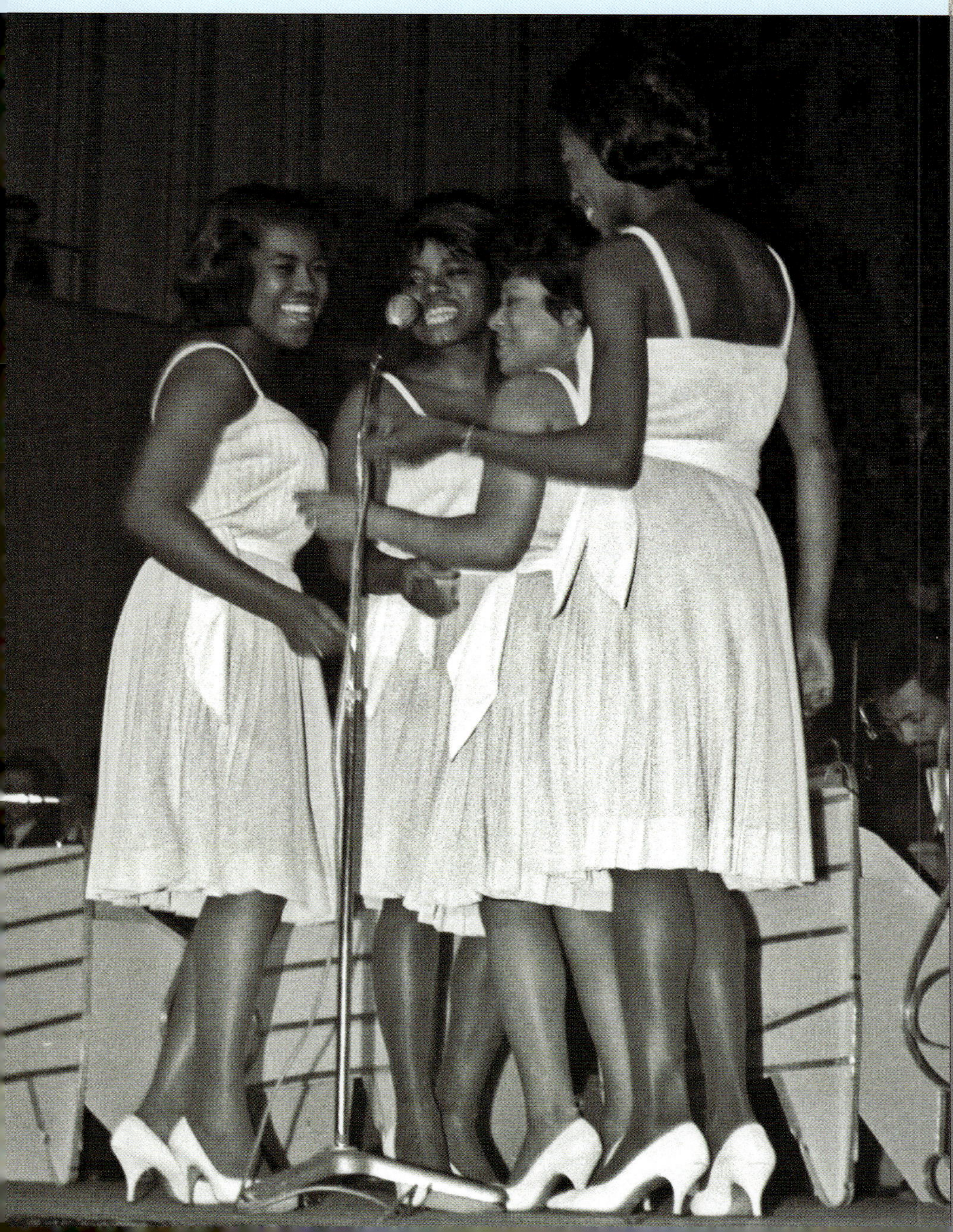

The Raelets had backed Ray Charles for several years by the time of his and their first visit to the UK. Brian saw the shows (they did two, early evening 6.15pm and 8.45pm) at the Free Trade Hall on May 18th 1963 and nervous of upsetting FOH staff took just this one photograph of Ray's backing singers. He also snapped Ray but the flash misfired and ruined the frame. At the time The Raelets comprised Gwen Berry, Margie Hendricks, (second from right), Pat Moseley Lyles and Darlene McCrea.

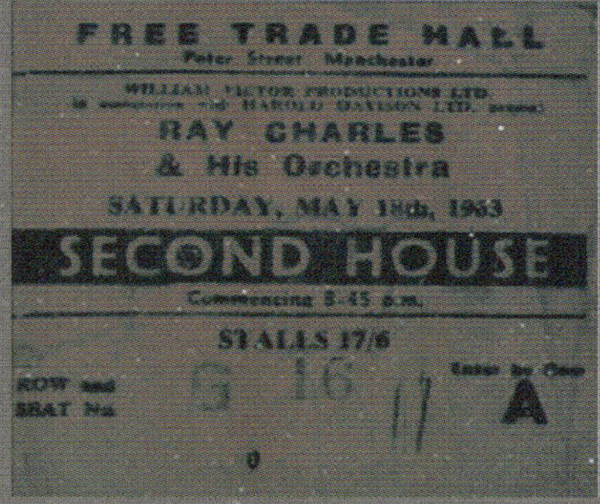

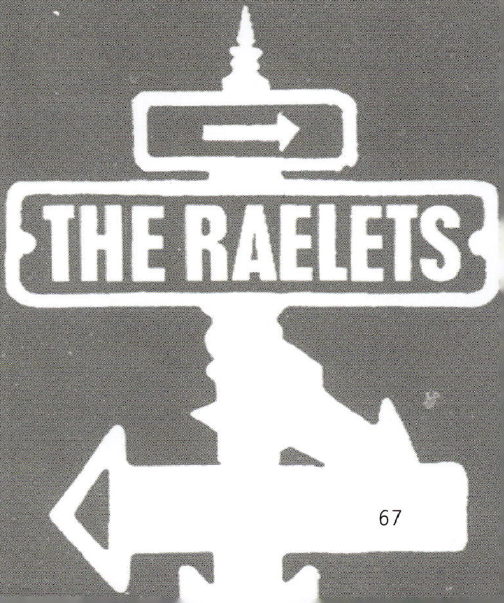

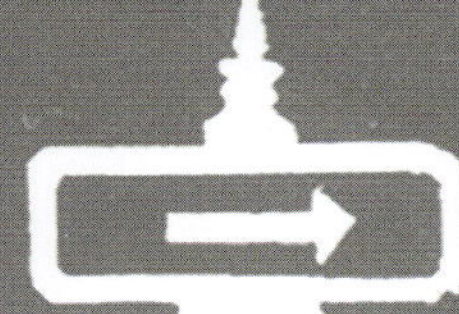

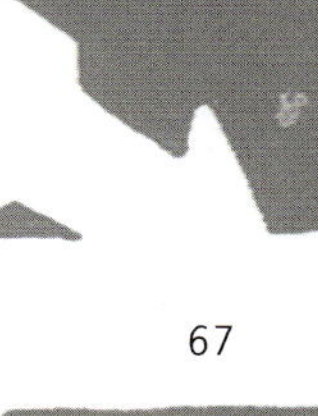

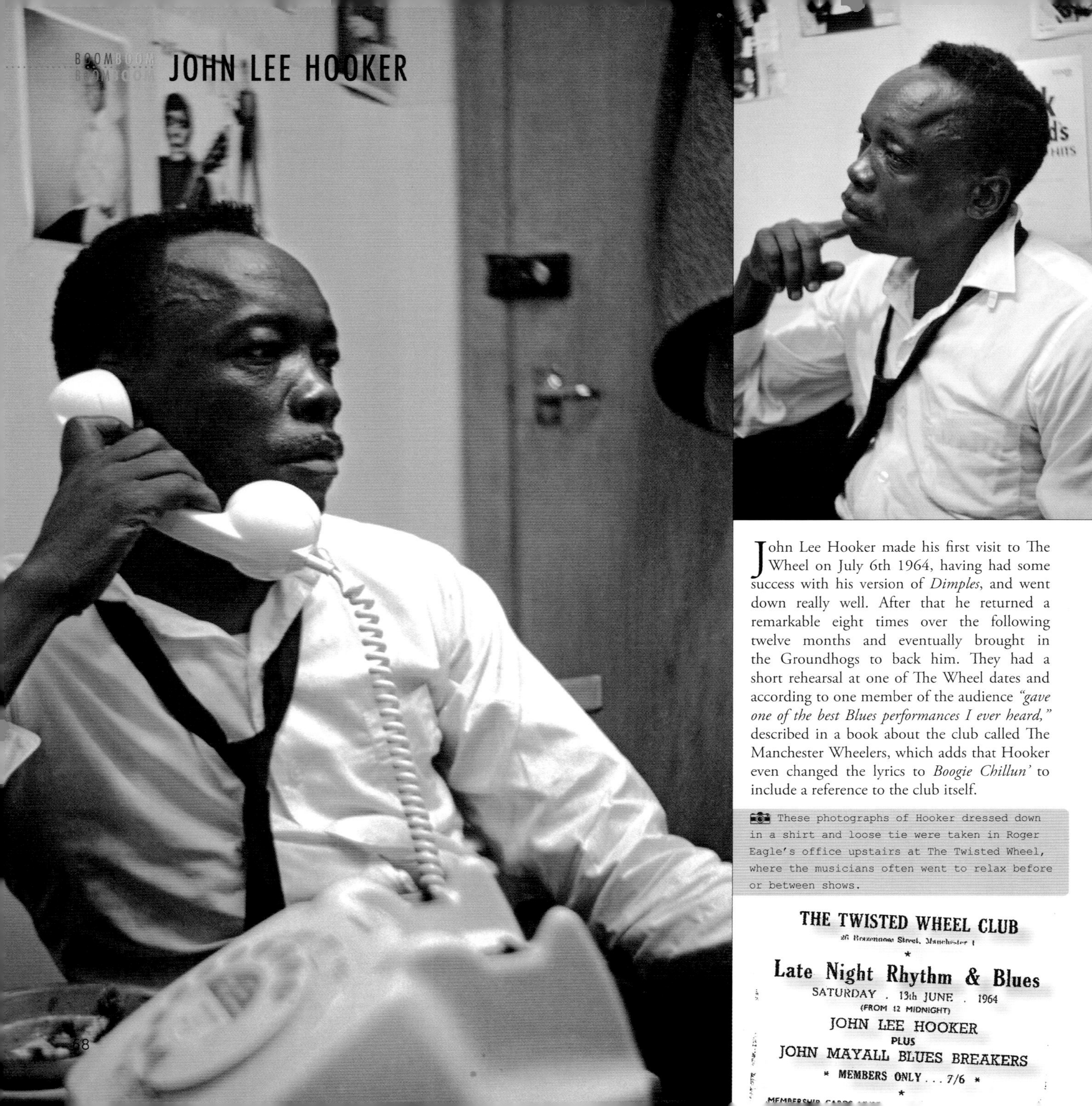

JOHN LEE HOOKER

John Lee Hooker made his first visit to The Wheel on July 6th 1964, having had some success with his version of *Dimples*, and went down really well. After that he returned a remarkable eight times over the following twelve months and eventually brought in the Groundhogs to back him. They had a short rehearsal at one of The Wheel dates and according to one member of the audience *"gave one of the best Blues performances I ever heard,"* described in a book about the club called The Manchester Wheelers, which adds that Hooker even changed the lyrics to *Boogie Chillun'* to include a reference to the club itself.

These photographs of Hooker dressed down in a shirt and loose tie were taken in Roger Eagle's office upstairs at The Twisted Wheel, where the musicians often went to relax before or between shows.

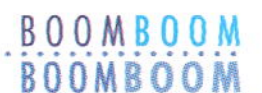 Hooker on-stage at Manchester Free Trade Hall,
October 22nd 1962, the first AFB Festival. Low
lighting made it difficult but for a first go with
his camera at a concert, Brian didn't do too badly.
These images are restored from old prints.

The American Folk and Blues Festival saw eight acts, each doing a handful of songs, watched by fans like Mick Jagger, Keith Richards, Brian Jones and Jimmy Page. *"When Hooker came out he looked very cool; the crowd stood up and started clapping wildly, he seemed rather chuffed by his reception!"* remembers Brian Smith. He took a few photographs from the stalls and the balcony. *"I had pretty much the run of the place that evening, from the local promoter. He had been helpful over two earlier Chris Barber gigs that sadly didn't happen, Howlin' Wolf and Louis Jordan (who was ill on the night). But I didn't yet have the nerve to go backstage.....!"*

This was Hooker's first visit to Britain . He returned in 1964 and on both visits found himself idolised by many British musicians. His music was always being played at The Twisted Wheel and while the track was not a big hit here, *Boom Boom* seemed to sum the era up for us when looking for a book title. Tony McPhee, featured in this book, later wrote *Mr Hooker, Sir John*, a moving acoustic blues tribute to his mentor.

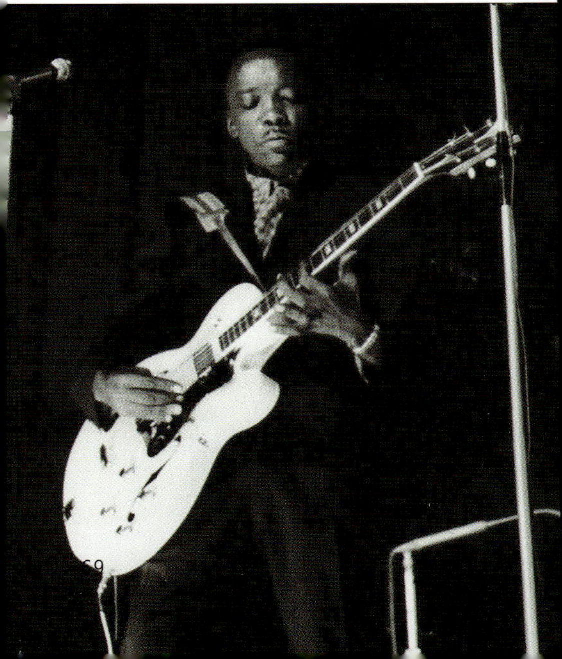

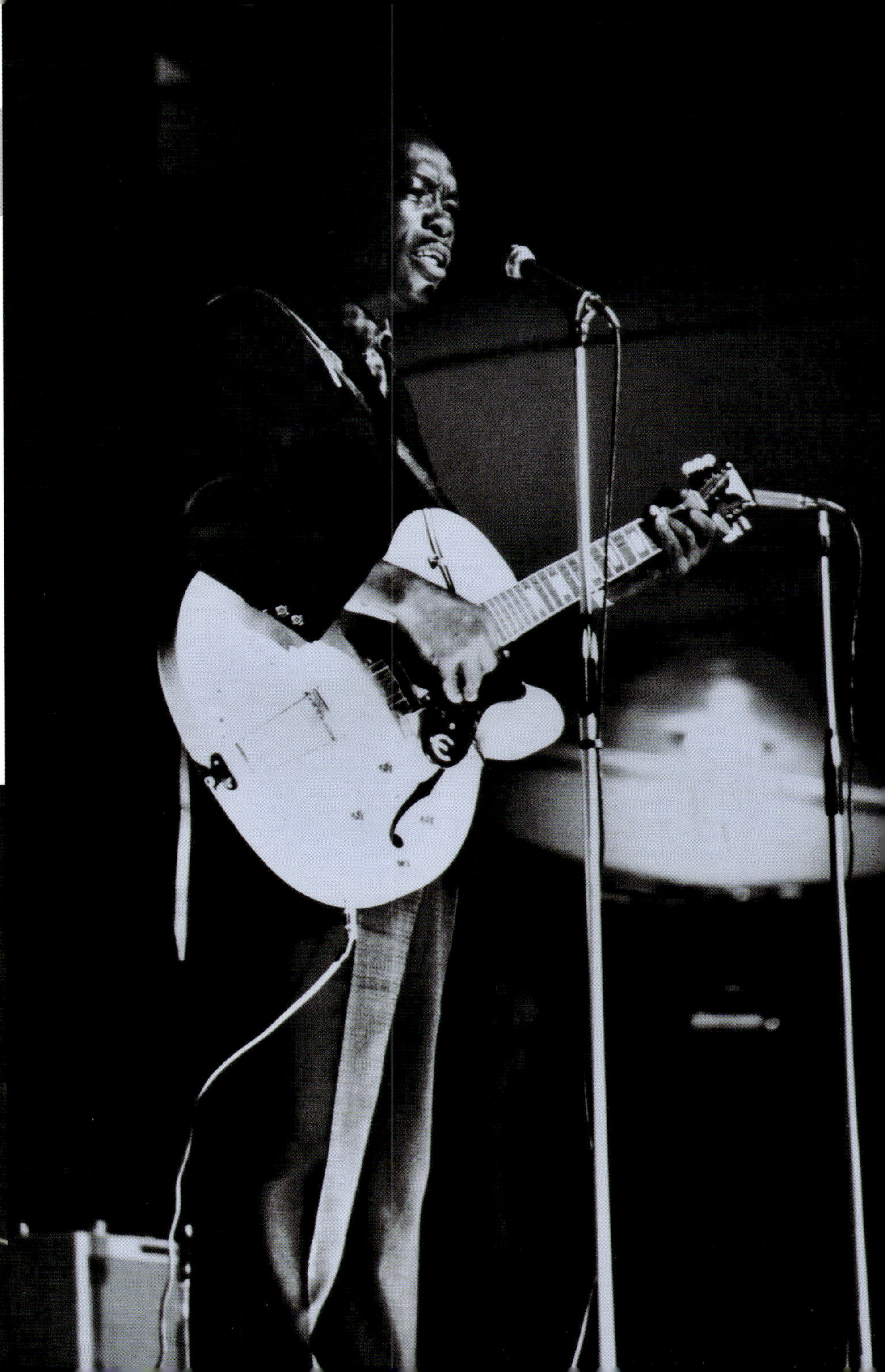

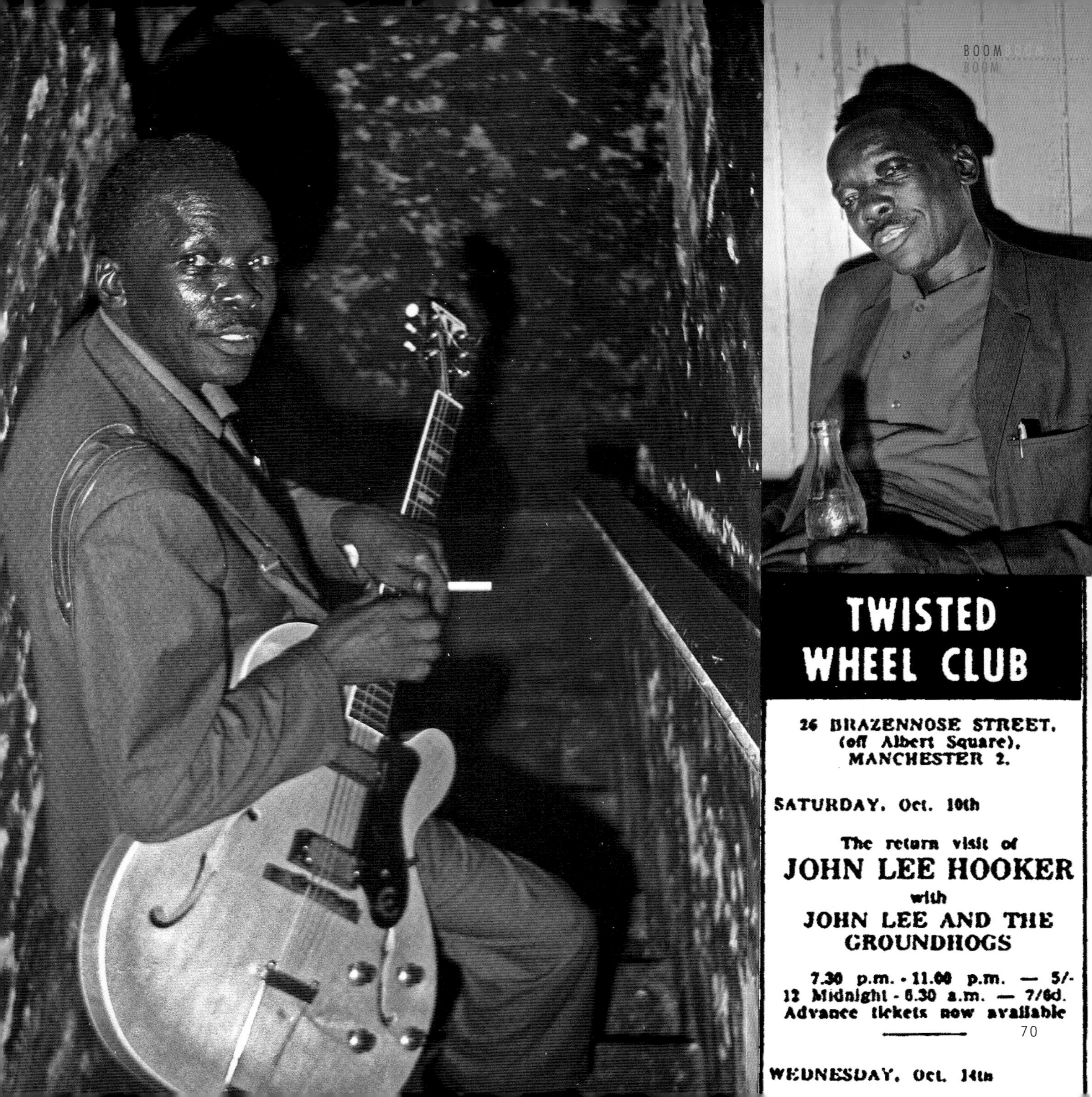
BOOM BOOM
BOOM

TWISTED
WHEEL CLUB

26 BRAZENNOSE STREET,
(off Albert Square),
MANCHESTER 2.

SATURDAY, Oct. 10th

The return visit of
JOHN LEE HOOKER
with
JOHN LEE AND THE
GROUNDHOGS

7.30 p.m. - 11.00 p.m. — 5/-
12 Midnight - 6.30 a.m. — 7/6d.
Advance tickets now available

WEDNESDAY, Oct. 14th

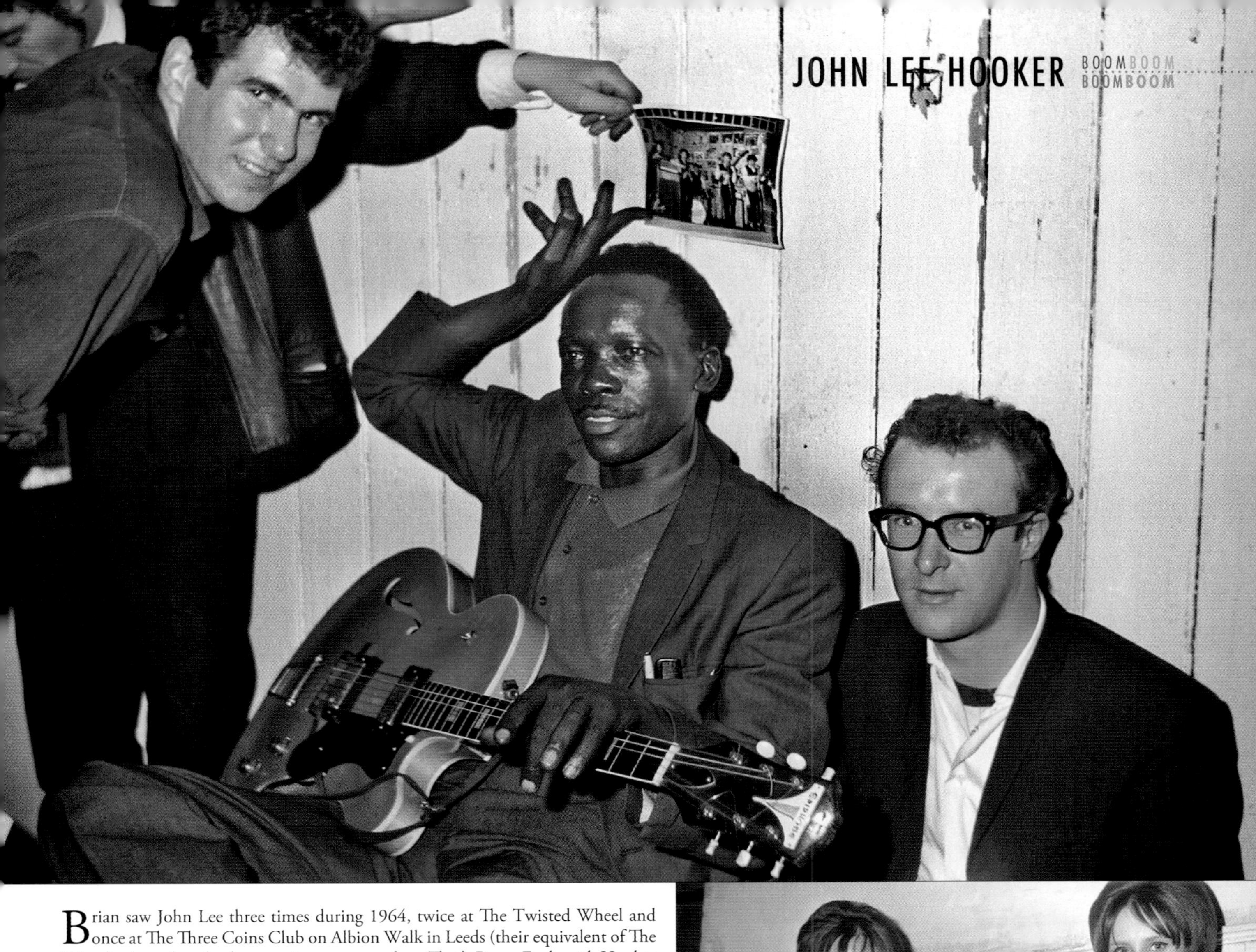

Brian saw John Lee three times during 1964, twice at The Twisted Wheel and once at The Three Coins Club on Albion Walk in Leeds (their equivalent of The Wheel) where these back-stage pictures were taken. That's Roger Eagle with Hooker above and Roger Fairhurst on the right. We don't know what the significance of the magazine photo they are pointing to is, and which the two young female fans getting autographs are also holding. They are very much dressed in the sort of clothes (and hairdos) favoured by hipper teenage girls of the time, note the CND badge.

Brian also photographed Hooker on the stairs leading down to the club in the basement; you can see the landlords certainly didn't spend much on interior decor. That photo (left) is usually said to be at The Twisted Wheel, but these stairs are stone and the walls are painted brick, so we're fairly sure it is also from The Three Coins Club.

71

JOHN LEE HOOKER

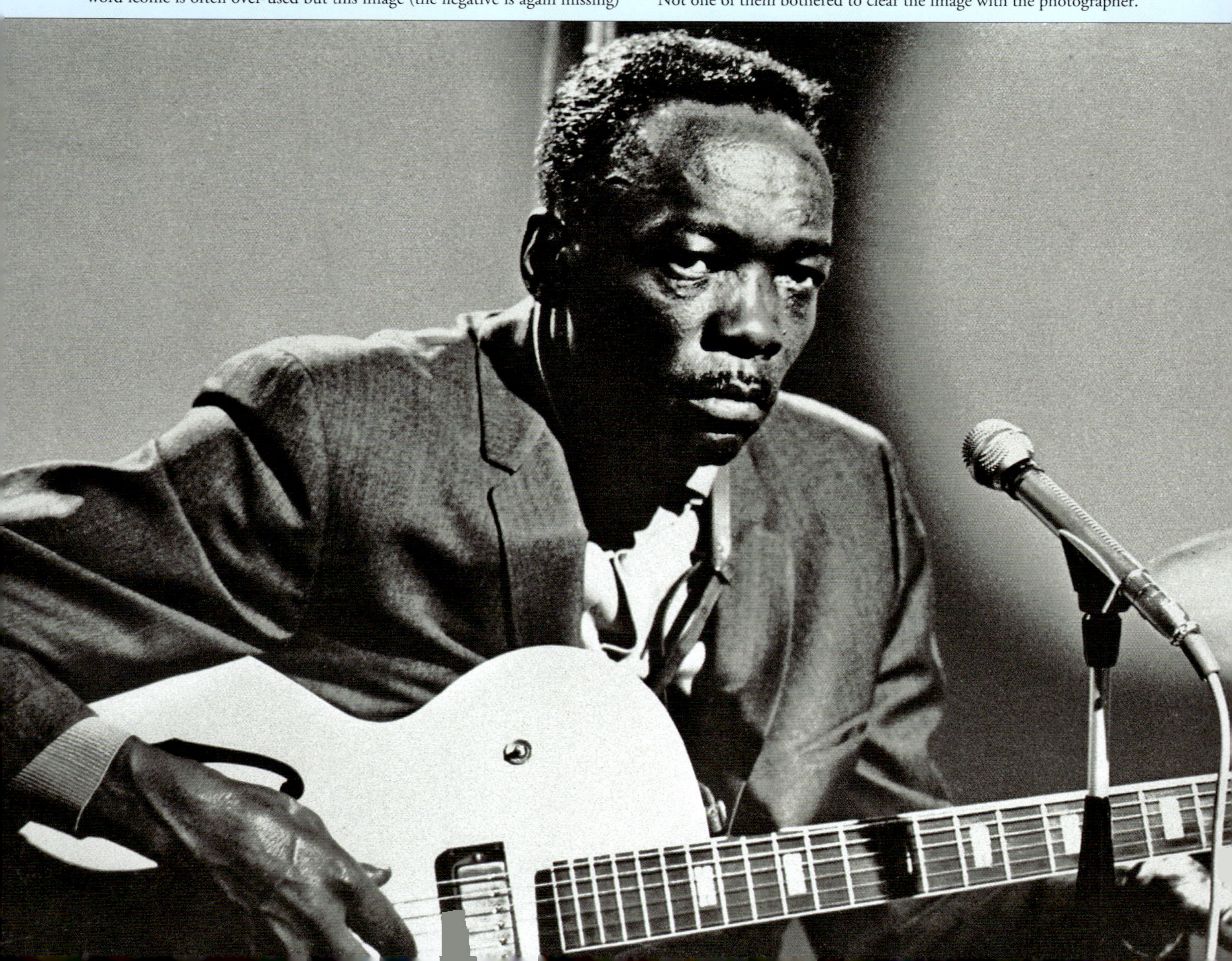

Brian took this moody photograph of John Lee during a camera rehearsal at Granada TV studios for *Scene At 6.30* aired on June 12th 1964. (Nelson Mandela was sentenced to life imprisonment the same day.) The word iconic is often over-used but this image (the negative is again missing) has been seen all over the world as this selection opposite (by no means comprehensive) of album, compact disc, MP3 and download sleeves all based on the original image demonstrates.

Not one of them bothered to clear the image with the photographer.

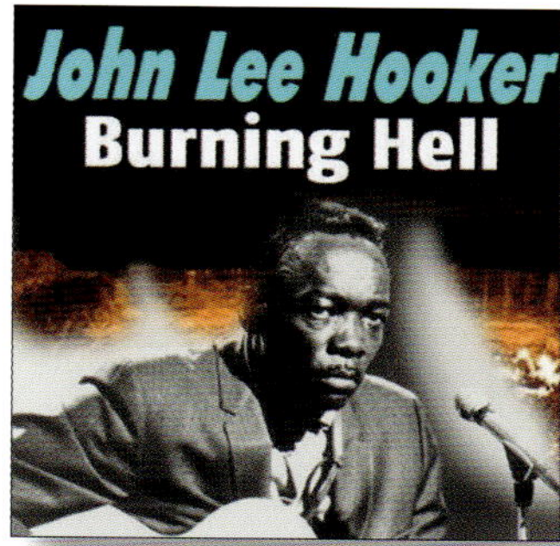
John Lee Hooker
Burning Hell

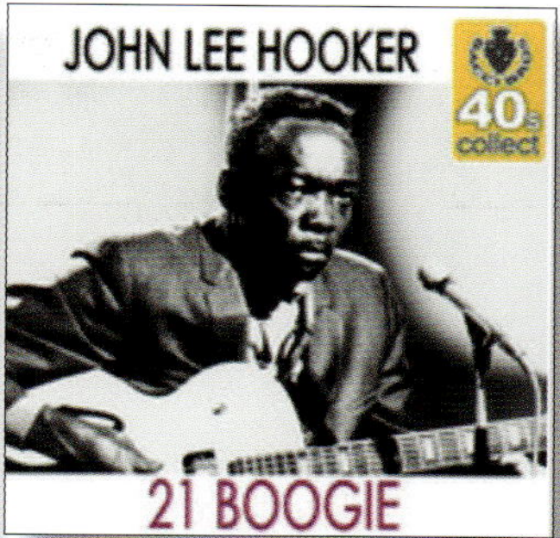
JOHN LEE HOOKER
40s collect
21 BOOGIE

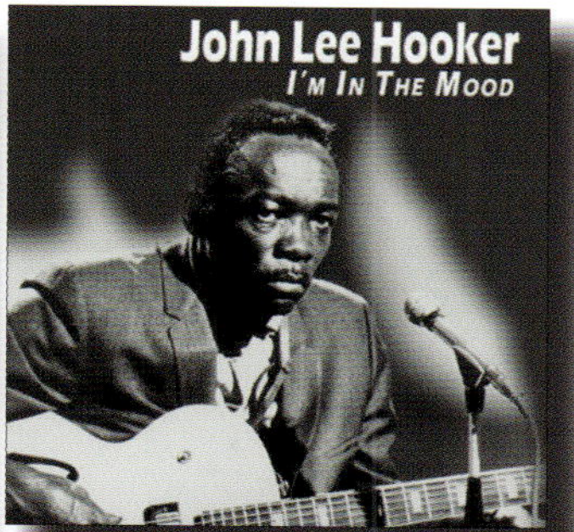
JOHN LEE HOOKER
I'M IN THE MOOD

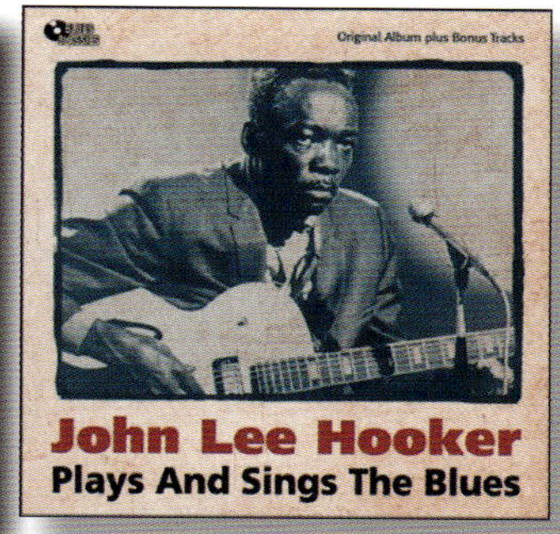
Original Album plus Bonus Tracks
John Lee Hooker
Plays And Sings The Blues

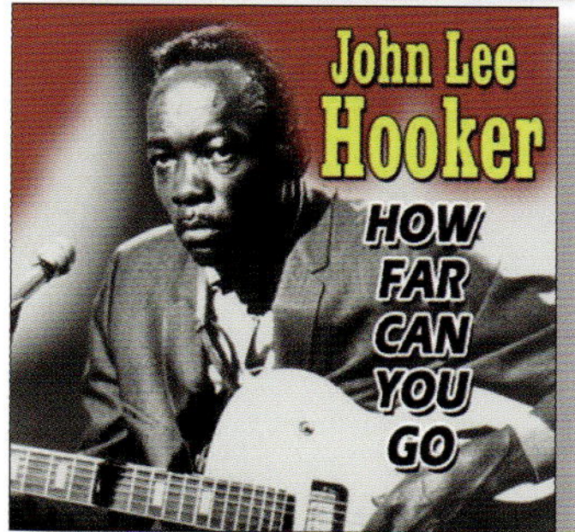
John Lee
Hooker
HOW
FAR
CAN
YOU
GO

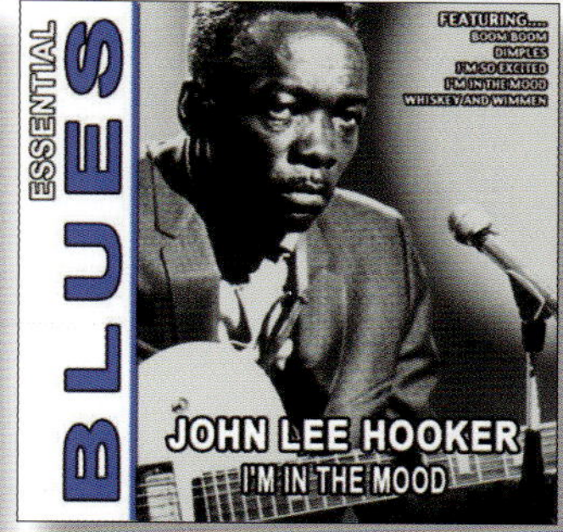
ESSENTIAL
BLUES
FEATURING....
BOOM BOOM
DIMPLES
I'M SO EXCITED
I'M IN THE MOOD
WHISKEY AND WIMMEN
JOHN LEE HOOKER
I'M IN THE MOOD

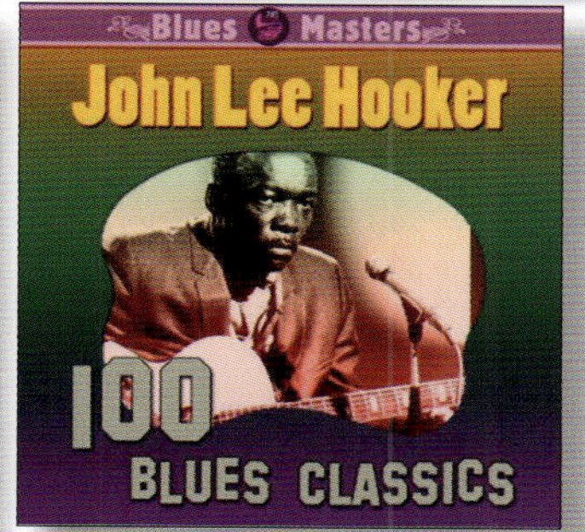
Blues Masters
John Lee Hooker
100
BLUES CLASSICS

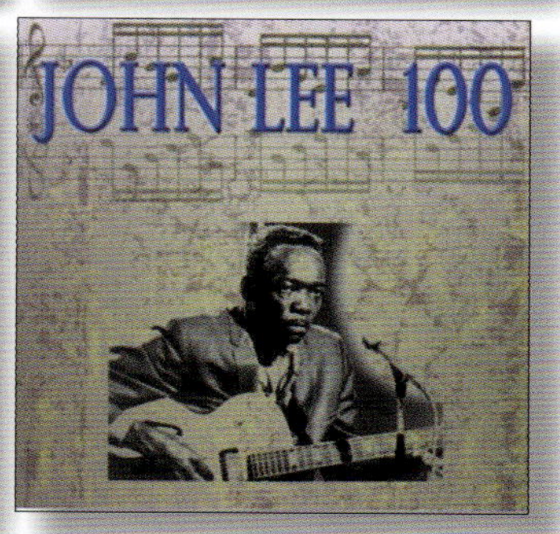
JOHN LEE 100

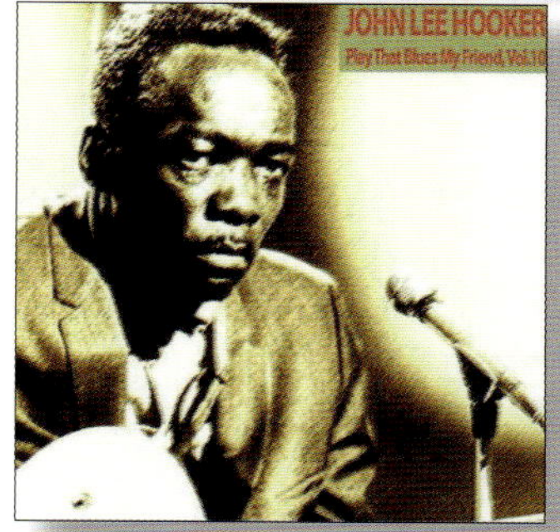
JOHN LEE HOOKER
Play That Blues My Friend, Vol.10

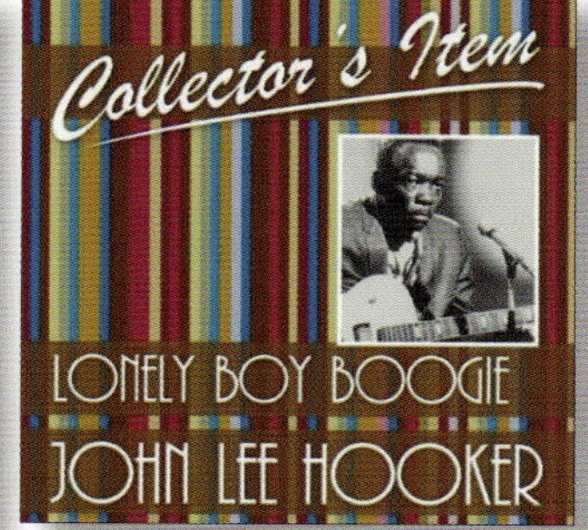
Collector's Item
LONELY BOY BOOGIE
JOHN LEE HOOKER

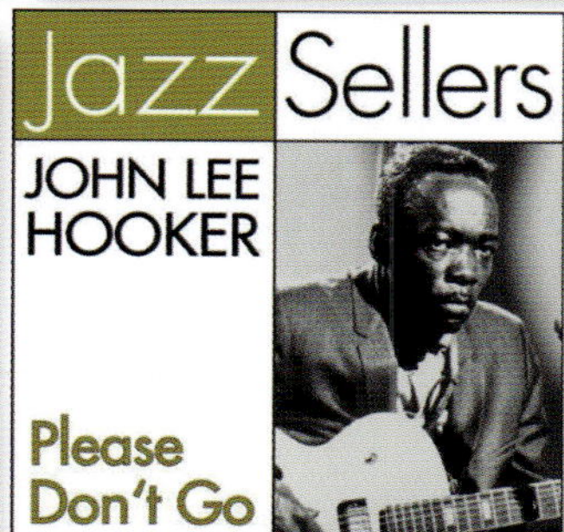
Jazz Sellers
JOHN LEE
HOOKER
Please
Don't Go

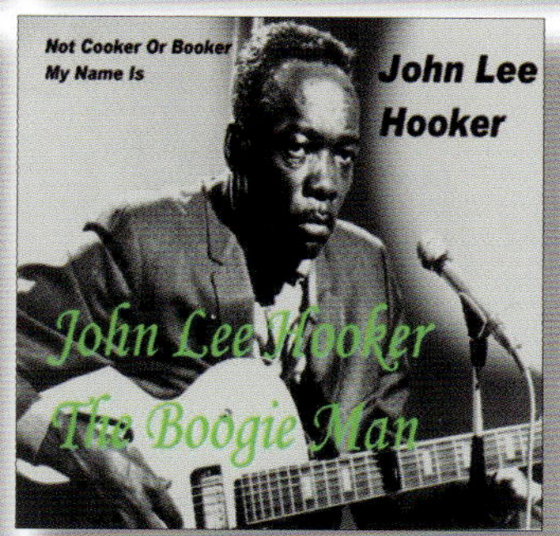
Not Cooker Or Booker
My Name Is
John Lee
Hooker
John Lee Hooker
The Boogie Man

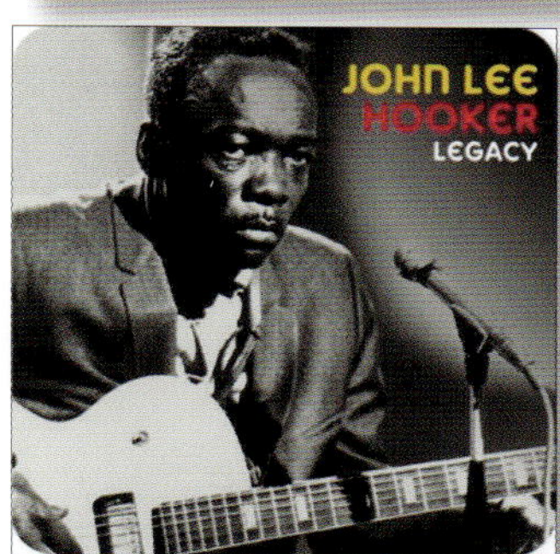
JOHN LEE
HOOKER
LEGACY

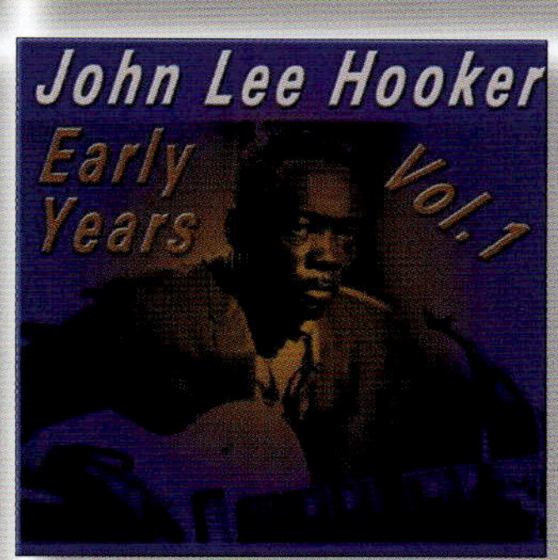
John Lee Hooker
Early
Years
Vol.1

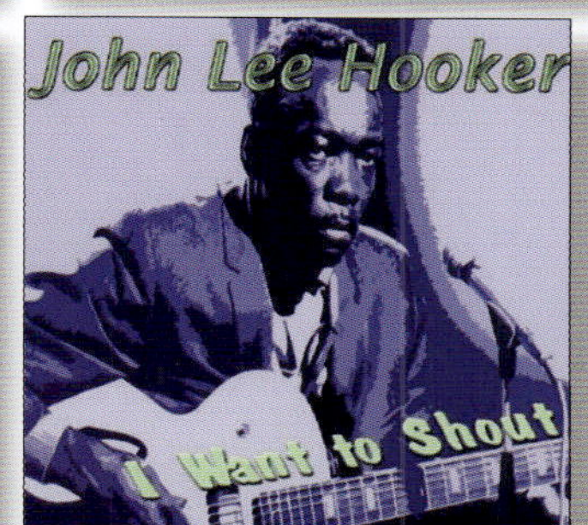
John Lee Hooker
I Want to Shout

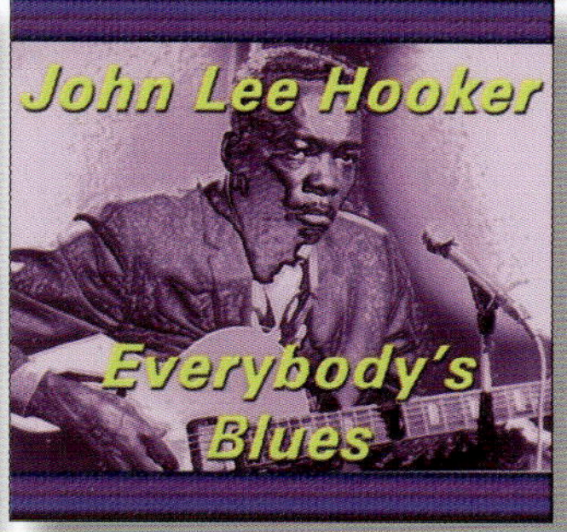
John Lee Hooker
Everybody's
Blues

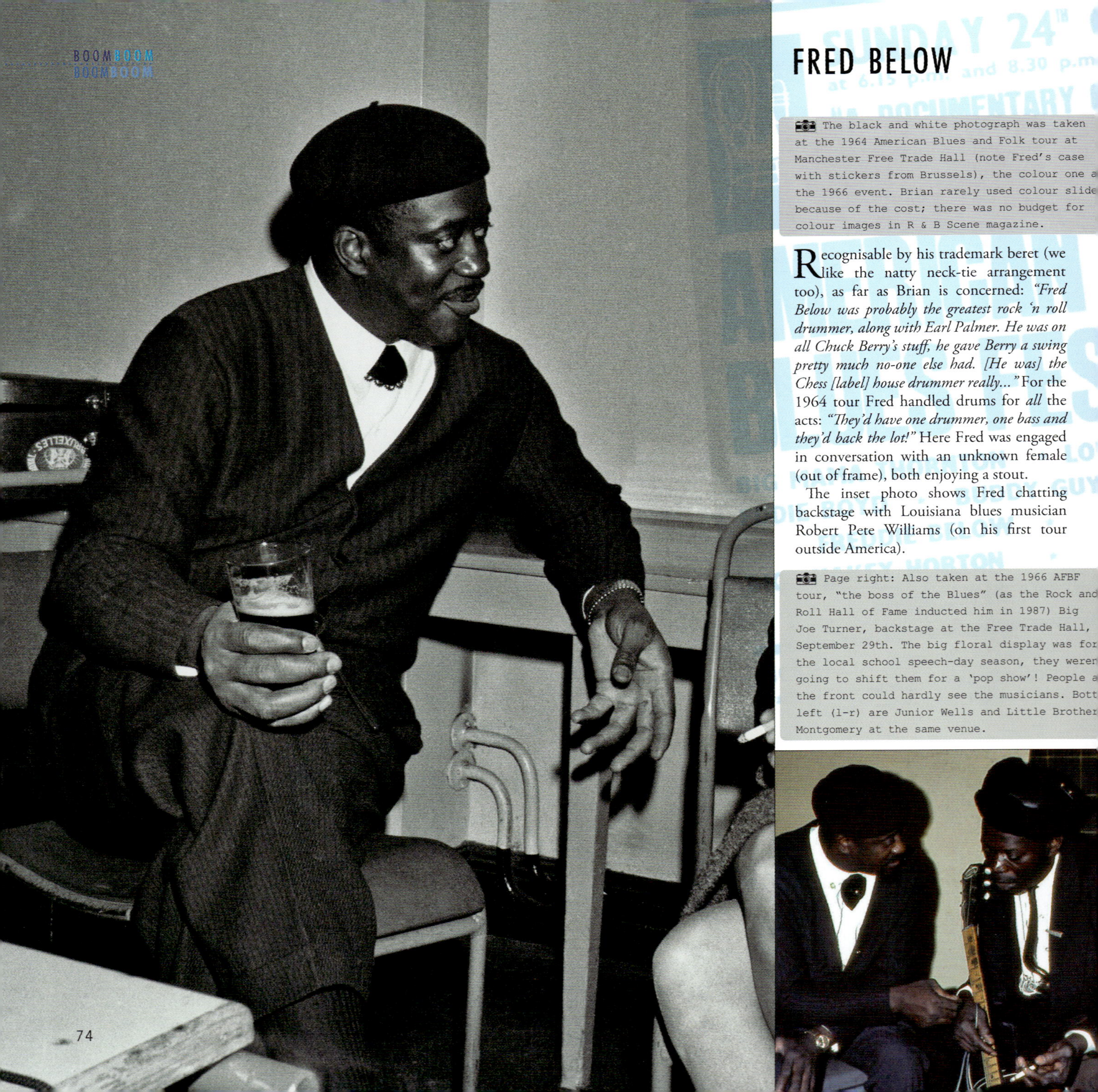

FRED BELOW

📷 The black and white photograph was taken at the 1964 American Blues and Folk tour at Manchester Free Trade Hall (note Fred's case with stickers from Brussels), the colour one a the 1966 event. Brian rarely used colour slide because of the cost; there was no budget for colour images in R & B Scene magazine.

Recognisable by his trademark beret (we like the natty neck-tie arrangement too), as far as Brian is concerned: *"Fred Below was probably the greatest rock 'n roll drummer, along with Earl Palmer. He was on all Chuck Berry's stuff, he gave Berry a swing pretty much no-one else had. [He was] the Chess [label] house drummer really…"* For the 1964 tour Fred handled drums for *all* the acts: *"They'd have one drummer, one bass and they'd back the lot!"* Here Fred was engaged in conversation with an unknown female (out of frame), both enjoying a stout.

The inset photo shows Fred chatting backstage with Louisiana blues musician Robert Pete Williams (on his first tour outside America).

📷 Page right: Also taken at the 1966 AFBF tour, "the boss of the Blues" (as the Rock and Roll Hall of Fame inducted him in 1987) Big Joe Turner, backstage at the Free Trade Hall, September 29th. The big floral display was for the local school speech-day season, they weren't going to shift them for a 'pop show'! People a the front could hardly see the musicians. Bott left (l-r) are Junior Wells and Little Brother Montgomery at the same venue.

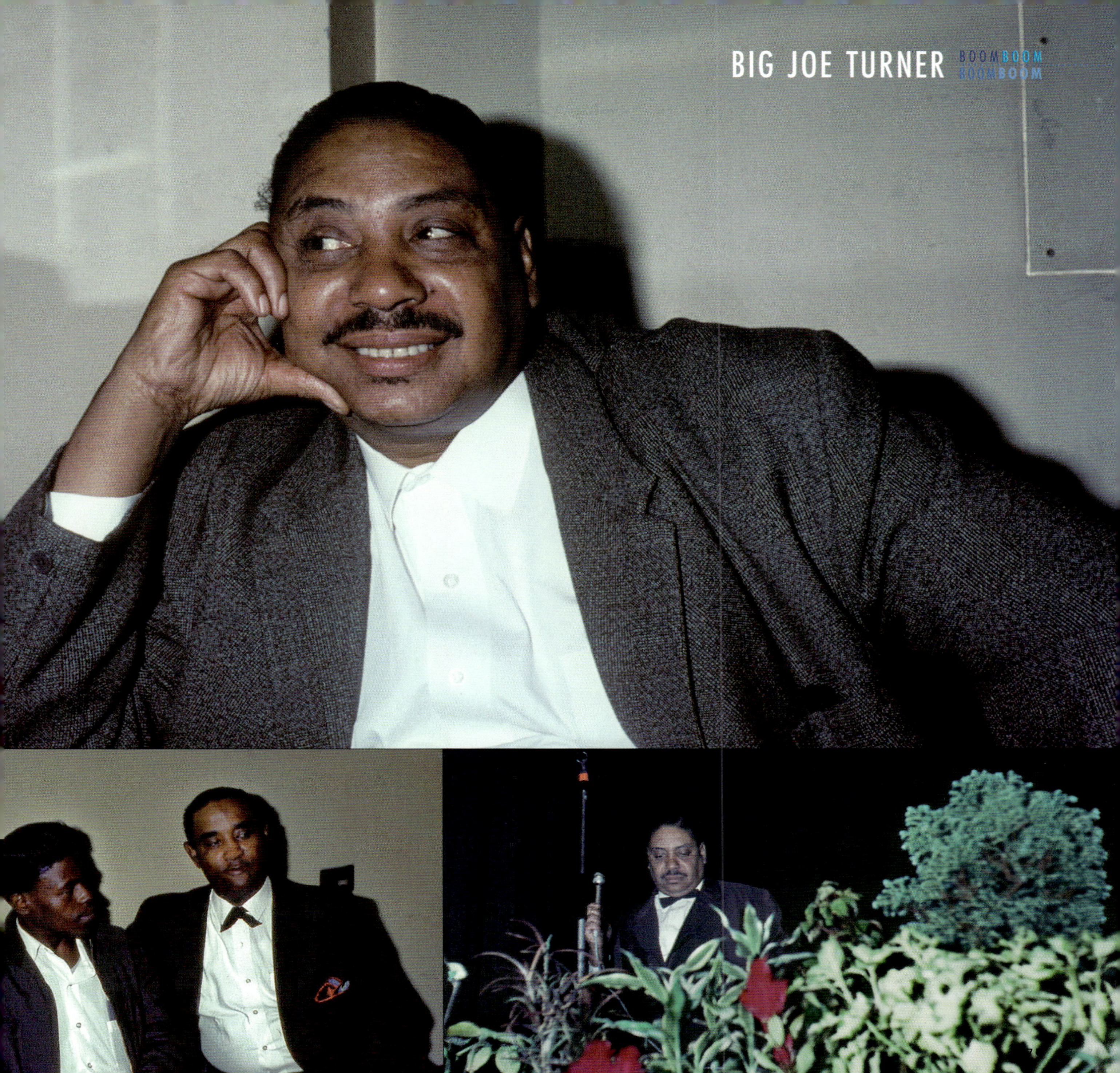
BIG JOE TURNER BOOMBOOM BOOMBOOM

JIMMY REED
and the
GROUNDHOGS

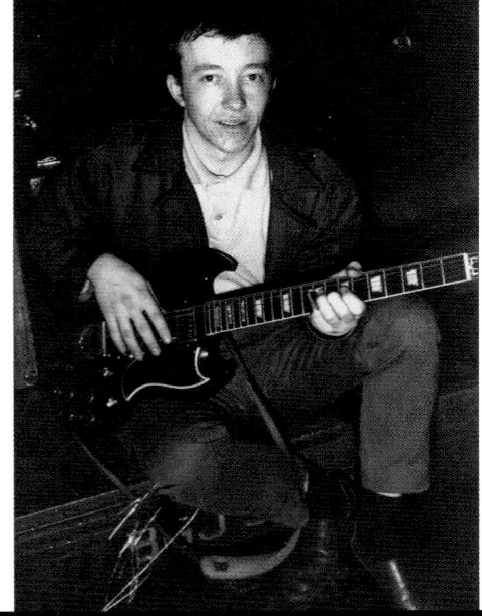

The Groundhogs were formed in 1962 and named after the title of a John Lee Hooker song by their new guitarist Tony McPhee, who was very much influenced by American black blues players. They were booked to back a number of visiting blues musicians as they knew the material so well, touring with John Lee Hooker in 1964 (as John Lee's Groundhogs), Little Walter, Champion Jack Dupree and here with Jimmy Reed. The photo was taken beside their touring dormobile outside the Twisted Wheel Club on 21st November 1964 (plus one of Tony inside). Roger Eagle was already a big fan of Reed and played his records in the club all the time. We asked Tony what he recalled about the line-up: *"Bob Hall had a good day job at Dolby so didn't want to go pro like the rest of us. So we advertised for another blues piano player and Tom Parker got the job, not as good as Bob (who played - and still plays - fantastic boogie piano) but willing to go on the road. So left to right is Tom Parker, piano; me (with bad acne!), guitar; Dave Boorman, drums; John Cruickshank, singer (I didn't sing until late '60s); Jimmy Reed and finally Pete Cruickshank, bass, in front of our Commer van. He used to drive us, our gear and on one tour John Lee Hooker, who liked to travel with us, which was fantastic!"*

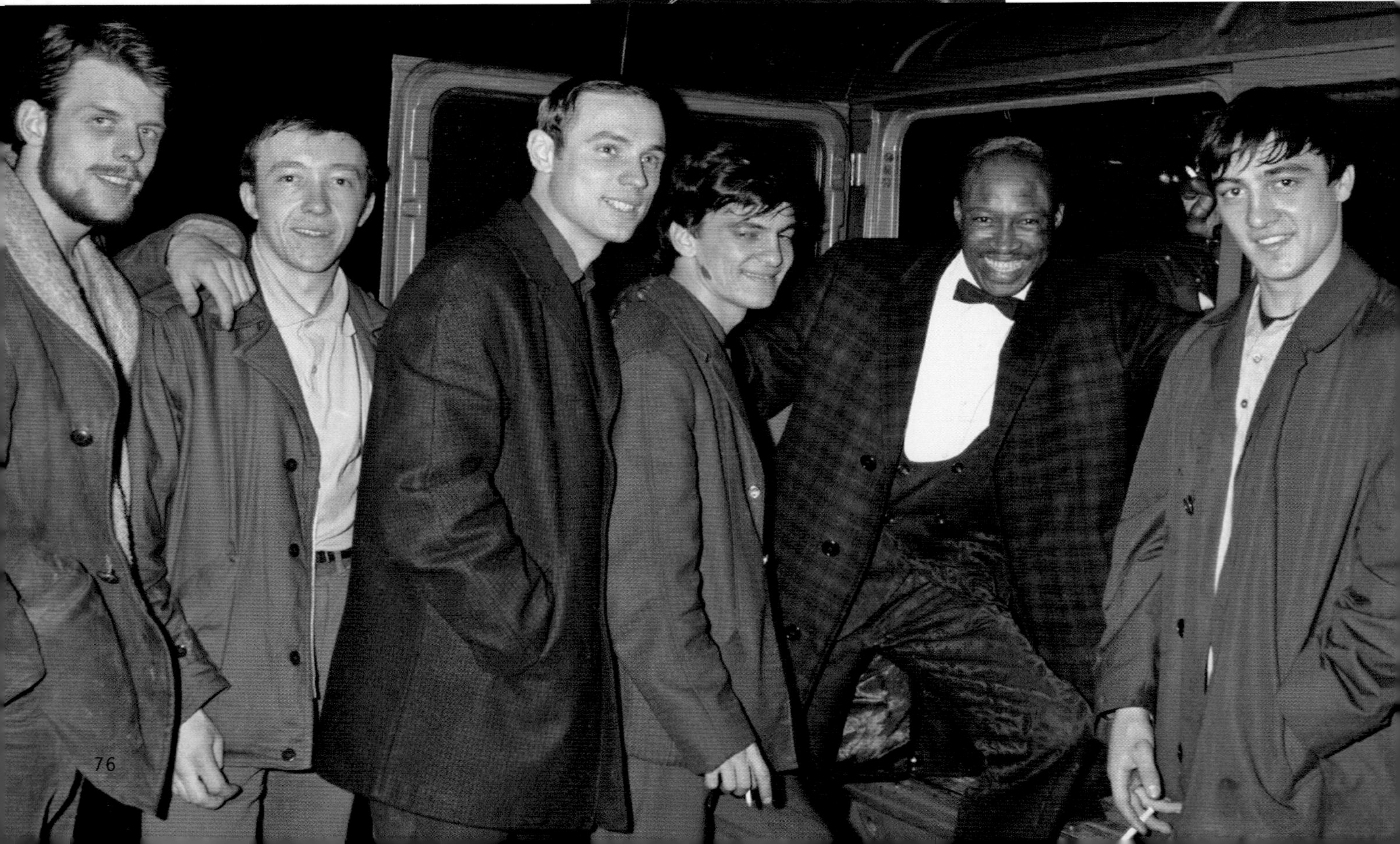

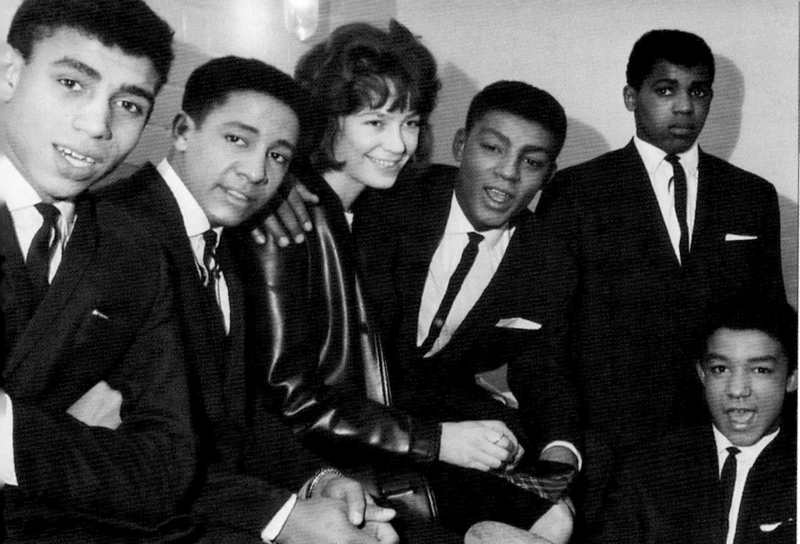

Two photographs taken backstage at Manchester Apollo (with an unknown female fan) on Dec 12th 1963.

The CHANTS

Not well remembered today, smart looking black Liverpool doo-wop quintet The Chants formed in 1962, featuring Joe Ankah, Eddie Ankah, Nat Smeda, Alan Harding and Chris Amoo. Brian photographed them on a package tour headed by Helen Shapiro with Bobby Rydell. The Chants were popular live and on disc at The Twisted Wheel as Brian recalls; *"I saw them at the Princess Club too, all in a line at front, stomping out I Don't Care, storming stuff!"* The Chants (still known then as The Shades) did several songs at The Cavern at their first show, backed by The Beatles in late 1962 (at Paul McCartney's suggestion) and were signed to NEMS as a result. Musically respected, and produced by Tony Hatch for Pye, they never got their chart break. Lead singer Eddie later formed The Real Thing who did have considerable success.

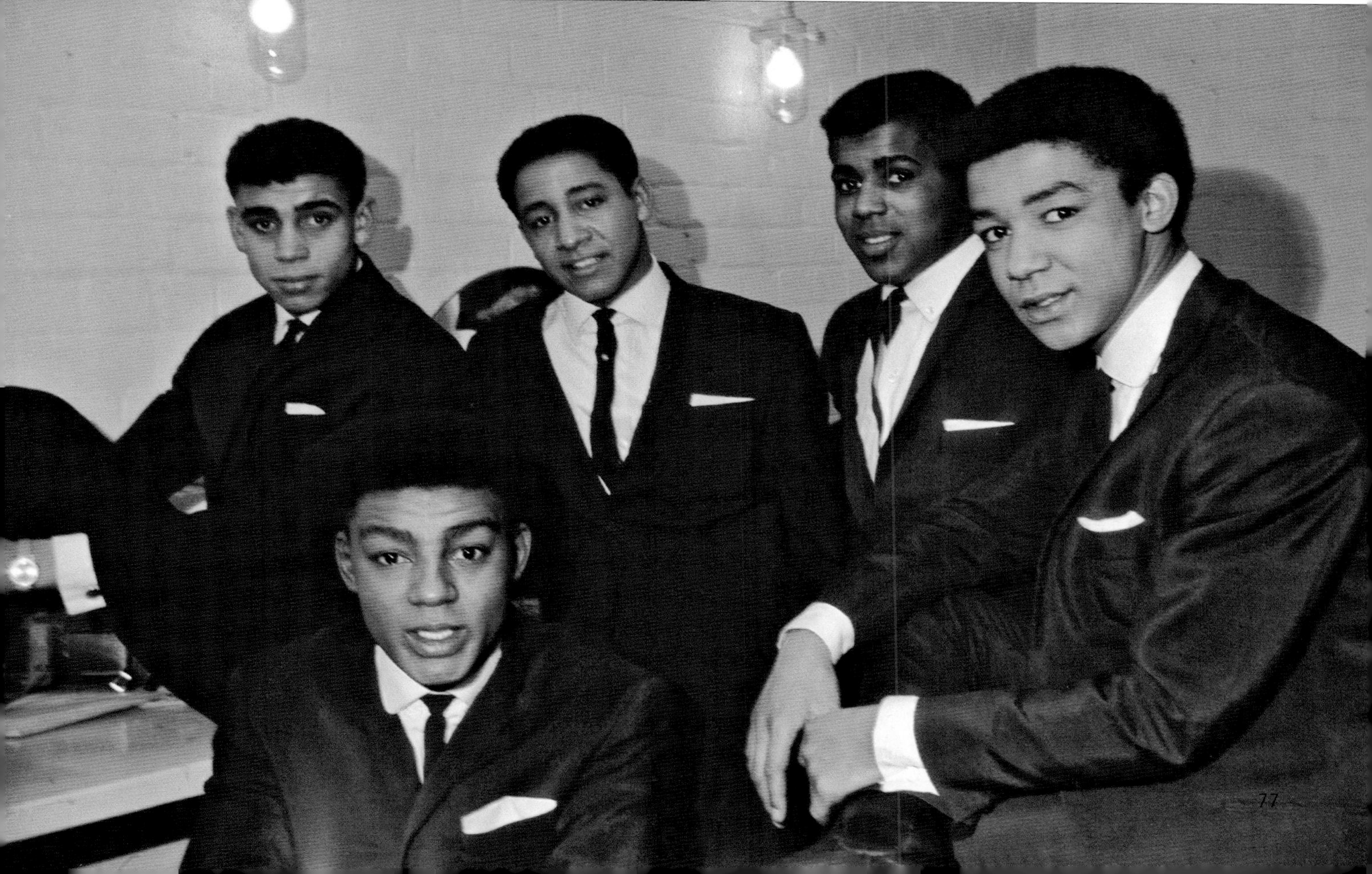

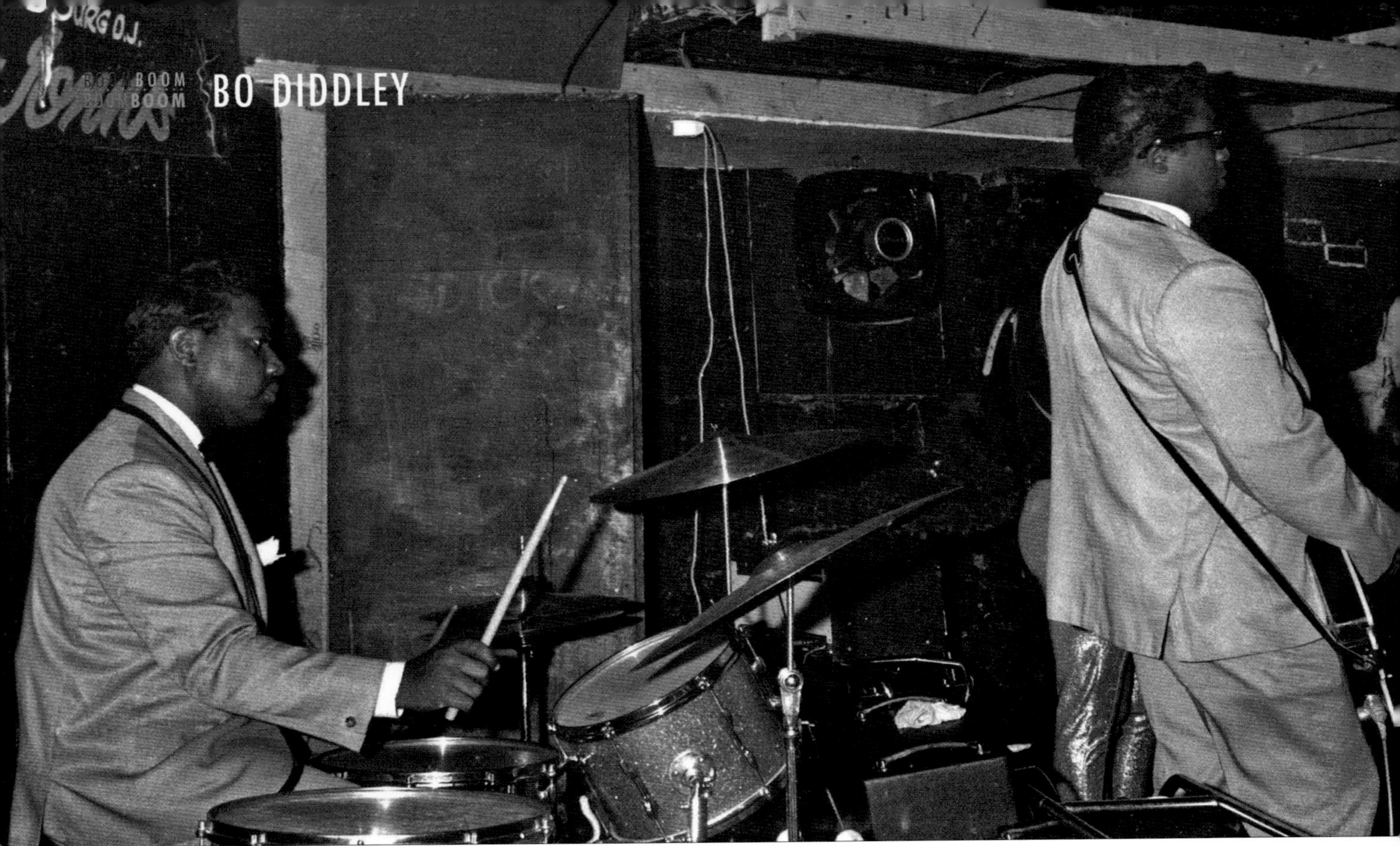

Although Bo Diddley played on a number of package tours, Brian Smith also managed to see him play some of the more intimate venues as a headliner. The rare photograph opposite was taken on October 16th 1963 backstage at Manchester Odeon when Diddley, fon his irst British tour, was second on the bill to the Everly Brothers, with Mickie Most, The Rolling Stones and Julie Grant in supporting roles. Although known today for his important chart production work, Most had been a pop singer and toured for five years or so before concentrating on production work in 1964. Jerome Green was an important part of the Diddley sound, and had worked with him for over a decade as a percussionist, also contributing vocals to a few of his recordings as well.

The atmospheric photograph above and on the second page following were taken at The Jigsaw Club in Manchester, with Brian squeezing in at the side of the low platform performance area (or 'stage'!) next to drummer Clifton James to avoid being jostled by the packed crowd. The Jigsaw had actually opened as The Cavern on May 19th 1964 and was downstairs on Cromford Court (now the site of the grim Arndale centre) off Market Street. It changed name to The Jigsaw Club the following year with Dave Lee Travis as their regular DJ. Roger Eagle worked here at times, then in 1968 began putting

events on in a basement room next door known as The Magic Village (in tune with the changing times).

Diddley here was touring with his rhythm guitarist, known simply as The Duchess, though frustratingly for lovers of her impressive gold lame stage outfit she was out of camera sight for most of the concert. Brian did manage to include the great Clifton James in the frame, who contributed much to the iconic Bo Diddley beat. Clifton was recently listed in the top thirty greatest drummers of all time by Rolling Stone, but also worked with many of the blues greats featured in this book. The date was October 1st 1965 (most gig lists have this Jigsaw show still incorrectly attributed to The Cavern) and Brian recalls the show because he was there with Eagle and spent the afternoon scouring electrical shops for fittings as the place was so poorly set up the band didn't have enough sockets. *If you look closely you'll see several white flexes feeding into 'Fitall' plugs into the ceiling, a bloody death-trap!*". Brian also recalls that Bo Diddley did two shows; the second was a late nighter at Stockport's Manor Lounge ten miles down the road (*"My friend Neil Carter did the DJ job there for a while and was there that night.Neil, Roger Eagle and me even went out for tea with The Duchess and Clifton,"* recalls Brian. *"God knows why I took no pics of that!"*

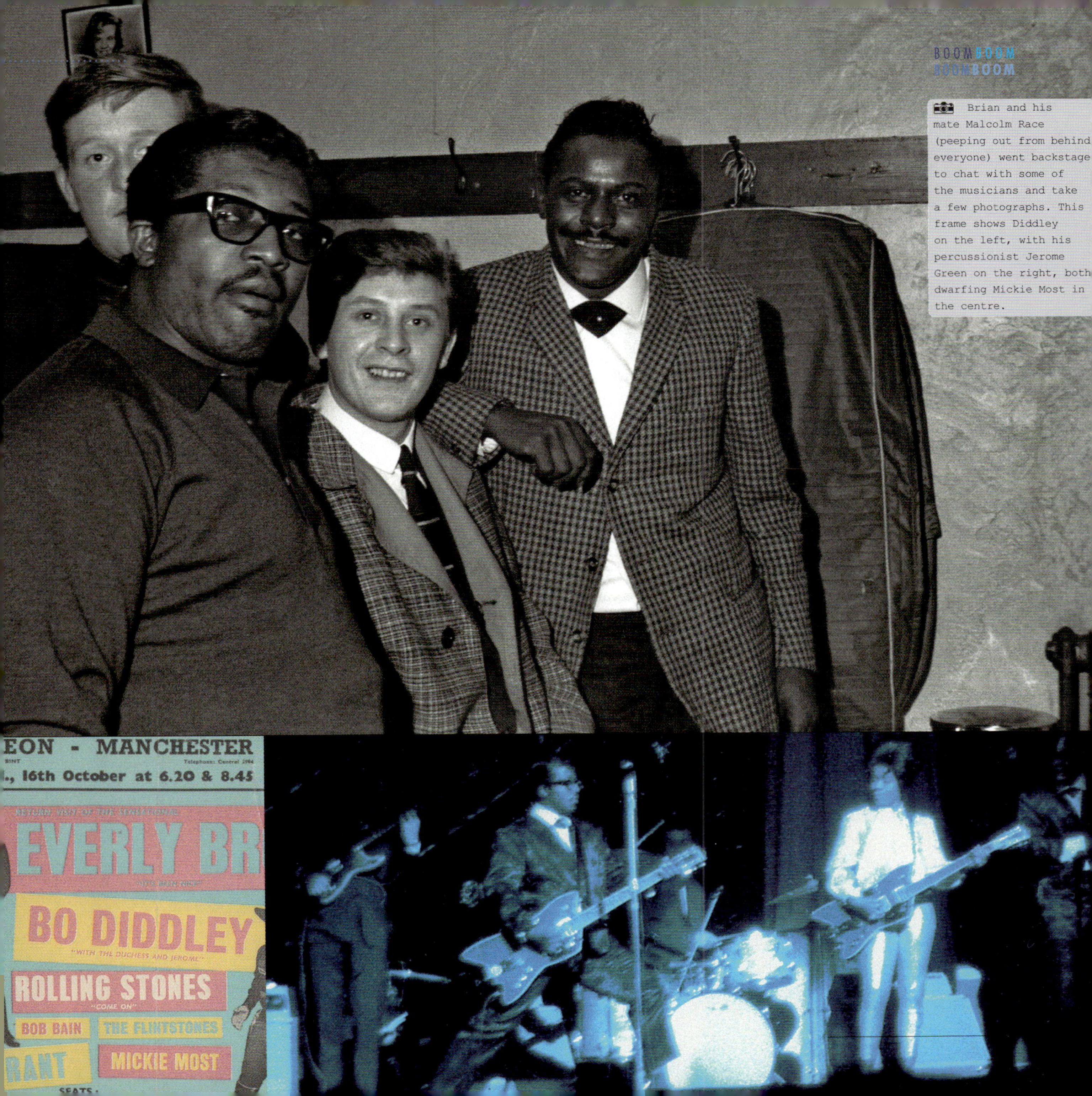

Brian and his mate Malcolm Race (peeping out from behind everyone) went backstage to chat with some of the musicians and take a few photographs. This frame shows Diddley on the left, with his percussionist Jerome Green on the right, both dwarfing Mickie Most in the centre.

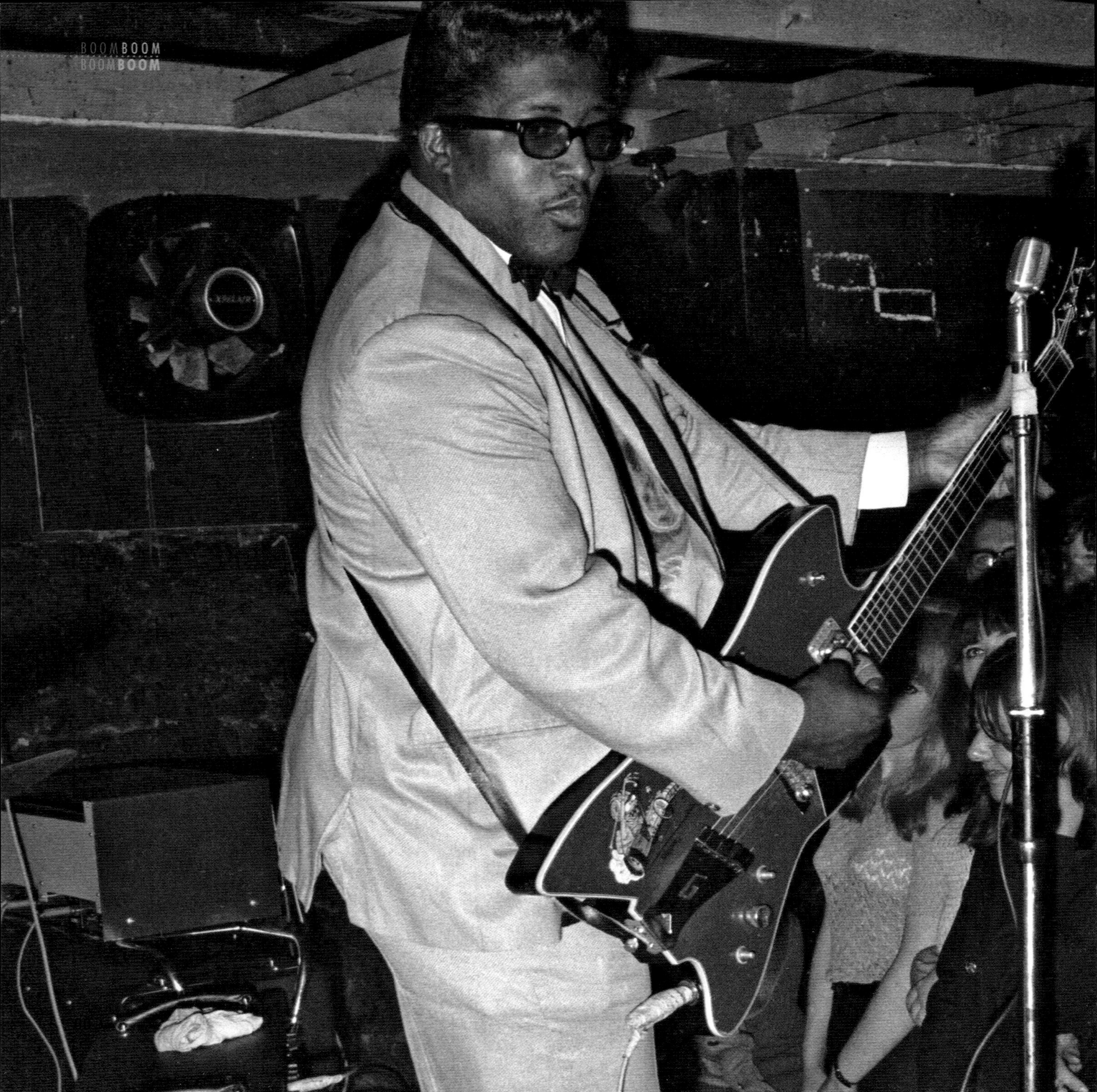
BOOM BOOM
BOOM BOOM

BO DIDDLEY

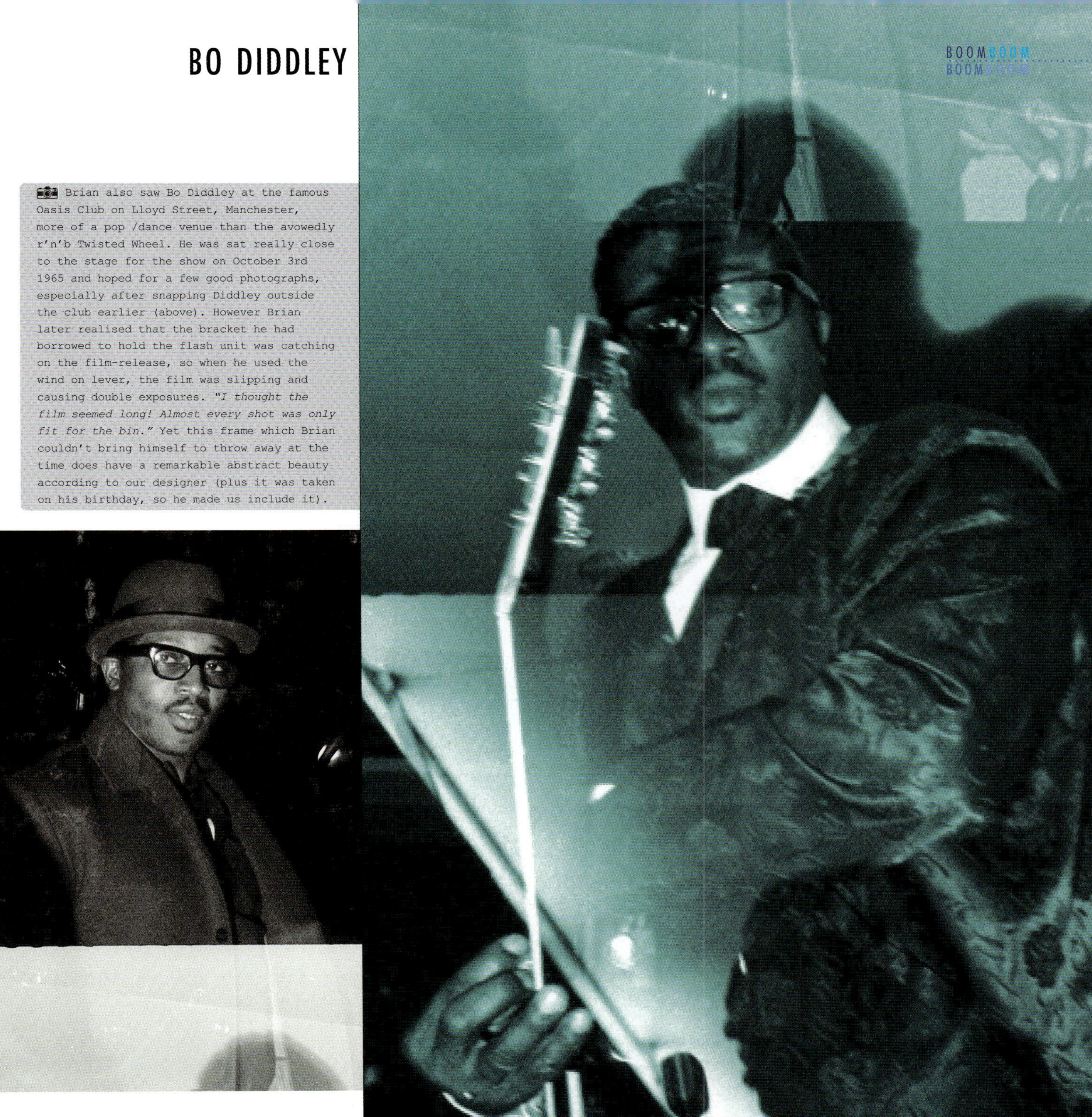

Brian also saw Bo Diddley at the famous
Oasis Club on Lloyd Street, Manchester,
more of a pop /dance venue than the avowedly
r'n'b Twisted Wheel. He was sat really close
to the stage for the show on October 3rd
1965 and hoped for a few good photographs,
especially after snapping Diddley outside
the club earlier (above). However Brian
later realised that the bracket he had
borrowed to hold the flash unit was catching
on the film-release, so when he used the
wind on lever, the film was slipping and
causing double exposures. *"I thought the
film seemed long! Almost every shot was only
fit for the bin."* Yet this frame which Brian
couldn't bring himself to throw away at the
time does have a remarkable abstract beauty
according to our designer (plus it was taken
on his birthday, so he made us include it).

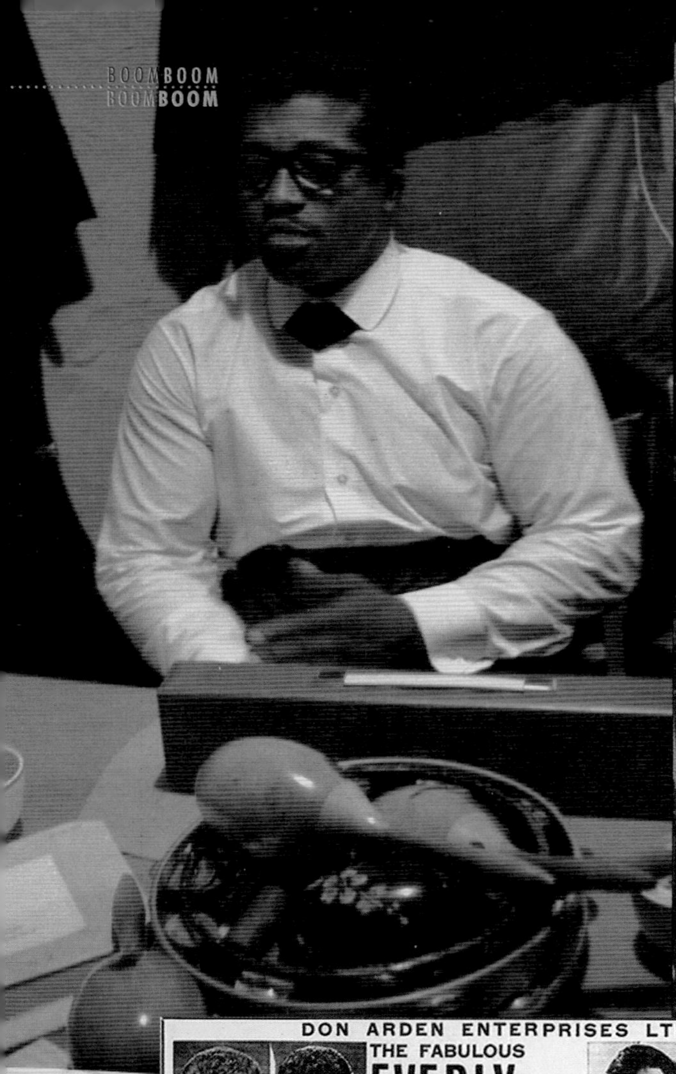

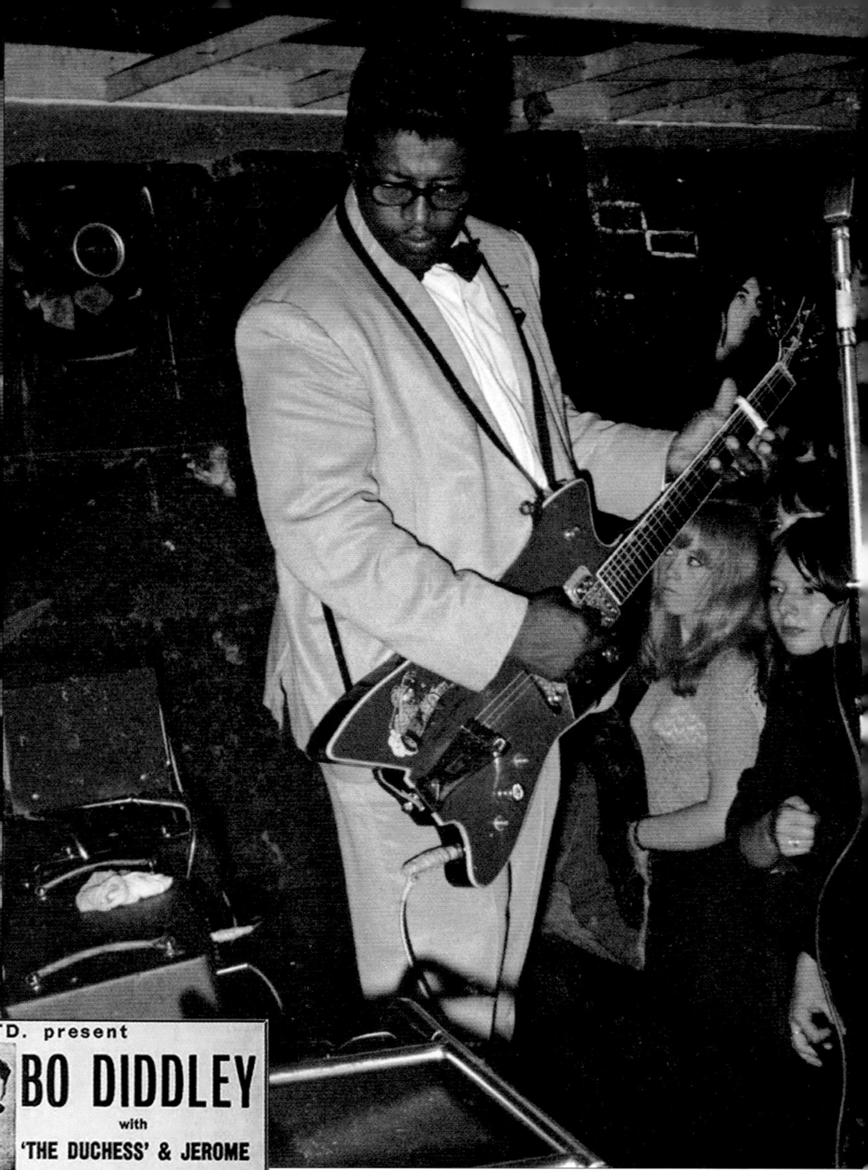

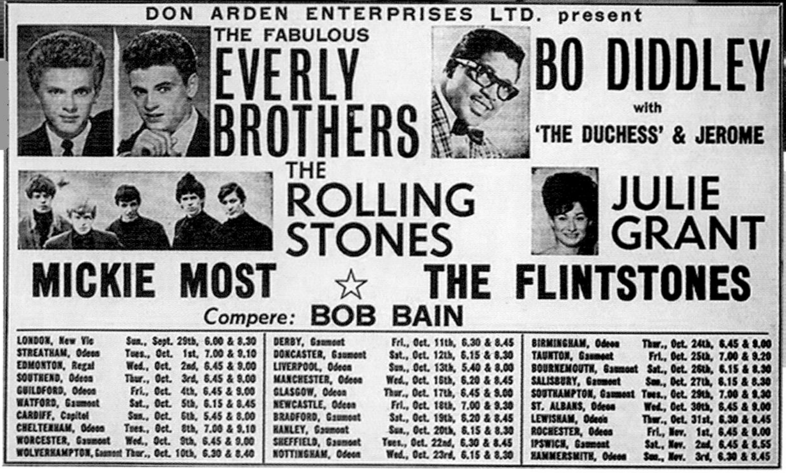

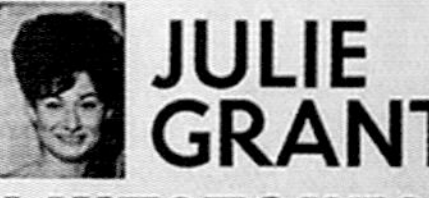

DON ARDEN ENTERPRISES LTD. present

THE FABULOUS EVERLY BROTHERS

BO DIDDLEY
with 'THE DUCHESS' & JEROME

THE ROLLING STONES

JULIE GRANT

MICKIE MOST ☆ THE FLINTSTONES
Compere: BOB BAIN

LONDON, New Vic	Sun., Sept. 29th, 6.00 & 8.30	DERBY, Gaumont	Fri., Oct. 11th, 6.30 & 8.45	BIRMINGHAM, Odeon	Thur., Oct. 24th, 6.45 & 9.00
STREATHAM, Odeon	Tues., Oct. 1st, 7.00 & 9.10	DONCASTER, Gaumont	Sat., Oct. 12th, 6.15 & 8.30	TAUNTON, Gaumont	Fri., Oct. 25th, 7.00 & 9.20
EDMONTON, Regal	Wed., Oct. 2nd, 6.45 & 9.00	LIVERPOOL, Odeon	Sun., Oct. 13th, 5.40 & 8.00	BOURNEMOUTH, Gaumont	Sat., Oct. 26th, 6.15 & 8.30
SOUTHEND, Odeon	Thur., Oct. 3rd, 6.45 & 9.00	MANCHESTER, Odeon	Wed., Oct. 16th, 6.20 & 8.45	SALISBURY, Gaumont	Sun., Oct. 27th, 6.15 & 8.30
GUILDFORD, Odeon	Fri., Oct. 4th, 6.45 & 9.00	GLASGOW, Odeon	Thur., Oct. 17th, 6.45 & 9.00	SOUTHAMPTON, Gaumont	Tues., Oct. 29th, 7.00 & 9.30
WATFORD, Gaumont	Sat., Oct. 5th, 6.15 & 8.45	NEWCASTLE, Odeon	Fri., Oct. 18th, 7.00 & 9.30	ST. ALBANS, Odeon	Wed., Oct. 30th, 6.45 & 9.00
CARDIFF, Capitol	Sun., Oct. 6th, 5.45 & 8.00	BRADFORD, Gaumont	Sat., Oct. 19th, 6.20 & 8.45	LEWISHAM, Odeon	Thur., Oct. 31st, 6.30 & 8.45
CHELTENHAM, Odeon	Tues., Oct. 8th, 7.00 & 9.10	HANLEY, Gaumont	Sun., Oct. 20th, 6.15 & 8.30	ROCHESTER, Odeon	Fri., Nov. 1st, 6.45 & 9.00
WORCESTER, Gaumont	Wed., Oct. 9th, 6.45 & 9.00	SHEFFIELD, Gaumont	Tues., Oct. 22nd, 6.30 & 8.45	IPSWICH, Gaumont	Sat., Nov. 2nd, 6.45 & 8.55
WOLVERHAMPTON, Gaumont	Thur., Oct. 10th, 6.30 & 8.40	NOTTINGHAM, Odeon	Wed., Oct. 23rd, 6.15 & 8.30	HAMMERSMITH, Odeon	Sun., Nov. 3rd, 6.30 & 8.45

Brian took this informal shot (left) in Bo Diddley's dressing room at the Odeon concert on October 16. 1963; you can see Jerome's precussion gear on the table. The slive shot above (and on page 80 and 179) were taken in Manchester's Jigsaw Club. If you thought the Twisted Wheel was run down..!

Dr. ISIAH ROSS

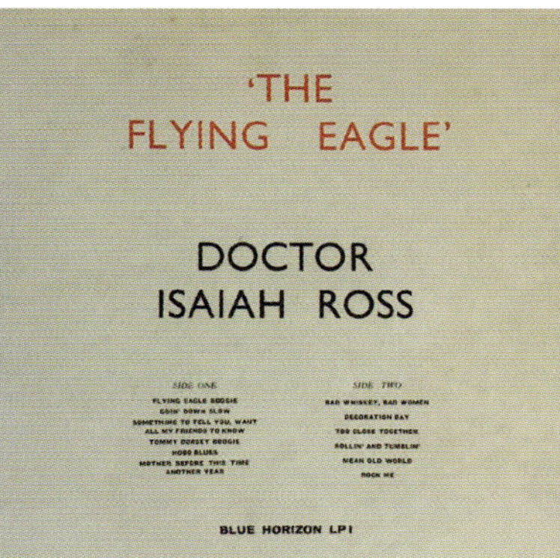

Another of Brian's one-off negatives, harmonica blues man Dr. Isiah Ross backstage at the Free Trade Hall in 1965 on the AFBF tour. This was Isiah's first visit to Europe, during which he also cut his debut LP, *Flying Eagle*, for Mike Vernon's Blue Horizon label (their first ever release, now a £1,000+ item). Something of a one-man band he is holding his harmonica neck stand in the photo but also sang, played guitar and drummed. Recording for both Chess and Sun in the Fifties, he was not a real doctor but carried his harmonicas in a doctor's bag (and also earned the nickname "The Harmonica Boss").

Brian caught up with Isiah again on one of his last visits in 1990 when he played in Burnley (his music was always more popular here than in America). He discovered that Isiah had never stopped working at his Detroit car plant job and had several labour union badges pinned inside his guitar case. Brian had discovered an unlikely family connection: *"I was able to tell him the union had been founded by my great-uncle Matt in 1934, after he emigrated to USA having been black-listed here by the engineering employers during the General Strike (and for which he remained General Secretary till he died in 1958). Isiah was quite tickled by this unlikely coincidence and gave me one of his badges!"*

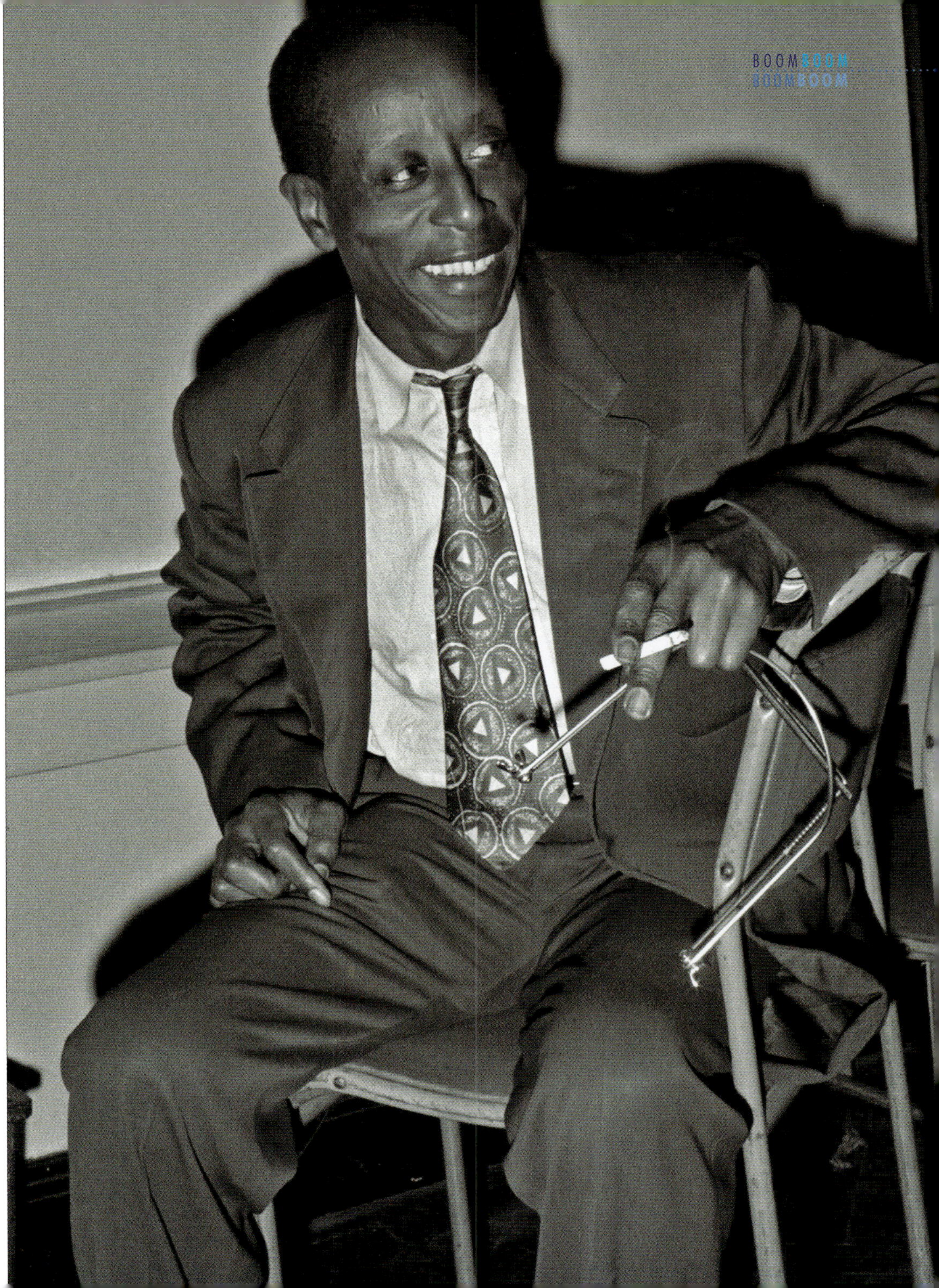

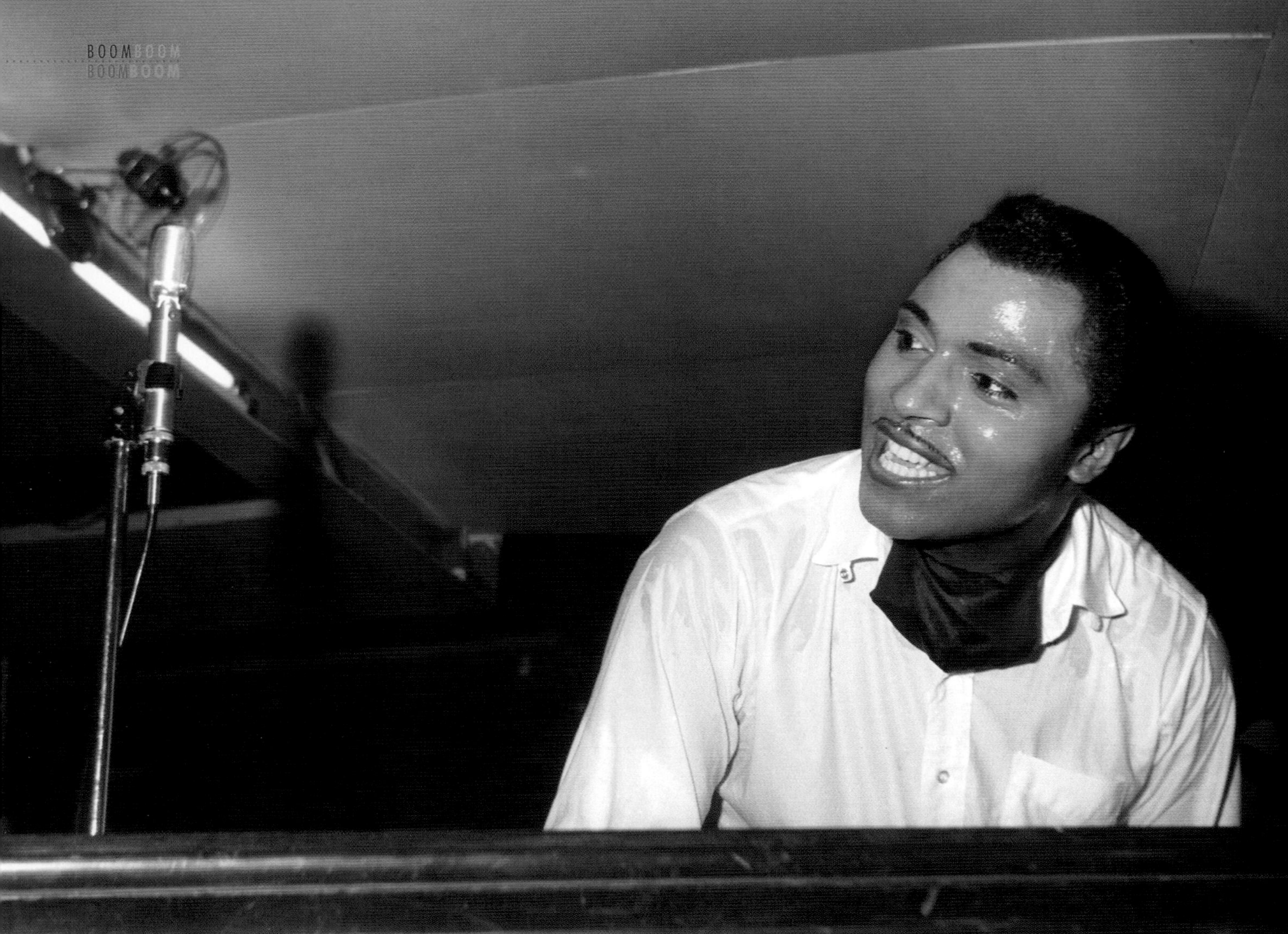

LITTLE RICHARD

📷 These remarkable photographs were taken at the Oasis Club on Lloyd Street, Manchester, May 10th 1964. They really capture the atmosphere of the show well, with the adoring crowd looking very into it and Little Richard putting everything into his performance.

Little Richard had toured bigger halls the year before, 1963, so this was a chance to see him in a more intimate setting at an 'extra' afternoon gig, promoted by the Oasis club. Don and Dewey were added to the bill at some shows on this tour but not at The Oasis. Richard's regular touring band took a day off (though Brian recalls Don 'Sugarcane' Harris and Richard's guitarist Glenn Willings came along to watch) and it was a local outfit called The Bo Weevils (whose drummer had played behind Bo Diddley at his Oasis gig) who did the honours. *I later tracked down Terry Betts, the bass player, and he confirmed this,"* remembers Brian. The band were Jim Hollingsworth, Trevor Jones, Alan Forbes and Terry Betts. Backstage Brian was chatting with Richard and Don on the day and actually quizzed him about Screaming Jay Hawkins who Roger Eagle was keen to track down. Don had met up with him not long before and had his address, which eventually led to the Twisted Wheel crew getting Hawkins over to Britain.

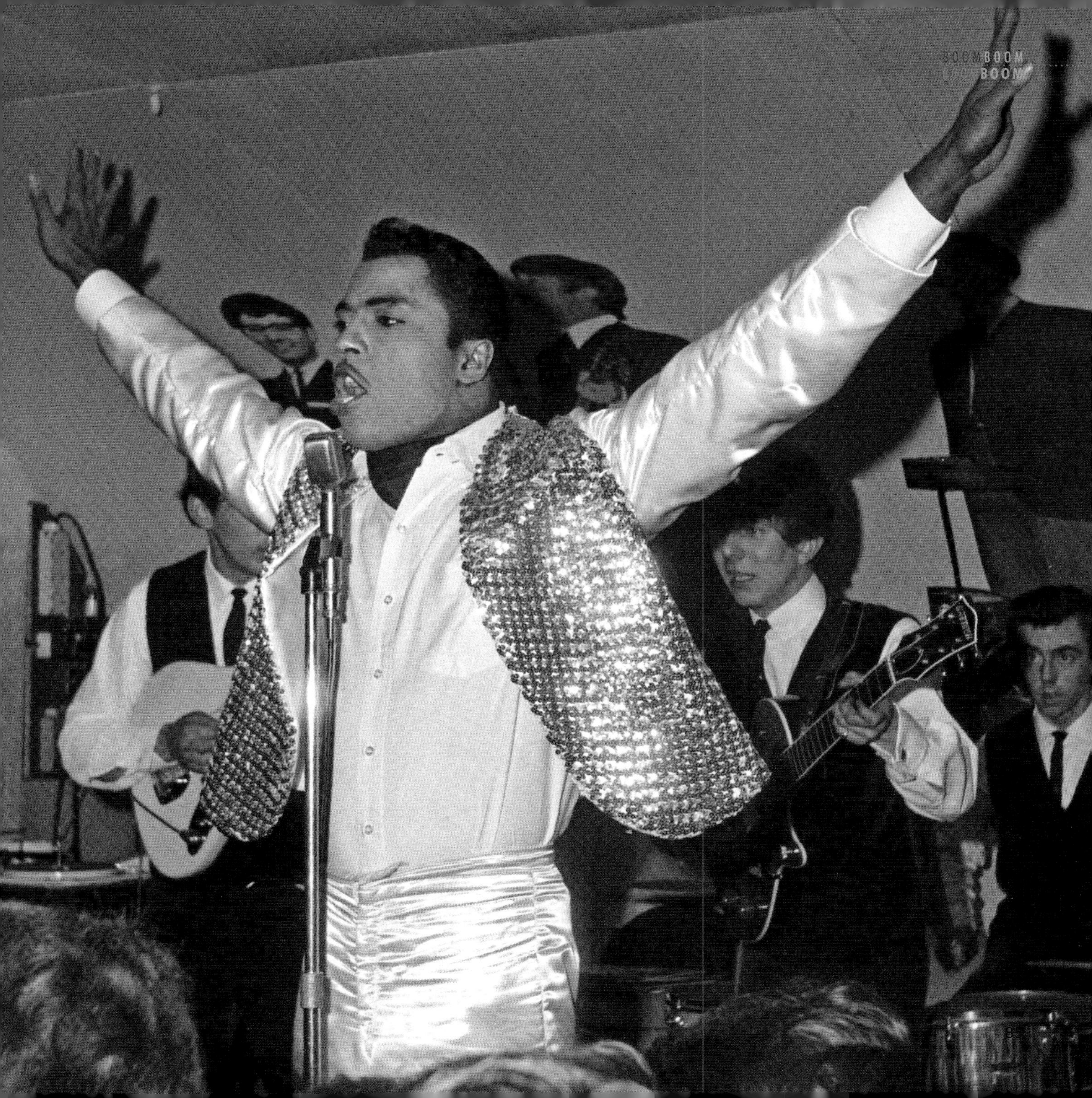
BOOM·BOOM
BOOM·BOOM

LITTLE RICHARD

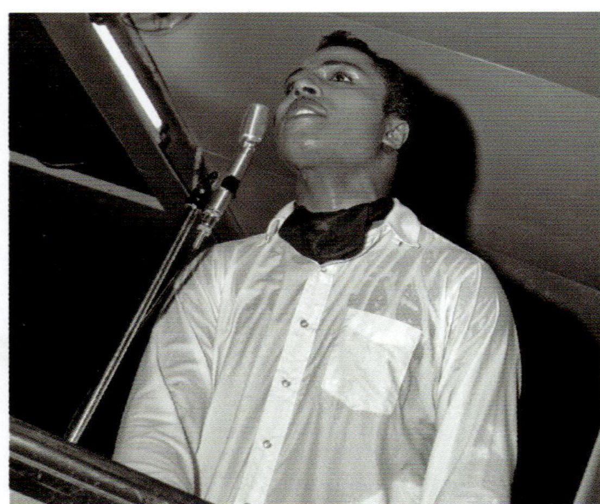

The Oasis Club was another of Manchester's famour Sixties venues, sited at 45 / 47 Lloyd Street off Albert Square. It opened in 1960 as The 2J's Jazz Club but changed to The Oasis a year later, billed as "Manchester's Most Fab Club for Young People" and more than likely helped inspire The Twisted Wheel (just round the corner) a couple of years later, although it was always more of a pop venue than The Wheel's r'n'b focus. It is famous today for The Beatles playing there only a couple of months after it opened. The club lasted through into 1967 when it was renamed Sloopys (and later Ye Father's Moustache!). The stage backdrop is quite impressive, a montage of Beatles photographs plus Freddie Garrity of The Dreamers. The hand painted poster advertises the club's Whitsuntide programme - Lord Sutch and The Savages, supported by local band The Stylos, then The Mojos plus The Invictas and lastly The Stylos (who were popular enough to have their own fan club locally) headlining the Monday night.

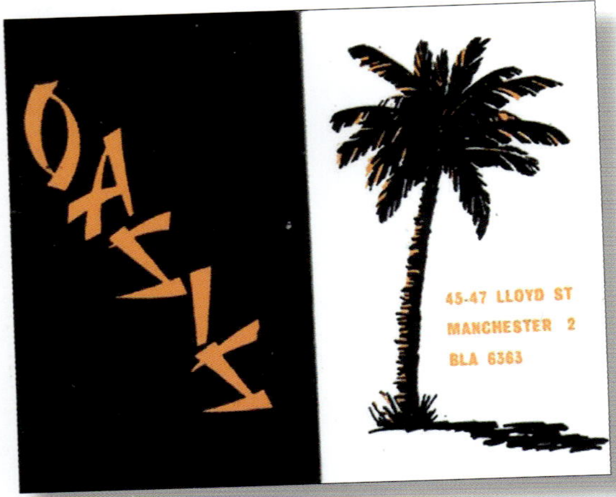

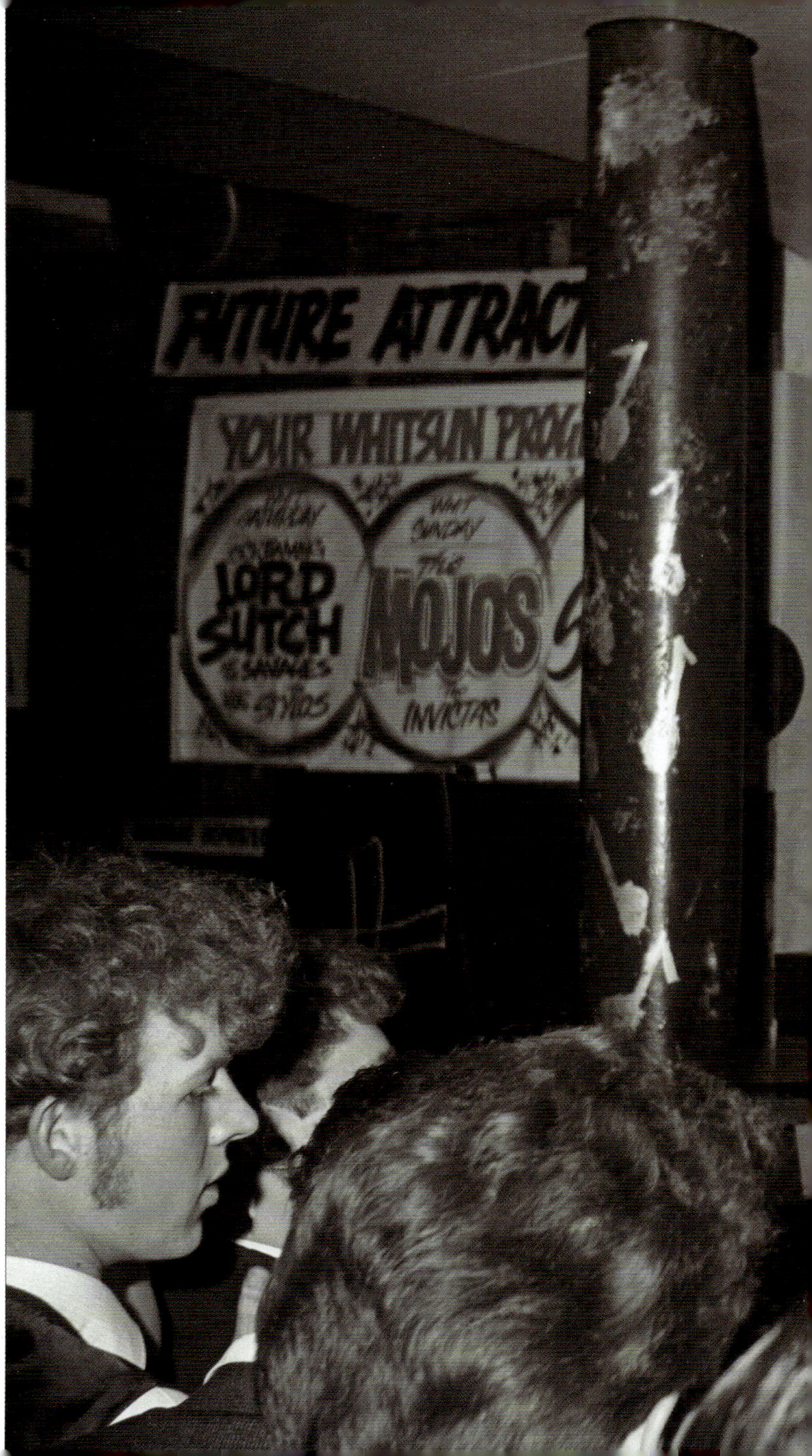

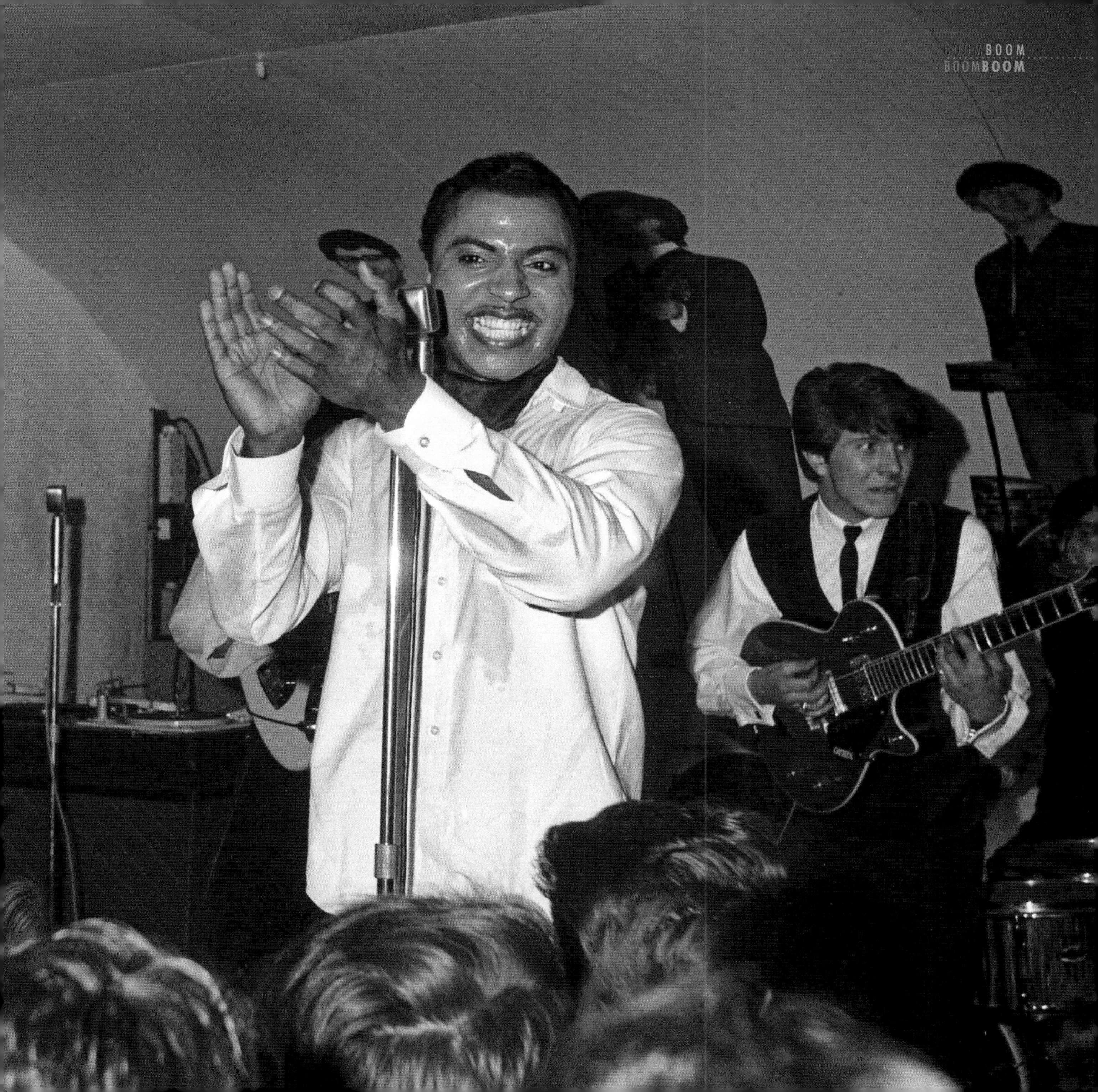
BOOMBOOM
BOOMBOOM

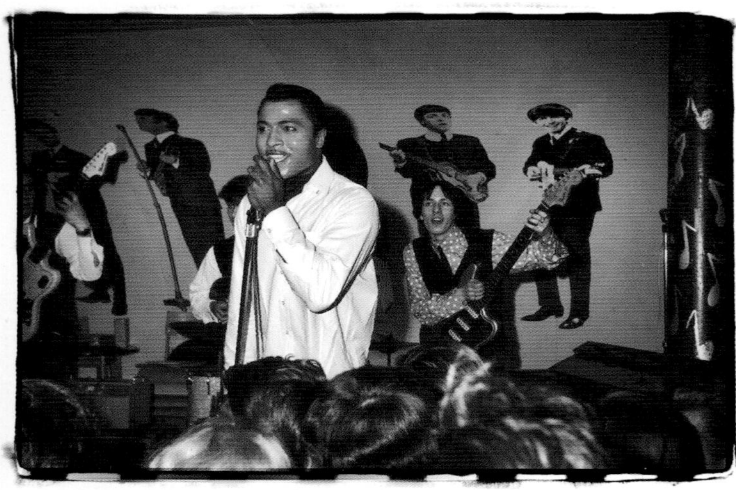
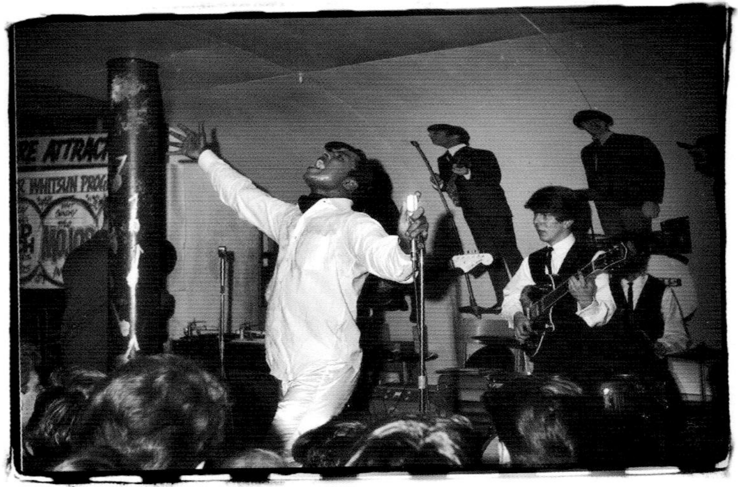
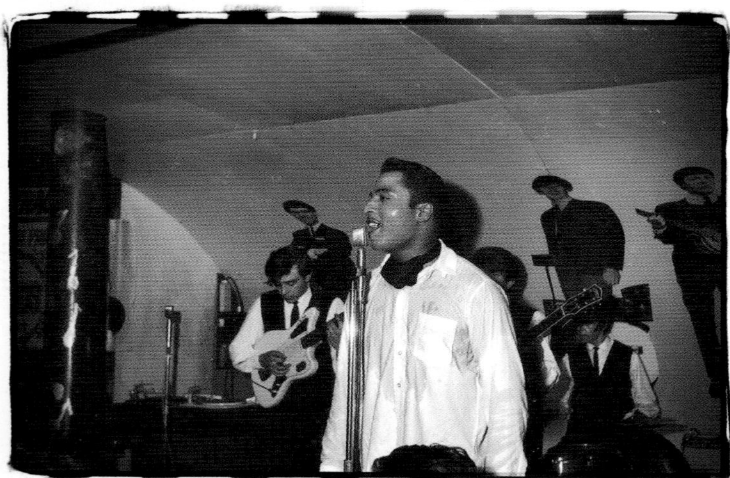
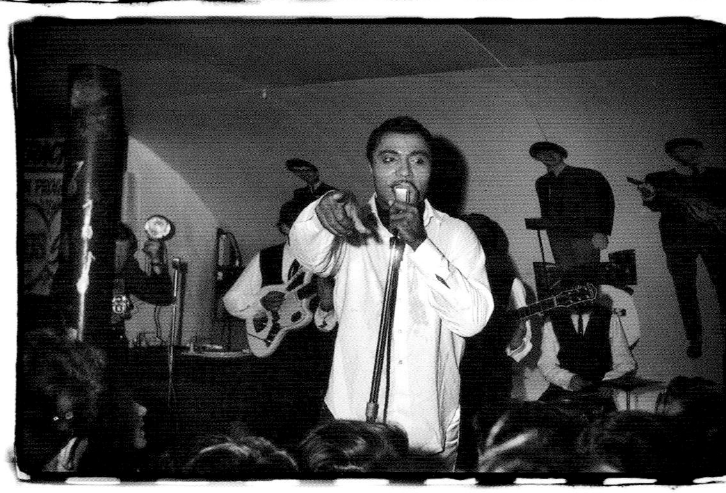
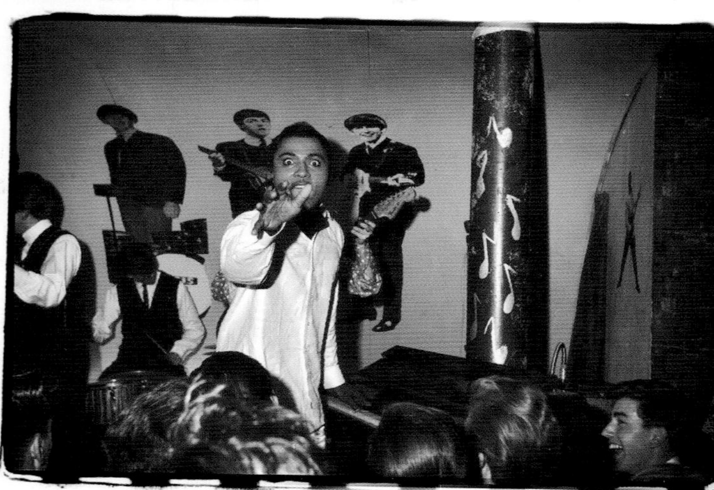
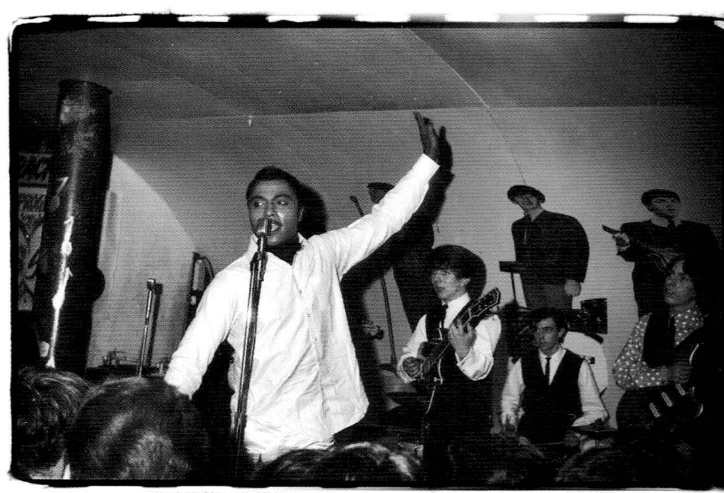

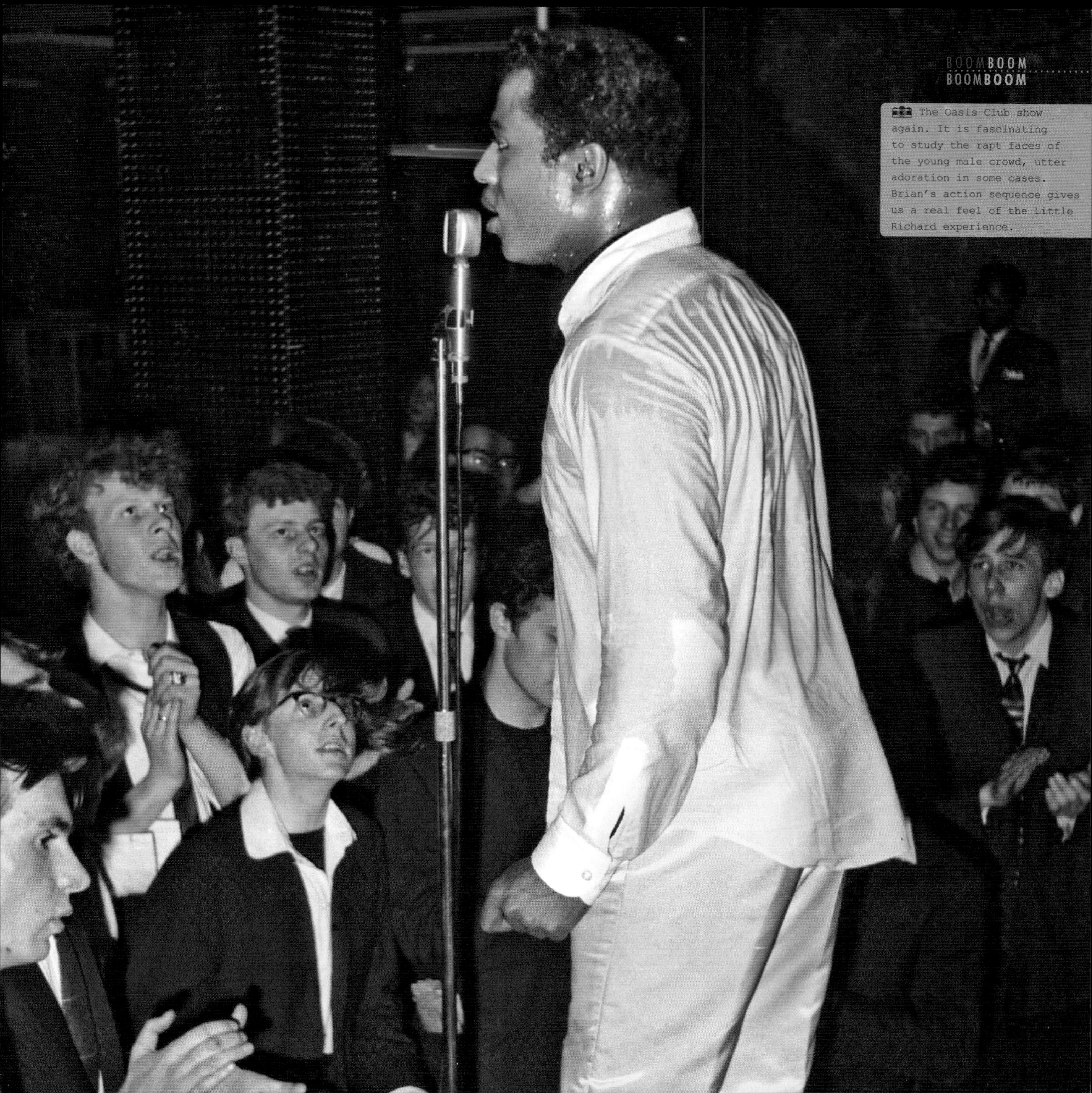

The Oasis Club show again. It is fascinating to study the rapt faces of the young male crowd, utter adoration in some cases. Brian's action sequence gives us a real feel of the Little Richard experience.

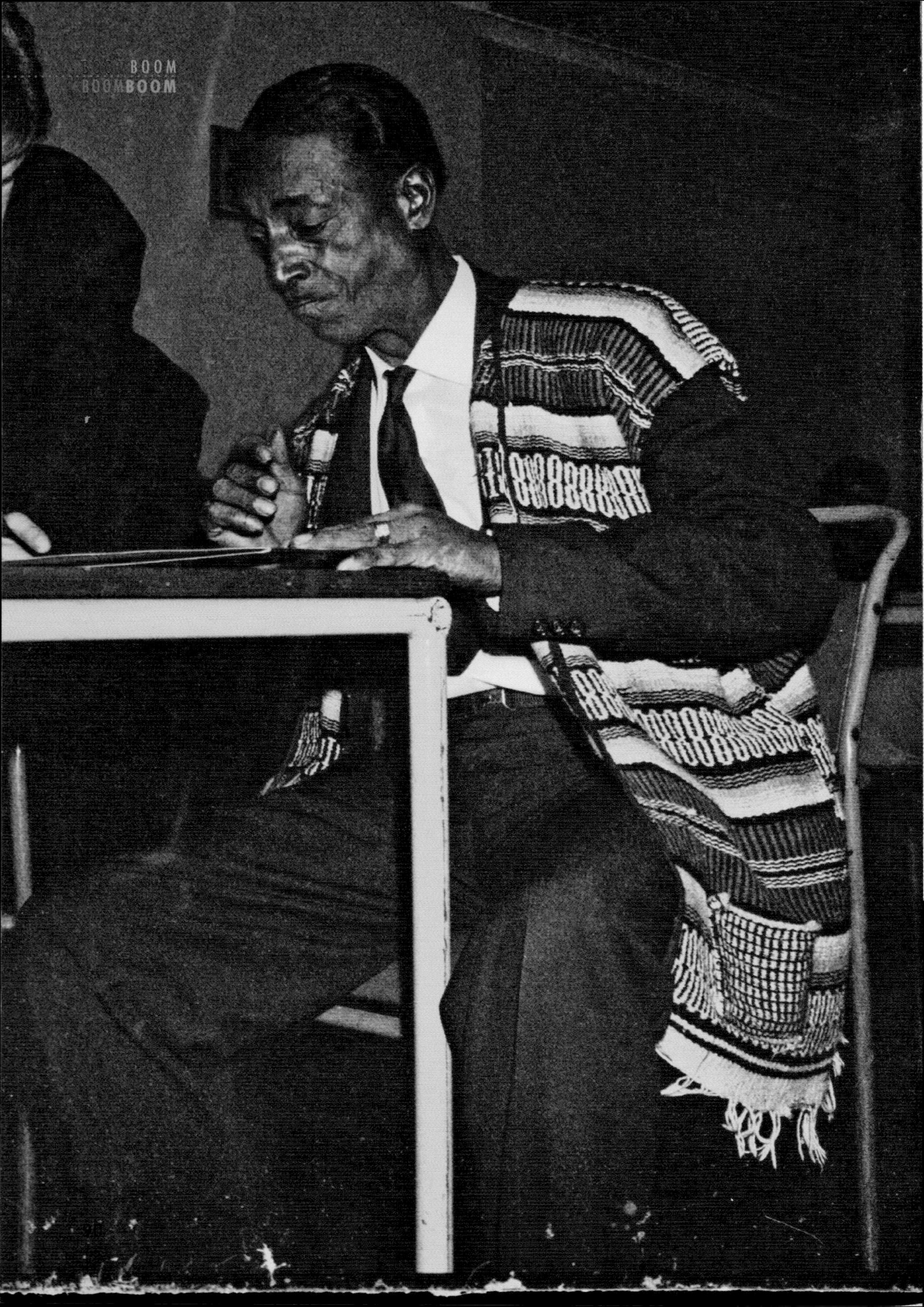

FRED McDOWELL

Brian's kit let him down a bit on this one photograph of Fred McDowell, taken, like the images of Lenoir on the previous pages, backstage at the fourth American Folk Blues Festival tour at the Free Trade Hall in 1965. The flash failed to go off properly, leaving Brian with a flat dense negative which he filed away. Taking a look at the very unpromising results after we did a new scan, we were also about to consign it to the 'reject' folder but decided to try passing it through some Photoshop filters. With some careful retouching, this rare if very grainy picture emerged. McDowell wore the groovy poncho-style jacket during the set as well (sadly Brian's three live pictures were out of focus and now lost, though we include one below out of interest). Here McDowell was signing an album for one of Brian's mates at the times: *"This picture taken of McDowell on his own has just been used in a great bio-film about him, so as always, throw nothing away....!"*

A true original, McDowell farmed for most of his life and played only semi-professionally until re-discovered by Alan Lomax in the late 1950s.

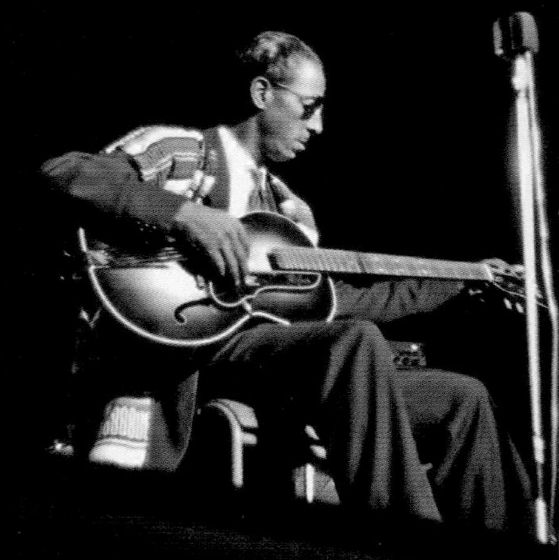

HUBERT SUMLIN

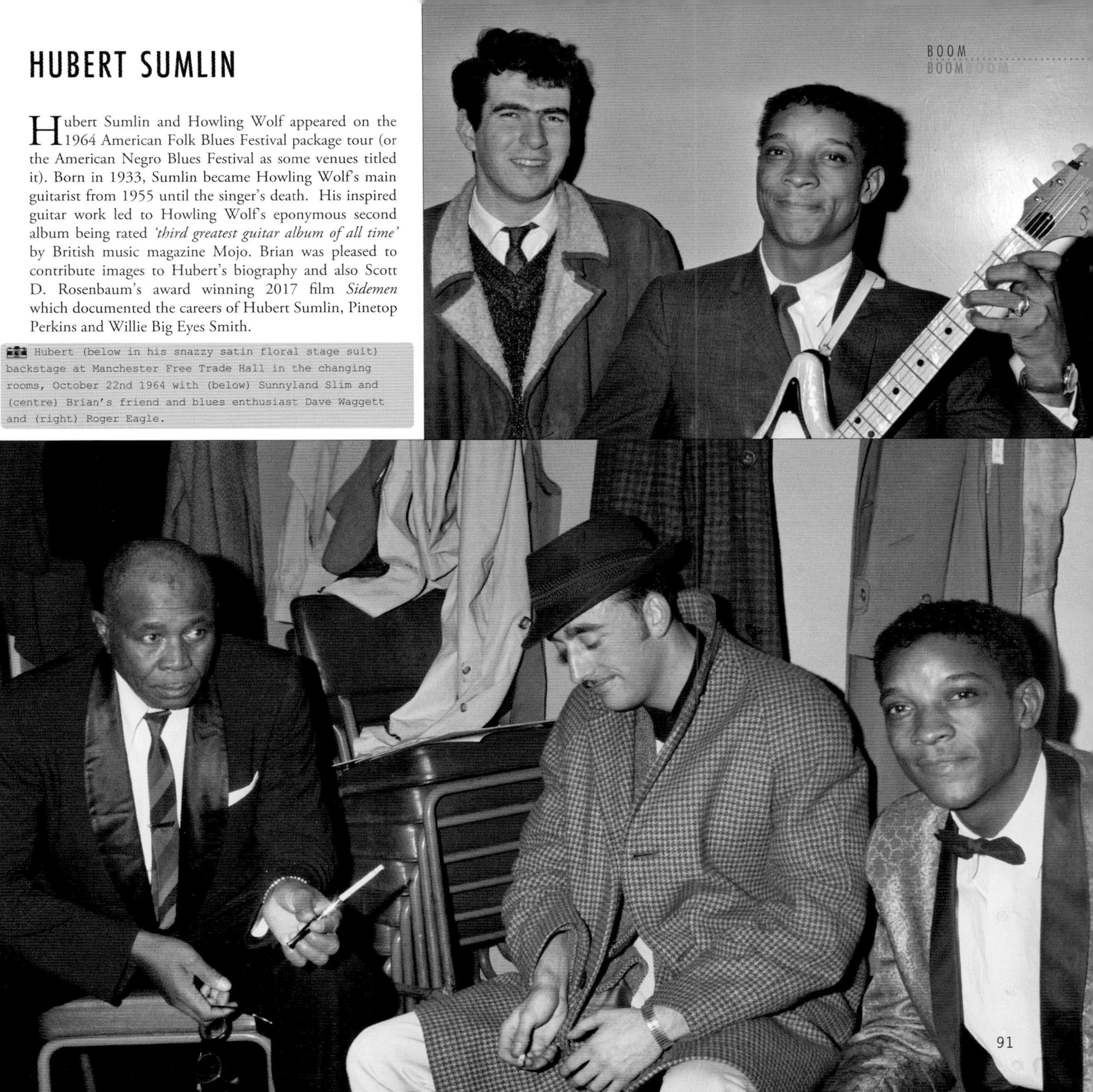

Hubert Sumlin and Howling Wolf appeared on the 1964 American Folk Blues Festival package tour (or the American Negro Blues Festival as some venues titled it). Born in 1933, Sumlin became Howling Wolf's main guitarist from 1955 until the singer's death. His inspired guitar work led to Howling Wolf's eponymous second album being rated *'third greatest guitar album of all time'* by British music magazine Mojo. Brian was pleased to contribute images to Hubert's biography and also Scott D. Rosenbaum's award winning 2017 film *Sidemen* which documented the careers of Hubert Sumlin, Pinetop Perkins and Willie Big Eyes Smith.

Hubert (below in his snazzy satin floral stage suit) backstage at Manchester Free Trade Hall in the changing rooms, October 22nd 1964 with (below) Sunnyland Slim and (centre) Brian's friend and blues enthusiast Dave Waggett and (right) Roger Eagle.

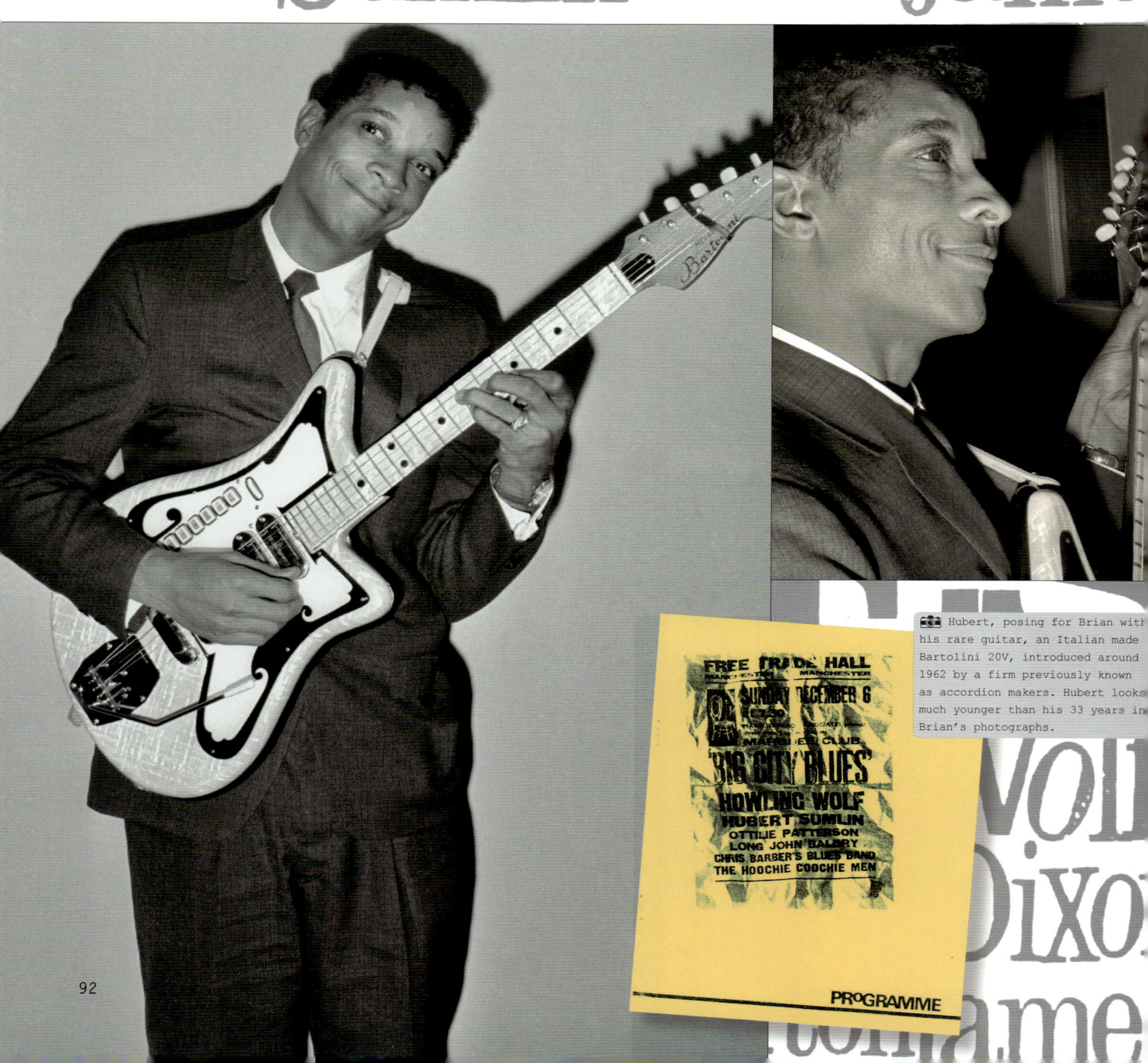

Hubert, posing for Brian with his rare guitar, an Italian made Bartolini 20V, introduced around 1962 by a firm previously known as accordion makers. Hubert looks much younger than his 33 years in Brian's photographs.

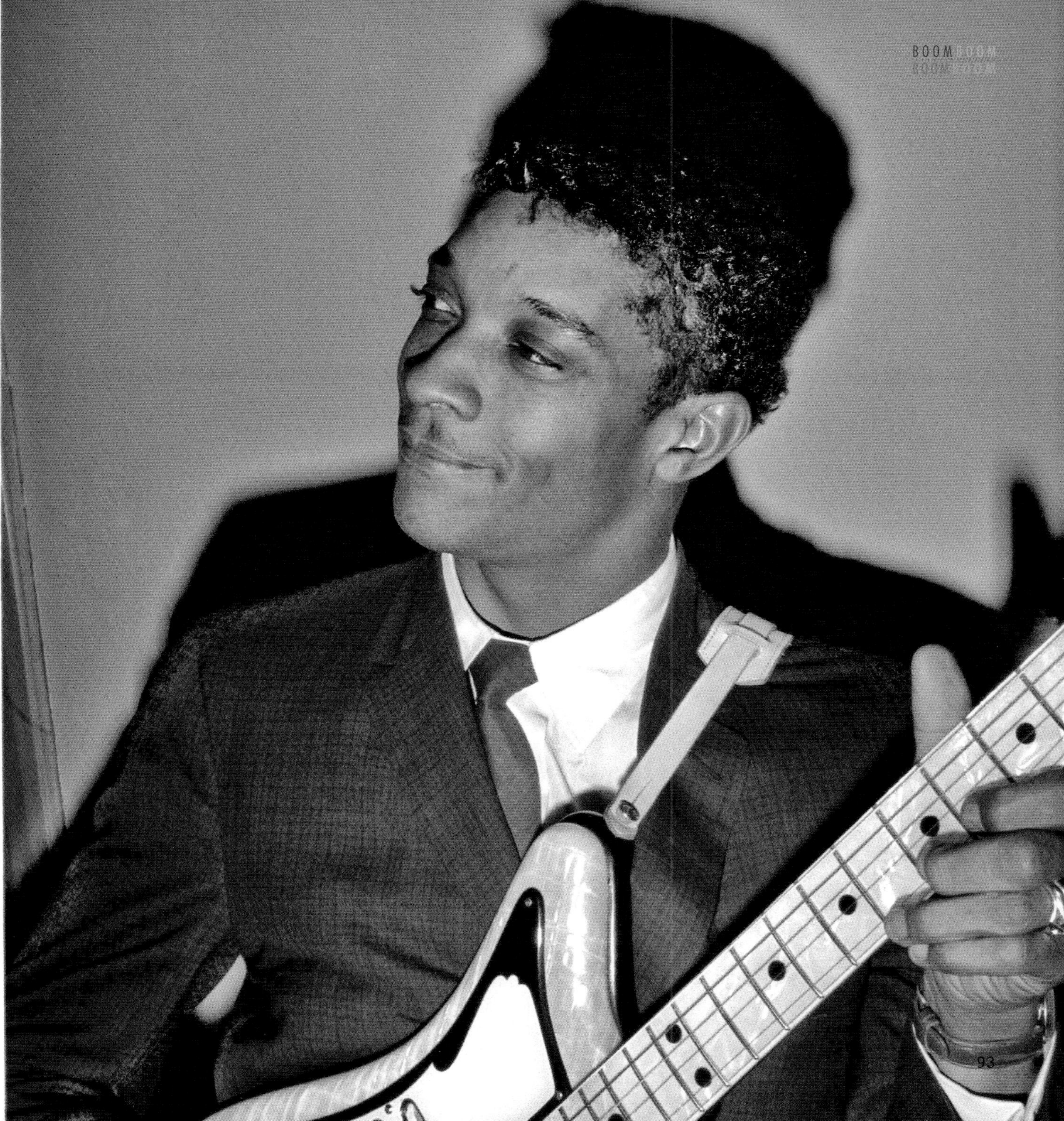

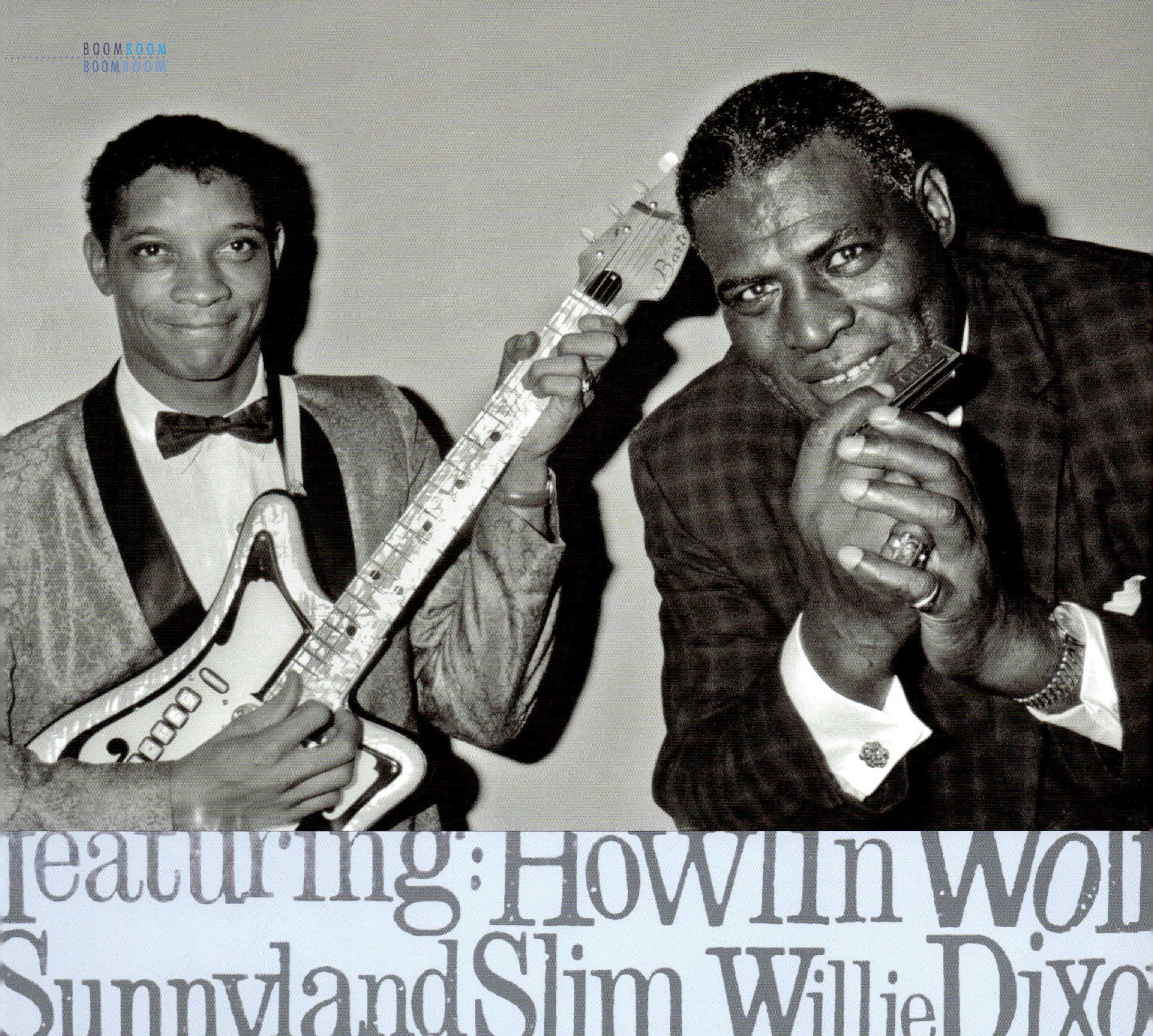
featuring: Howlin Wolf
Sunnyland Slim Willie Dixo
Hubert Sumlin Clifton Jame

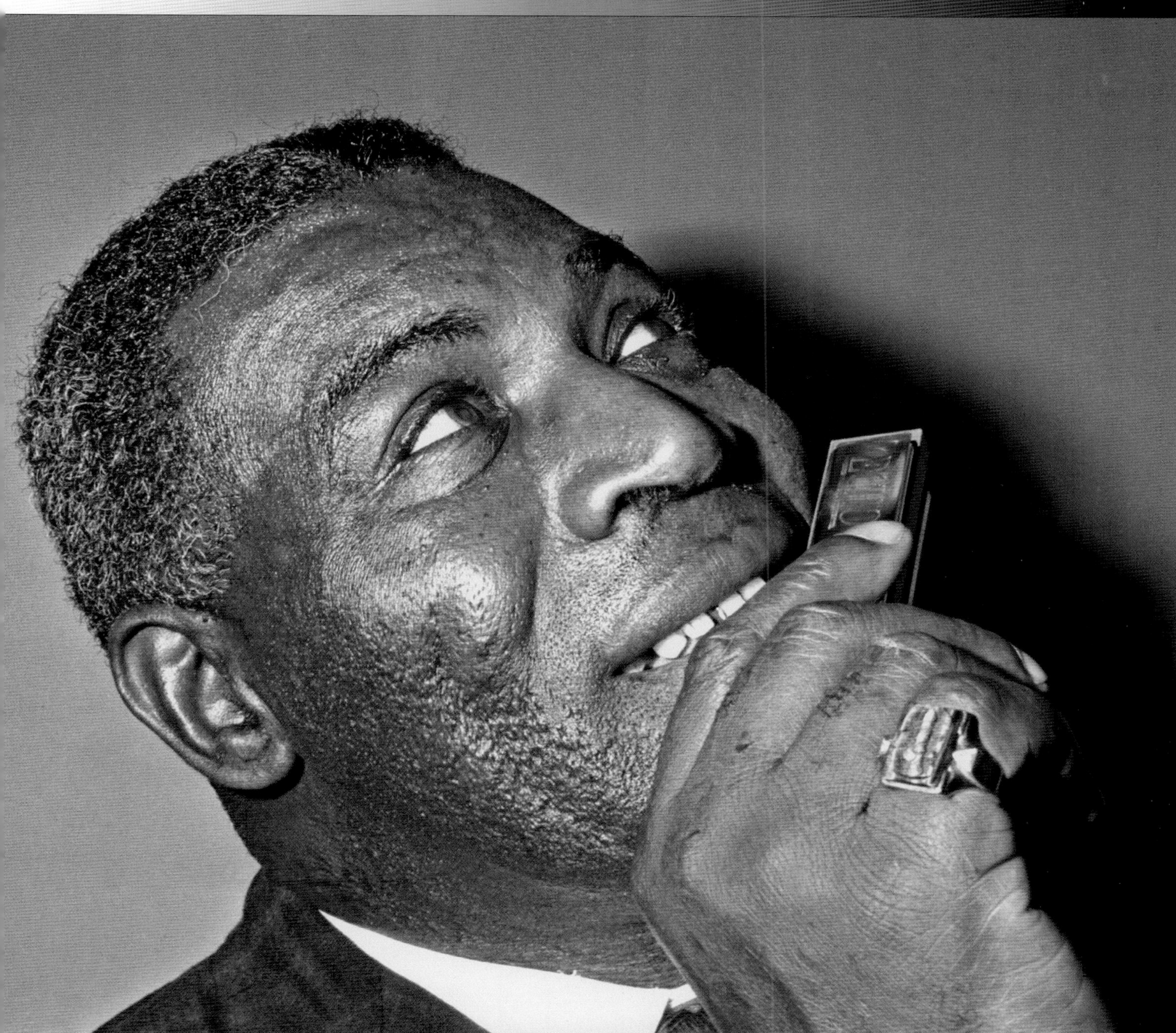

Brian's photograph of Wolf here is rightly regarded as a classic image of the man, again taken in the Free Trade Hall on October 22. 1964. The previously lost negative was found as we prepared this book and newly scanned.

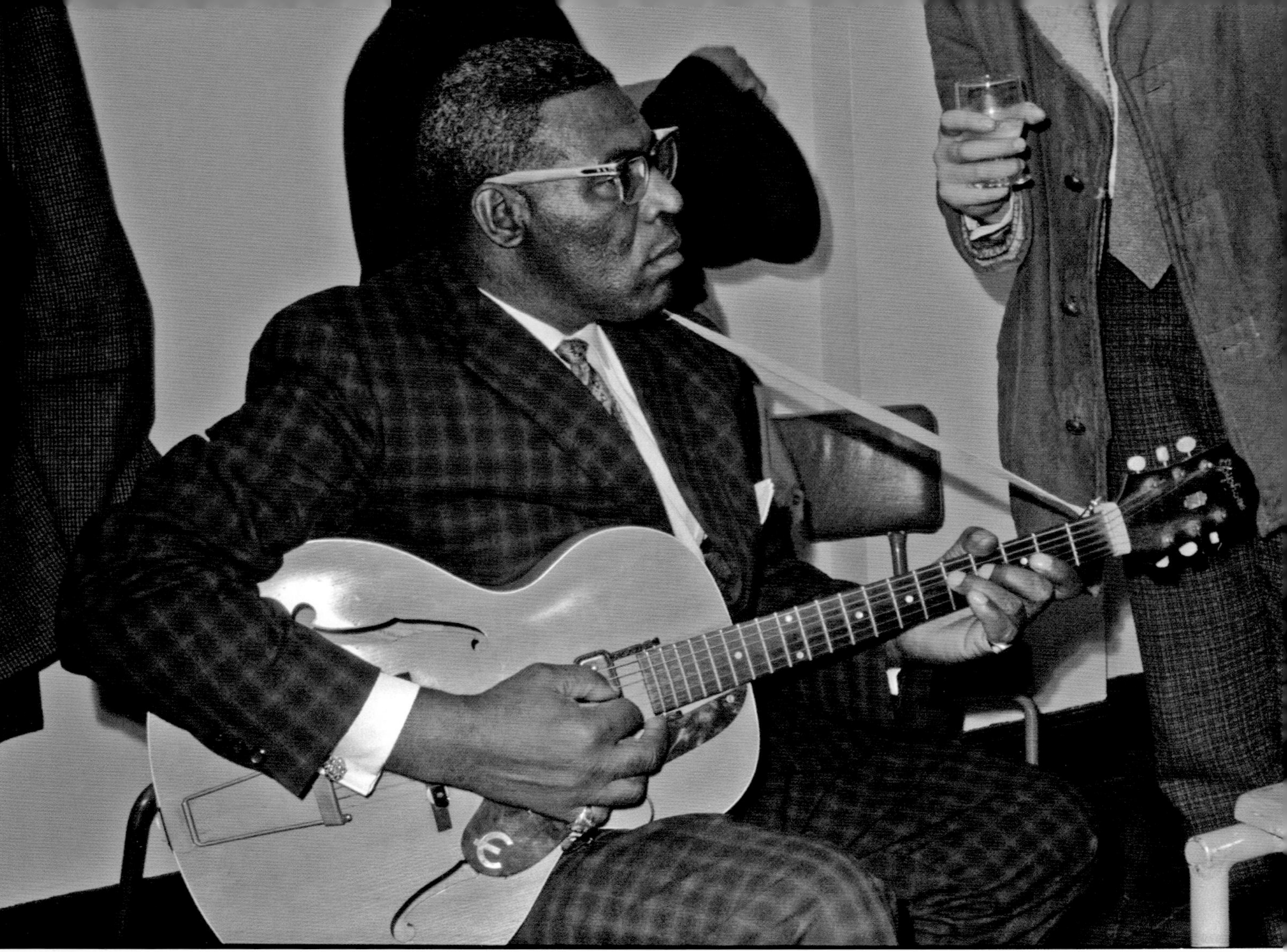

THE RAVINGEST, SWINGINGEST, MOST ENTERTAINING
RHYTHM AND BLUES MAN IN THE WORLD !

Chester
'Howling Wolf'
Bernett

DON'T MISS HIM ON SUNDAY, MARCH 25th with CHRIS BARBER

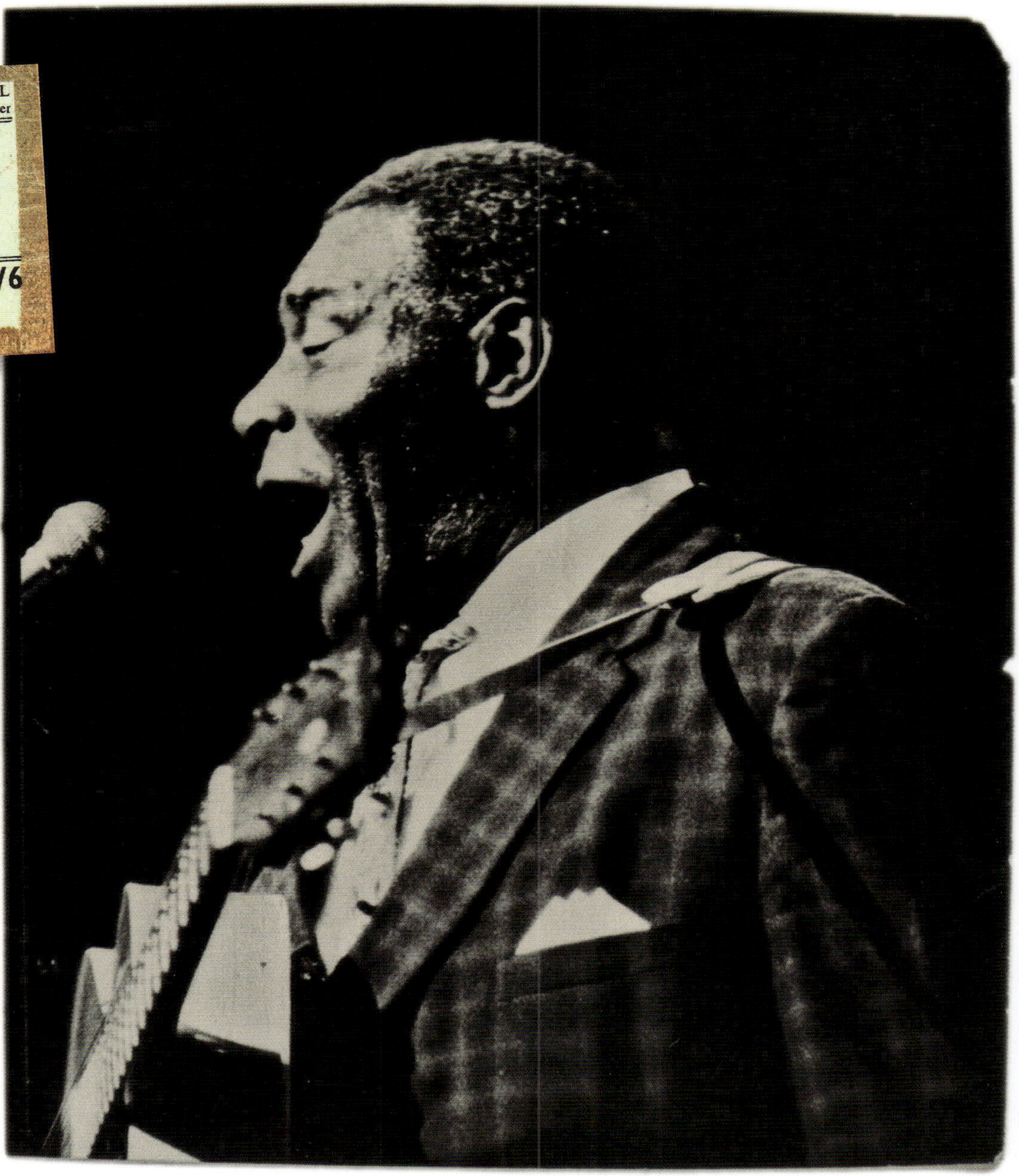

BOOMBOOM
BOOMBOOM

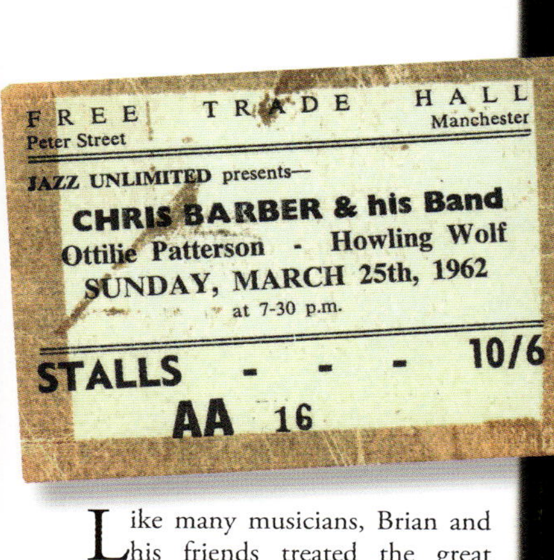

Like many musicians, Brian and his friends treated the great Chester 'Howling Wolf' Bernett with near reverence. There is something quite touching about the young Manchester lads mixing with these legendary musicians and Wolf seemed to appreciate their enthusiasm, happy to let Brian snap away backstage.

Wolf was first due to play in Manchester as a guest of Chris Barber in March 1962. Brian had been able to afford a front row ticket (they were not especially cheap, 10/6d in 1962 was no small investment; that's his prized ticket above). However Wolf became ill two days before travelling and Clinton Ford stepped in to replace him.

When Wolf finally got to Europe, it was as part of the blues package tour in 1964 and Brian, Neil and Roger were finally able to meet one of their heroes. I'm sure Brian would argue that his photographs were *just taken for the magazine'* and came out so well by good fortune, but they are rightly regarded as classic Blues images today and - like the John Lee Hooker shot on page 72 - some have been used over and over.

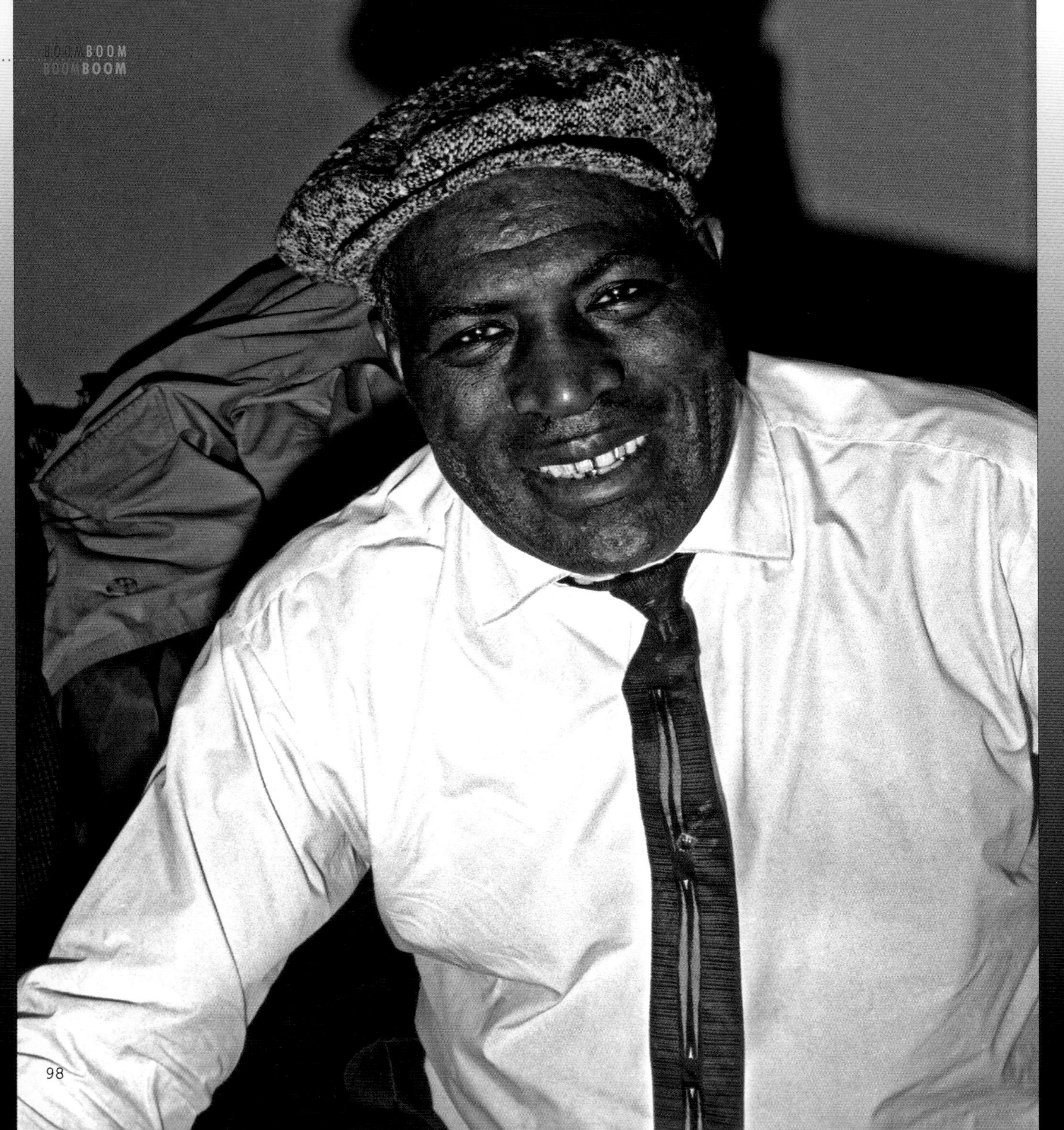

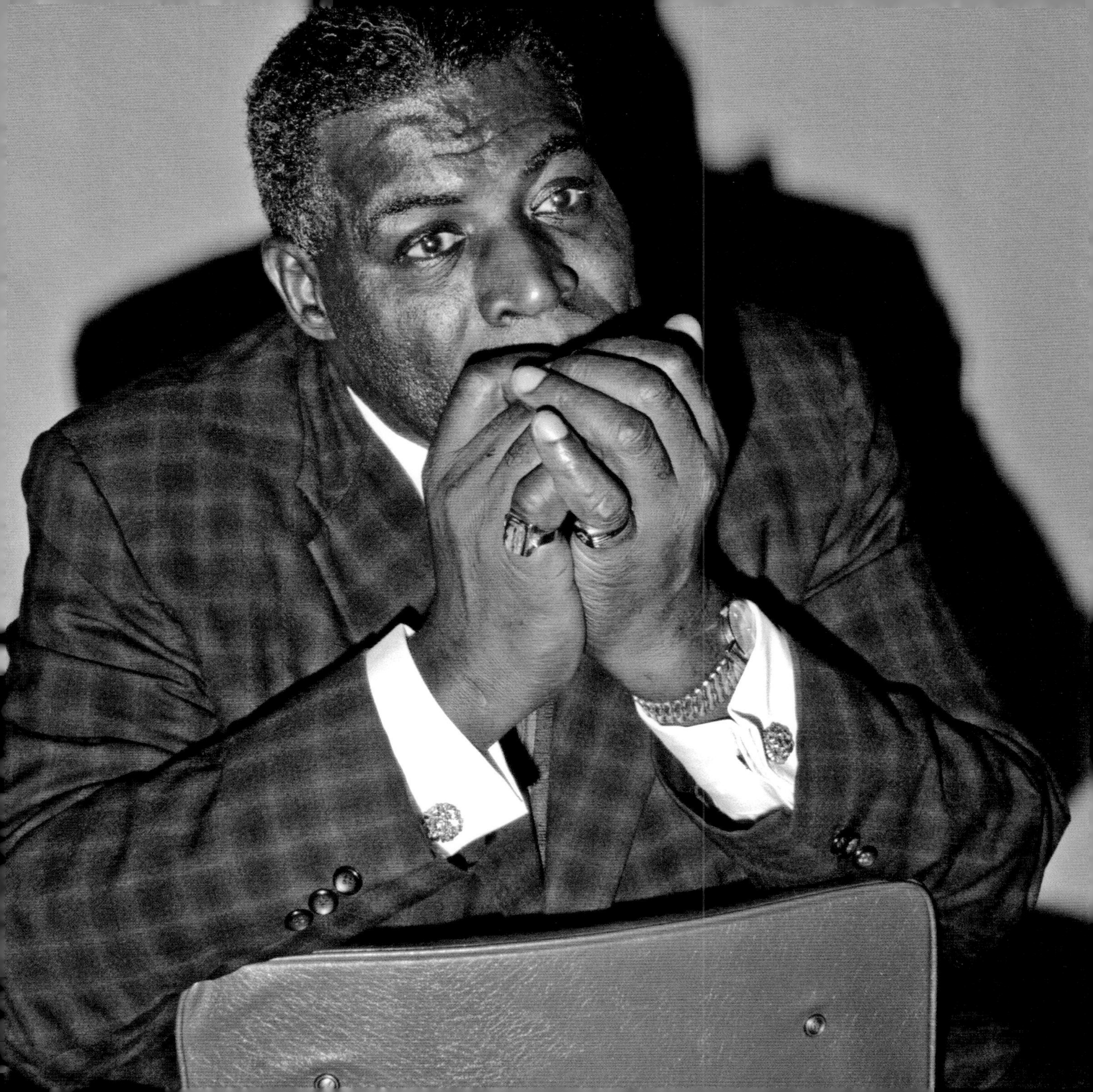

JIMMY REED

Jimmy (Mathis James) Reed was an important tick on Brian Smith's must-see blues players list. Roger Eagle was also a huge fan and played his records regularly at The Twisted Wheel, so all the Wheel regulars were on hand when Jimmy was booked to appear there on 21st November 1964.

Jimmy was happy to co-operate with the lads from R & B Scene magazine and posed with his harmonica, his varnished guitar and an impressive cigar.

He also signed autographs and sleeves for them all, though he had never learned to read or write.

Brian's photographs of Jimmy backstage over these three pages are very evocative and the negatives have mostly survived in good shape with only one (top left page 102) missing (restored from a print).

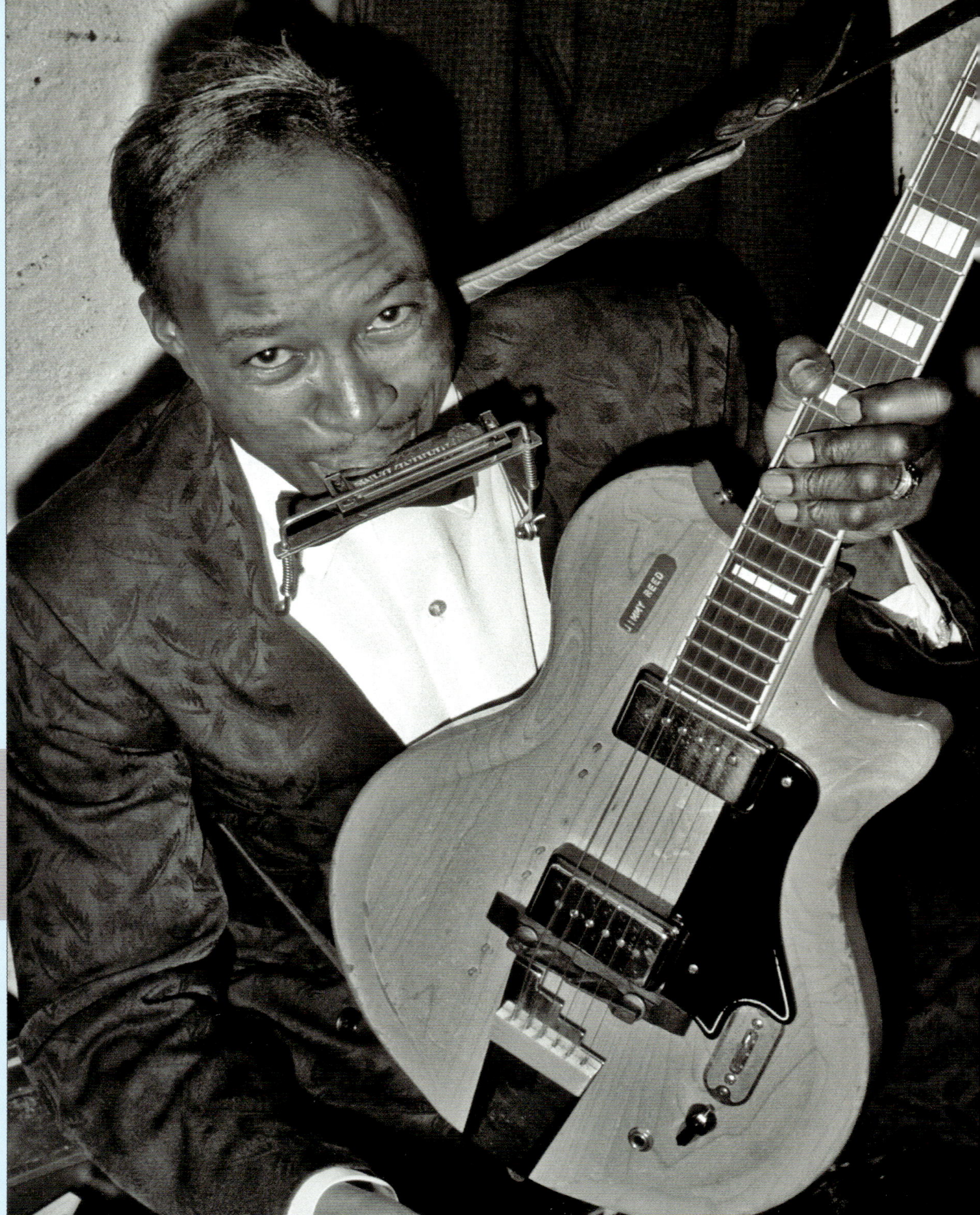

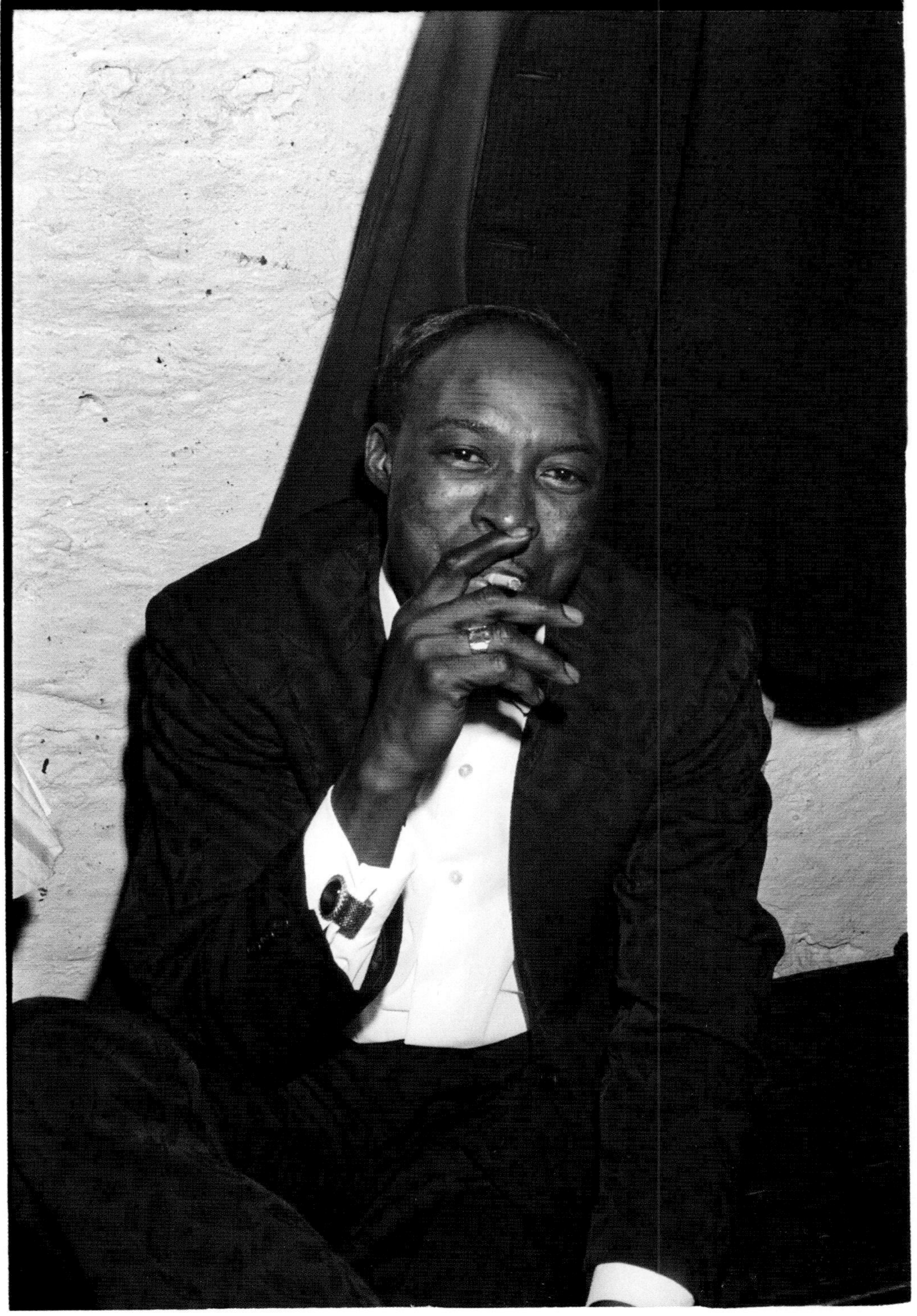

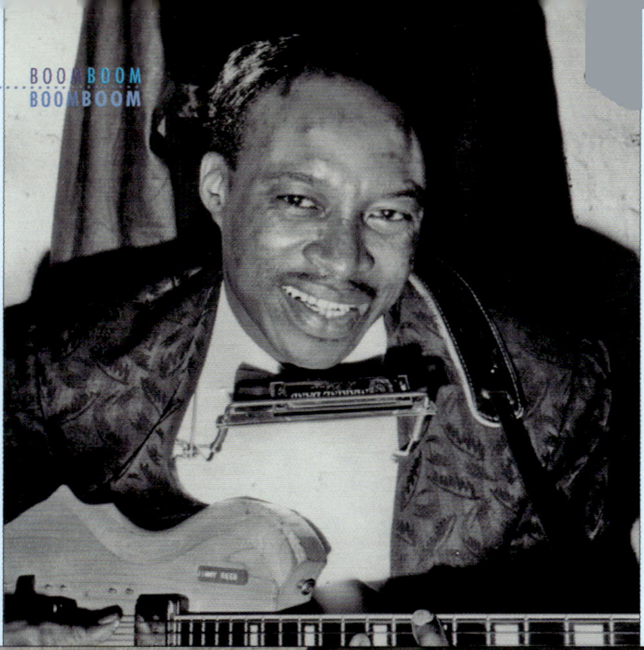

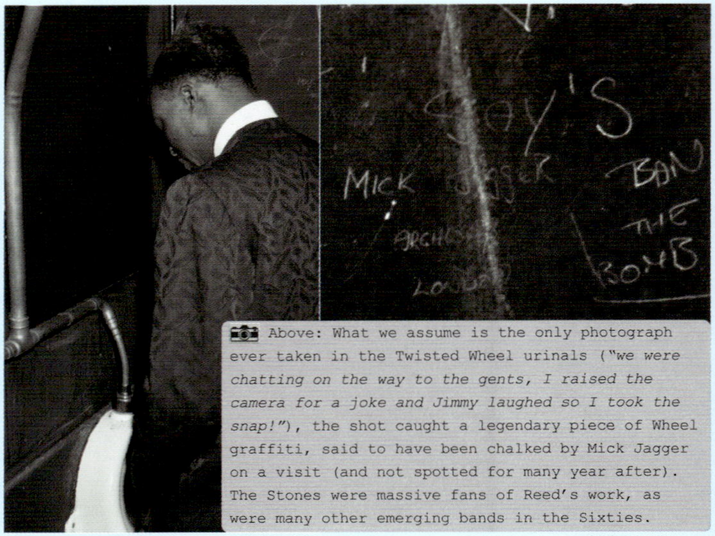

Above: What we assume is the only photograph ever taken in the Twisted Wheel urinals ("*we were chatting on the way to the gents, I raised the camera for a joke and Jimmy laughed so I took the snap!*"), the shot caught a legendary piece of Wheel graffiti, said to have been chalked by Mick Jagger on a visit (and not spotted for many year after). The Stones were massive fans of Reed's work, as were many other emerging bands in the Sixties.

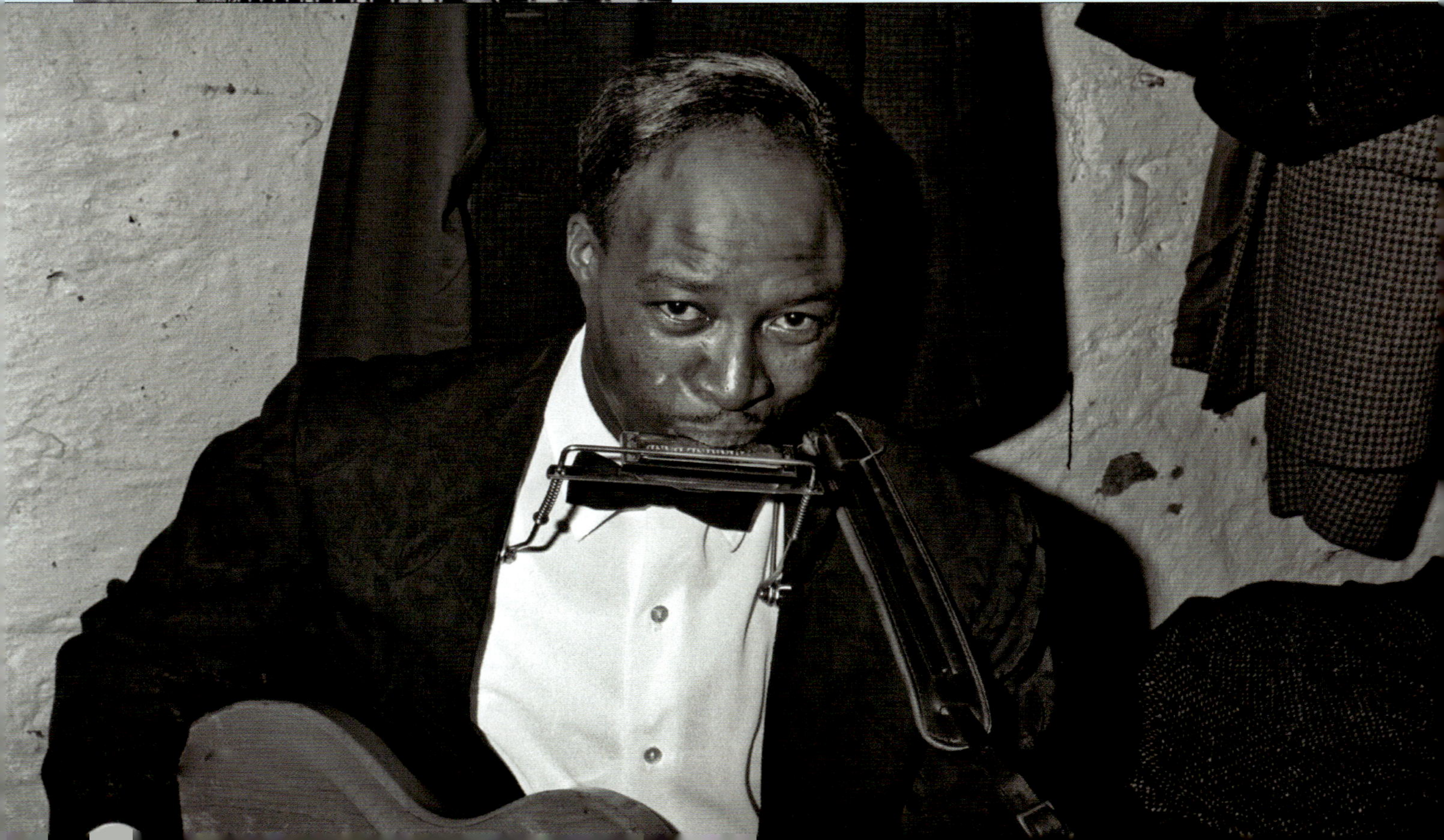

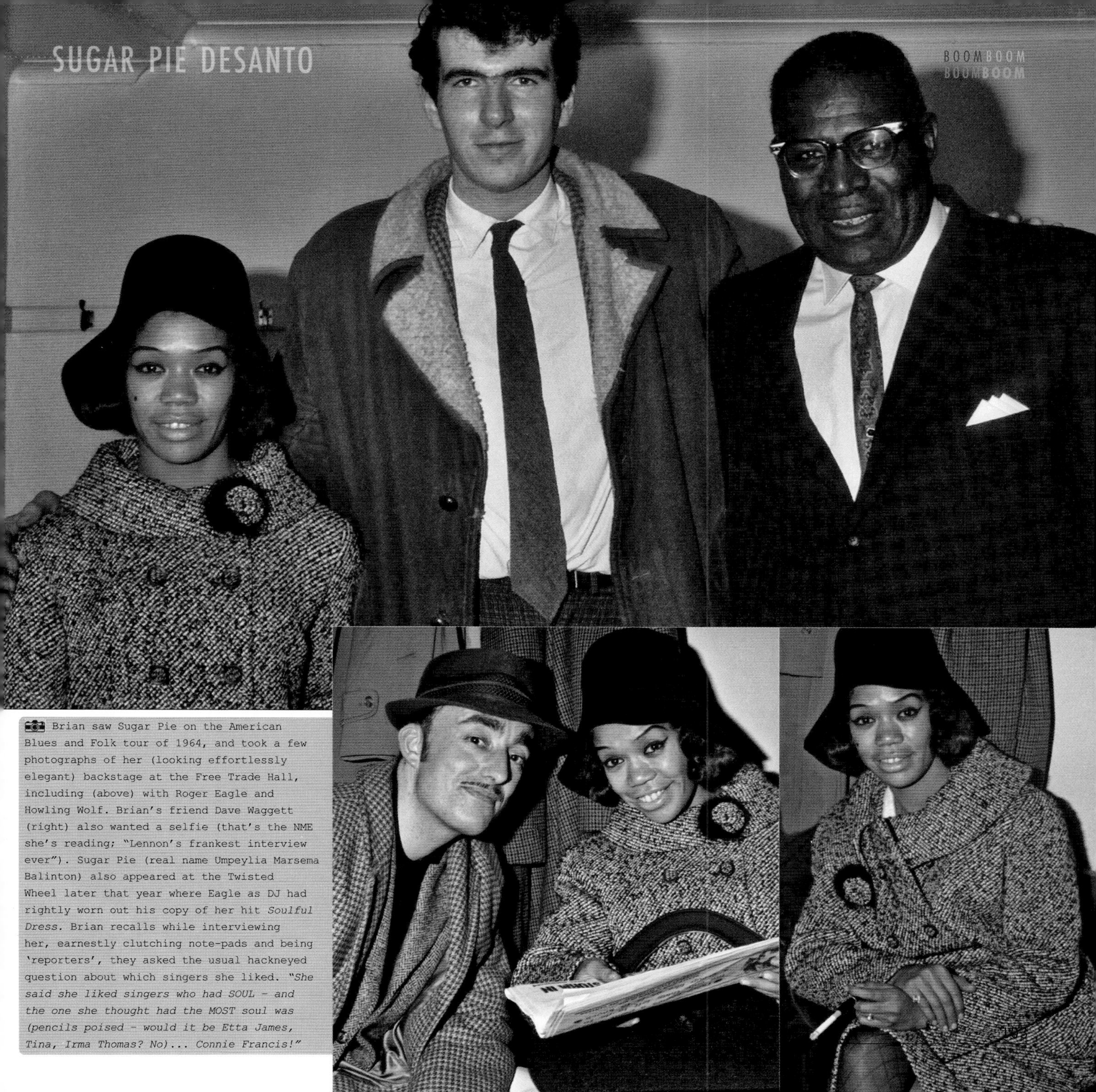

📷 Brian saw Sugar Pie on the American Blues and Folk tour of 1964, and took a few photographs of her (looking effortlessly elegant) backstage at the Free Trade Hall, including (above) with Roger Eagle and Howling Wolf. Brian's friend Dave Waggett (right) also wanted a selfie (that's the NME she's reading; "Lennon's frankest interview ever"). Sugar Pie (real name Umpeylia Marsema Balinton) also appeared at the Twisted Wheel later that year where Eagle as DJ had rightly worn out his copy of her hit *Soulful Dress*. Brian recalls while interviewing her, earnestly clutching note-pads and being 'reporters', they asked the usual hackneyed question about which singers she liked. *"She said she liked singers who had SOUL - and the one she thought had the MOST soul was (pencils poised - would it be Etta James, Tina, Irma Thomas? No)... Connie Francis!"*

Rev. GARY DAVIS

Born in 1896, the Reverend Gary Davis was certainly one of the elder statesmen of the blues when he appeared at the Free Trade Hall in Manchester on May 8th 1964 with the Blues and Gospel Caravan tour. Having first recorded back in the 1930s, Davis became blind as a young child. He was later ordained, hence his stage name, and enjoying a period of rediscovery at this time. His early material was covered by The Grateful Dead, Dylan and The Rolling Stones. Remarkably his Free Trade set was taped, released on CD over forty years later with Brian's iconic (that word again) photo on the cover.

Granada TV arranged to have the artists appear at a special performance the day before but the Rev. was too poorly to appear and preferred to rest before the live concert.

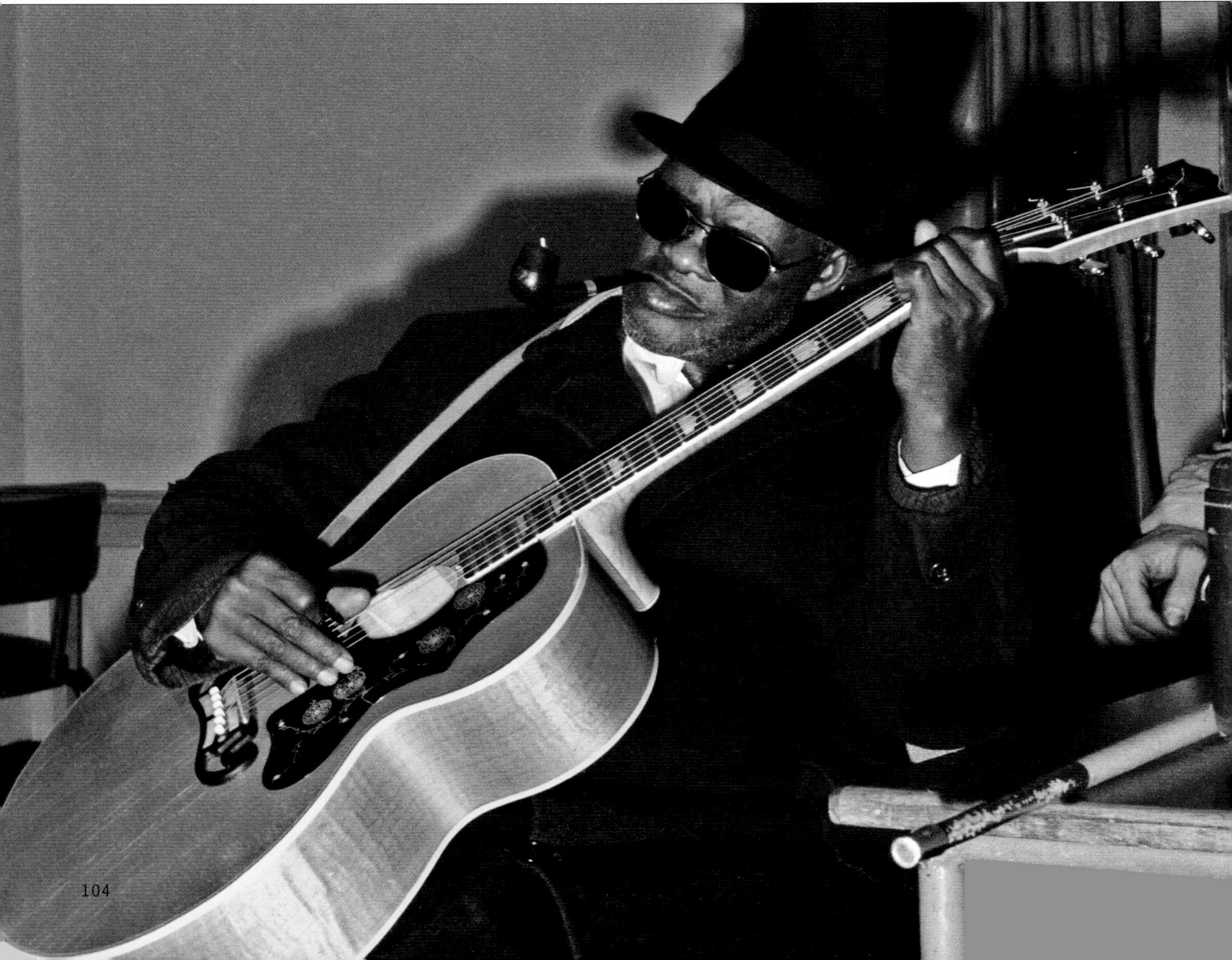

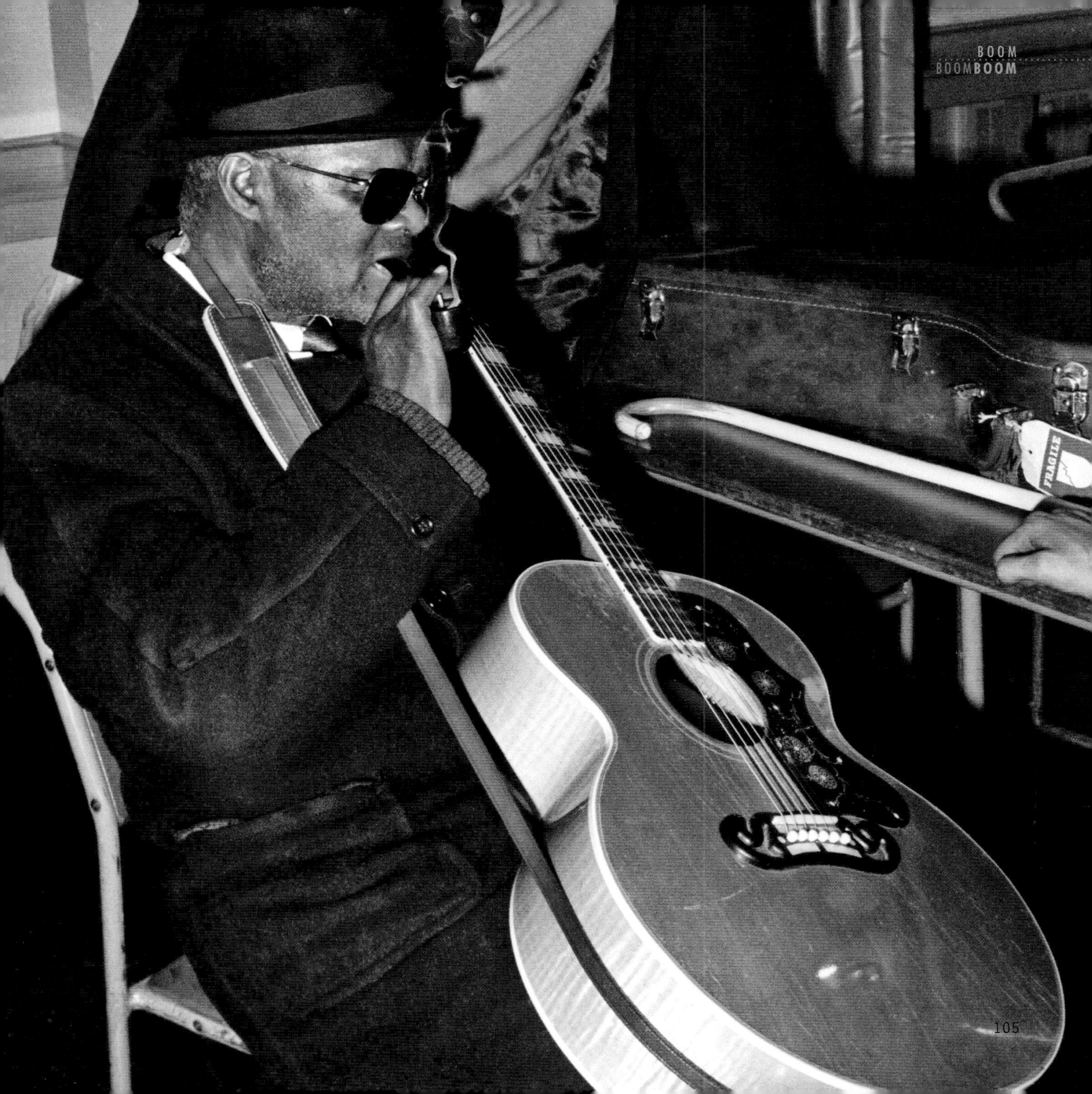
BOOM
BOOMBOOM
FRAGILE

FATS DOMINO, BROOK BENTON, EDDIE TAYLOR

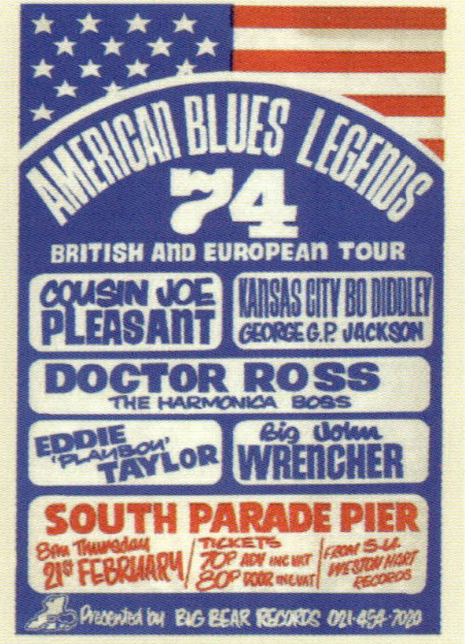

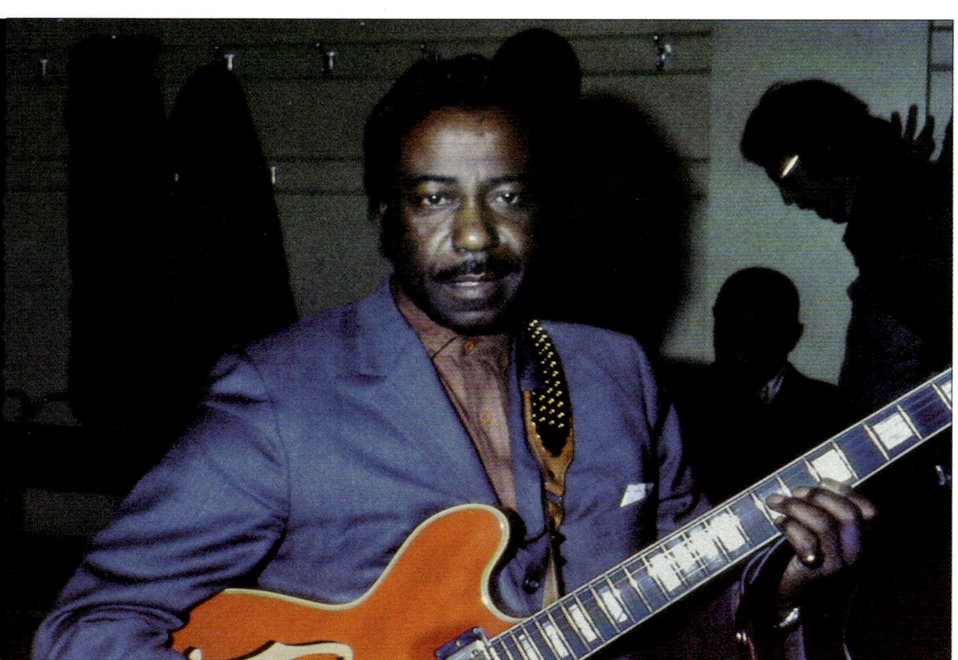

ON THE LEFT, though less well known than some of the Chicago based bluesmen, singer and guitarist Eddie Playboy Taylor's work with Jimmy Reed was very influential. The photograph was taken backstage in Manchester on the 1974 Blues Legends tour, put together by Bear Records. Taylor continued to work and record into the 1980s.

THIS IS Fats Domino, photographed in poor light outside the Palace Theatre in Manchester (April 2nd 1967) while he was signing autograph books for fans. On the far right is Brook Benton, with Brian's flash until playing up on his one frame. It was taken at Manchester Odeon in October 1963 (at the same show as the Lesley Gore and Dion photographs).

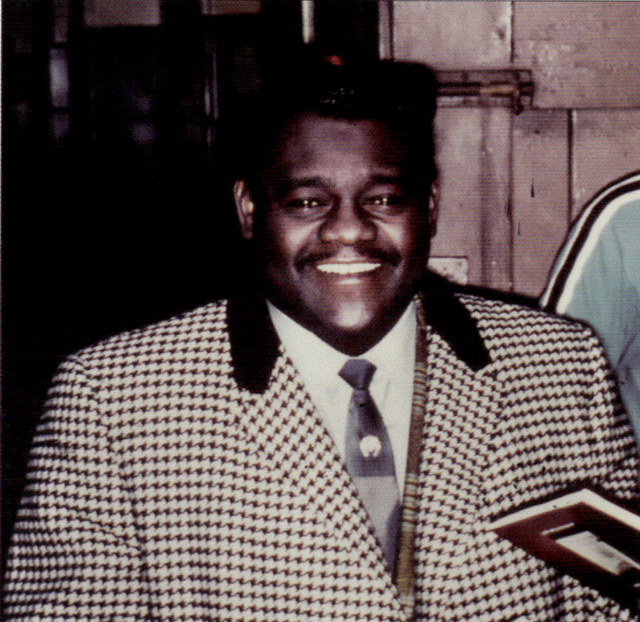

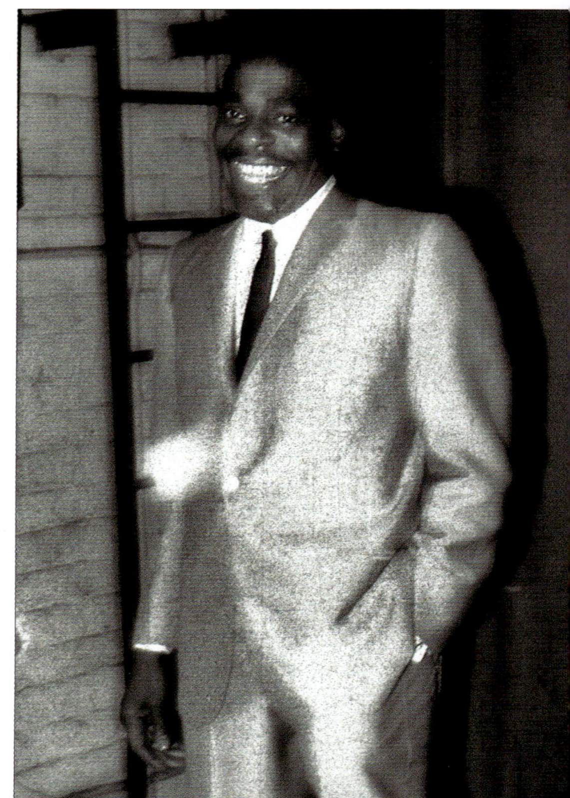

WILLIE DIXON BOOMBOOM BOOMBOOM

ABC TV arranged with the promoters of the 1962 American Folk and Blues Festival to film a show at the Free Trade Hall on October 21st for their Sunday afternoon arts show *Tempo*. This package tour was not originally going to come to the UK but local promoter Paddy MacKiernan and Melody Maker managed to persuade them it was worth doing, under the Jazz Unlimited banner Paddy had used for shows there in the past. This gave Brian one of his first chances to see some of the blues legends, and take photographs. He admits he went as he heard that T-Bone Walker played like Chuck Berry and thought it might be good, and soon realised it was in fact Berry who had based himself on Walker...

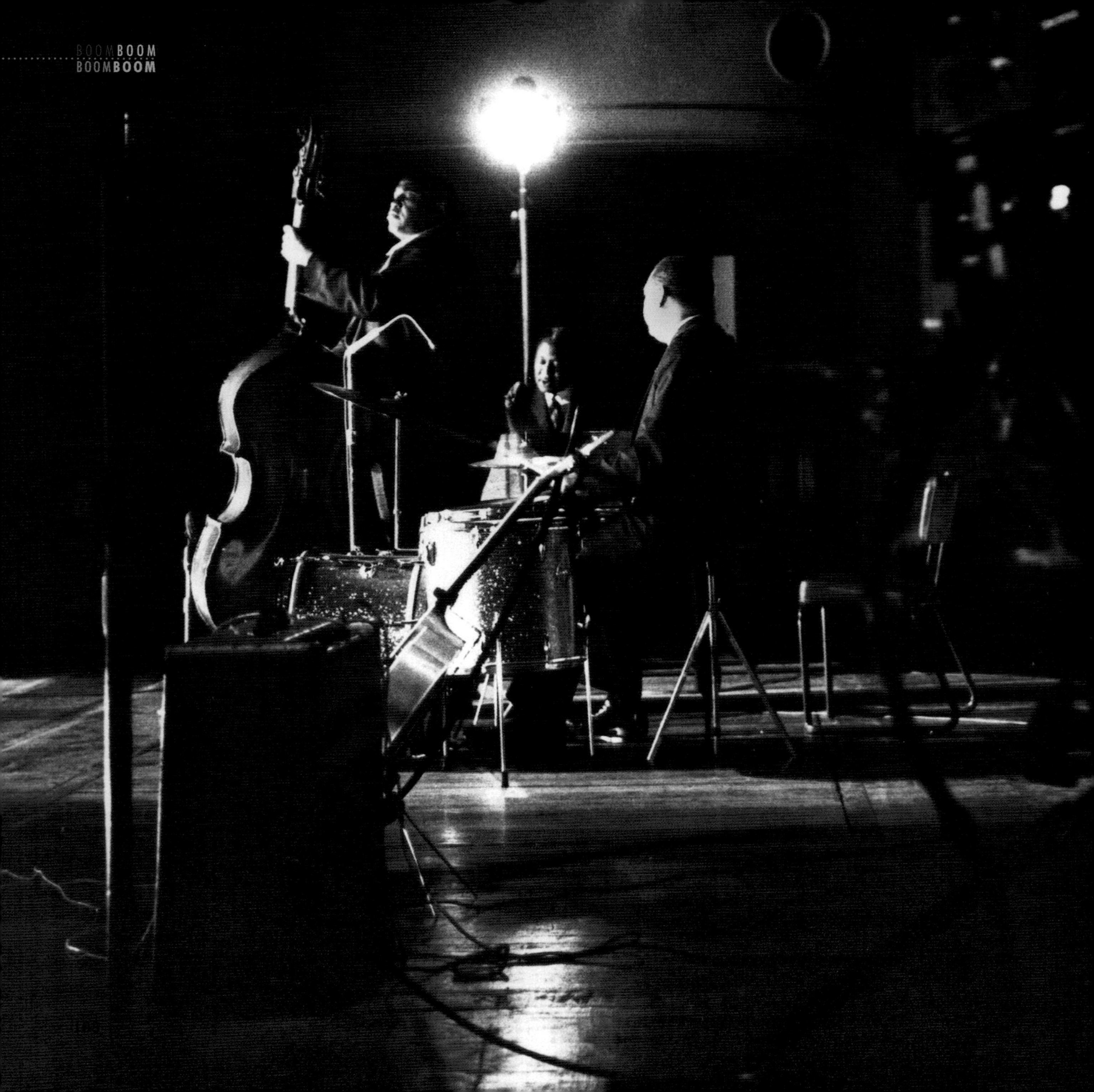

BOOMBOOM
BOOMBOOM

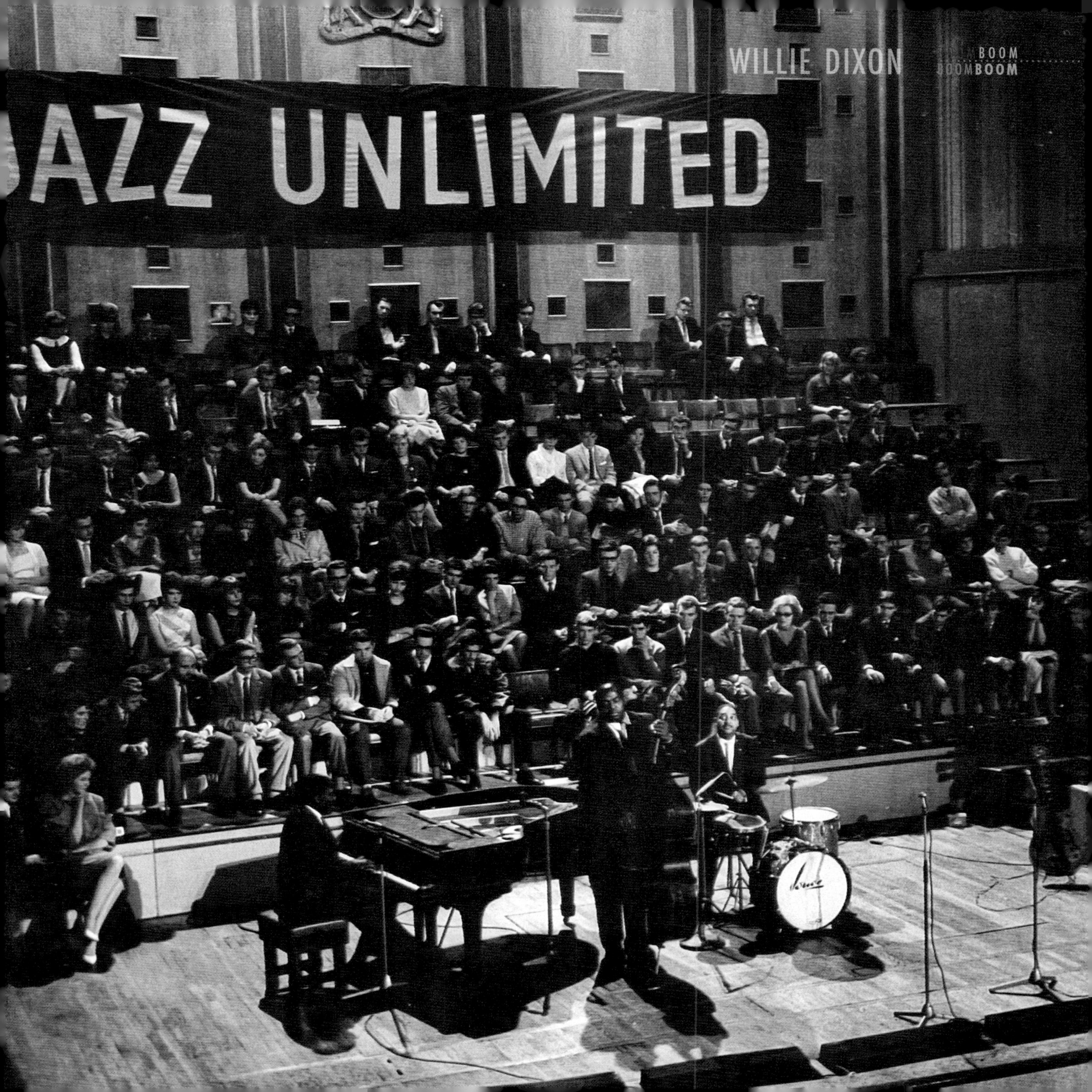

JAZZ UNLIMITED
WILLIE DIXON
BOOM
BOOMBOOM

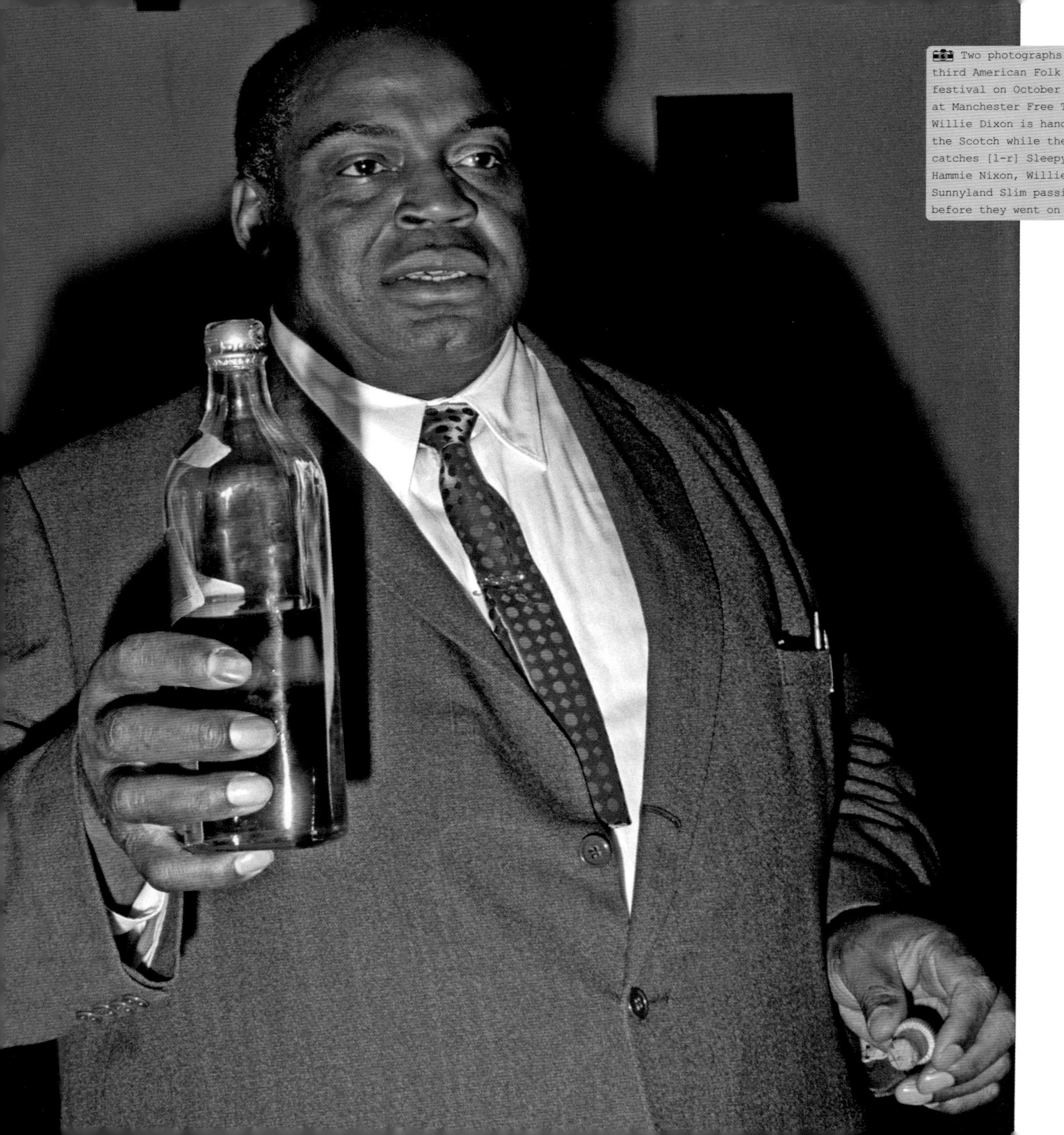

Two photographs from the
third American Folk Blues
festival on October 22. 1964
at Manchester Free Trade Hall.
Willie Dixon is handing round
the Scotch while the group ima
catches [l-r] Sleepy John Este
Hammie Nixon, Willie Dixon and
Sunnyland Slim passing time
before they went on stage.

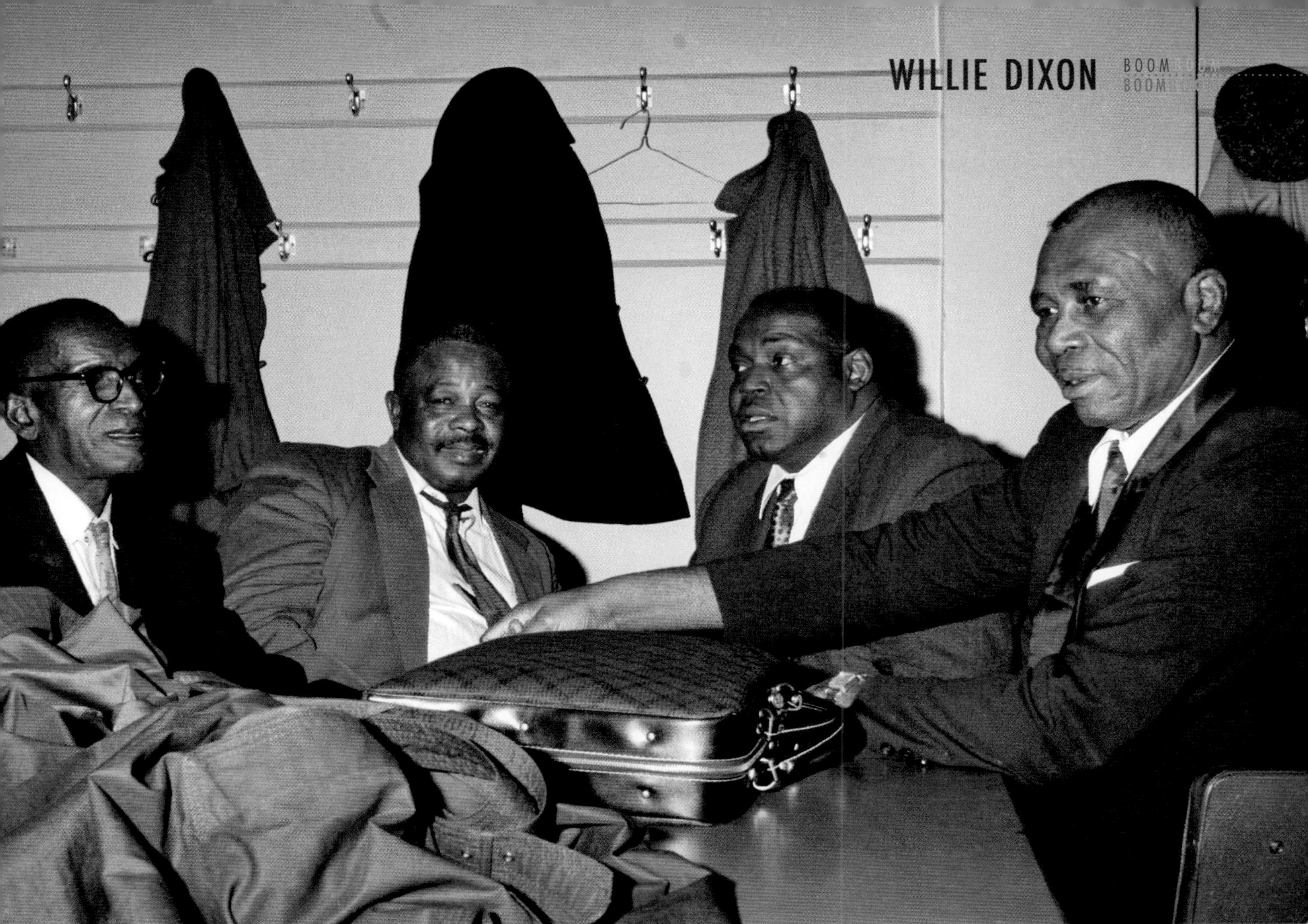

The 1962 shot taken from the gods looking down at the stage (page 109) shows the raked seating at the back where some of the audience were able to watch the acts from up close, which will evoke memories for anyone who used to go to this great hall for concerts. Brian had good access during the show, wandering around more or less at will, and took the shots from the front and side of the stage. He still has a set of battered 10" by 8" prints he had done at the time: *"I used to do this and then if they came back to town I would try and give them copies and perhaps get one signed."*

Blues fans from all over the country travelled to the two 1962 performances (matinee and evening). David Williams (in his book *The First Time We Met The Blues*) recalls: *"We could hardly believe that real blues artists were going to appear here in our country. They were regarded somewhat like mystic gods within our circle."* His circle included Jimmy Page and several members of The Rolling Stones.

Brian also recalls that the musicians caused a stir when the connecting flight from Heathrow to Manchester landed and fans had gathered to greet them. Willie Dixon had travelled with his own double bass which saw raised eyebrows at customs. *"He carried it without a case as it was, and you know, big fella he was... when they came to Manchester they were getting out to meet some of the people who wanted to say hello, and some official realised that they hadn't been through customs during this continental trip. So they had to hastily put up a load of tables and they went through and there was a lovely moment where they were shining torches through the frets of his bass to see if any substances were taped inside!"*

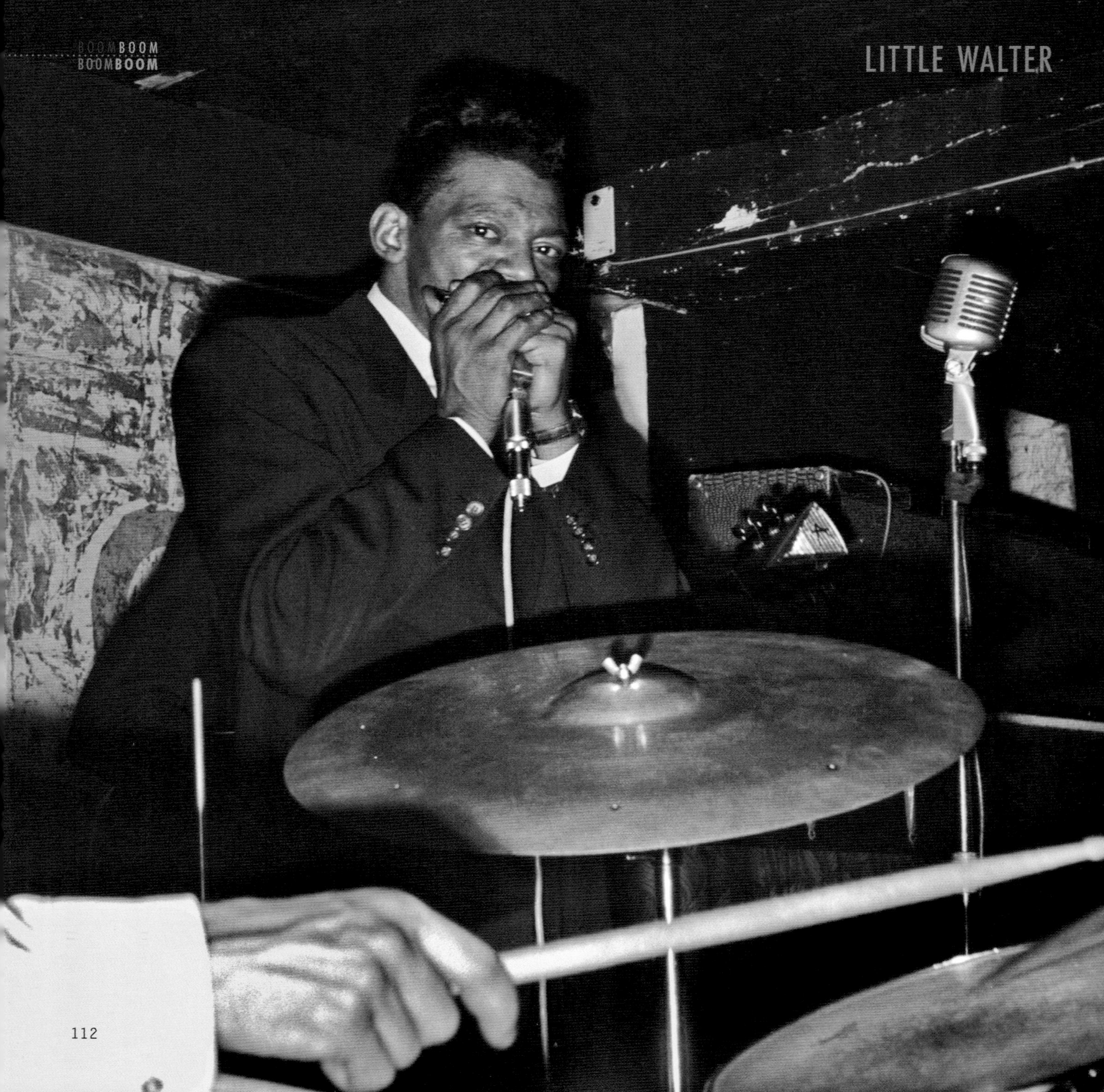

BOOMBOOM
BOOMBOOM
LITTLE WALTER
112

Little Walter played The Twisted Wheel Club on October 3rd 1964. Walter was something of a legendary harmonica player by this time, having played it close to a microphone and overloading the amplifier to experiment with distortion back in the 1940s. This was the first of only two trips to Europe, so fans were keen to see him on his Manchester debut. He played a number of the small blues venues while over, including The Cavern in Liverpool, The Alley Club in Cambridge, The Black Prince and Marquee clubs in London, the Borough Assembly Hall in Aylesbury and the Esquire in Sheffield. He even got booked to play on the BBC2 pop show *Beat Room*.

During the tour Walter was supported by various scratch or local groups and Alexis Korner did the honours for the Manchester date (and a support set), though is directly behind Walter on the live shot (left). Before long Korner had got himself a twice monthly residency at The Wheel Club through much of Autumn 1964, which became twice weekly for a time the following year.

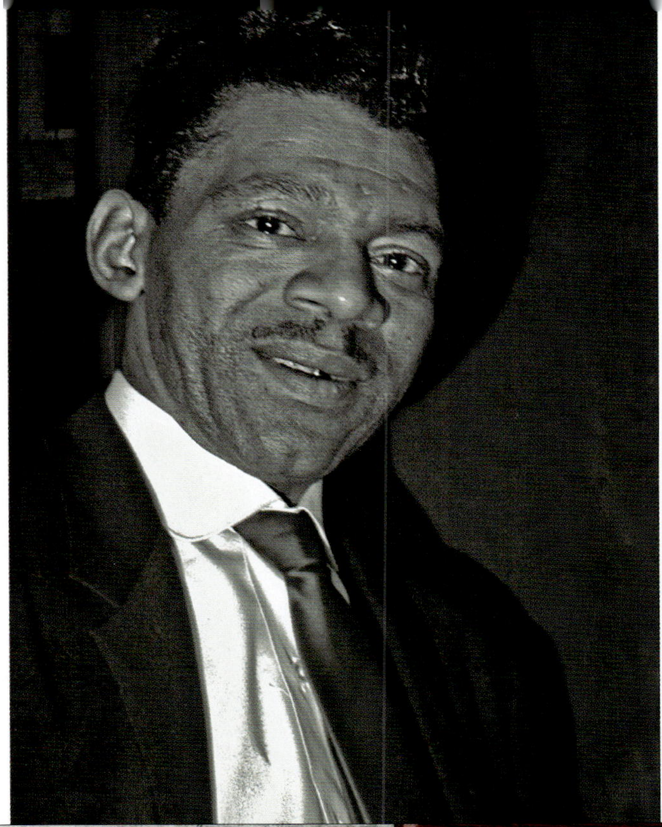

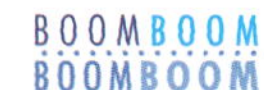

Brian went to take photographs for R & B Scene magazine as usual, including a few before the concert. Almost on top of the drum kit for the show, he was also battling a temperamental flash unit, then his roll of film ran out, so he only got three live photographs (and one of those was ruined by the drum stick in front of Walter's face!). Two of Korner's band can be seen in the backstage shot (below) but we've not been able to identify them yet. The great shot of Walter and Eagle negotiating fees for a return gig was taken by the main entrance of The Wheel Club.

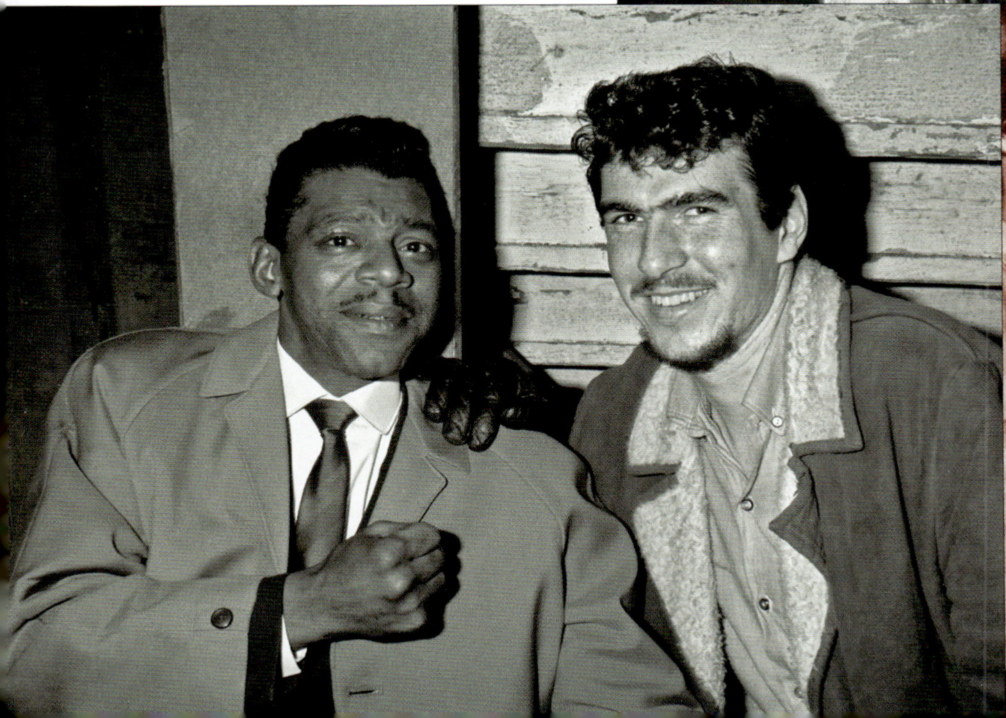

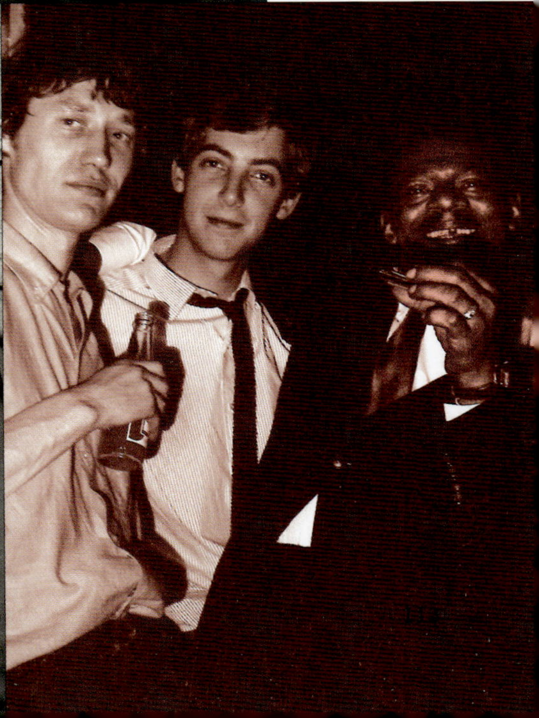

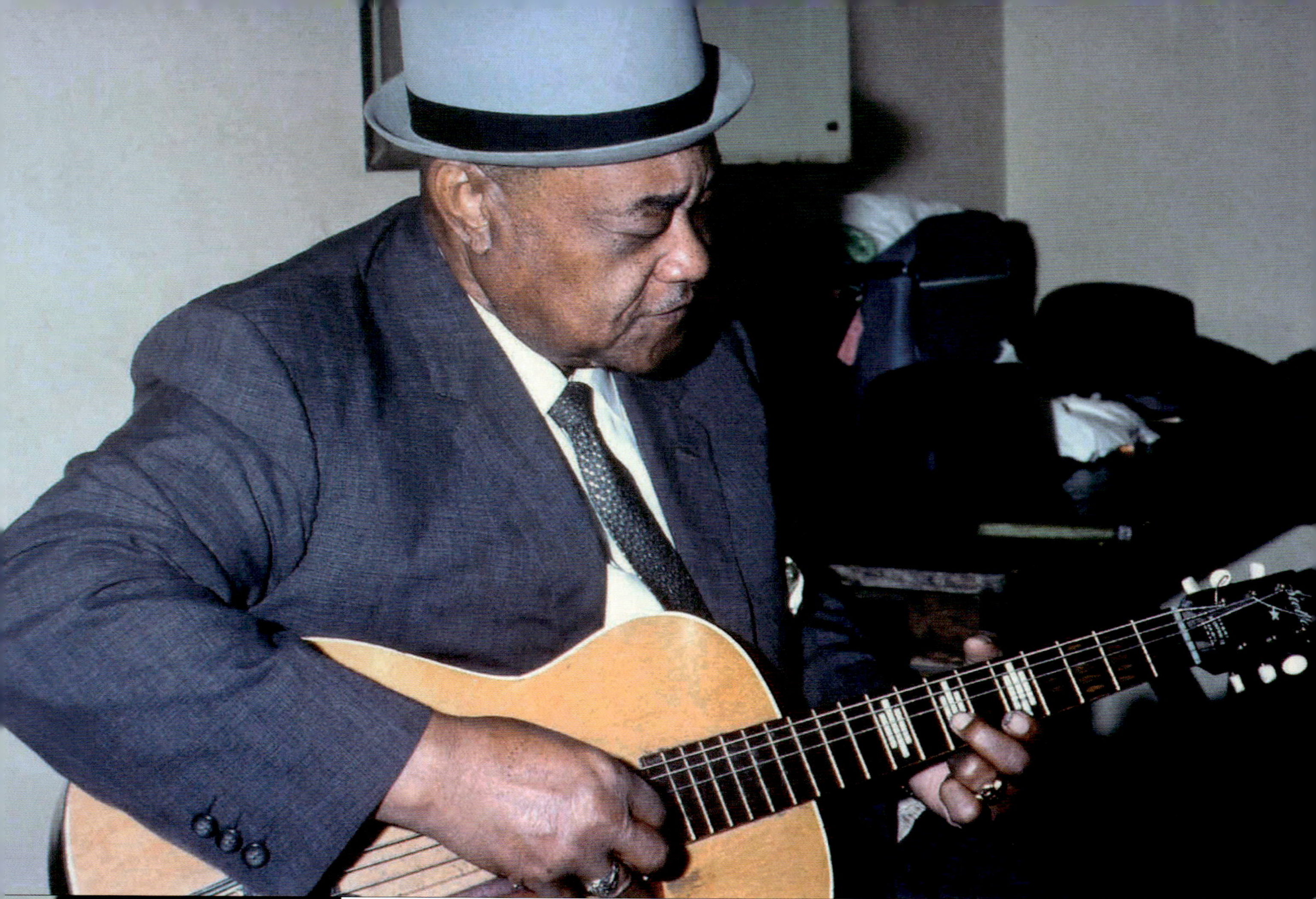

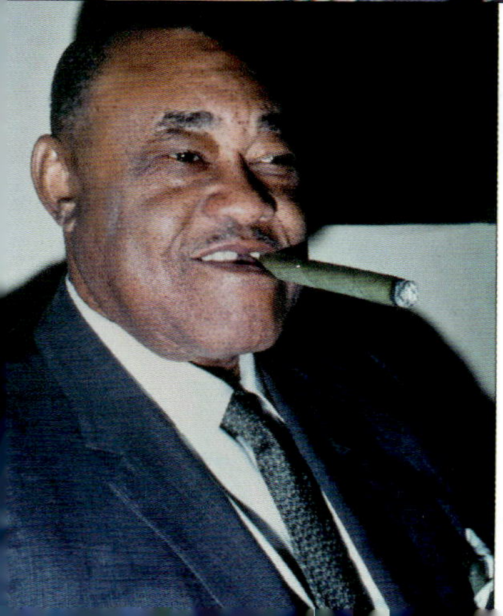

ROOSEVELT SYKES

Boogie pianist Roosevelt Sykes played the UK twice, on the AFBF tours of 1964 and 1966 (some of which was filmed by Granada TV) and Brian got to see him both time. Sykes' recording career spanned several decades, starting in 1929, but he didn't score a hit until 1945 with his band The Honeydrippers. Thanks to the AFBF tours his career was sustained in Europe with a succession of blues albums.

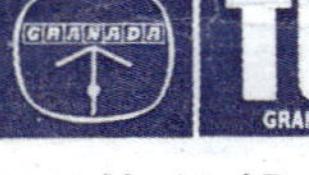 Brian took a couple of colour slides at the 1966 show, a great one (above) of Sykes warming up backstage at the Free Trade Hall and one of him with his trademark cigar. The black and white of Sykes raising a glass in the Free Trade Hall bar is from 1964.

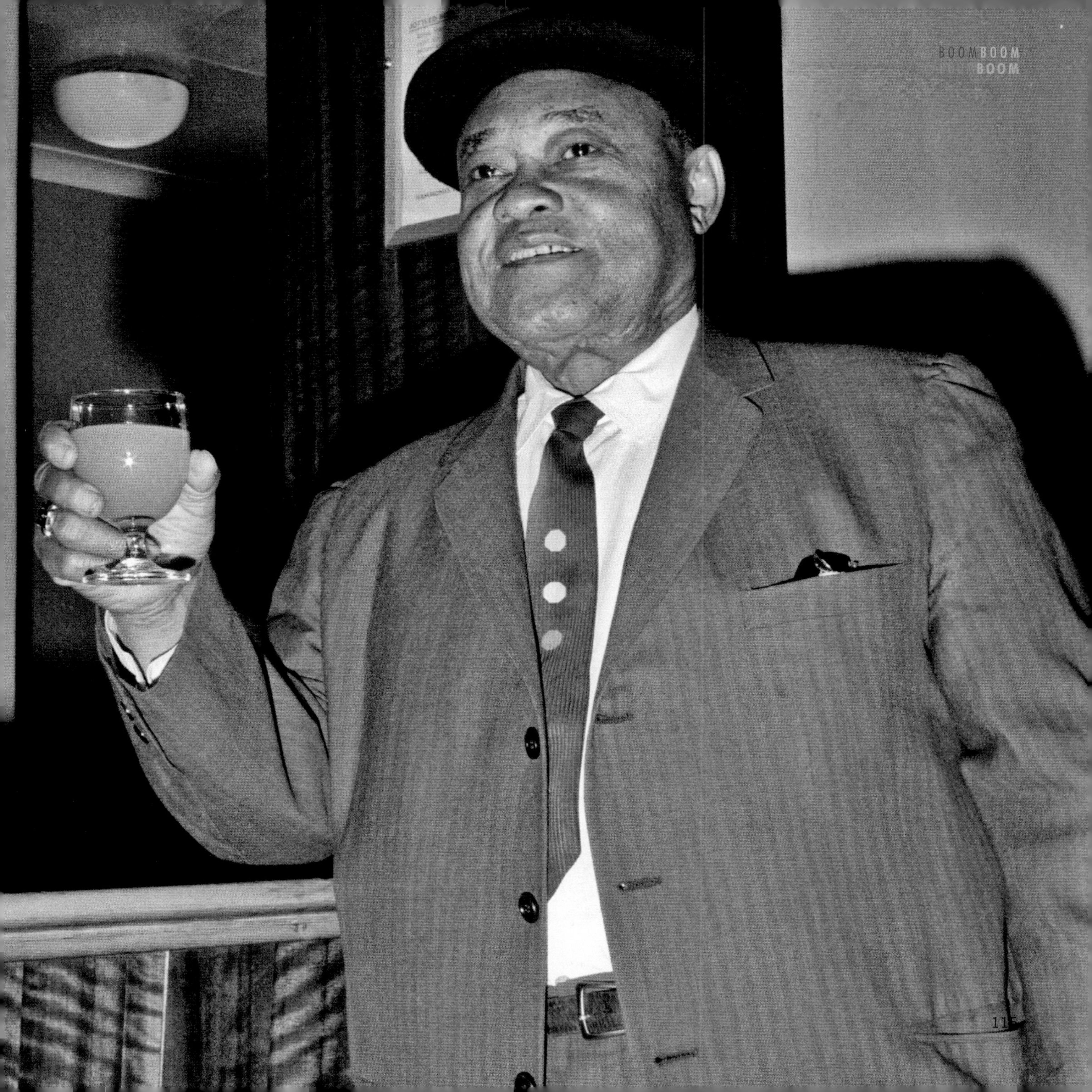
BOOM BOOM
BOOM BOOM

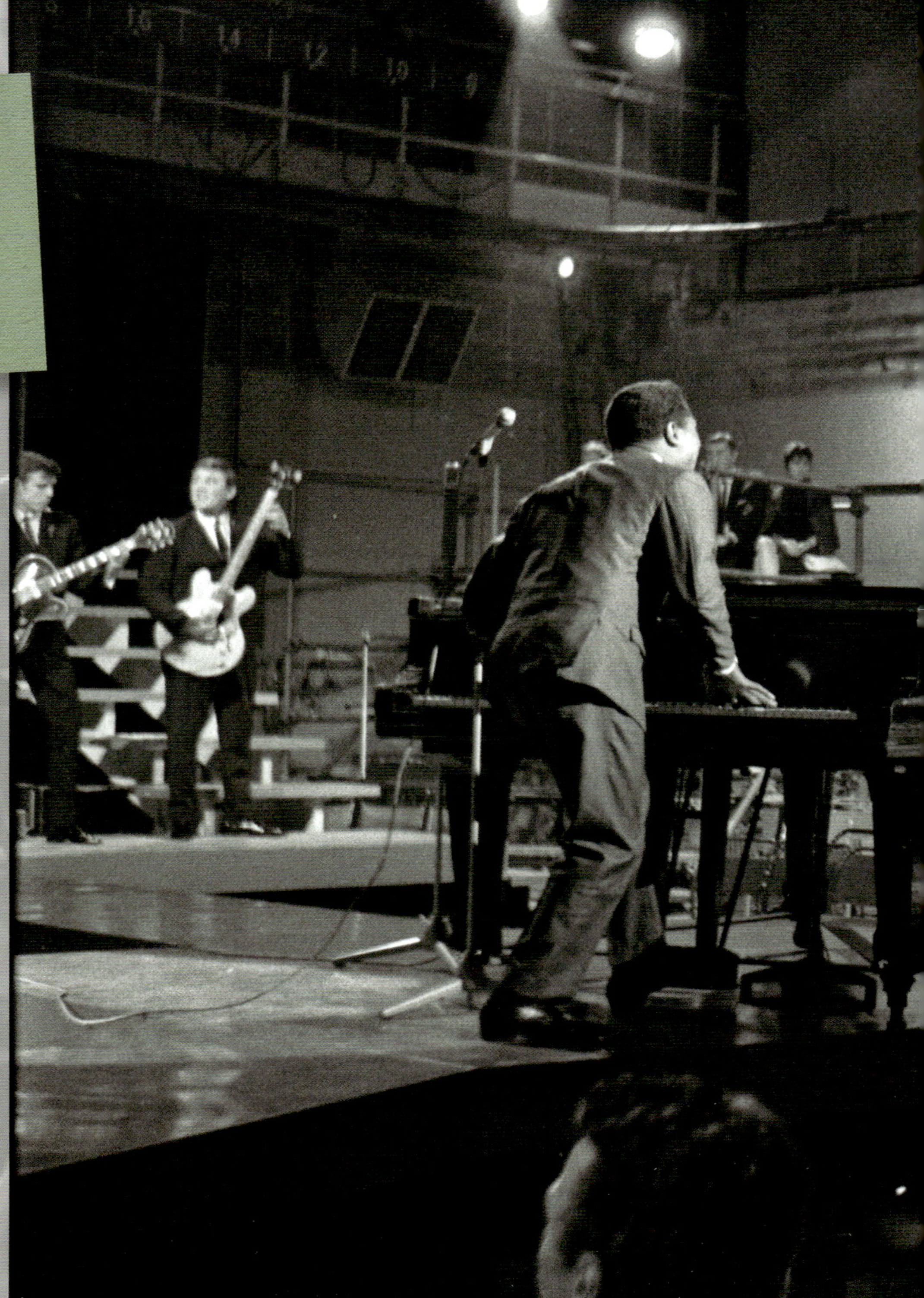

Broadcast on January 8. 1964, *It's Little Richard* was another of Granada's remarkable Sixties pop programmes, indeed many regard it as their best. Little Richard was due in town as part of his long November 1963 British tour and Granada organised the TV recording around this. The format was simple; a basic stage, unadorned studio walls, racked seating made from scaffolding and all the focus on the musicians.

Richard was backed by British band Sounds Incorporated and The Shirelles sang with him on the gospel song *Joy Joy Joy*. Happily the programme has survived, along with this great image (one of just two by Brian, seated near the front) taken during the rehearsals; he didn't want to stand up too often in case it risked him being thrown out! The photograph really captures what it was like to be in the audience that night. The Shirelles (see also next page over) also added a dynamic visual edge to the show and sashayed their way through a couple of tracks on their own. Already a very influential quartet, many credit them as having invented the girl group long before Motown.

Sounds Incorporated were a versatile and very well respected six man sax-led instrumental group who issued early singles produced by Joe Meek, but they backed many visiting American acts, and the sax section also played on one of the Beatles' *Sgt. Pepper* album tracks.

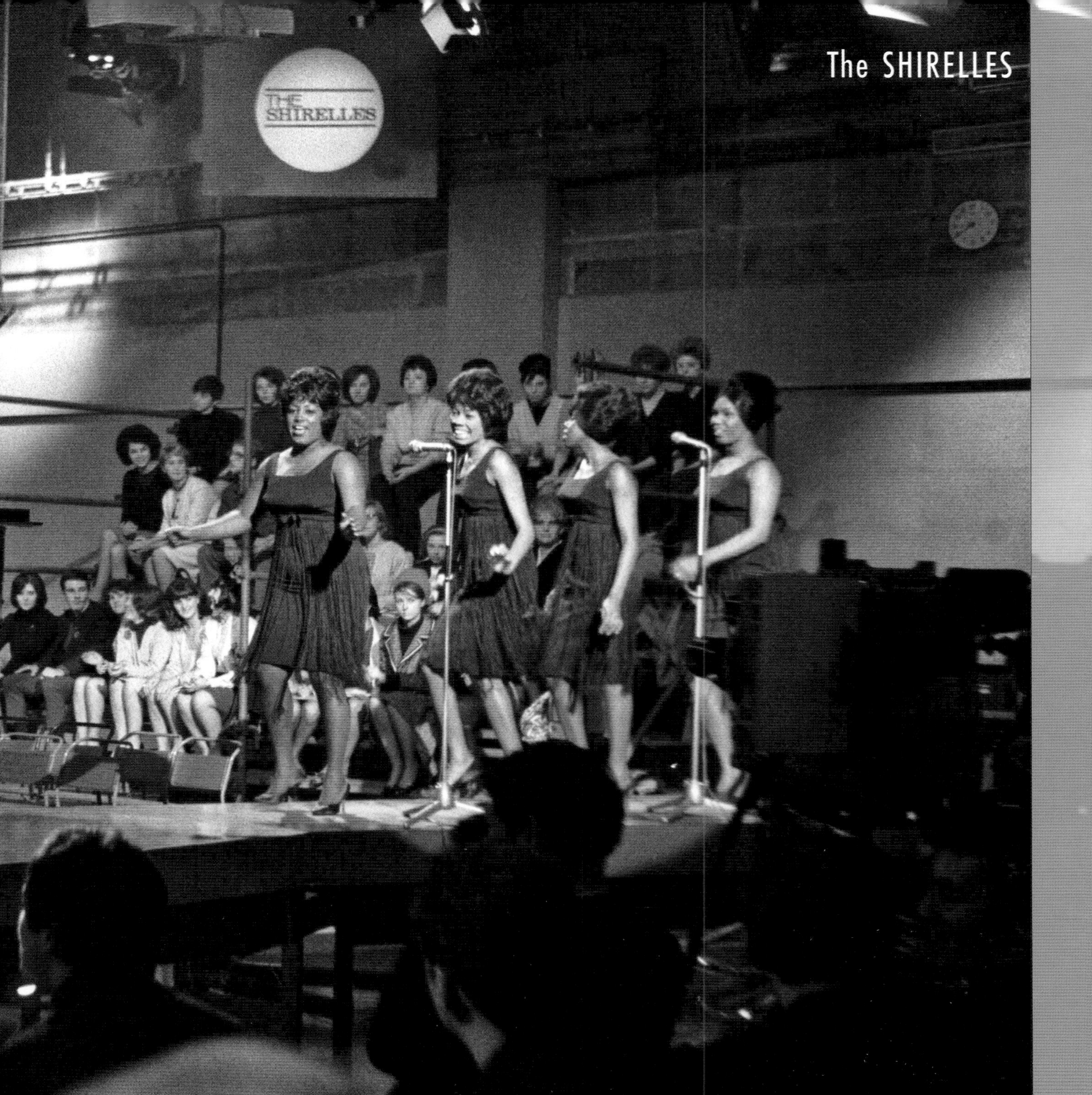
THE SHIRELLES
The SHIRELLES

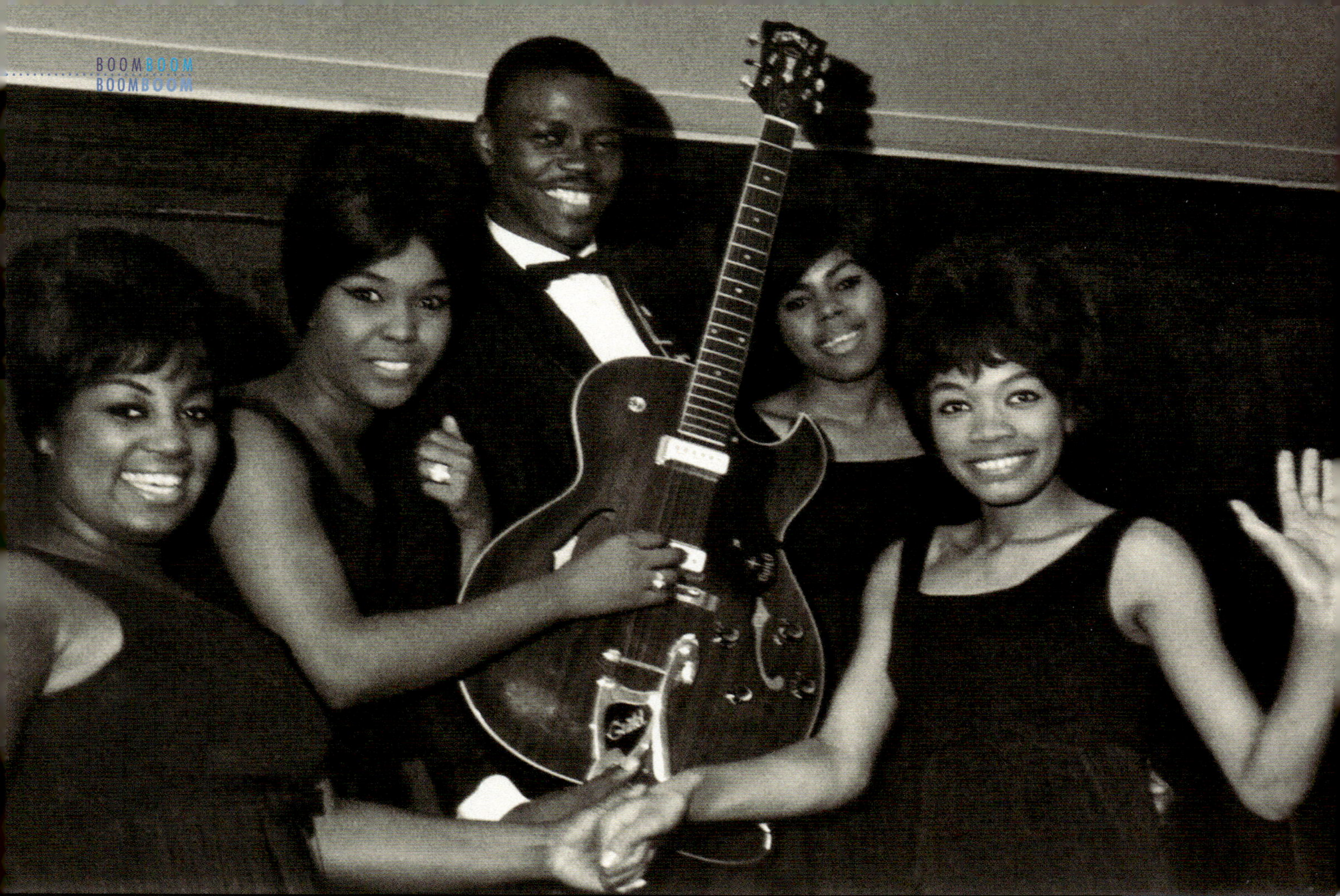

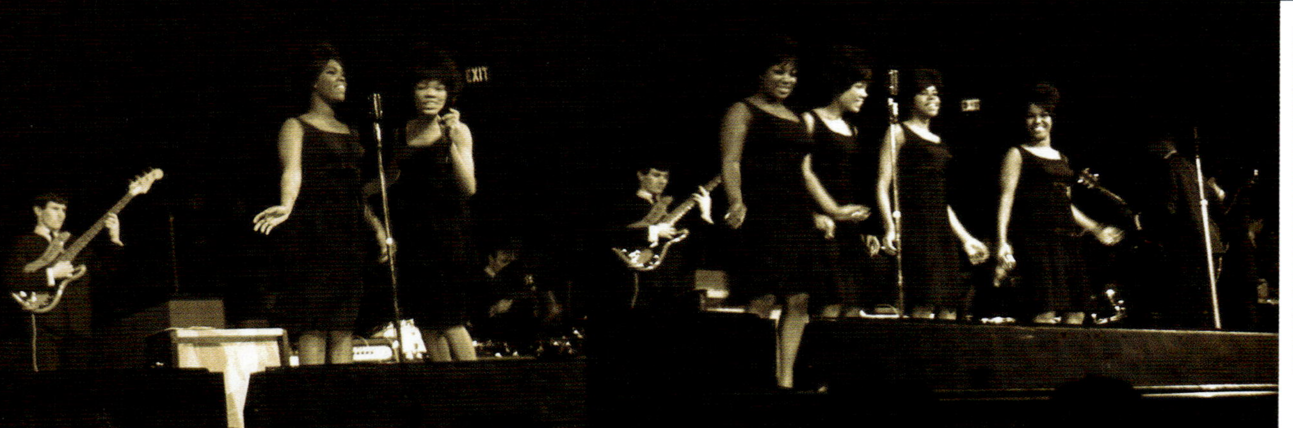

Brian took the lovel shot of The Shirelles with their guitarist Joe Richardson in the dressi room at Sheffield City Hall in 1963, where he'd gone to catch the Duane Eddy tour. This and the distant stage shots give a flavour of their stage set-up. The backstage sh only survives as a poor scan off a battered prin but is such a nice image wanted to include it.

SONNY TERRY / BROWNIE McGHEE

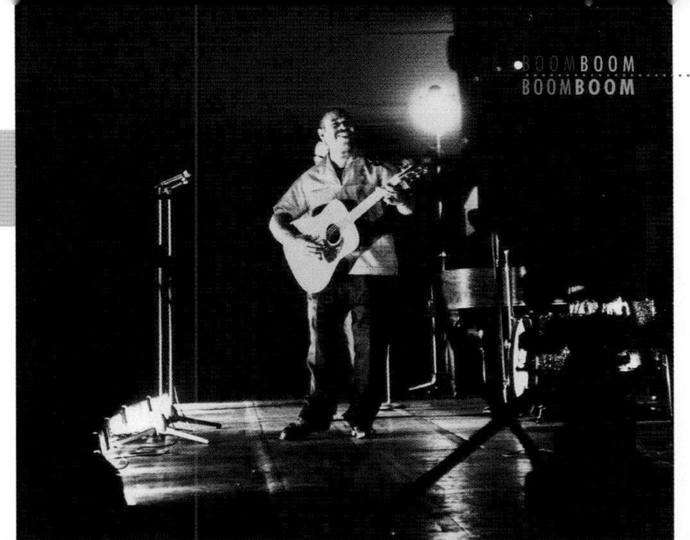

📷 Both negatives here are lost. The live shot has been restored from a vintage print, the backstage one from an early scan.

Two photographs of Brownie McGhee, one on stage at the Free Trade Hall during the filming of ABC TV's 1962 special, with their camera looming over the shot. The backstage image is very informal with McGhee on the left, Sonny Terry and a representative from the concert promotion agency Harold Davison, backstage at the Free Trade Hall on the Blues and Gospel Caravan in May 1964. Like the photo of The Shirelles opposite, Brian managed to get a relaxed portrait despite unpromising surroundings, and recalls the moment: *"We were passing albums around for people to sign but were a bit unsure about asking Sonny, being blind, until he piped up 'Hey, I sign them too!' He pulled out a John Bull printing outfit stamp and inkpad, with YOURS TRULY SONNY TERRY set up, and everyone queued up!"*

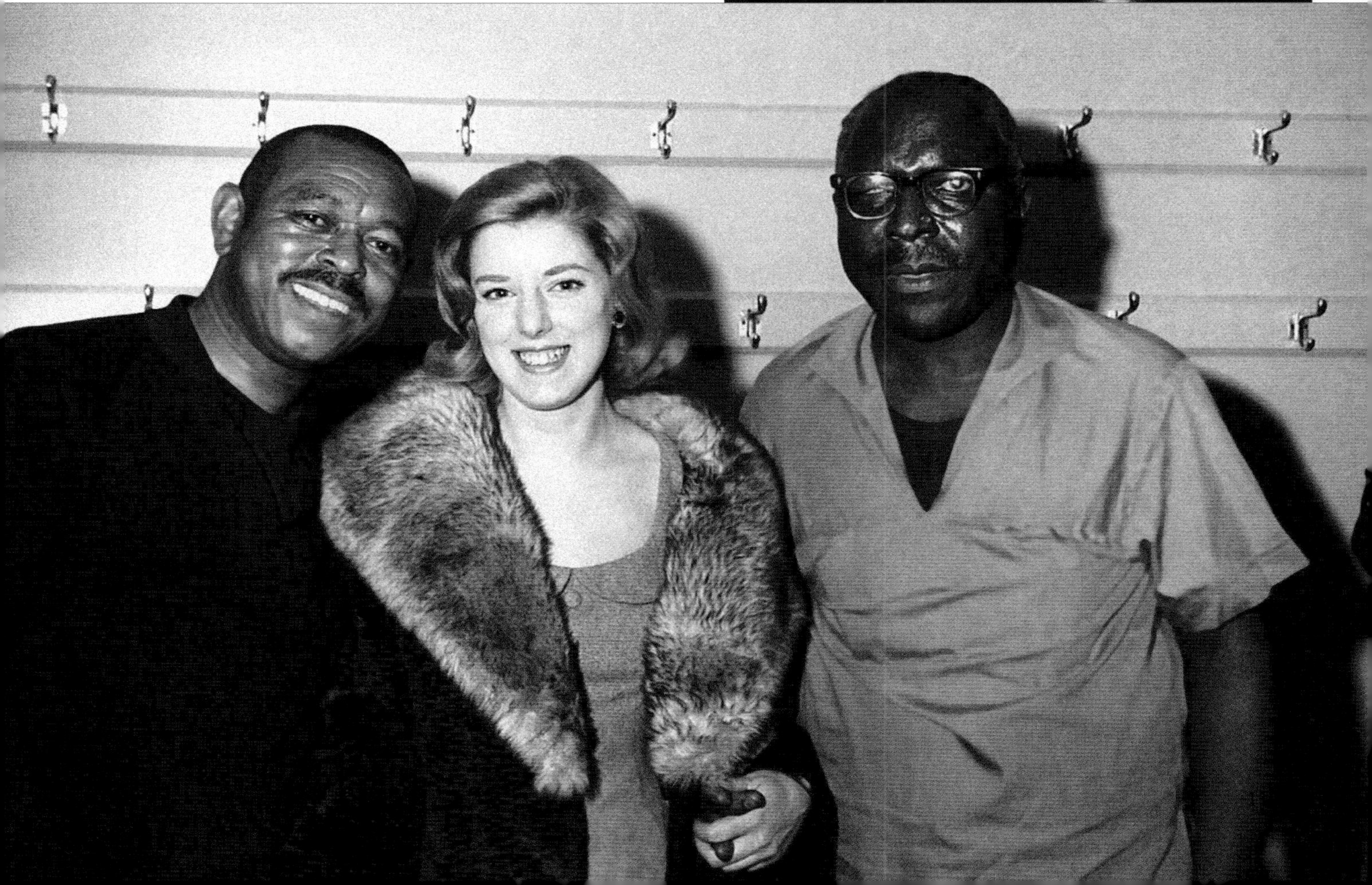

GARY U.S. BONDS

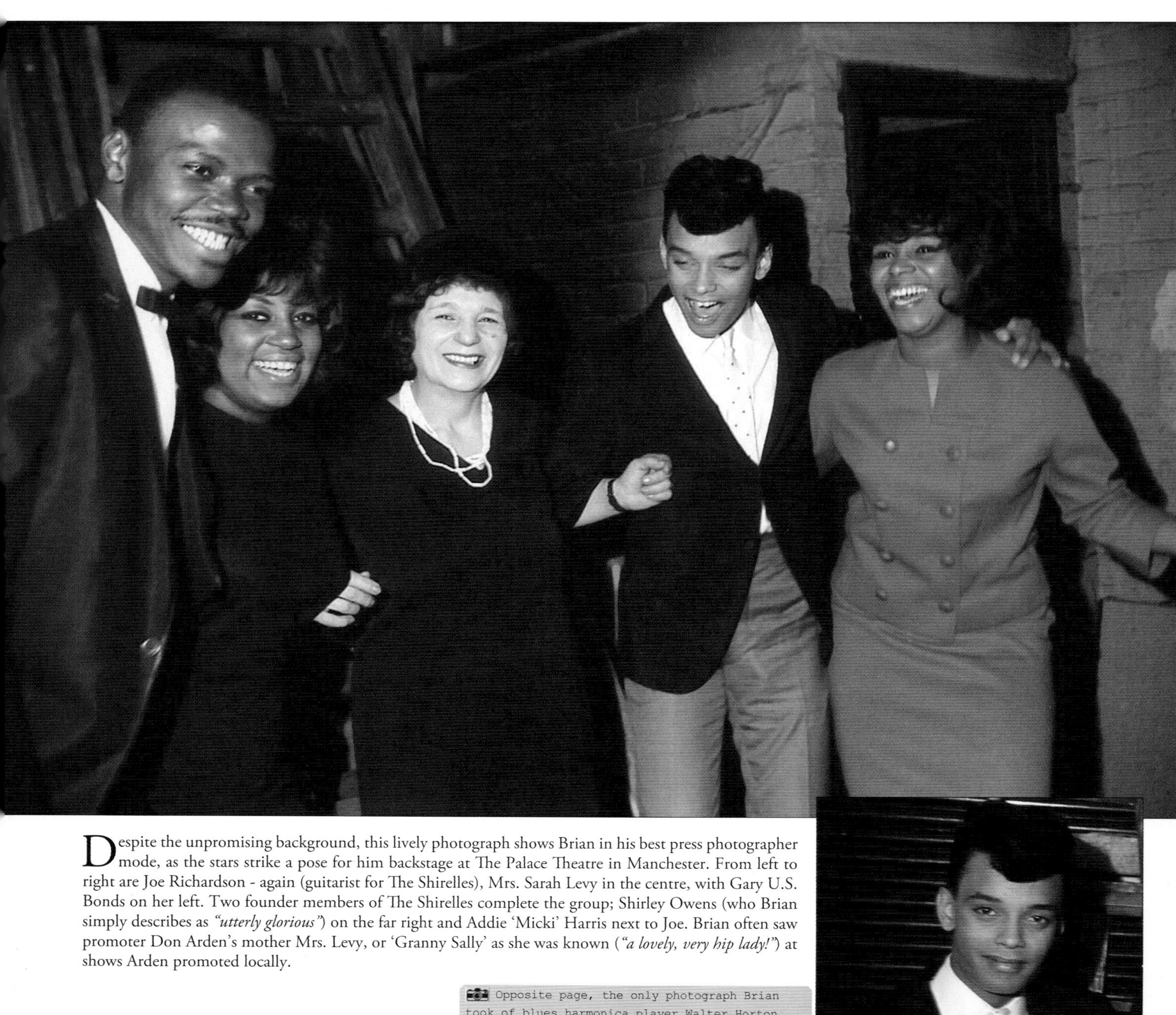

Despite the unpromising background, this lively photograph shows Brian in his best press photographer mode, as the stars strike a pose for him backstage at The Palace Theatre in Manchester. From left to right are Joe Richardson - again (guitarist for The Shirelles), Mrs. Sarah Levy in the centre, with Gary U.S. Bonds on her left. Two founder members of The Shirelles complete the group; Shirley Owens (who Brian simply describes as *"utterly glorious"*) on the far right and Addie 'Micki' Harris next to Joe. Brian often saw promoter Don Arden's mother Mrs. Levy, or 'Granny Sally' as she was known (*"a lovely, very hip lady!"*) at shows Arden promoted locally.

Opposite page, the only photograph Brian took of blues harmonica player Walter Horton, backstage at the Manchester Free Trade Hall.

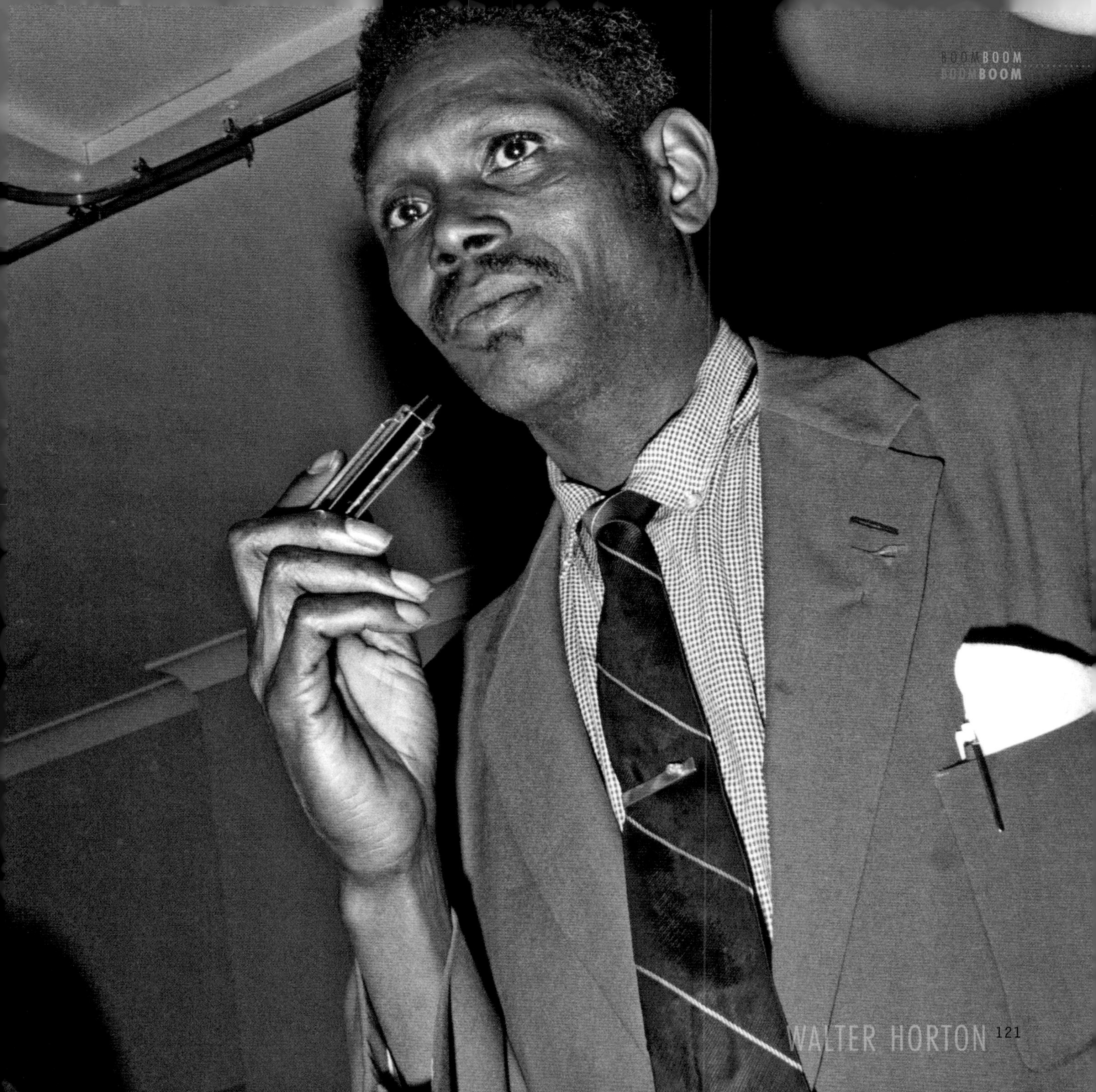

BOOM BOOM
BOOM BOOM
WALTER HORTON
121

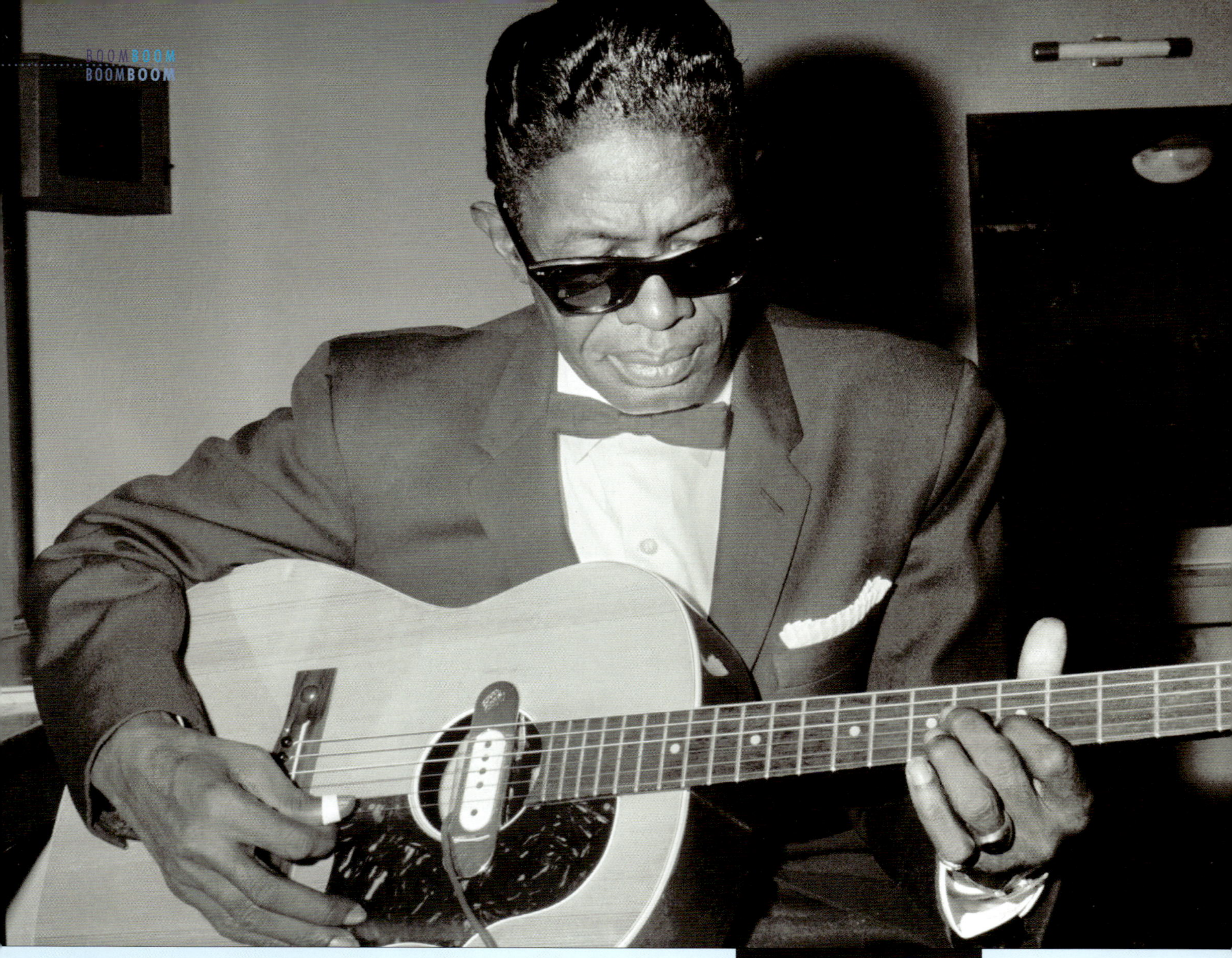

Brian got to see Lightning Hopkins at Manchester Free Trade Hall in 1965 while he was touring on the AFBF bill that year. This was Hopkins' only tour in the UK, which came as interest in his enormous contributions to blues music were at last being properly recognised. Brian took the photo of him here strumming on the acoustic and another of Hopkins signing a Crown label album for him. Hopkins was not always so responsive to such requests, Alan Balfour writing in the NME remembered trying to get one of his albums signed on the same tour. *"Boy, everybody's bin asking me one damn thing or another,"* came the reply. *"I'll sing you something from that record when I get out there. You're here to hear me* sing, *ain't ya?"*

122

LIGHTNING HOPKINS

Left: While Brian's back-stage negatives have survived, his live photos of Hopkins have been lost apart from this one contemporary print.

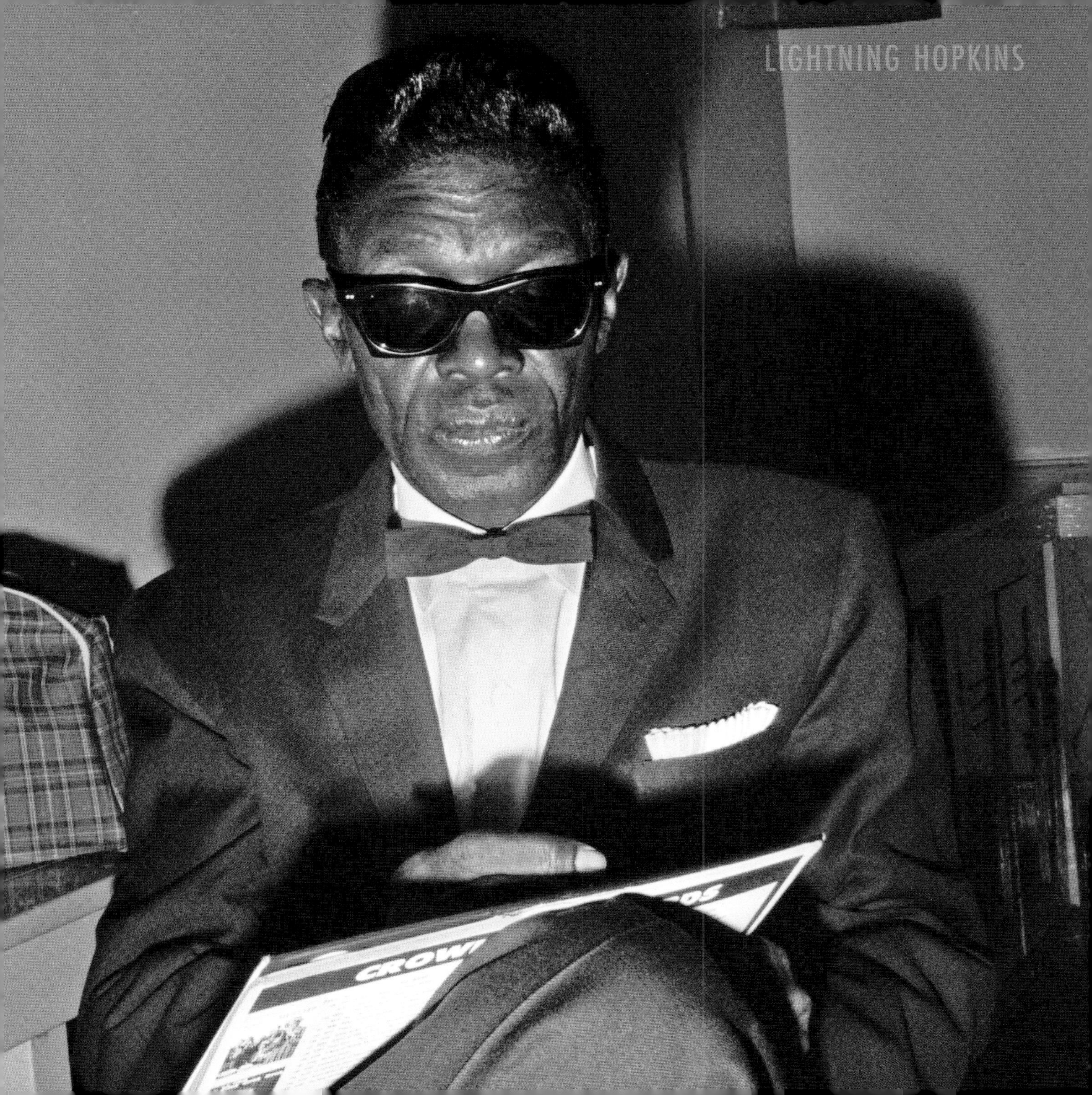
LIGHTNING HOPKINS

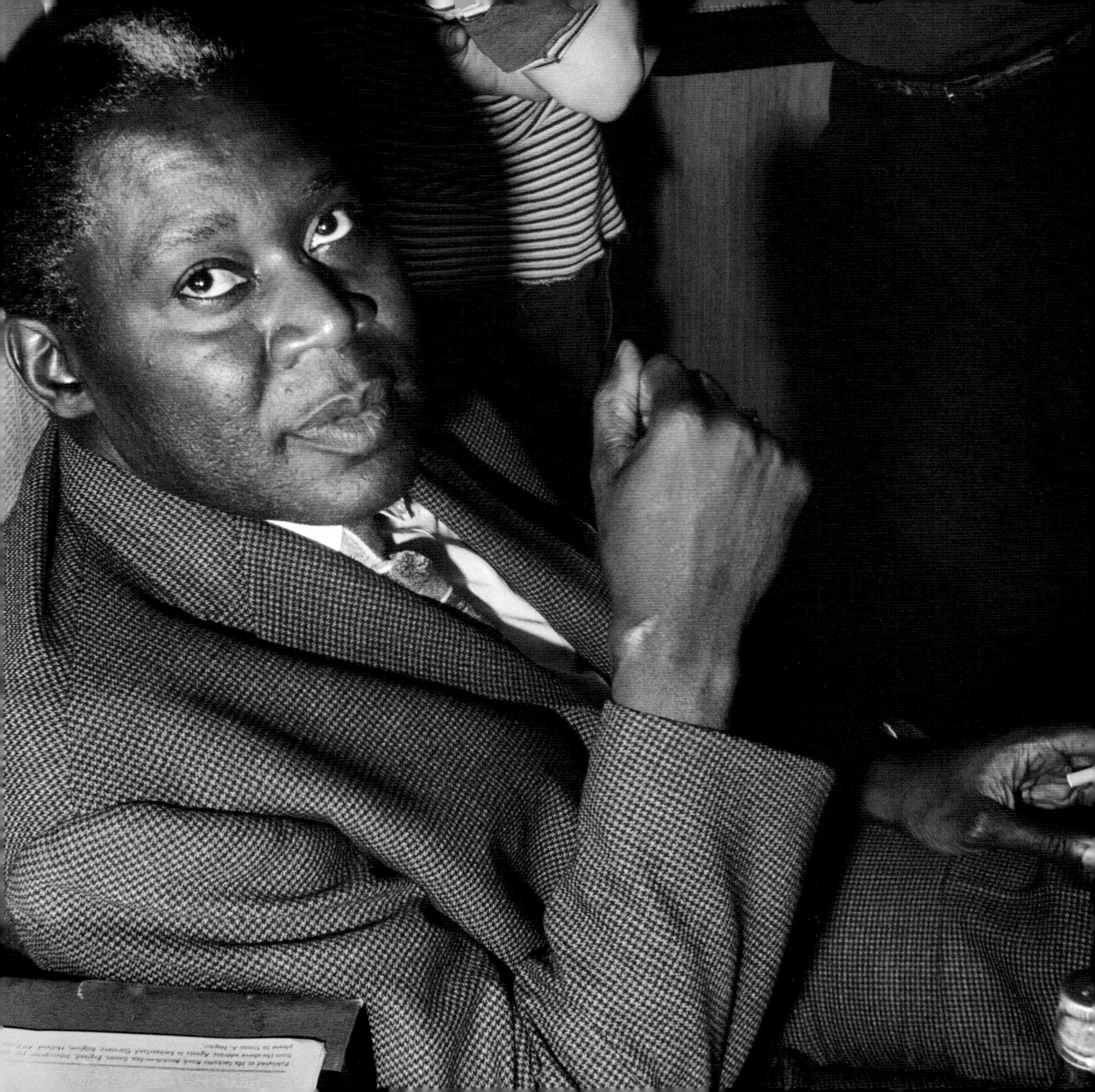

MEMPHIS SLIM

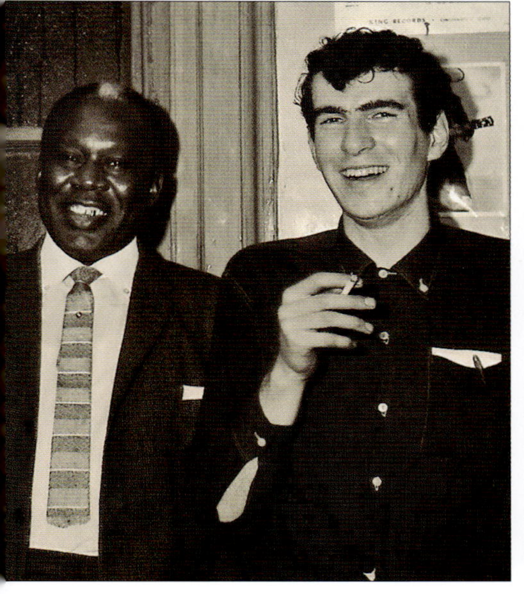

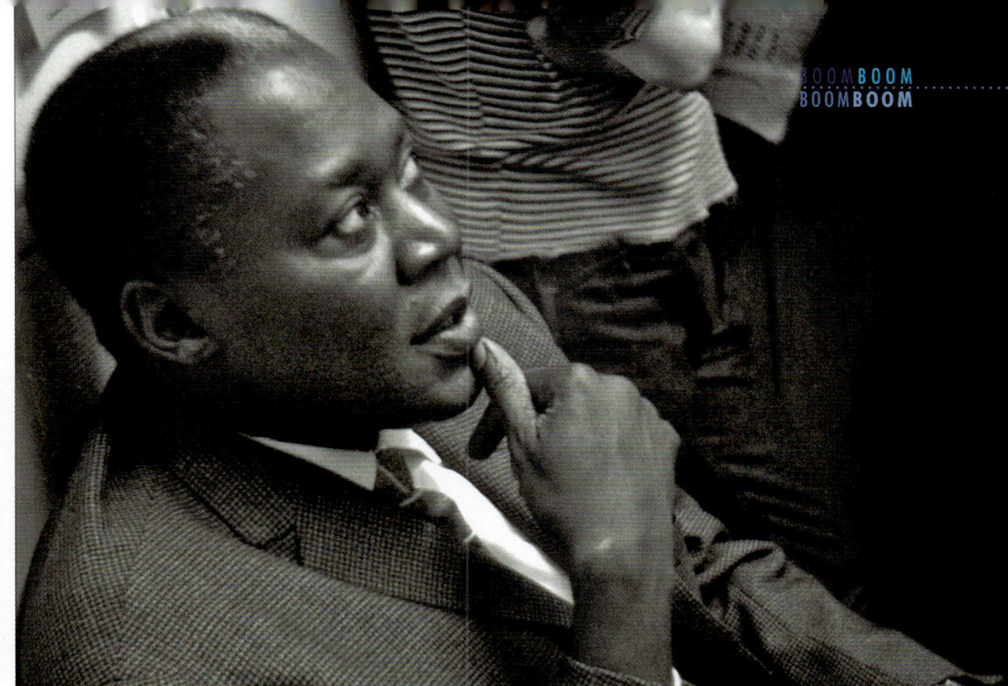

Memphis Slim was another of the musicians on the first American Folk and Blues festival tour in 1962, making that important stop off in Manchester on October 22nd. Indeed Slim liked Europe so much that he decided to move permanently to Paris after this trip. He appeared on the next year's festival in Croydon (advertised as the "only appearance in Britain") and did a Granada TV special.

Slim then came over twice in 1964 to headline smaller venues (and the National Jazz & Blues Festival) with pick-up bands; naturally Roger Eagle (seen above with Slim in the club) was quick to book him for The Twisted Wheel. Slim duely appeared on May 9th with Zoot Money's Big Roll Band and returned on September 5th 1964 for one of Eagle's all-nighter weekend events. Georgie Fame and the Blue Flames played the opening set, then backed Slim for his performance.

Before the September show, Brian was able to take these great images up in Roger's office, plus a couple of Slim soundchecking on the club's old piano (overleaf). Roger Fairhurst was the D.J. for this particular evening, and cuts from the rare Memphis Slim album *The World's Foremost Blues Singer* were played frequently in the run up to the show.

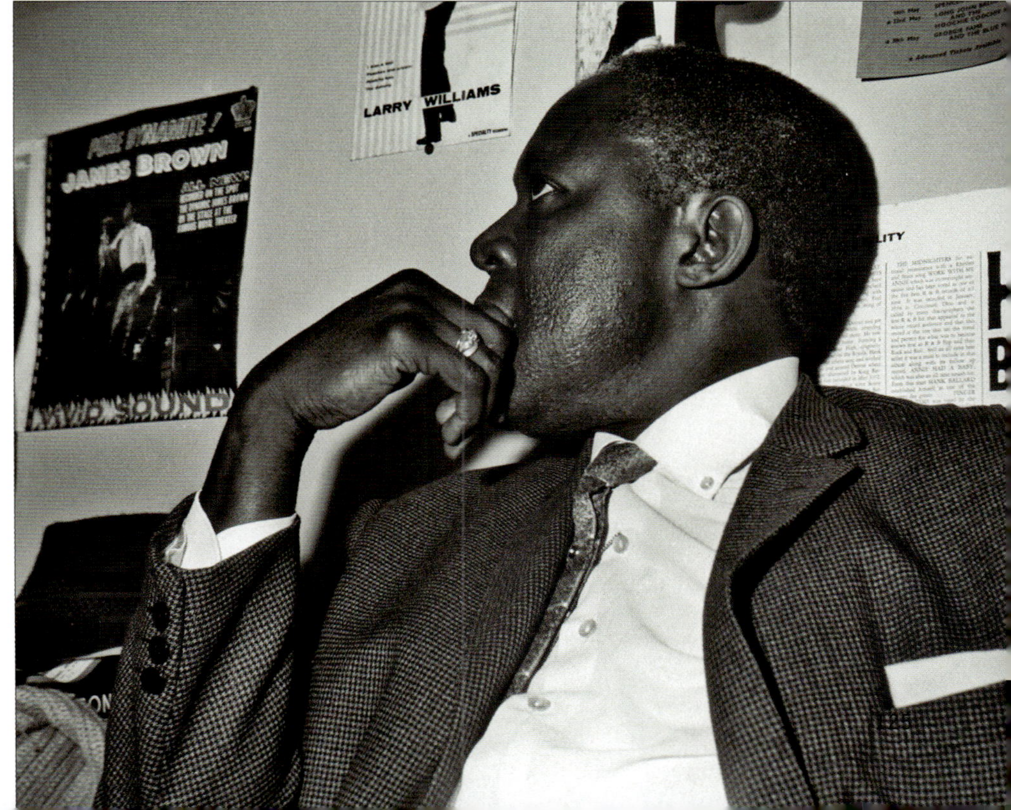

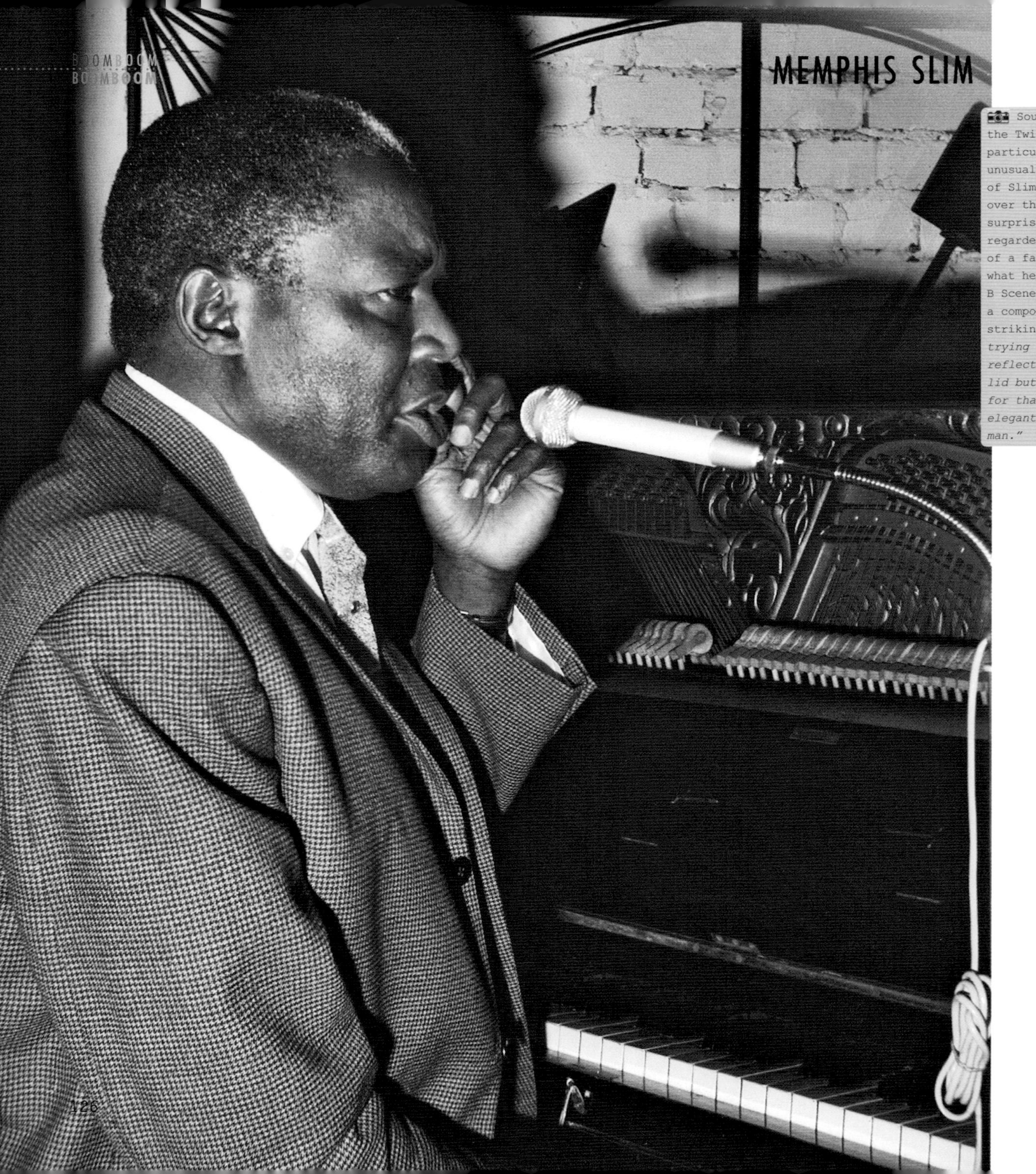

Sound-checking in the Twisted Wheel. We particularly like the unusually cropped image of Slim's head peeping over the piano, and were surprised to learn Brian regarded this as a bit of a failure in terms of what he needed for R & B Scene magazine. But as a composition it is very striking: "I think I was trying to capture his reflection in the piano lid but the flash did for that idea! A lovely, elegant and erudite man."

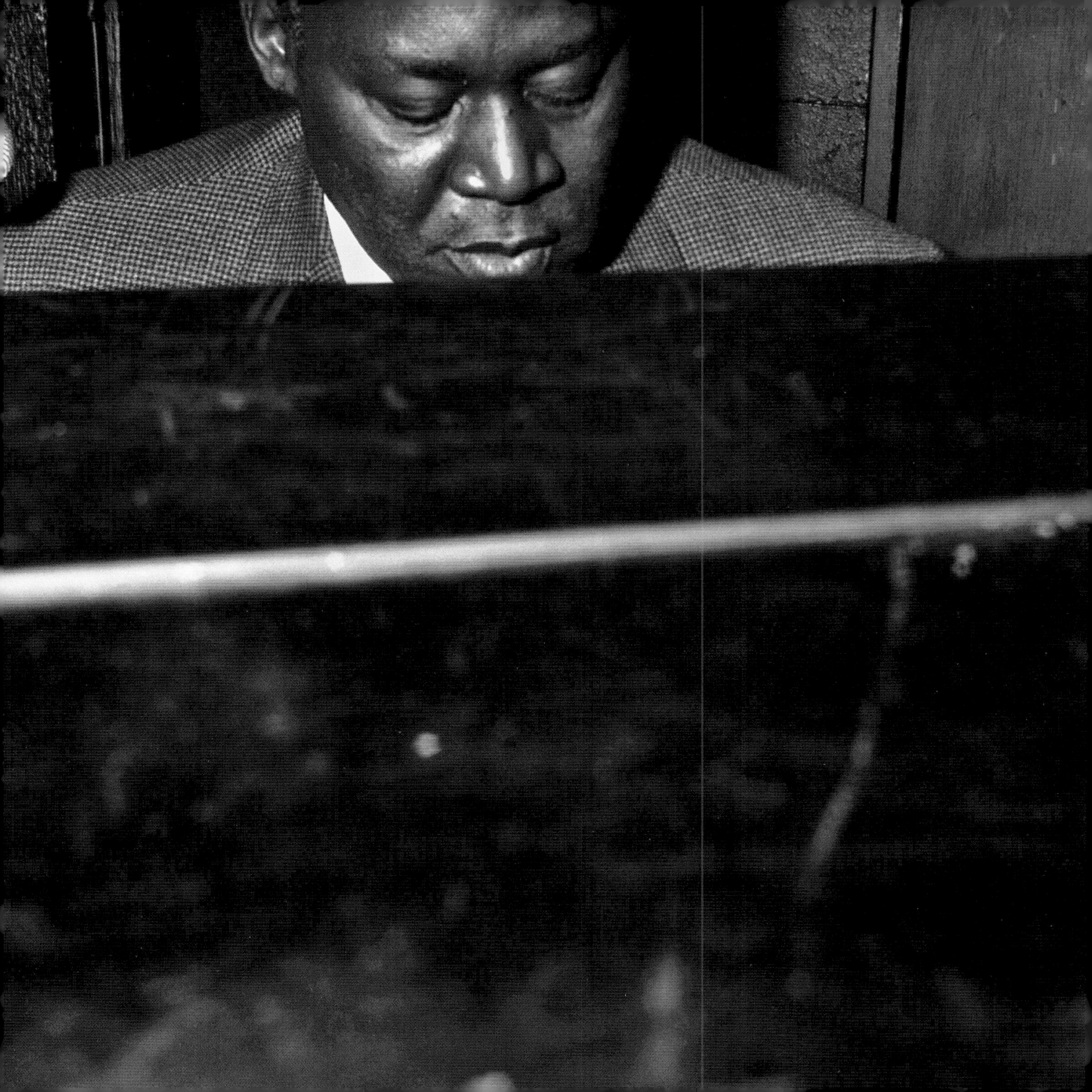

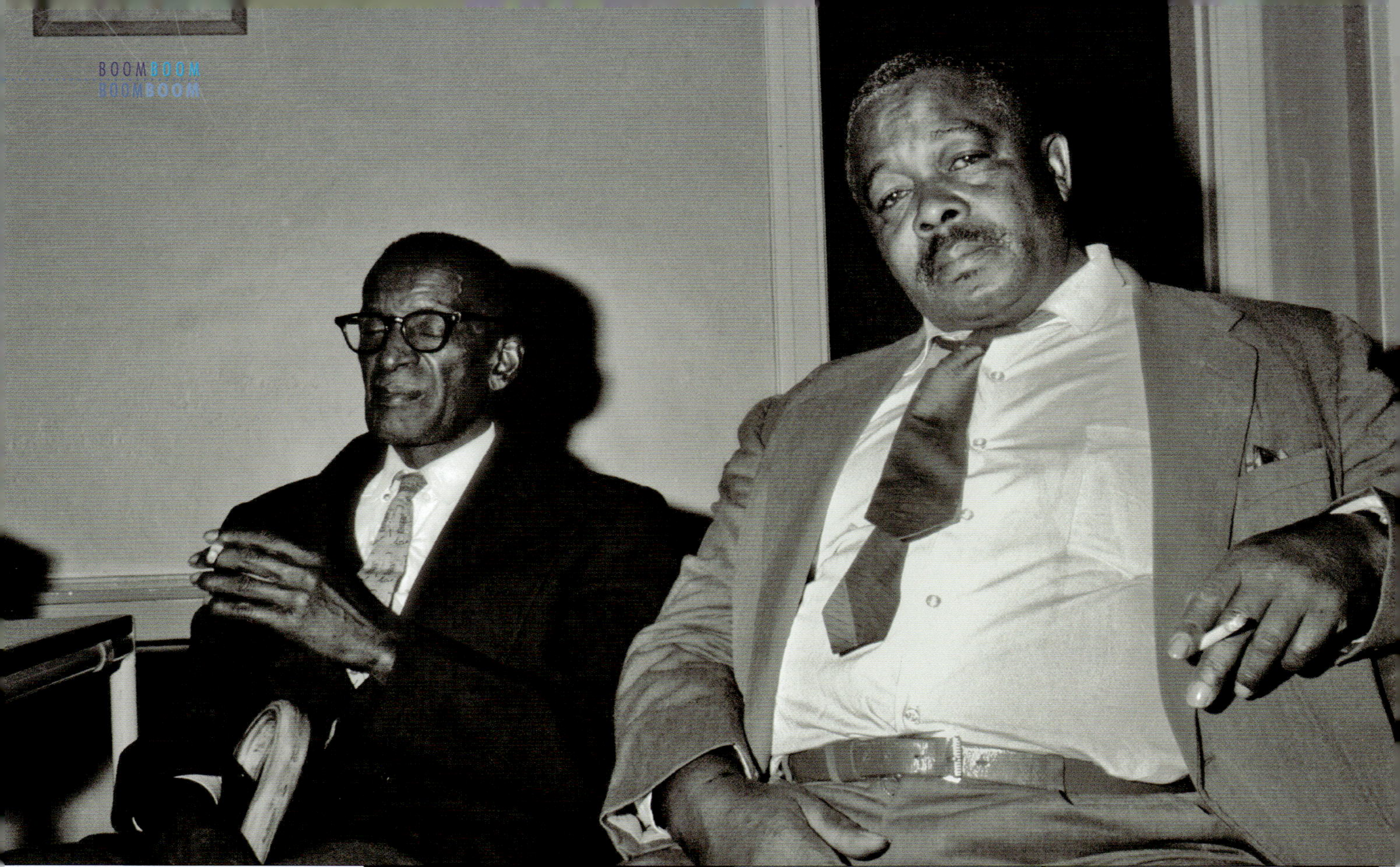

JOHN ESTES
HAMMIE NIXON

After a decade in abject poverty brought on by the onset of blindness, blues singer and songwriter Sleepy John Estes was rediscovered in the early Sixties and began playing concerts with his music partner and companion, harmonica player Hammie Nixon. They joined the American Folk & Blues Festival tour in Manchester where Brian met them.

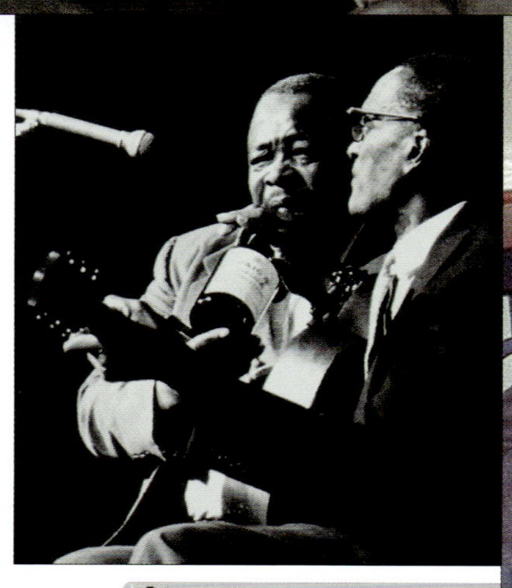

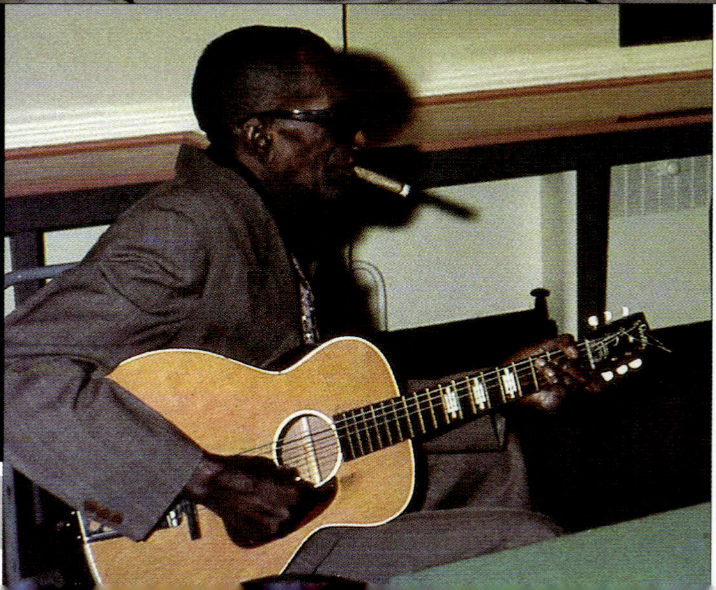

The black and white photos are from 1964, the colour slide (which is lost) from 1966.

JIMMIE LEE

Given Lee's nickname, Brian's only photograph of Lonesome Jimmie Lee is perhaps appropriate, showing Jimmie at the very back of the stage on his own, dressed in a knitted jumper and beret, and concentrating on his bass work. As well as doing a couple of his own tracks, Lee backed several of the other acts on the 1965 AFBF tour where this was taken at Manchester Free Trade Hall.

An in demand session player throughout the Fifties, by the end of the Sixties Lee, with the blues out of fashion, supplemented his musical career by opening a candy store in Chicago. He was 'discovered' again in the late 1980s by local blues fans and encouraged to start playing and eventually recording again.

The poster for this tour is shown below. (Without exception all the AFBF tour material was superbly designed; and it's surprising it has yet to be compiled.)

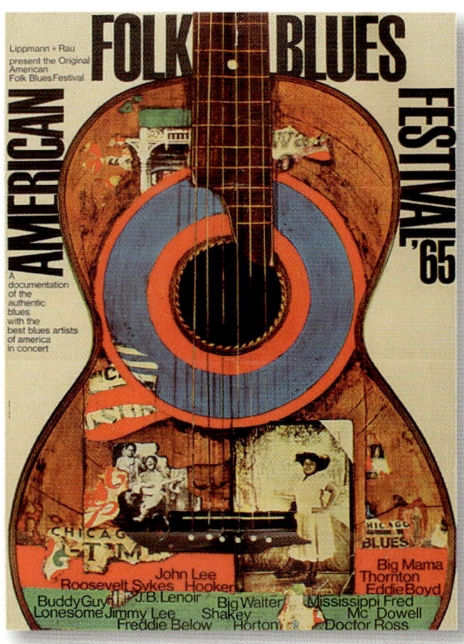

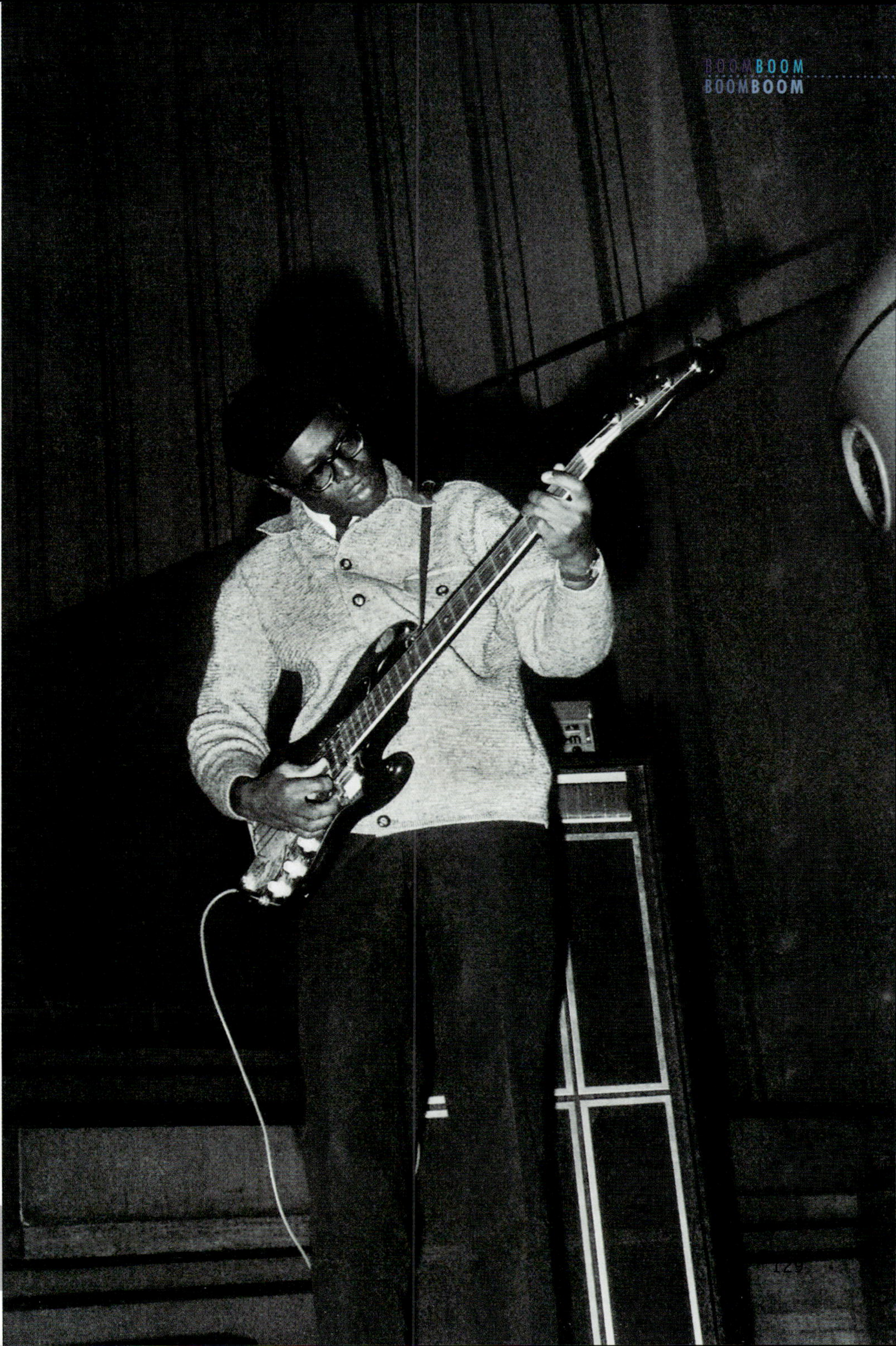

The negative for this photograph is and has been scanned from grainy print. The edge of the Free Trade Hall balcony in the top right corner confirms the venue (which is now a hotel).

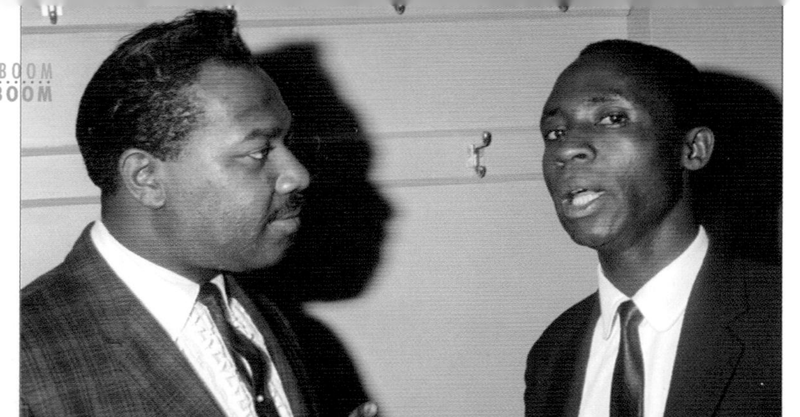

CLIFTON JAMES

Celebrated Chicago blues drummer Clifton James appeared on the 1964 American Folk Blues Festival and Brian took these two photographs of him backstage in Manchester. James was the go to drummer for the Chess and Checker labels for many years, so a natural to back the other musicians on this tour. He is seen below with Sunny Boy Williamson, and (right) with a so far unidentified musician : *"I've tried every source I can think of but nobody has been able to help…!"* If you can help solve the mystery do get in touch.

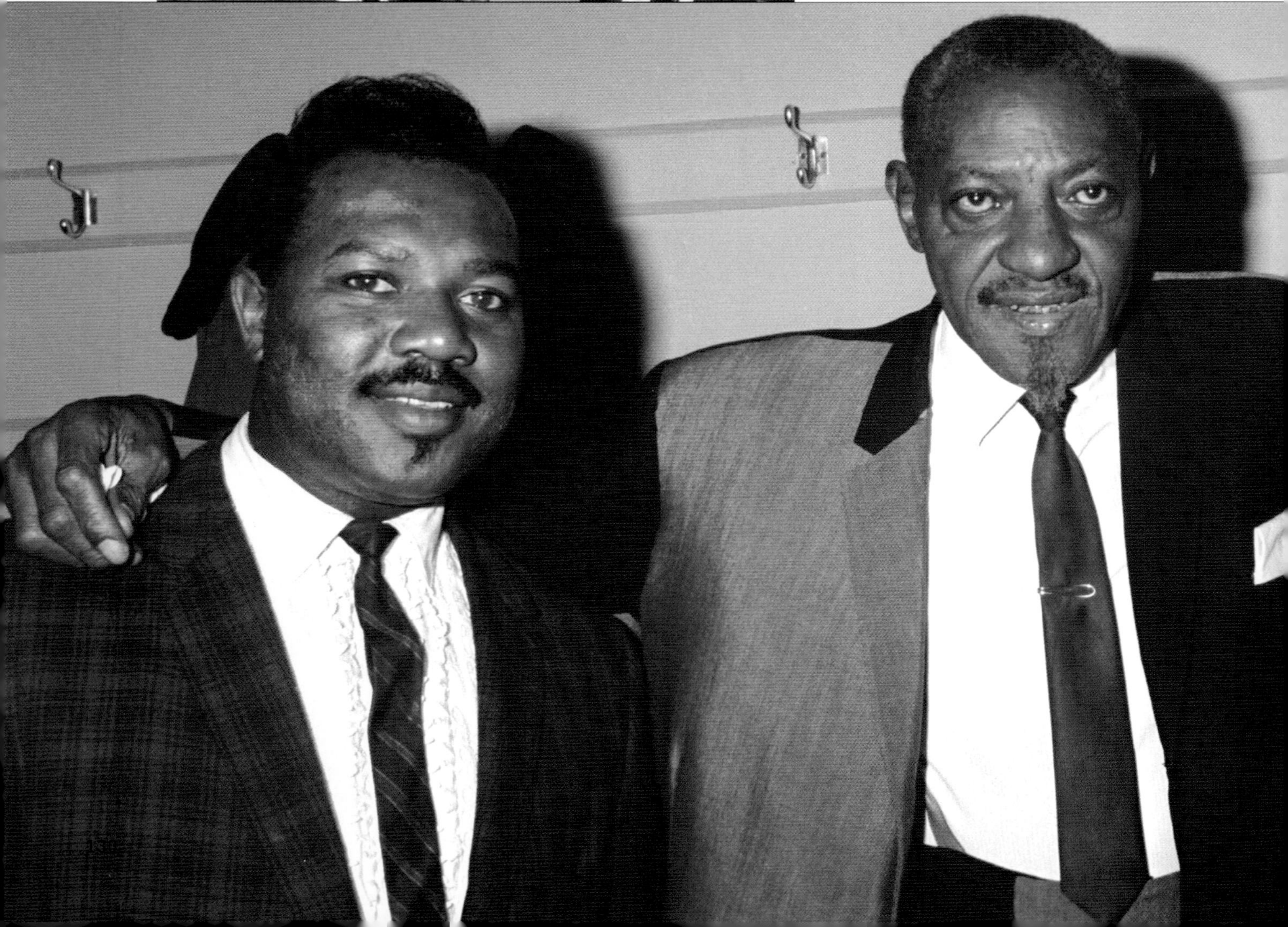

Brian could only take one photograph of Sunnyland Slim during the 1964 AFBF concert, which survives only as a print, the wear and tear adding to the sense of history (though the scratches and damage on the Free Trade Hall grand piano are for real).

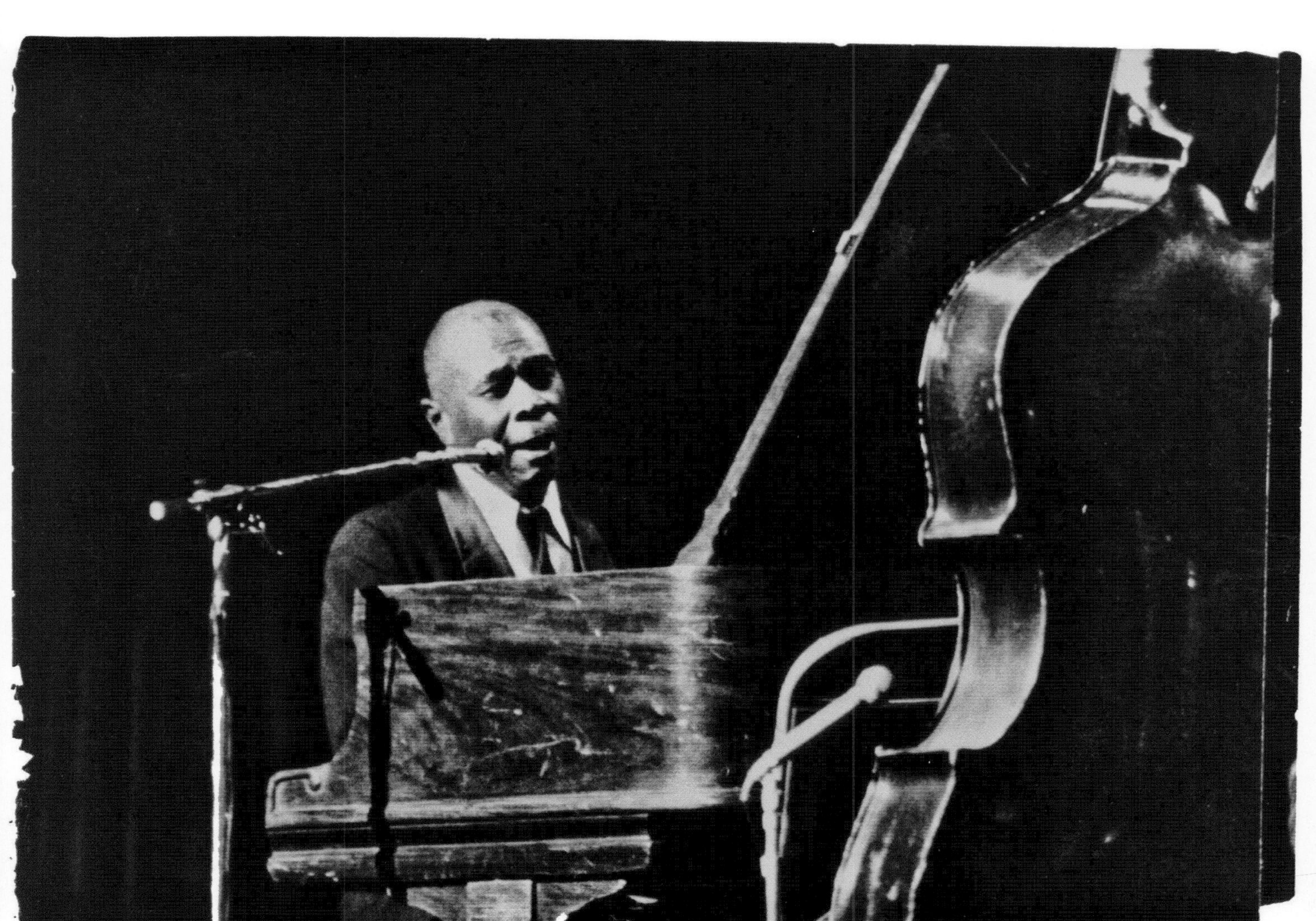

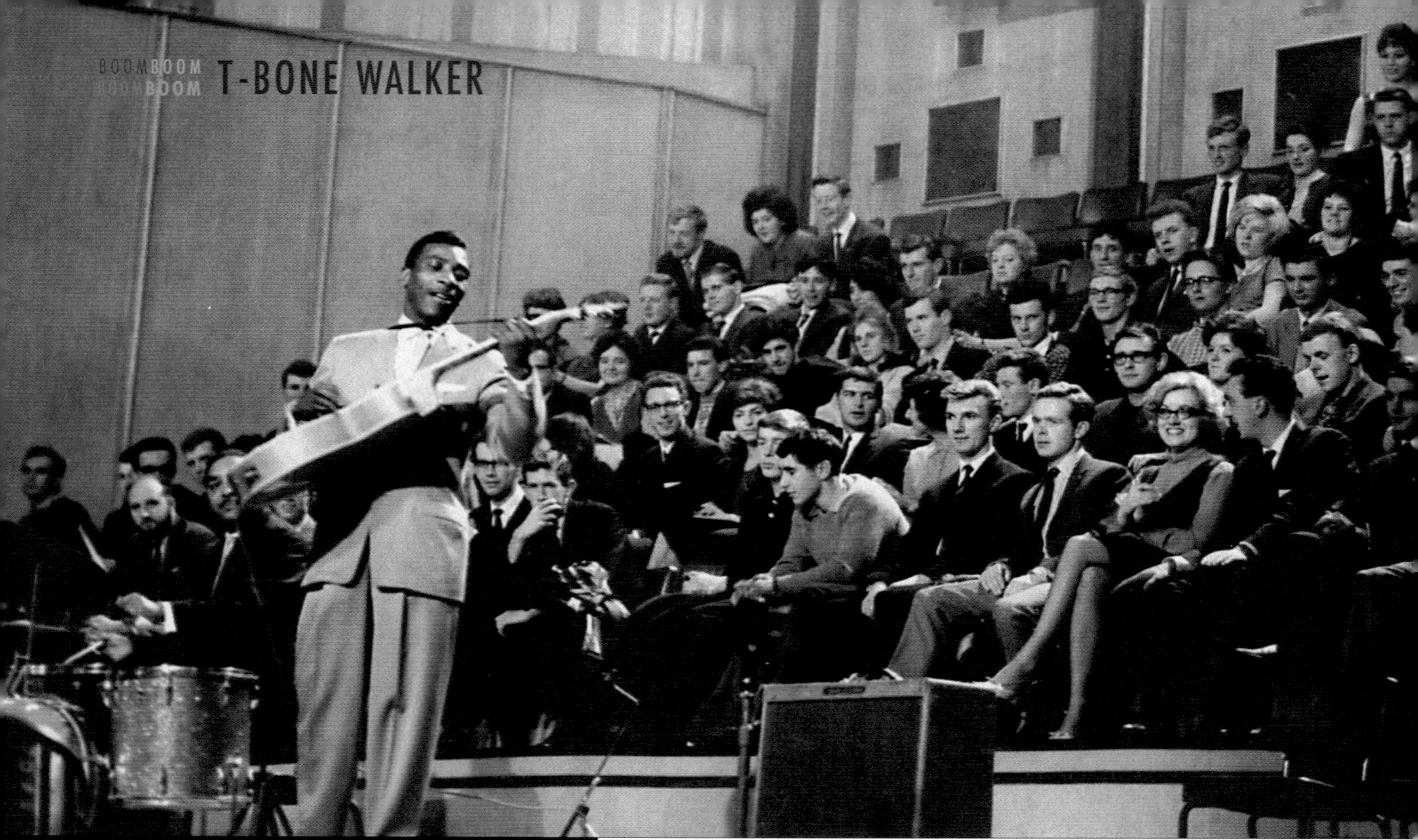

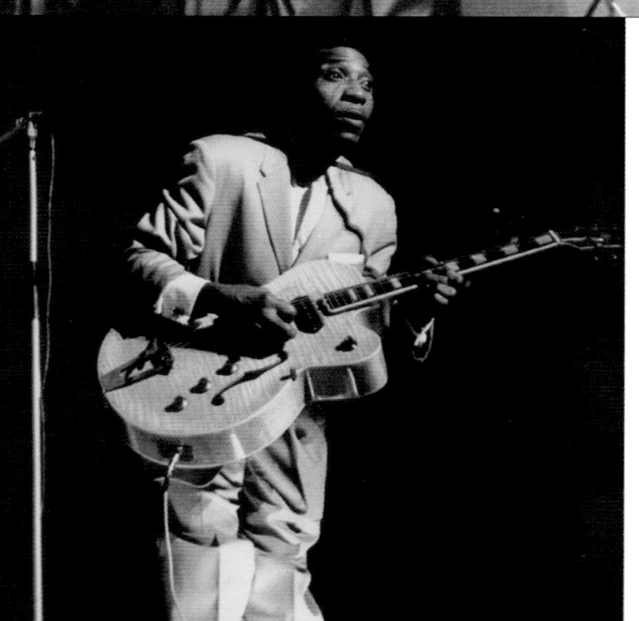

Brian saw T-Bone Walker on the first American Folk and Blues Festival in 1962, and this evocative picture above shows him in action on the big stage, with some of the audience sat in the raked seating behind, normally used for the orchestra. The show was being filmed by ABC TV (not Granada as many sources claim).

Walker came back to Manchester three years later to play The Twisted Wheel for the first time on March 27th 1965. This time Brian was able to take a few great portraits of this influential guitarist lurking in various corners of the club, and seen over the next three pages. Walker did return to play the Wheel again after it had moved to its new home.

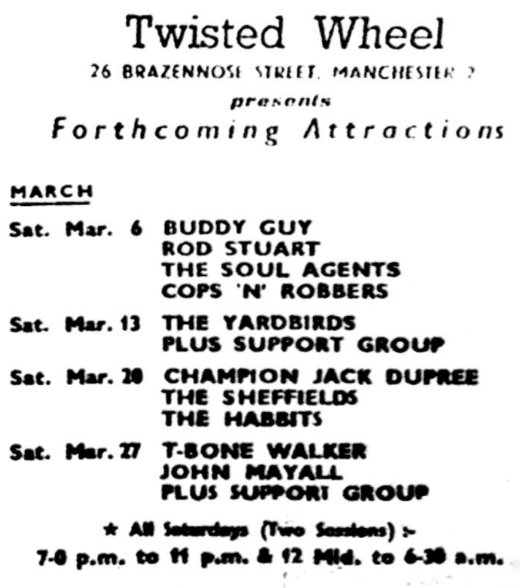

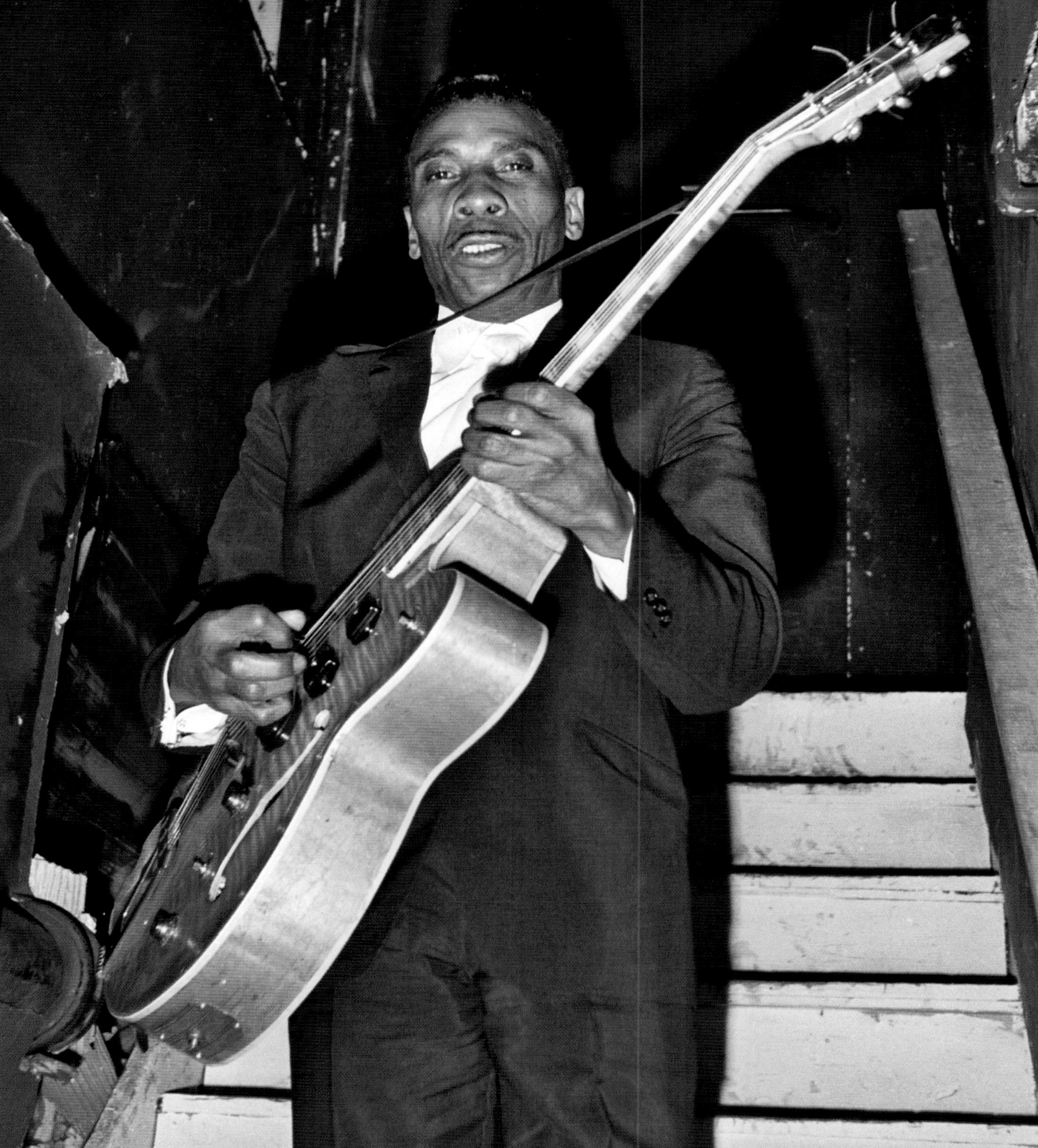

 # T-BONE WALKER

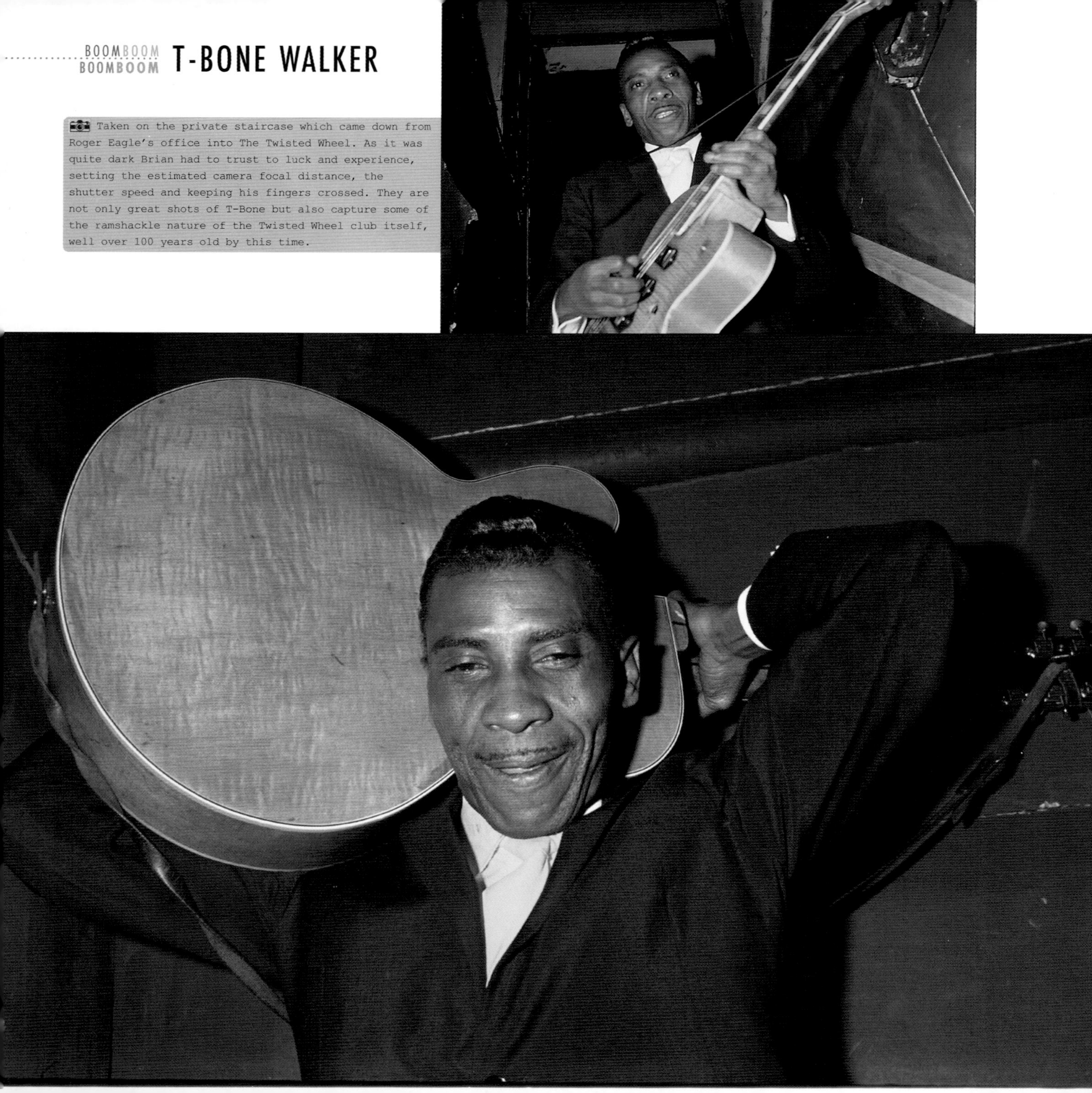

Taken on the private staircase which came down from Roger Eagle's office into The Twisted Wheel. As it was quite dark Brian had to trust to luck and experience, setting the estimated camera focal distance, the shutter speed and keeping his fingers crossed. They are not only great shots of T-Bone but also capture some of the ramshackle nature of the Twisted Wheel club itself, well over 100 years old by this time.

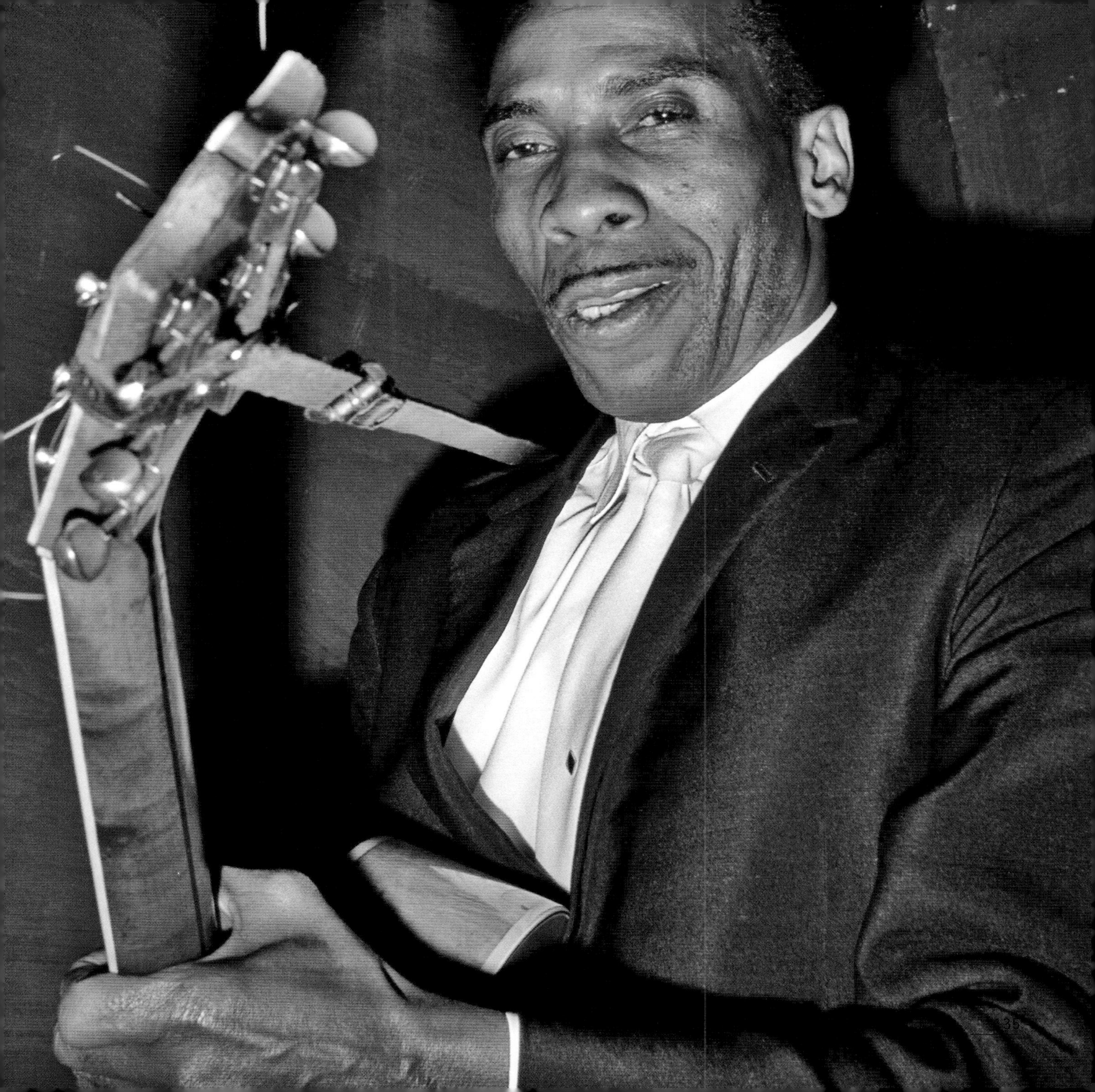

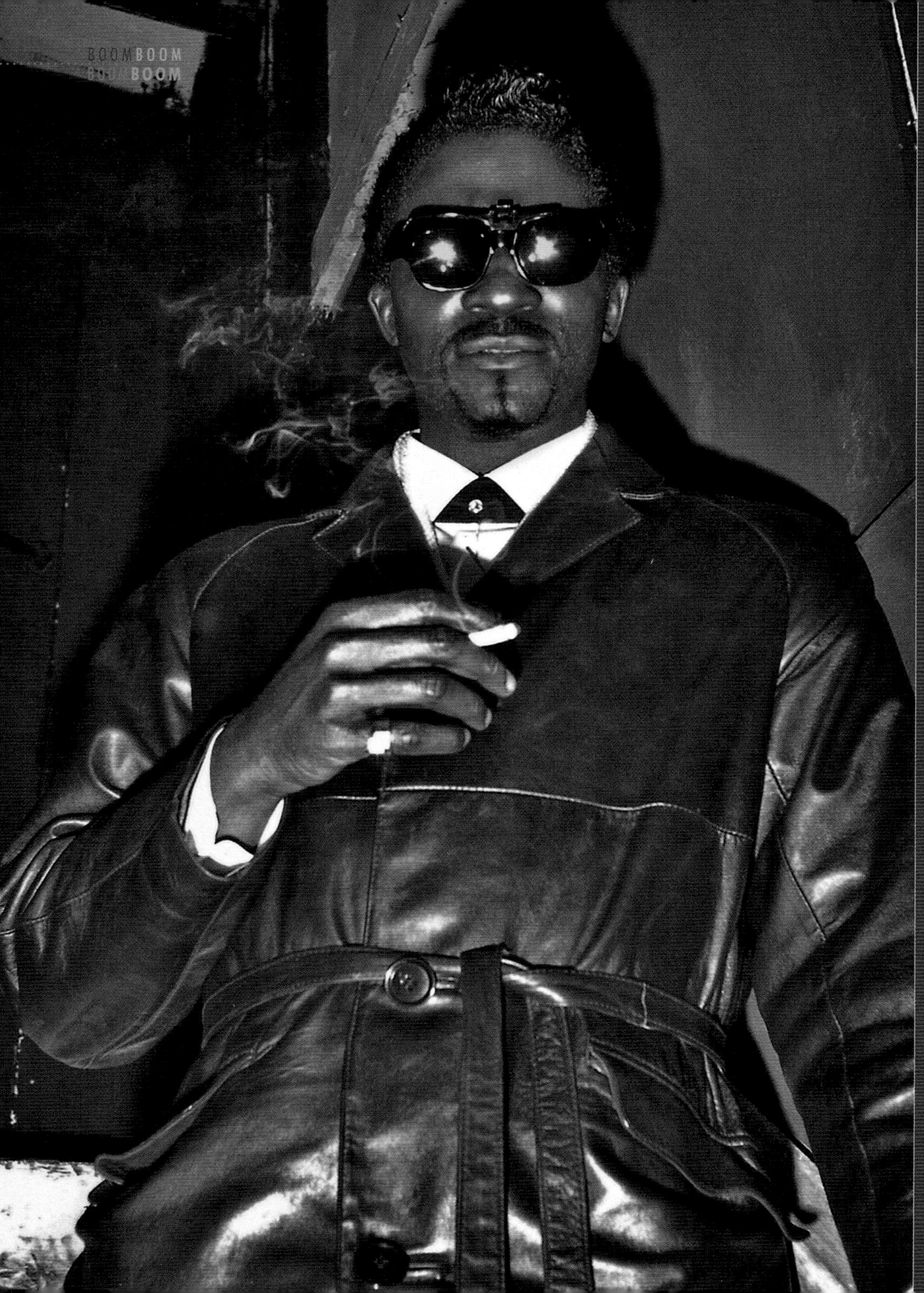

SCREAMING JAY HAWKINS

If we ran a 'coolest looking dude in the book' competition you would put money on Screaming Jay Hawkins to win. He had already created a stir at London airport when he and his modest entourage arrived. Clad in his exotic garb, with an even more exotic looking wife, plus his voodoo accessories, it was not your average customs job.

In the somewhat down at heel surroundings of the Twisted Wheel Club, Hawkins looked like he'd landed from another planet. Brian bravely battled on and this remarkable portrait was taken (like the one of T-Bone Walker) on the private staircase leading down from Roger Eagle's office. Not surprisingly when the designers of a book on the history of The Wheel were looking for their cover star, they didn't need to look any further.

On this occasion Hawkins was just along for a visit, as his friend Walker was playing that evening. The audience spotted him, so it wasn't long before Walker invited Hawkins on-stage (page 138) where he did a rousing version of the Bobby Lewis number *Mumbles Blues*. *"It saved T-Bone's set,"* reckons Brian. *"It had been a bit lukewarm up to then to be honest, which was unusual."*

Hawkins then headlined at the Twisted Wheel on February 20. 1965, an all-nighter backed by Leigh based Wheel regulars The Beat Boys, now renamed Ronnie Carr's Blu(e) Set (Georgie Fame had started out in Carr's group) and managed by The Abadis (support were The Falling Leaves). Hawkins did tracks including *I Put a Spell On You* and *I Hear Voices*, records frequently played by Roger Eagle at the club. *Picture Of A Man* and *The Whammy* are also remembered from the set. Hawkins, on a short UK tour, was quickly booked to return to the Wheel in April.

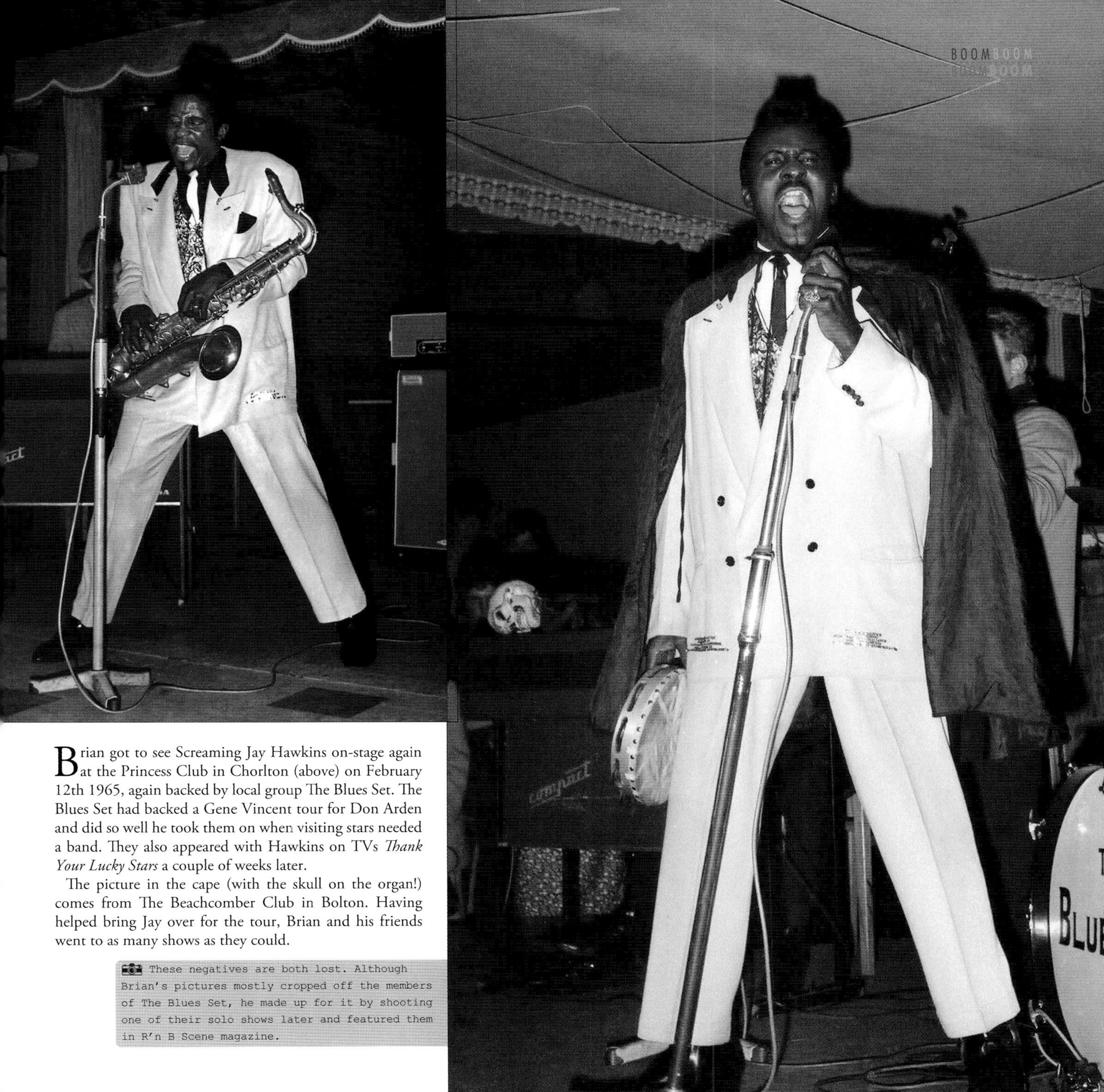

Brian got to see Screaming Jay Hawkins on-stage again at the Princess Club in Chorlton (above) on February 12th 1965, again backed by local group The Blues Set. The Blues Set had backed a Gene Vincent tour for Don Arden and did so well he took them on when visiting stars needed a band. They also appeared with Hawkins on TVs *Thank Your Lucky Stars* a couple of weeks later.

The picture in the cape (with the skull on the organ!) comes from The Beachcomber Club in Bolton. Having helped bring Jay over for the tour, Brian and his friends went to as many shows as they could.

These negatives are both lost. Although Brian's pictures mostly cropped off the members of The Blues Set, he made up for it by shooting one of their solo shows later and featured them in R'n B Scene magazine.

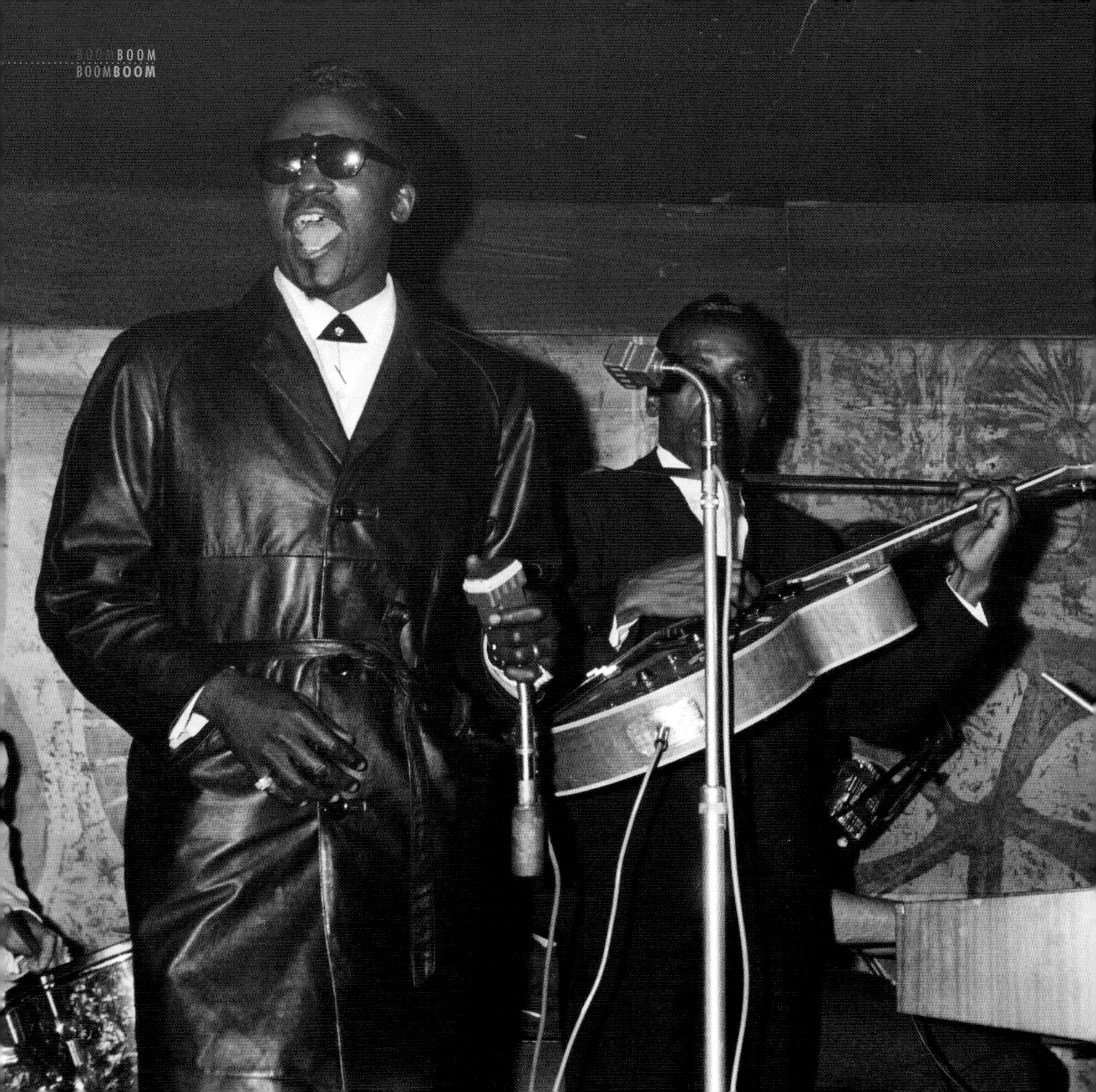

BOOM BOOM
BOOM BOOM

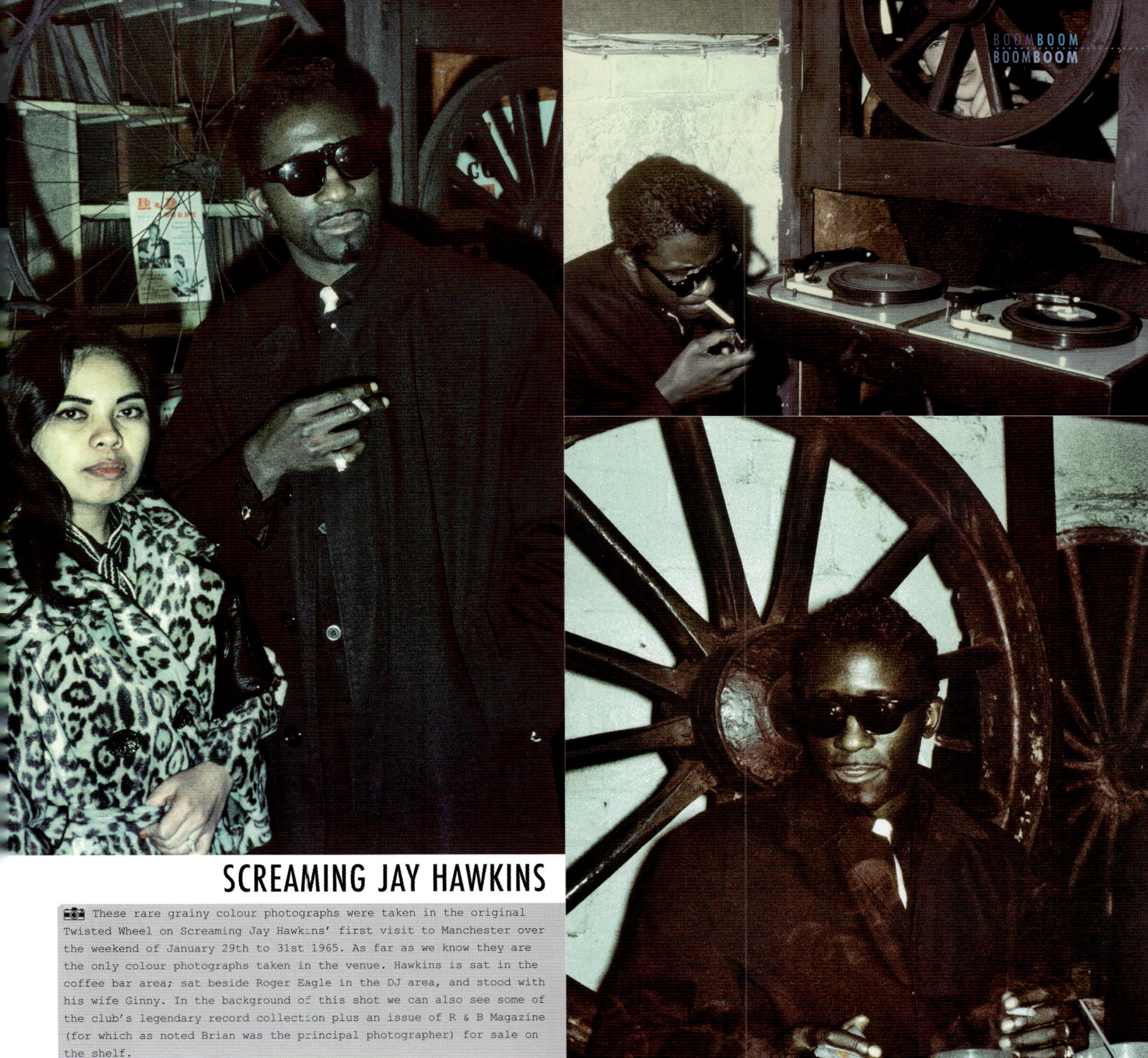

SCREAMING JAY HAWKINS

These rare grainy colour photographs were taken in the original Twisted Wheel on Screaming Jay Hawkins' first visit to Manchester over the weekend of January 29th to 31st 1965. As far as we know they are the only colour photographs taken in the venue. Hawkins is sat in the coffee bar area; sat beside Roger Eagle in the DJ area, and stood with his wife Ginny. In the background of this shot we can also see some of the club's legendary record collection plus an issue of R & B Magazine (for which as noted Brian was the principal photographer) for sale on the shelf.

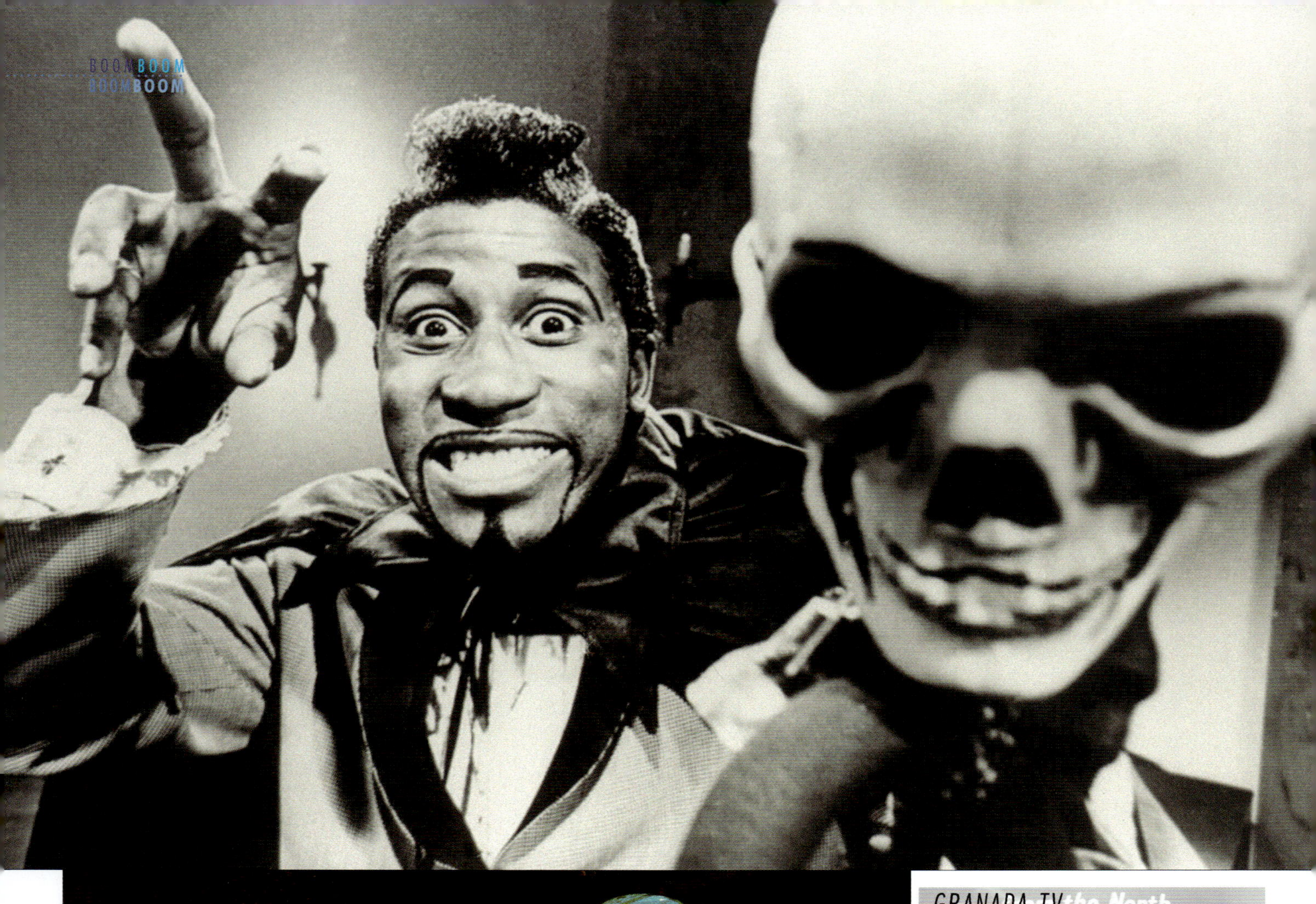

GRANADA TV in the North

On another visit to the North West, Granada were able to get Hawkins into their Quay Street studio for a TV spot on *Late Scene* and Brian was able to take a couple of (now lost) frames during the sound-check (above and opposite). It's not hard to see how much Hawkins influenced Arthur Brown and before that Screaming Lord Sutch (snapped here with Hawkins by Brian), who were both happy to cite him as a big influence in their stage performances.

SCREAMING JAY HAWKINS

This is a great shot, set-up by Brian at the hotel on January 26th and then taken by Roger Eagle as an unusual portrait. *"His manager John Cann had laid on a little reception do at the hotel for the press,"* says Brian. Screaming Jay Hawkins had actually come through customs with this strange skull stick; no wonder he had caused a stir!

It made such a great image that R & B Scene magazine used it on their cover (see page 19). The contrast between Brian's conservative work attire - cardigan, shirt and knitted tie - and Jay's more exuberant look is wonderful but led to ribbing as Brian points out: *"I have certainly come in for disparaging comments about the cardigan over the years, though fashion experts have told me it was the height of beat fashion at the time, even if it looks a bit grand-dad today!"*

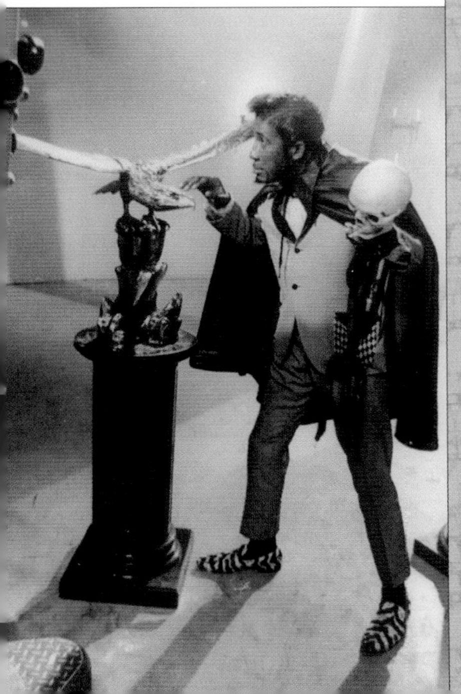

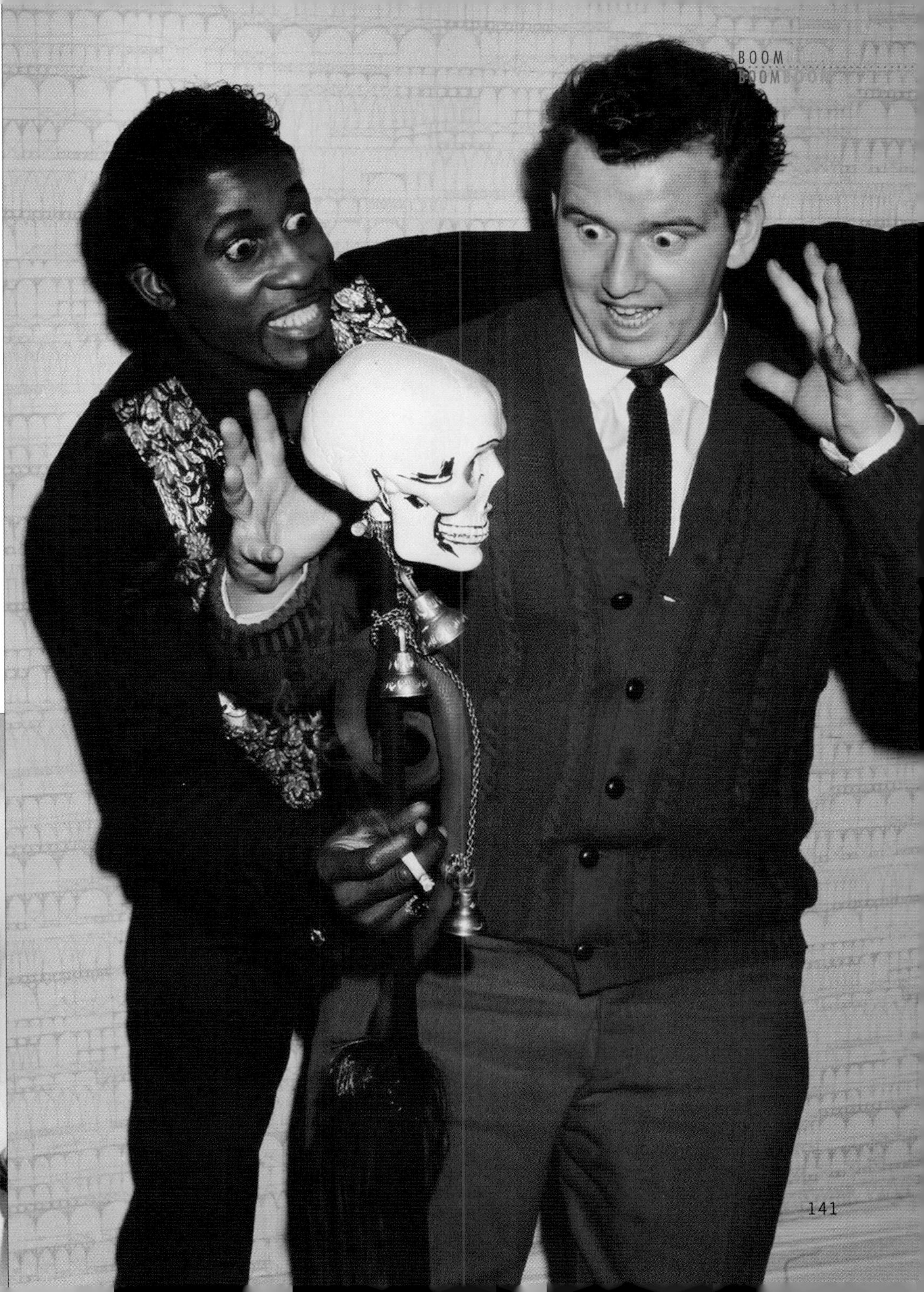

CHUCK JACKSON
GRANADA TV

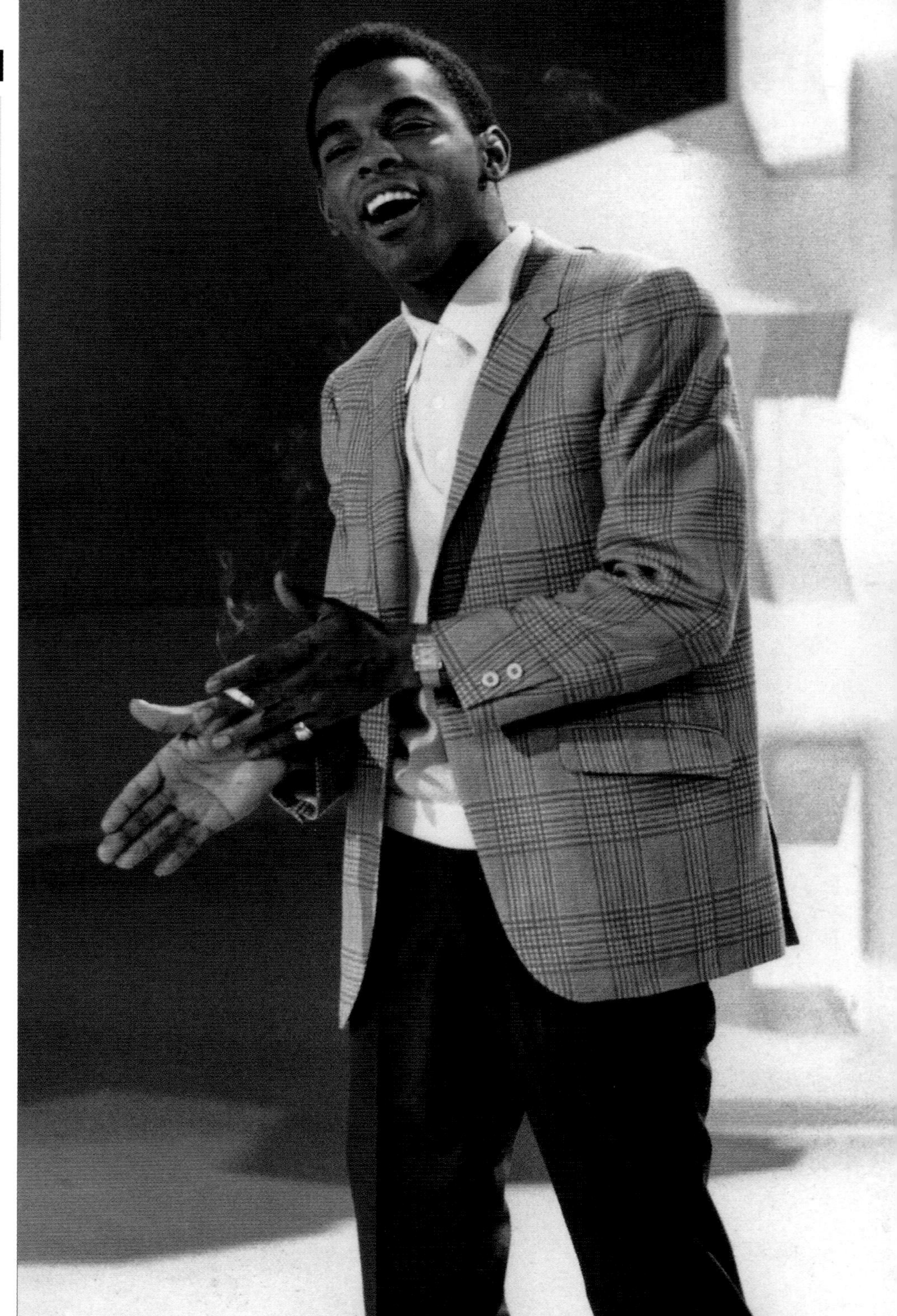

Manchester's local commercial TV station was Granada, who filmed hundreds of musicians from The Beatles on when they were in the area. The footage would usually be slotted in to their early evening news magazine programme *Scene At 6.30* (think *The One Show* but with clever reporting, hip musicians, interesting presenters - Bill Grundy, Michael Parkinson to name but two - and a sensible audience. So, nothing like *The One Show* then). Granada originally covered 'The North' but after Yorkshire TV and Tyne Tees got going, concentrated on the North West. Brian and his friends were often invited to make up audience numbers at the last moment and he was sometimes allowed to take one or two photographs during rehearsals (which survive now only as prints) which took between 3.00pm and 6.00pm. The show was broadcast from 6.30pm to 7.00pm in the Granada region. It had what one critic called *'a very irreverent northern anti-metropolitan feel'* and featured entertainment guests every night of the week. It ran for three years and producer Johnnie Hamp presented a feature called 'Pop Scene' every Wednesday starting in 1964. Bands would use this spot to promote singles weeks before the official release date.

Scene At 6.30 spawned a spin-off called *Late Scene* in November 1963, broadcast at 10.25pm. More laid back it also featured musical guests, sometimes using extra material shot for *Scene At 6.30*. Brian also went to a couple of these: *"The Screaming Jay clip they used was shot for Scene At 6.30 but editors left it out almost certainly because his miming was pretty bad, he'd simply not done much of it and never even sung one of the songs before. When it didn't appear we kept phoning Granada for a broadcast date and eventually they stuck it out on Late Scene. Roger (Eagle) and his girlfriend came round to my Mum's house to watch it as he had no telly!"*

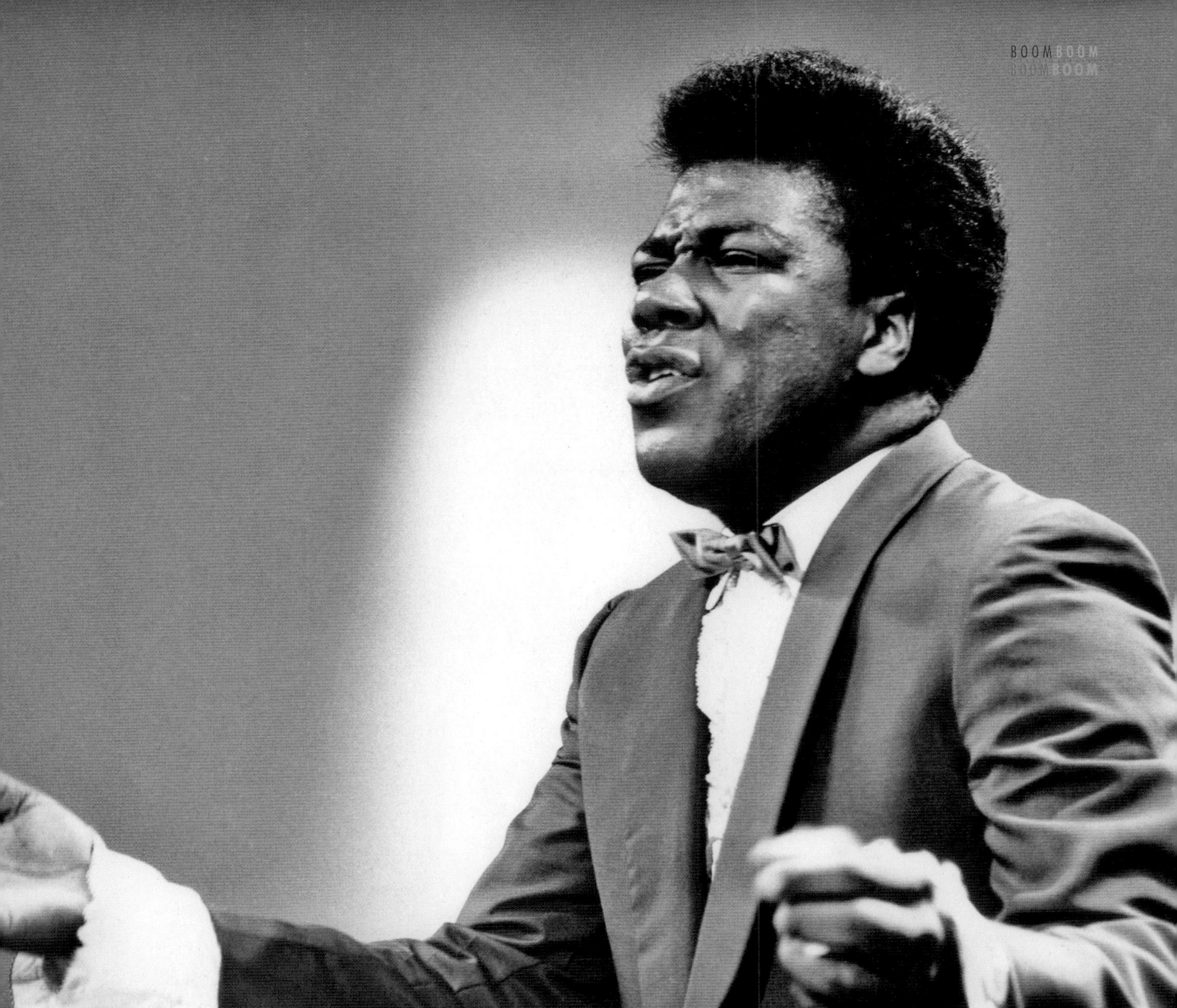

DON COVAY
GRANADA TV

Soul singer Covay is best remembered for his early hit *Mercy Mercy*, and seen here during rehearsals at Granada TV.

We have not been able to date Brian's Granada photographs. Most of the shows were wiped, though a few of The Beatles slots have been rescued from copies used on American TV. The Granada TV archives are returning to the city so may enable more research. Maybe they'll restore the building's iconic red logo while they're at it?

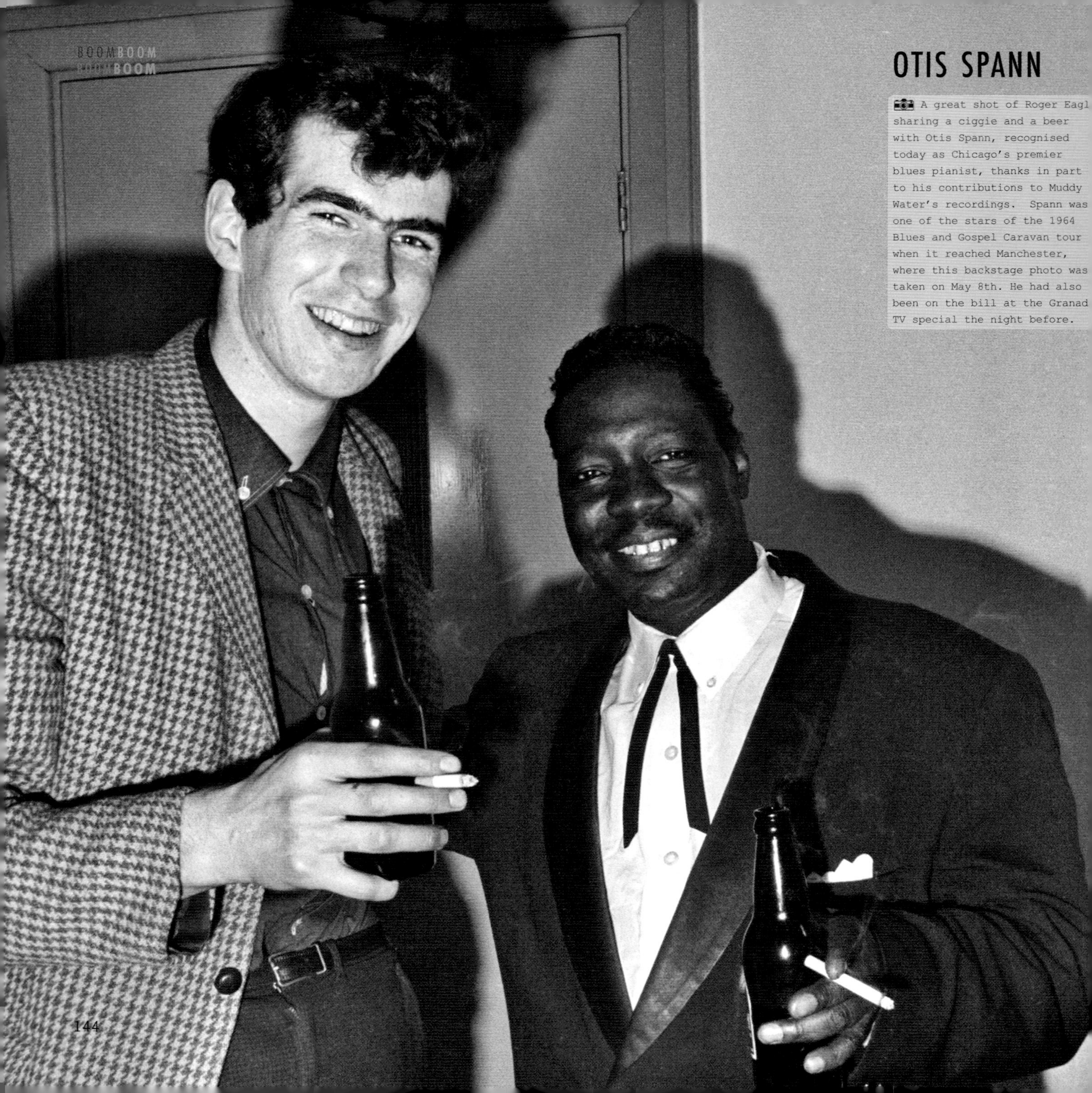

OTIS SPANN

A great shot of Roger Eagl sharing a ciggie and a beer with Otis Spann, recognised today as Chicago's premier blues pianist, thanks in part to his contributions to Muddy Water's recordings. Spann was one of the stars of the 1964 Blues and Gospel Caravan tour when it reached Manchester, where this backstage photo was taken on May 8th. He had also been on the bill at the Granad TV special the night before.

CARTER LEWIS & THE SOUTHERNERS BOOM BOOM BOOM BOOM

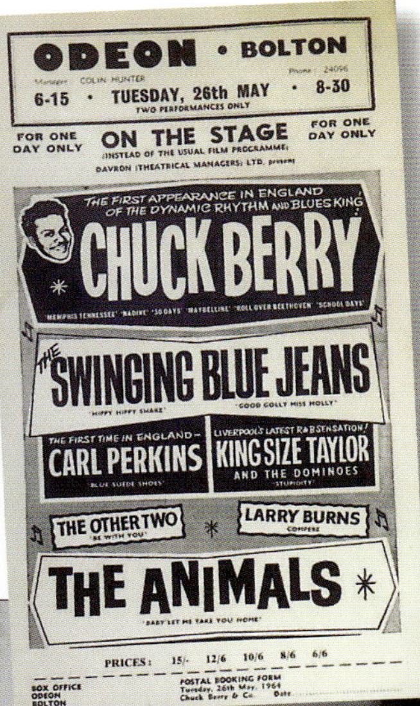

Although the focus of this book is on the visiting Black blues musicians, they rarely toured here in isolation. Many were supported by British acts such as The Animals (as on the flyer here, supporting Chuck Berry), The Rolling Stones and The Spencer Davis Group as well as white American players. All were huge admirers of the American blues musicians and had often begun their careers emulating the music. Brian Smith was a fan of many of the acts and the second part of this book is devoted to these photographs.

Originally a song-writing duo, John Carter and Ken Lewis cut a couple of singles produced by Joe Meek. Using session players to back their radio spots in 1962, they became known as Carter Lewis and The Southerners (after Southern Music, who published their material) in 1962. Lots of musicians came and went, though we think the line-up seen here backstage is Carter and Lewis with drummer Viv Prince in the rear and bass player Rod Clark. They worked on a number of package tours in 1963 and into 1964, before coming off the road to concentrate more on writing and recording.

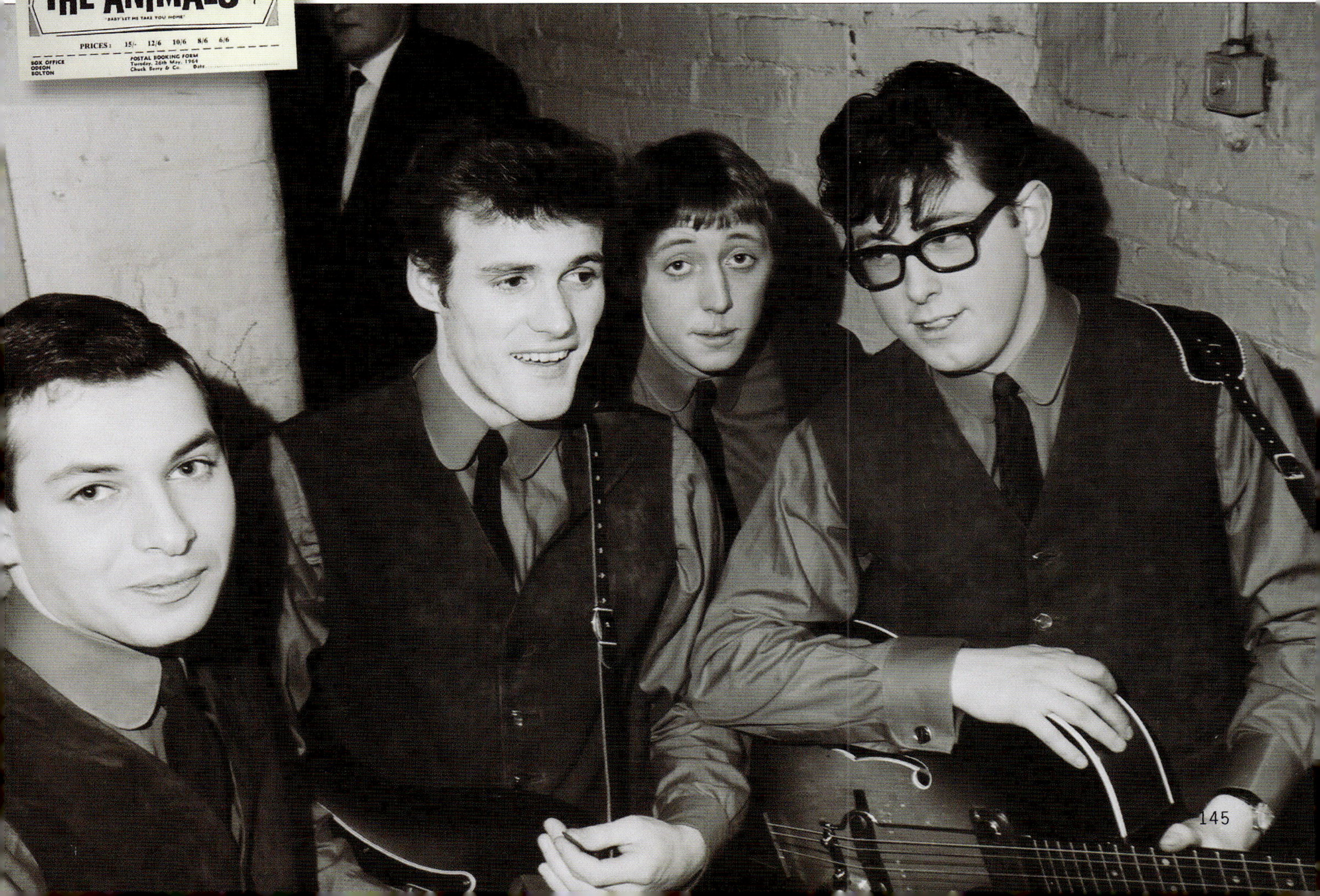

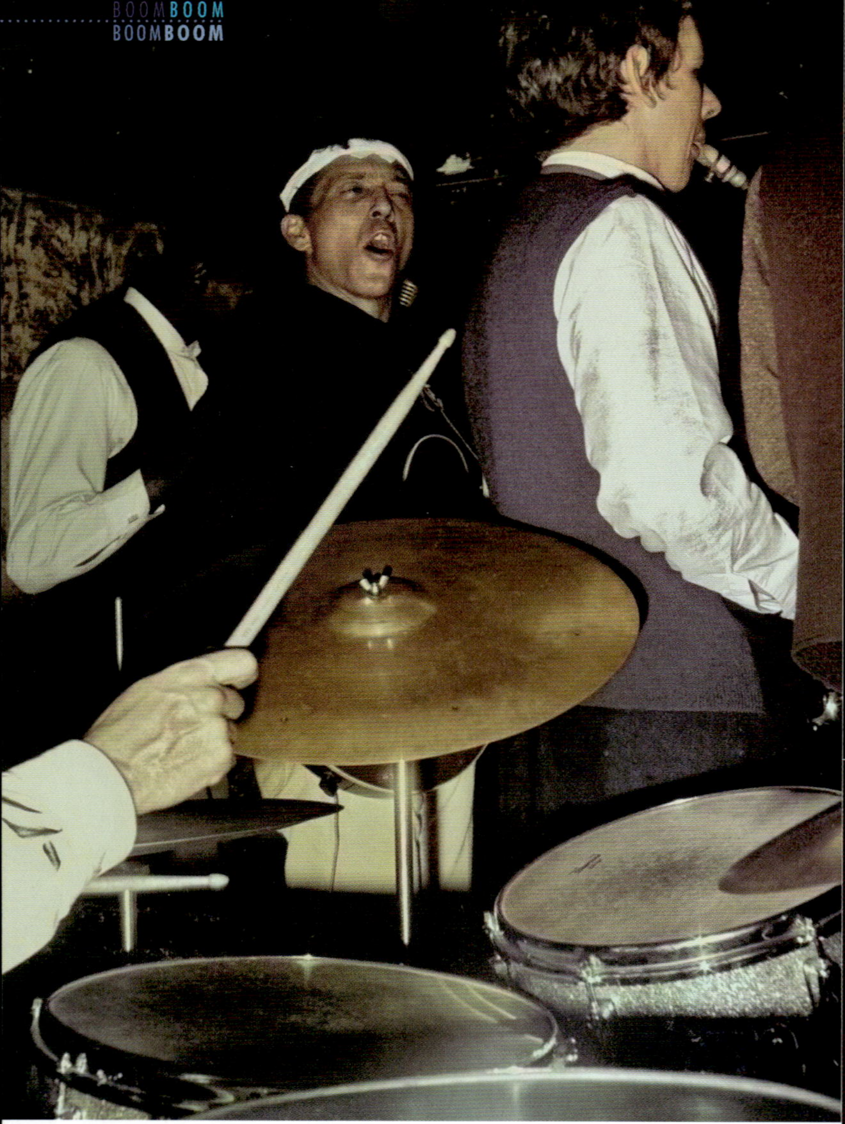

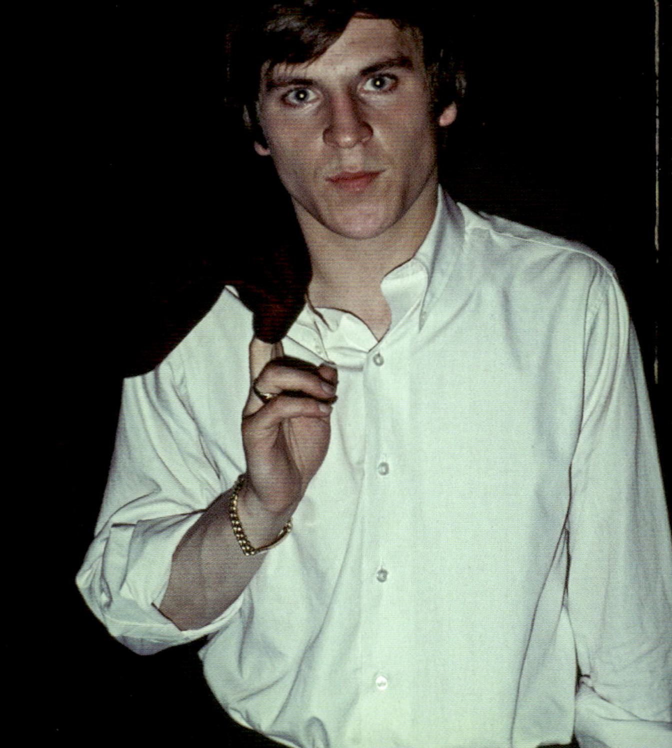

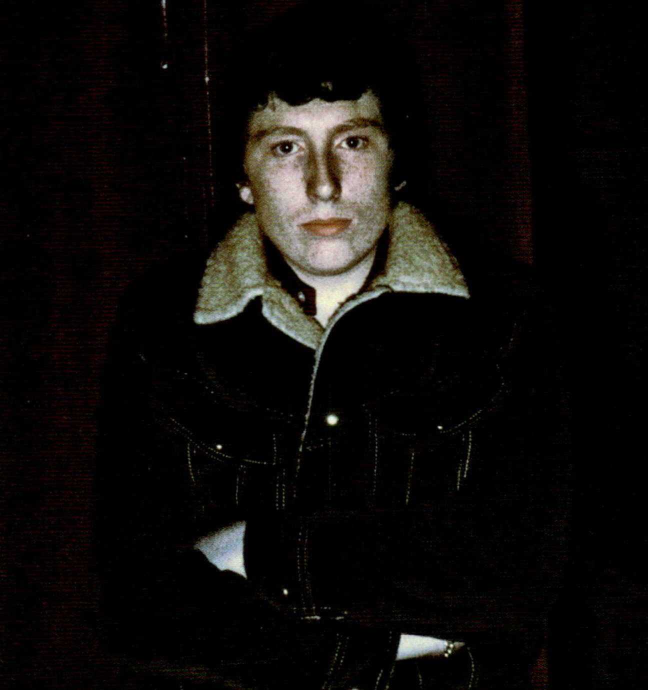

ALAN PRICE, CHRIS FARLOWE, ALEXIS KORNER

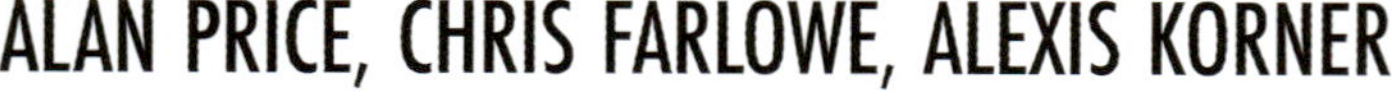 One-off slides of Alan Price (top right) and a very cold looking Chris Farlowe (right). Brian took three shots during the Alexis Korner performance (above) from behind the drum kit at the stage door, two showing the back of his head! This one frame was very underexposed, so has been restored here (and for fun tinted). As Brian said, the book wouldn't seem right without Alexis in.

JULIE GRANT

Singer Julie Grant, in a very mod leather coat and hair do, was added to the first Rolling Stones tour. She had just had a decent chart placing for a single *Up On The Roof* on Pye. But although the label kept releasing follow-ups, Julie found it hard to get proper label support and moved to America at the end of the Sixties to work the busy resort circuit and later run a booking agency. Brian remembers seeing her a lot: *"Julie Grant was never a big star, but she was always around, on a lot of bills and seems to have been well-remembered and well thought-about (and good looking too!). As this pic was on the Stones' first national tour of their own in May 1964, it gets talked about still"*.

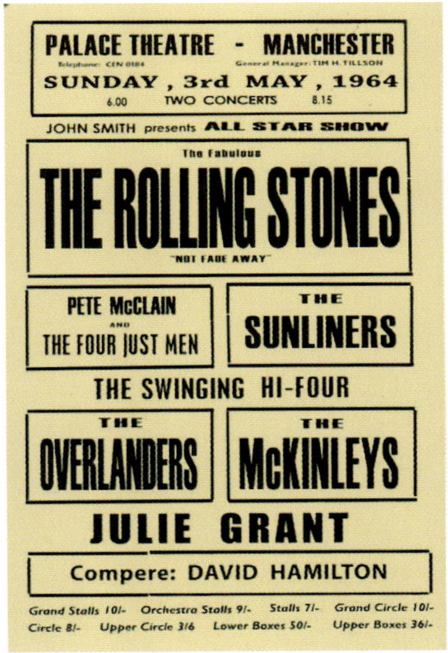

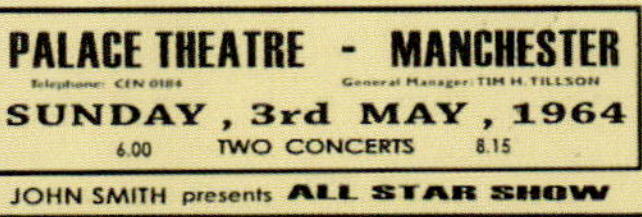

PALACE THEATRE - MANCHESTER

Telephone: CEN 0184   General Manager: TIM H. TILLSON

SUNDAY, 3rd MAY, 1964

6.00   TWO CONCERTS   8.15

JOHN SMITH presents **ALL STAR SHOW**

The Fabulous

THE ROLLING STONES

"NOT FADE AWAY"

PETE McCLAIN AND THE FOUR JUST MEN	THE SUNLINERS

THE SWINGING HI-FOUR

THE OVERLANDERS	THE McKINLEYS

JULIE GRANT

Compere: DAVID HAMILTON

Grand Stalls 10/-   Orchestra Stalls 9/-   Stalls 7/-   Grand Circle 10/-
Circle 8/-   Upper Circle 3/6   Lower Boxes 50/-   Upper Boxes 36/-

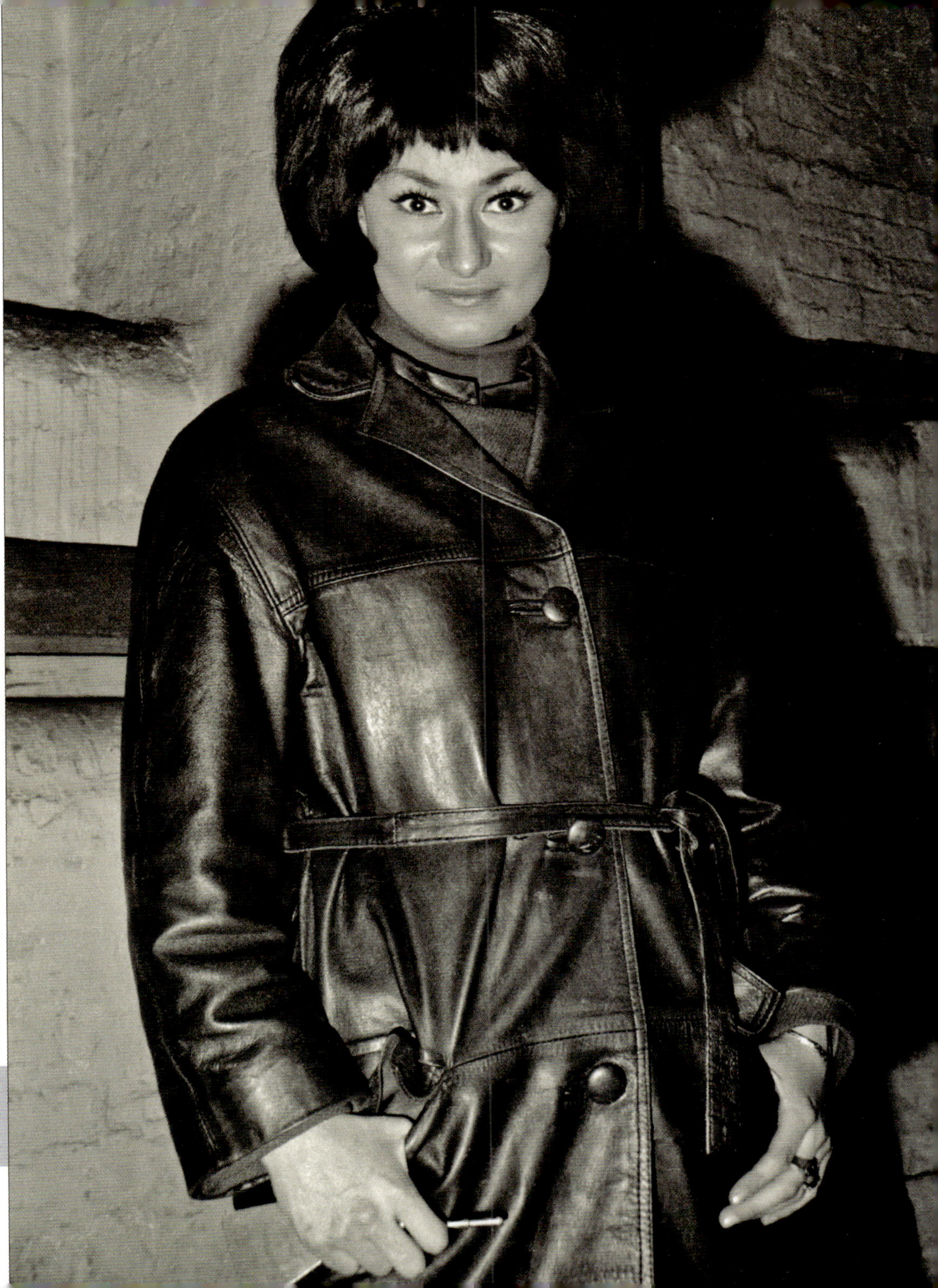

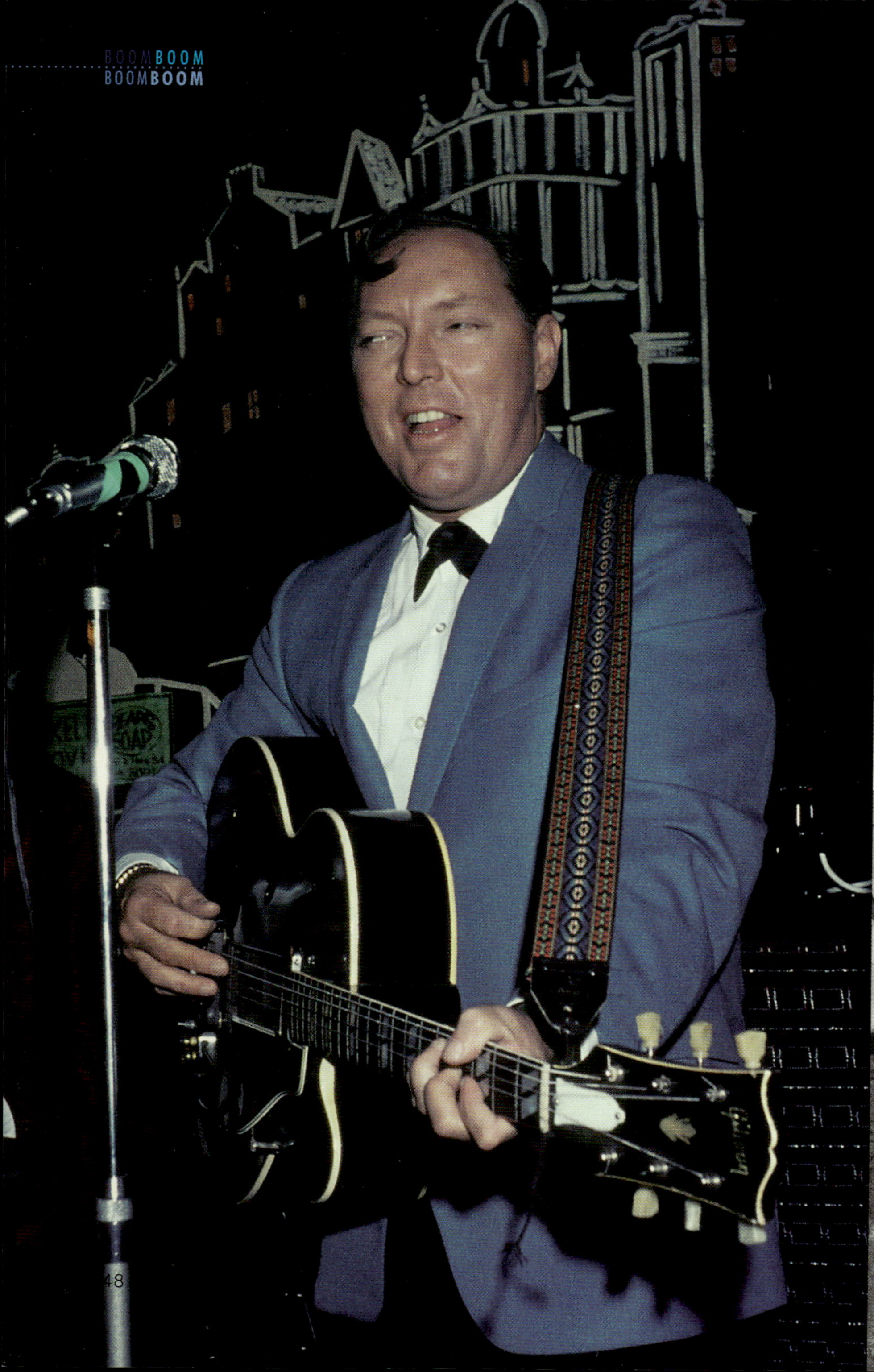

BILL HALEY

The colour photograph was taken at The Carlton in Warrington, the town's legendary night spot run by Bill Medland through the Sixties. Brian had a way in: *"My friend Dave Clarke was the DJ there at the time!"*

The backstage photographs (right) were taken four years earlier in 1964 on what was only Bill Haley and The Comets' second British tour. Brian and a few of the R & B Scene magazine crew got permission to do an interview when the tour came to the Manchester Odeon on October 9th.

"He was a real gentleman," is how Brian recalls Haley, and they were treated well backstage. While the others chatted, Brian took about half a dozen informal photographs which really capture the man's personality. He then took the fan snap of Roger Eagle with Haley's sax player, Rudy Pompilli (below). He had been with Haley since 1955, played on all the early records and worked with him until he became too ill to tour in 1975.

Taken on May 3rd 1968, this colour slide was the last time Brian took a camera to a concert for many years. He got married on June 1st...

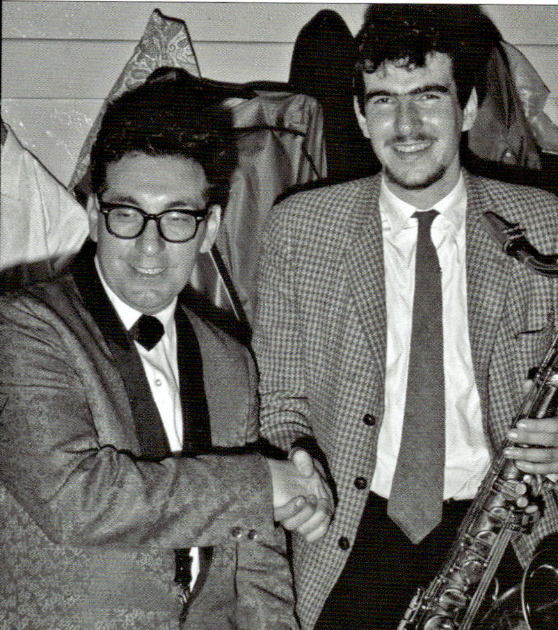

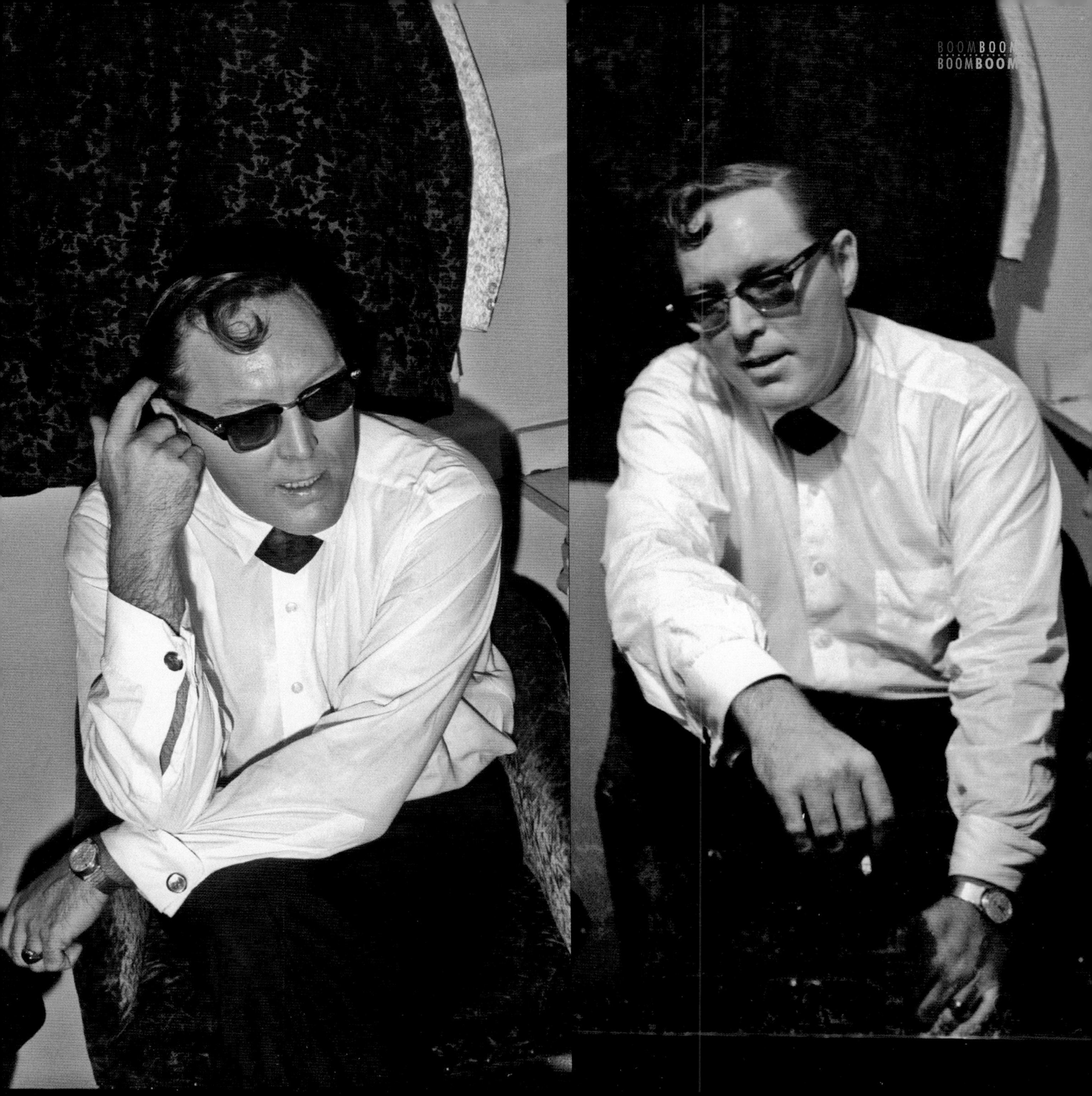

BOOMBOOM
BOOMBOOM

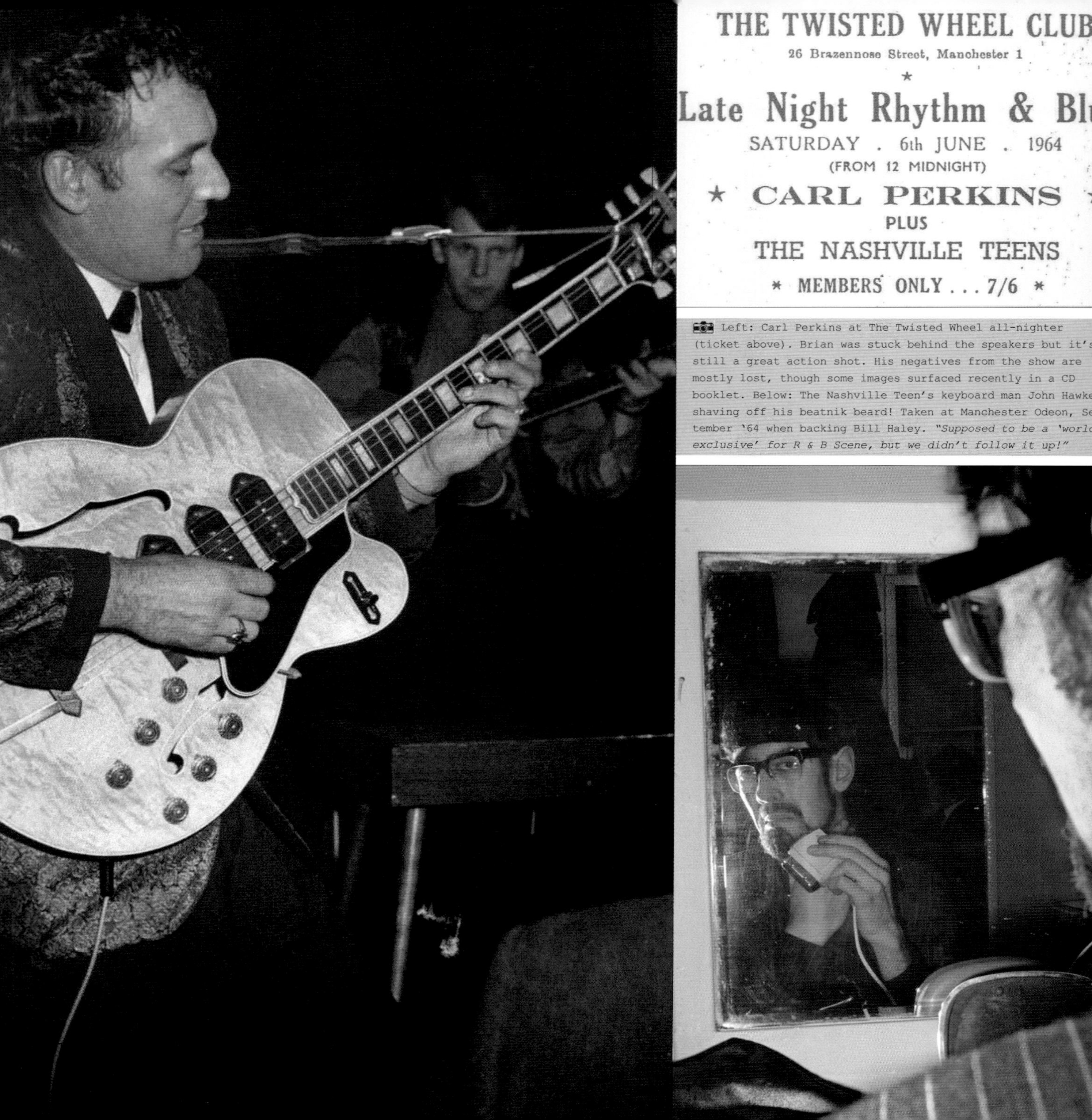

Left: Carl Perkins at The Twisted Wheel all-nighter (ticket above). Brian was stuck behind the speakers but it's still a great action shot. His negatives from the show are mostly lost, though some images surfaced recently in a CD booklet. Below: The Nashville Teen's keyboard man John Hawken shaving off his beatnik beard! Taken at Manchester Odeon, September '64 when backing Bill Haley. *Supposed to be a 'world exclusive' for R & B Scene, but we didn't follow it up!*

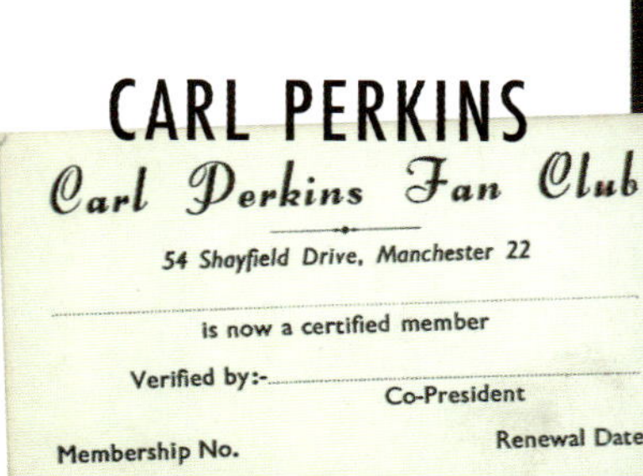

As one of the Million Dollar Quartet back in 1956, Carl Perkins was always assured of a place in rock and roll history. He was one of Brian Smith's favourite musicians, so much so that he persuaded Carl to let him and Dave Waggett start a fan-club together; he still has the hand-written agreement Carl signed for him (complete with Dave's fan art letterhead image done on the train from Blackpool to Manchester).

After the package tour ended, Perkins did three late bookings including the Twisted Wheel (with The Nashville Teens) in June 1964 (ticket next page). It shows the prestige of the venue that a big name would play there just a week after the Hammersmith Odeon. Says Brian: *"There was so little room on The Wheel stage that they set up the pianist John Hawkins elswhere in the room and shouted instructions to each other!"*

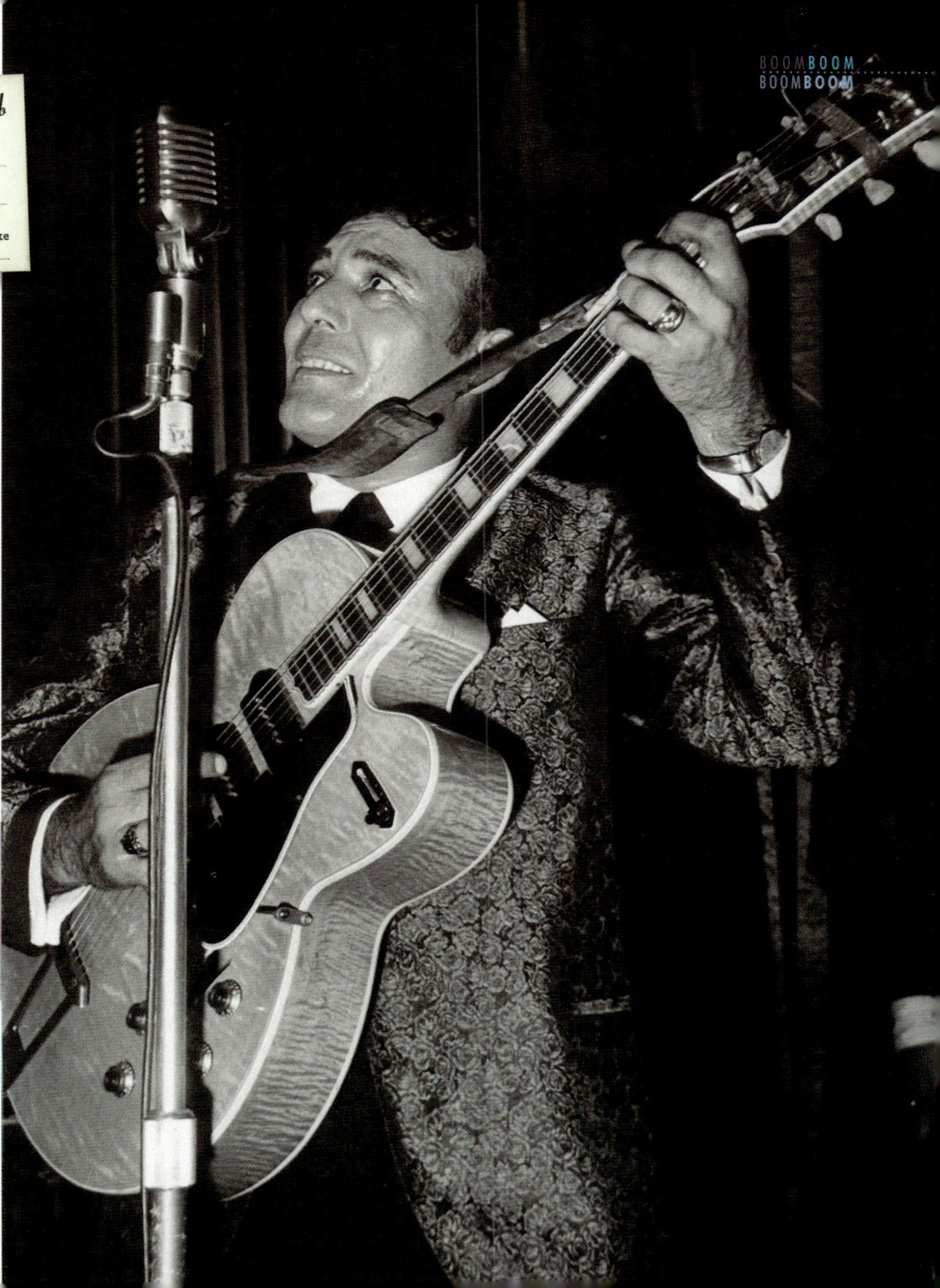

Right: This photograph was taken at the Manchester Odeon in May 1964 and used in the second issue of R & B Scene magazine. Perkins was coming off the stage after his set and the stage curtains had been drawn, when Brian asked him to pose, which is why the guitar strap is where it is. The negative is lost so this was restored from a very scratchy print.

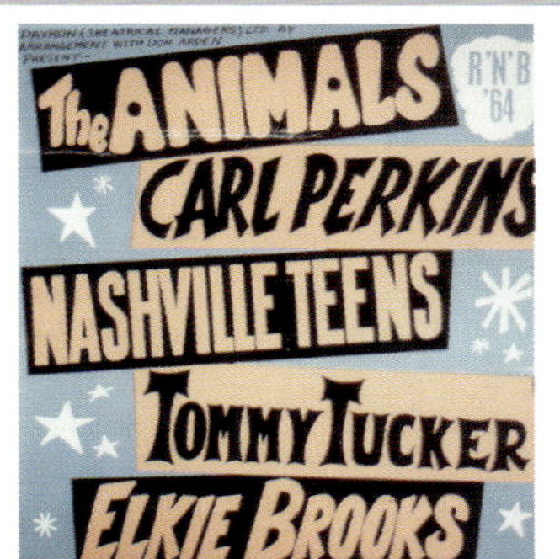

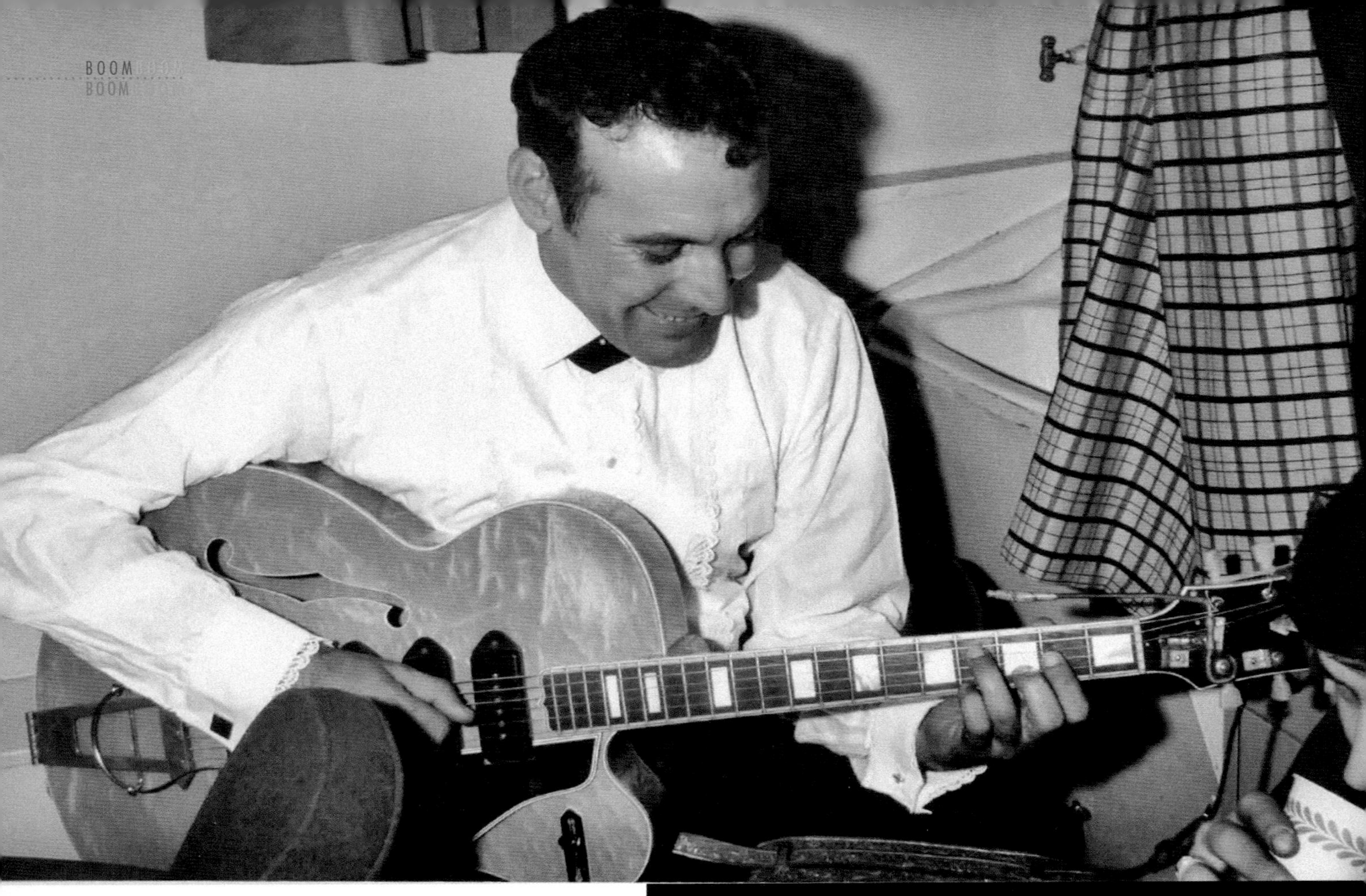

Brian photographed Carl Perkins here at the BBC TV Theatre in Shepherd's Bush during a recording for the pioneering BBC2 programme *Beat Extra* ("*Thirty minutes of non-stop beat and shake*" ran the Radio Times entry for this show, on October 22nd 1964), again backed by The Nashville Teens, who had just scored a huge hit covering *Tobacco Road* and did their own set. "*The Honeycombs and Dionne Warwick were also on. I'd gone down to meet Carl when he arrived the previous day. After the show, me and Carl went for a Chinese at The Lotus House (where we'd eaten on my 21st in June, after visiting Abbey Road to meet the Beatles, recording Carl's song Matchbox).*" Before you ask, that was the one time Brian did not have his camera with him...

CARL PERKINS

In 1964 after a BBC show in London, Brian travelled back on only Perkins' second train journey ever (right) to Manchester for a Granada TV recording. Cash co-headled with his wife June Carter-Cash and Carl Perkins on a UK tour in 1968, seen (below l-r Carl, June and Johnny) at Manchester Odeon.

Brian recently spotted one of his lost images from Perkins' 1964 Twisted Wheel show on this 1975 Italian Sun vinyl compilation. It cost him a tenner to buy back this piece of his history!

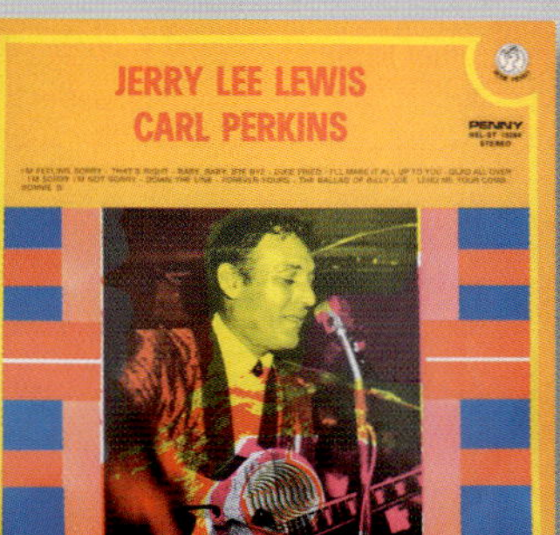

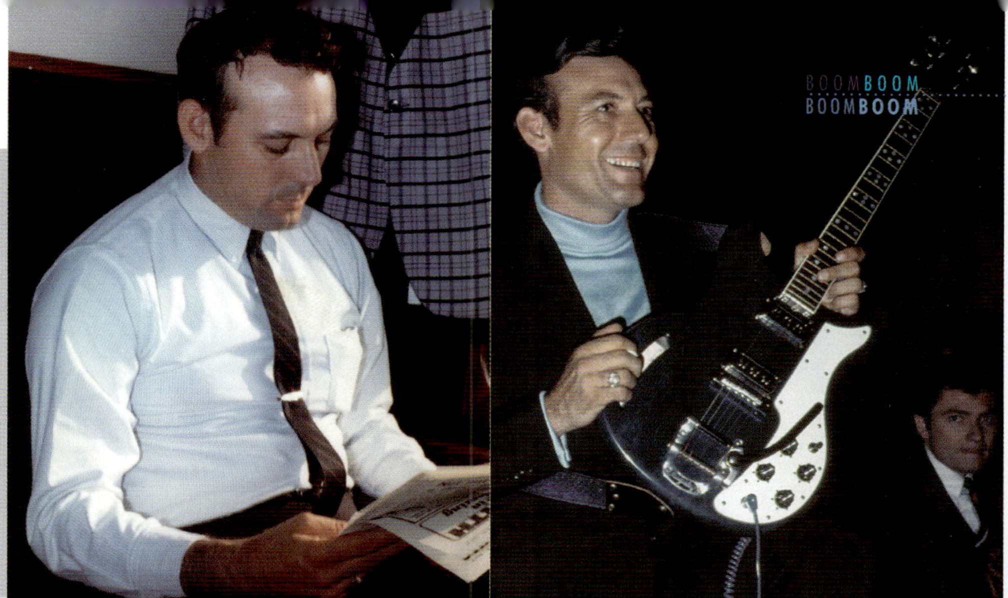

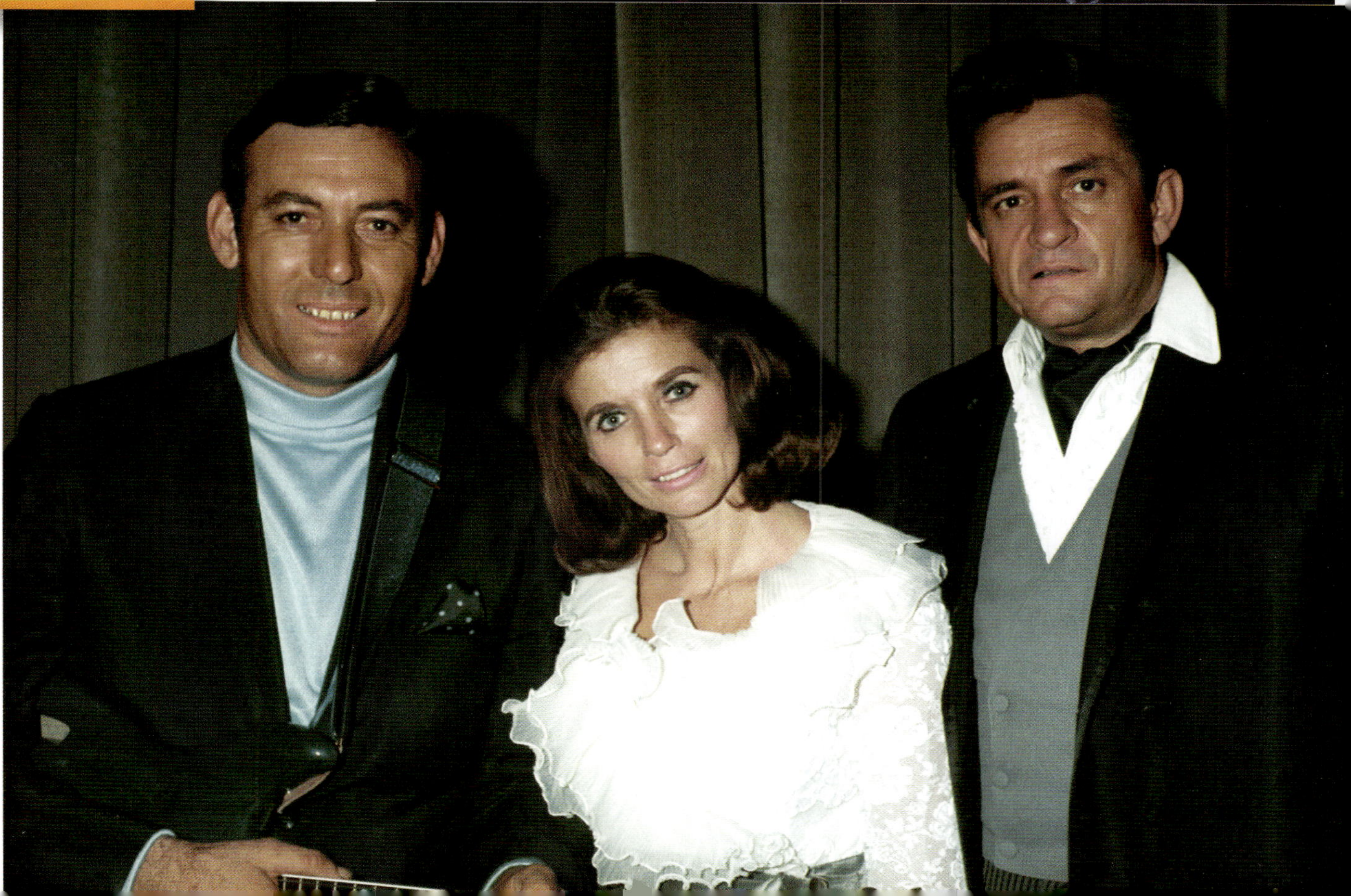

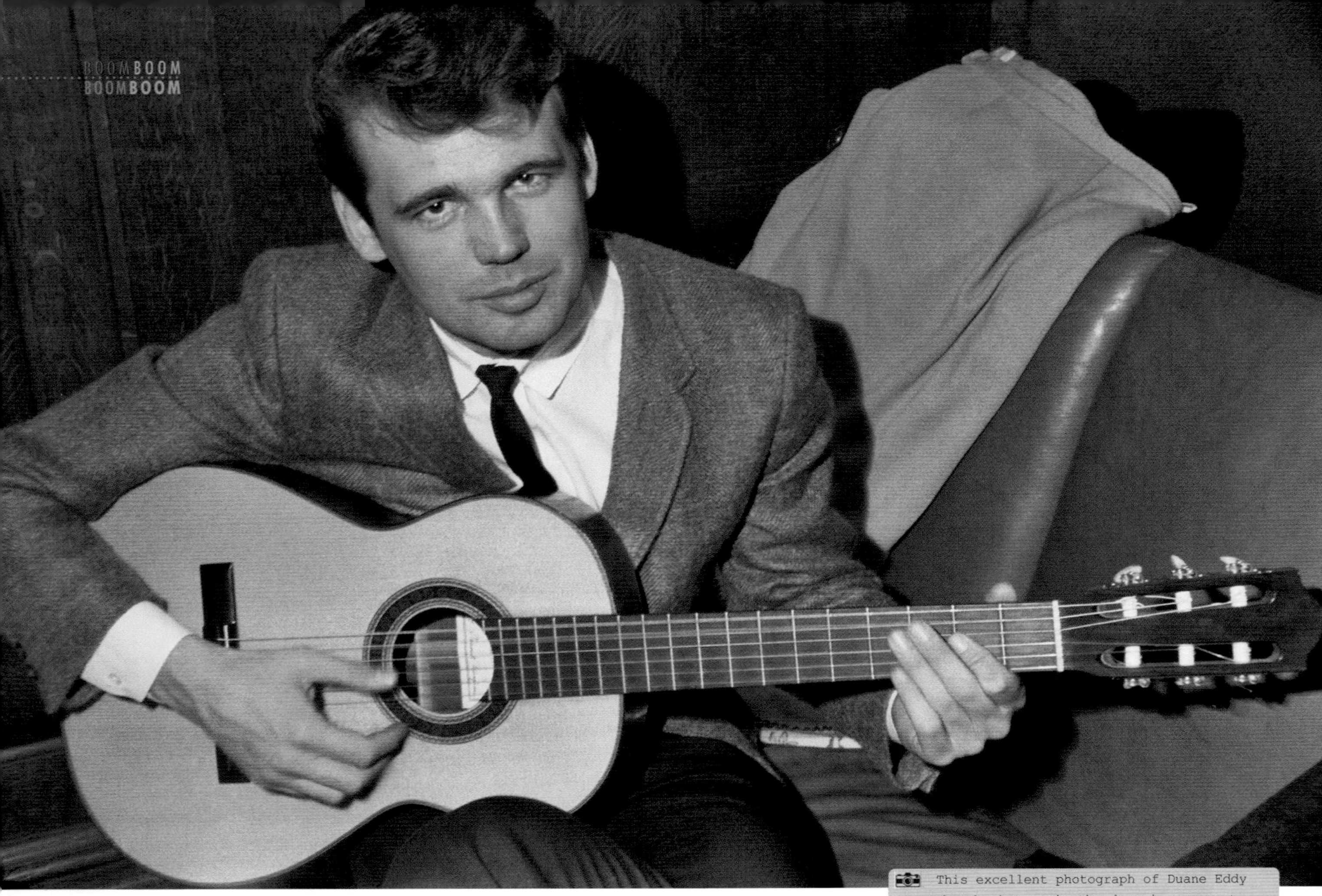

By 1963 Eddy had not played the UK for three years and the monster hits had dried up, but he still had a big following. Eddy brought his own band The Rebels with him but after three shows the Musicians Union heard about it. A particularly brave MU official was given the task of informing promoter Don Arden that, as he had not arranged a reciprocal tour of America for a British group, The Rebels could not continue on the tour.

Arden cast about and found The Hi-Fi's who stepped in at just two days notice. The photograph of them on the next page was also taken in the Sheffield dressing room. It shows Jim Horn, Bob Taylor, the legendary Al Casey (far right) and sax-man Rex Morris (second from left), an ex-jazzer and session man. *"They just gave him the records to learn,"* Brian recalls, being impressed: *"I complimented him on how well he played and he commented that he was costing (Don) Arden enough, so why not?!"*

The photograph of Duane Eddy with The Rolling Stones (overleaf) is unique. Brian went to see Eddy at Manchester Odeon on November 28th 1963. Brian and his mates would usually arrive before a show and ask to see the Odeon manager. *"He was very much the boss in those days. He would then give us the nod and we usually got the run of the building backstage."* What Brian didn't know was that The Rolling Stones were keen to meet Eddy, and were playing the same night at Northwich Memorial Hall. It was only 20 miles away, so they arranged to drive over, say hello, and get back for their show. They watched Eddy's early set from the wings and met up as he came off-stage. *"When it looked like they'd finished chatting, I jumped in and asked to take the photograph. It was very dark, I guessed a standard flash setting and took the shot, hoping for the best."* It was only when Brian then stepped into the brightly lit corridor and spotted Bill Wyman chatting up a girl, that

154

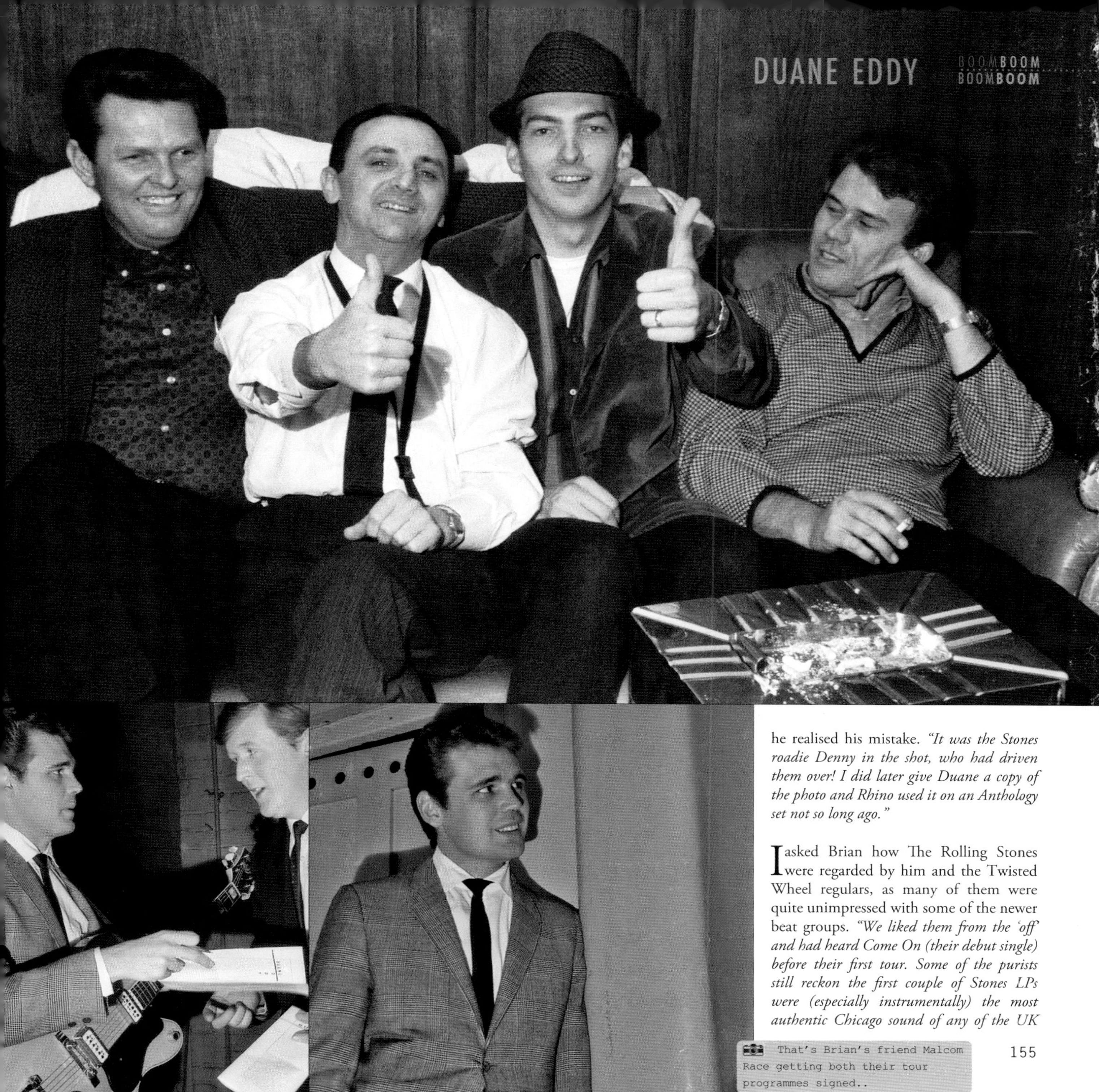

he realised his mistake. *"It was the Stones roadie Denny in the shot, who had driven them over! I did later give Duane a copy of the photo and Rhino used it on an Anthology set not so long ago."*

I asked Brian how The Rolling Stones were regarded by him and the Twisted Wheel regulars, as many of them were quite unimpressed with some of the newer beat groups. *"We liked them from the 'off and had heard Come On (their debut single) before their first tour. Some of the purists still reckon the first couple of Stones LPs were (especially instrumentally) the most authentic Chicago sound of any of the UK*

That's Brian's friend Malcom Race getting both their tour programmes signed..

155

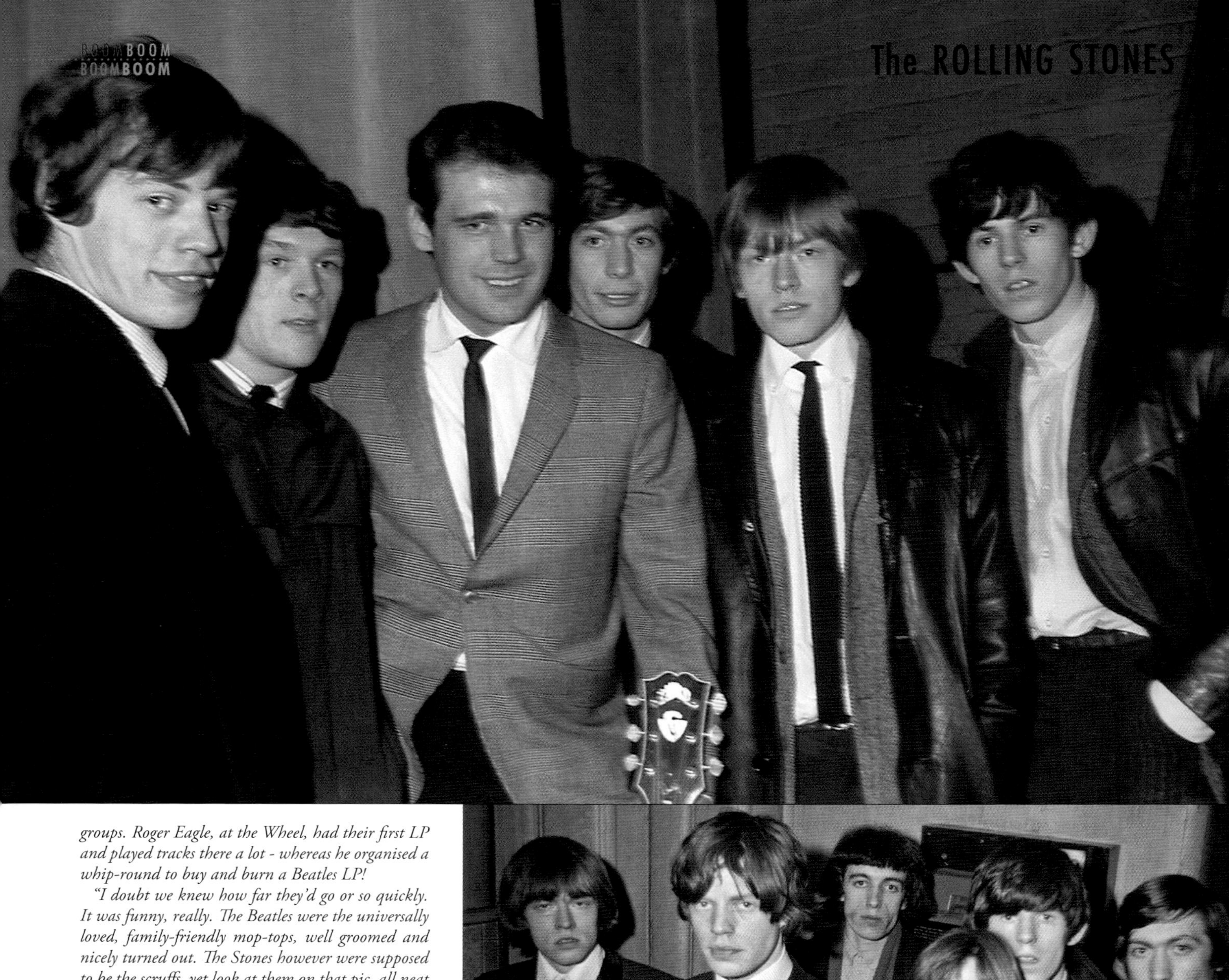

groups. Roger Eagle, at the Wheel, had their first LP and played tracks there a lot - whereas he organised a whip-round to buy and burn a Beatles LP!

"I doubt we knew how far they'd go or so quickly. It was funny, really. The Beatles were the universally loved, family-friendly mop-tops, well groomed and nicely turned out. The Stones however were supposed to be the scruffs, yet look at them on that pic, all neat shirts and suits."

In the photograph right, taken on the The Rolling Stones' own tour in January 1964 at Manchester Palace, the female guest is Brian's sister Val, who he managed to get in to meet the group and have her photograph taken, the envy of her schoolfriends as a result.

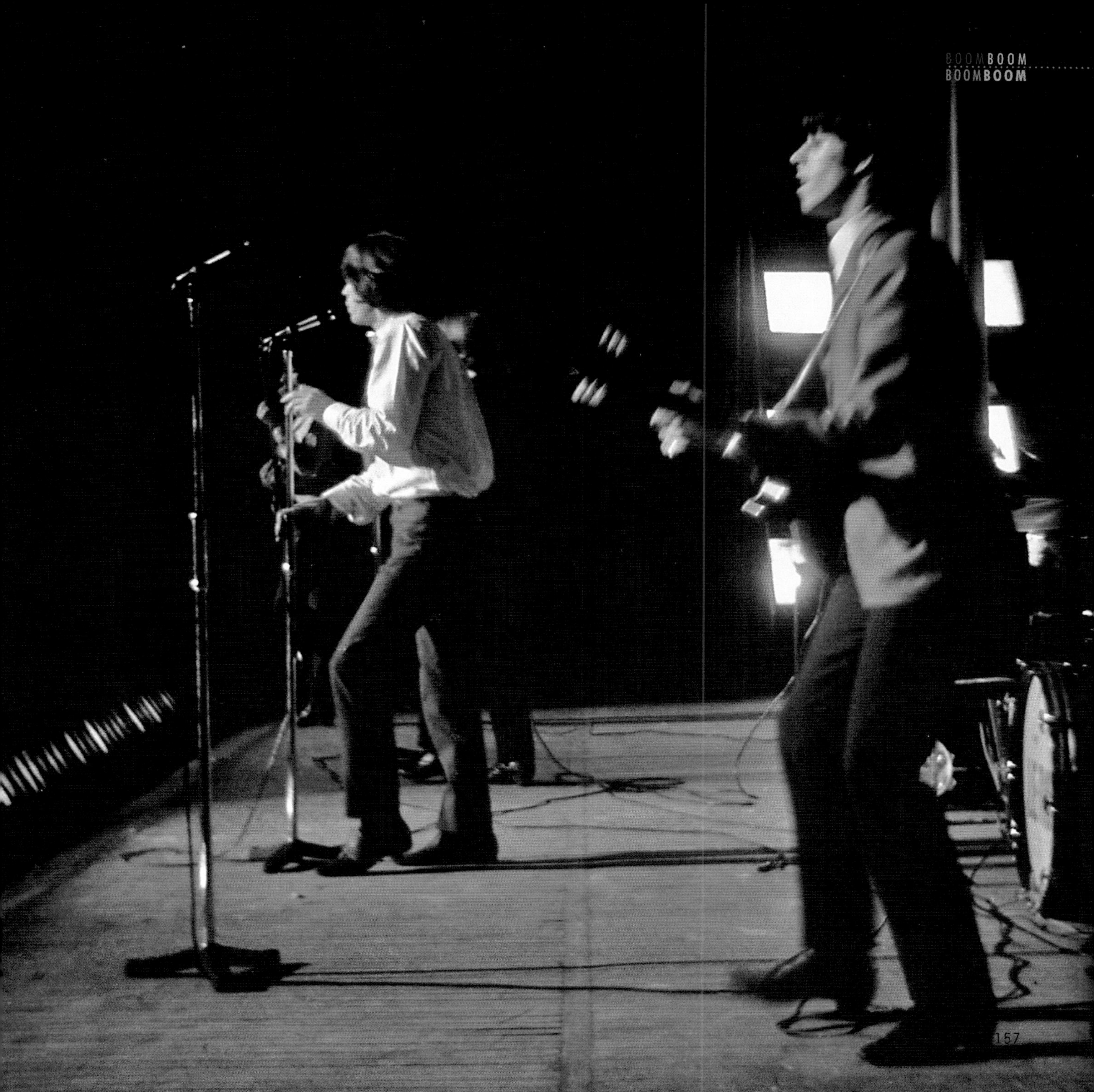

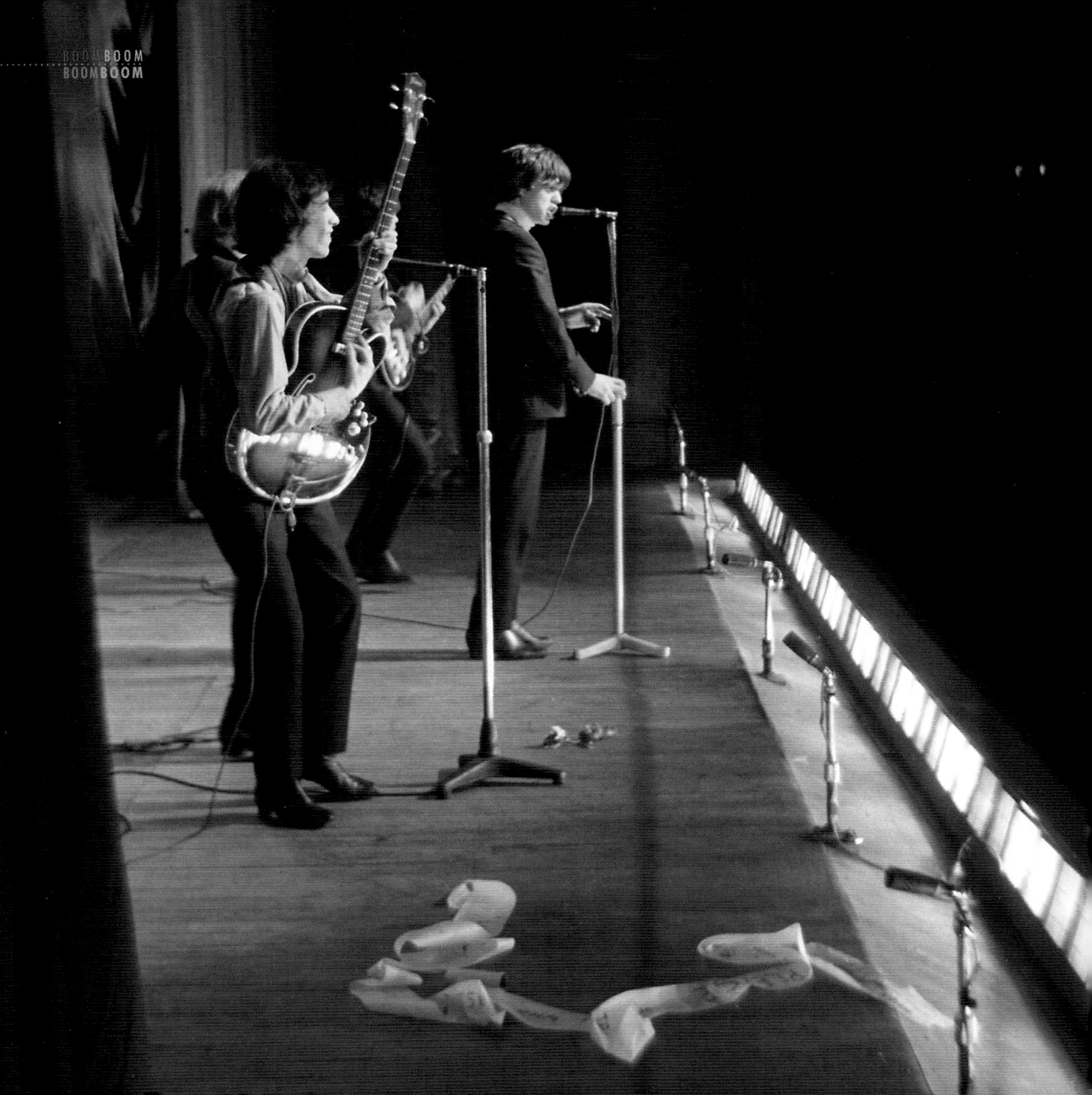
BOOMBOOM
BOOMBOOM

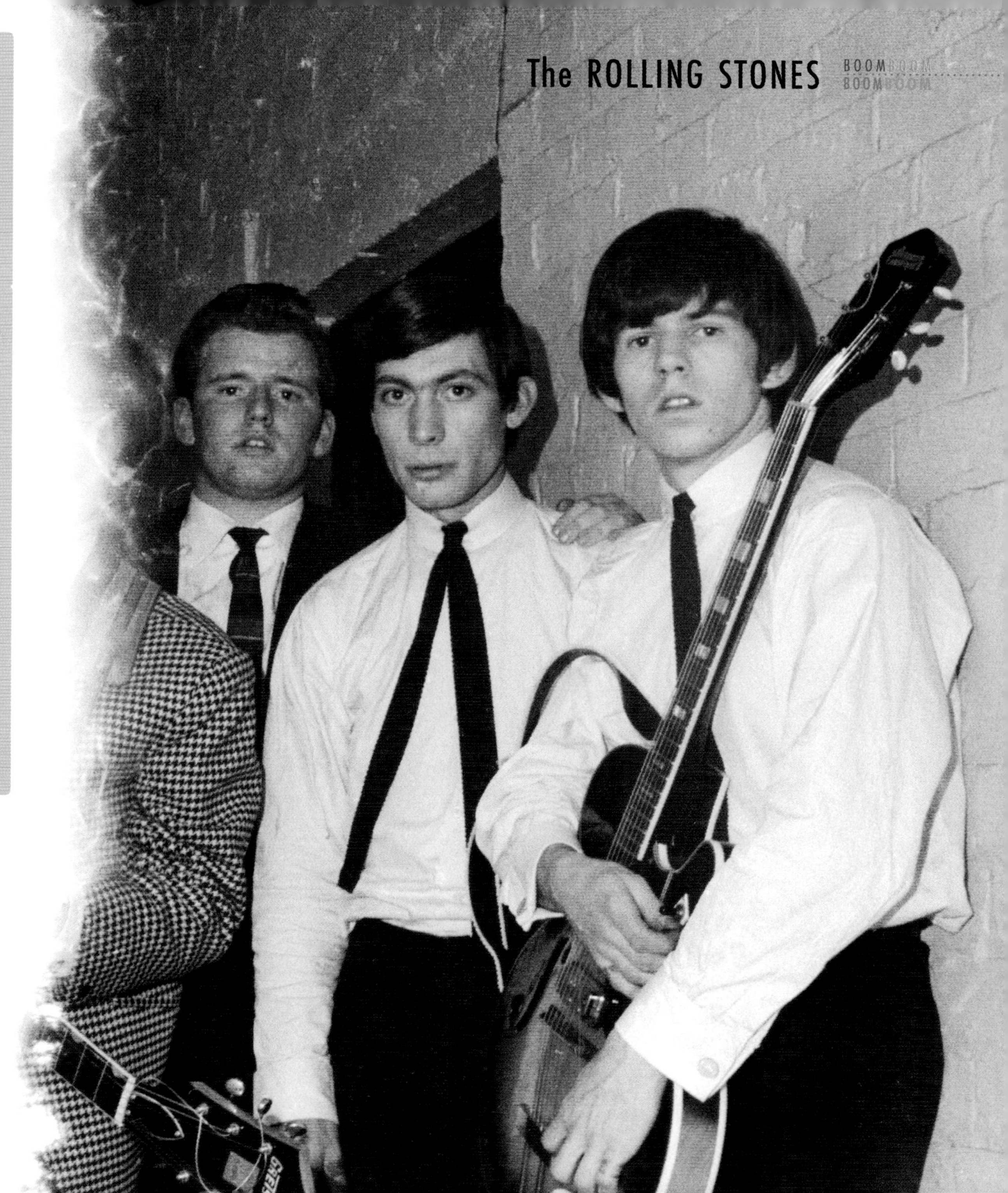

Brian was at the side of the stage for The Rolling Stones on their first headline British tour at Manchester Palace Theatre, May 3rd 1964, which is where the live shot (left) and on page 159 are from. Notice the heart felt messages written on toilet roll thrown onto the stage...!
Brian also caught The Stones as part of the Everly Brothers package tour in October 1963, at Manchester Odeon. This was very much a last minute deal and Brian quickly loaded the only film cassette he had and dashed over to the venue. He took a nice photo of a friend with the group in a corridor backstage afterwards, passing him the camera to return the favour. Brian clearly has a worried look about him, knowing the film was about to run out. Old school photographers everywhere will recognise that dreaded edge of the film cassette fogging... so here is Brian, with HALF The Rolling Stones!

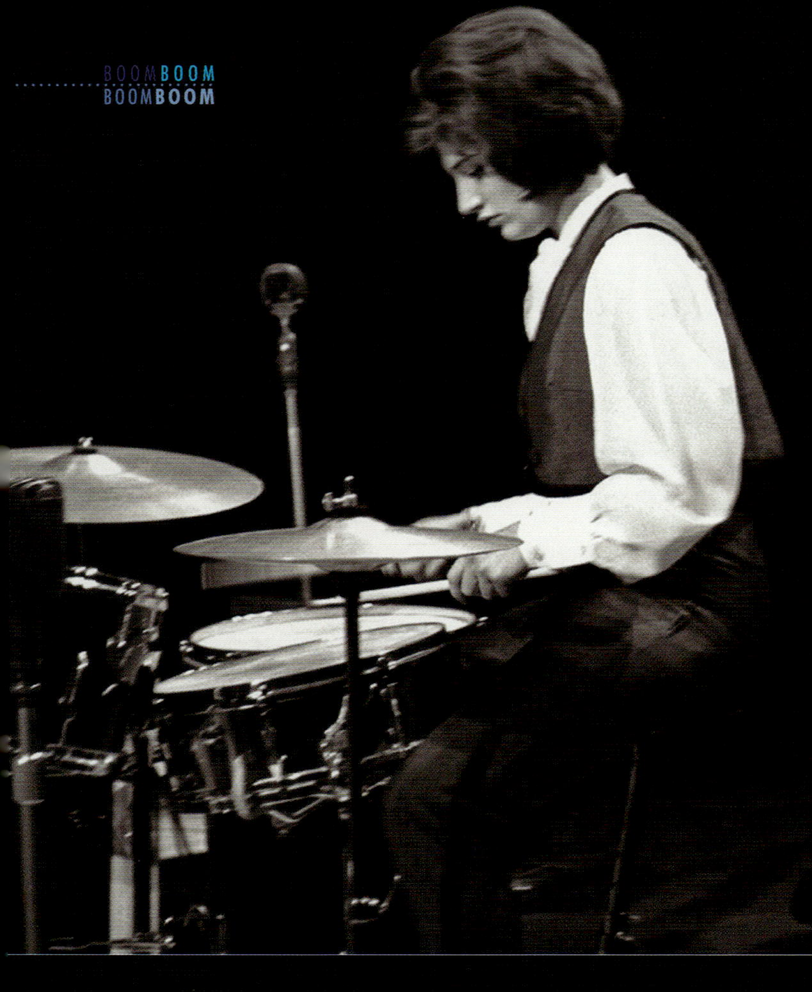

The NASHVILLE TEENS

Brian travelled down to London to photograph Carl Perkins on BBC's *Beat Extra* TV show (see page 154) but also took a couple of contrasty pictures of the other guests during their rehearsals for the same show, hence the big BBC TV cameras in the photo below. The episode (which seems to have been wiped) also featured Dionne Warwick but Brian wasn't allowed to take any photos of her. *"We were there for most of the day, there were frequent rehearsals, otherwise we were sat around with The Nashville Teens in the dressing room helping ourseklves to Kia-Ora orange juice and vodka! I sat up late in the hotel watching the election results coming in. I then watched Carl Perkins tackle his first British Rail Full English breakfast on the train up to Manchester the next morning!"*

There is a photo of Perkins on the train on page 153, (reading not eating!). The Nashville Teens are in the photographs below (they borrowed The Honeycombs drum kit) in the charts with their cover of Tobacco Road.

The Honeycombs fantastic debut single Have I The Right had reached Number 1 in the British charts, so having them on the show as well was quite a coup. The group were one of the first to feature a female drummer, the pioneering Honey Lantree (left), while the record was also notable for being produced by the inimitable Joe Meek at his independant RGM studio.

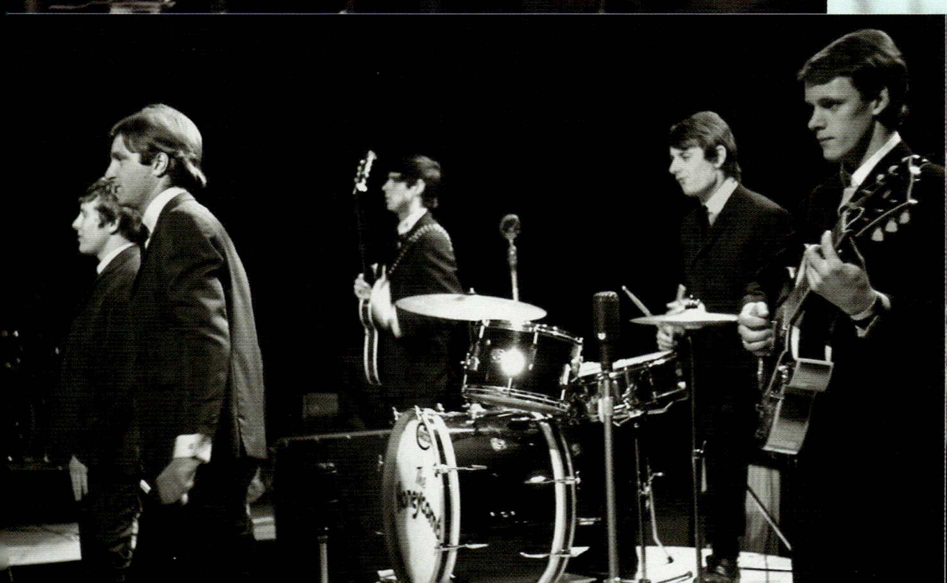

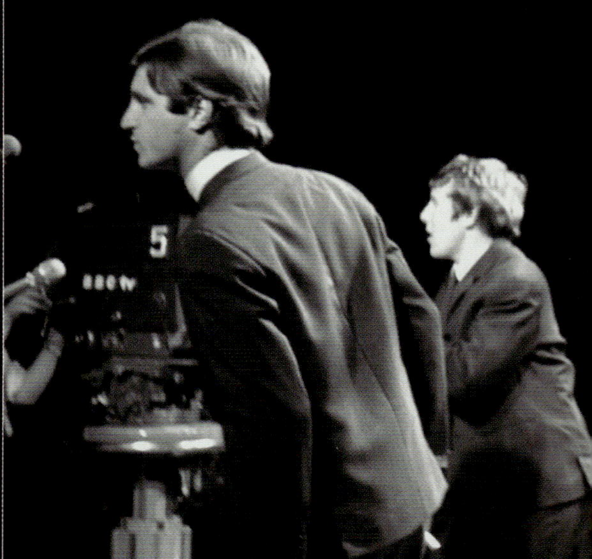

JACKIE FRISCO

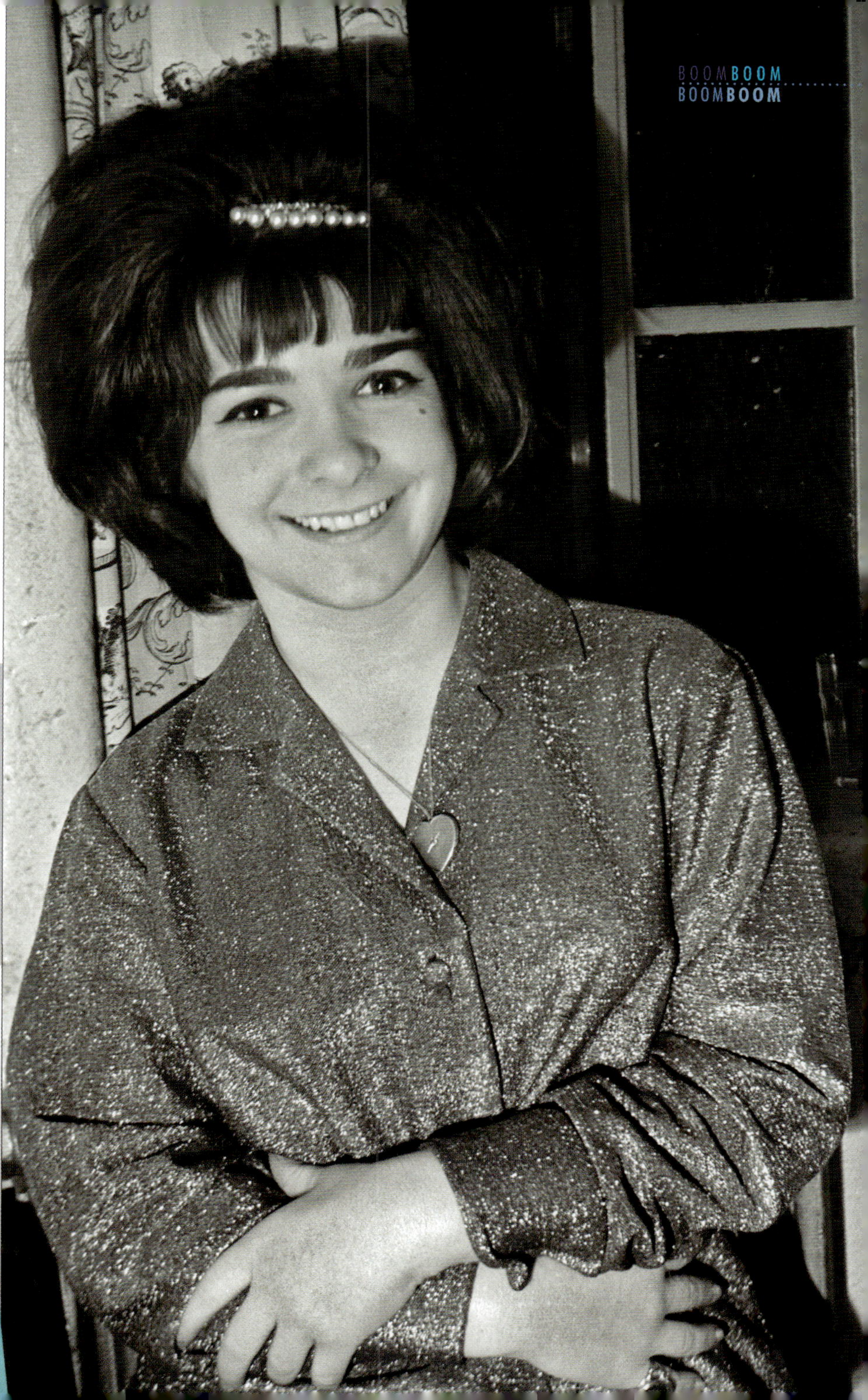

Jackie, whose real surname was Fusco, was born in England but her family emigrated to South Africa when she was a baby. Inspired by winning a local talent contest aged 5, her singing career proper began aged 15 at a rock jamboree in Johannesburg. She had a couple of modest hits in the South African charts, releasing an impossibly rare album for Rave Records in 1961 (see below) which was produced by Mickie Most, who had moved there (and married Jackie's sister Christina). When Mickie returned to the UK in 1962 he suggested Jackie might have more success with her pop career here. A deal for Decca produced two 45s in 1963 but neither made much of an impact.

Jackie began going out with Gene Vincent in 1964, they had met during his South African tour with Mickie Most and The Playboys back in 1961. They became engaged in July 1965, and she became his fourth and last wife (they split up around 1969).

This one-off photograph of Jackie was taken backstage at Manchester Odeon, on the Duane Eddy / Shirelles / Gene Vincent tour. Brian explained the circumstances: *"Jackie Frisco was not on the bill, but we asked if we could take some photographs and had just taken this one of her when Gene Vincent was called to go on, so they dashed off, but said we could pop back after his set and take some more. So we did, but I think we disturbed them! There was quite a bit of noise in the dressing room and she eventually let us in, but if looks could kill! So I took one shot of Gene, one of them together, then we beat a hasty retreat."* Sadly his shots of Vincent on (and off) stage were later lost.

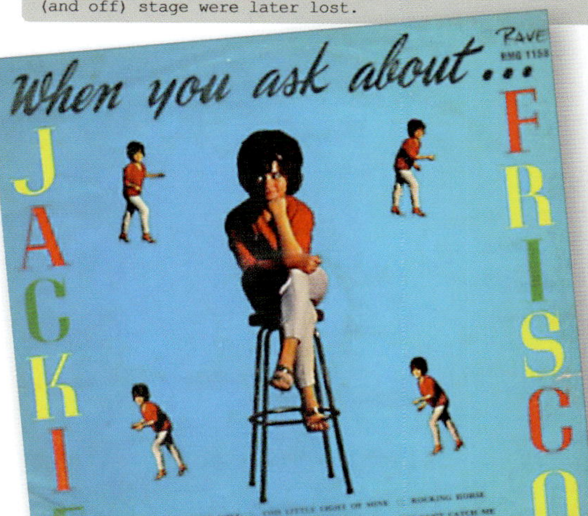

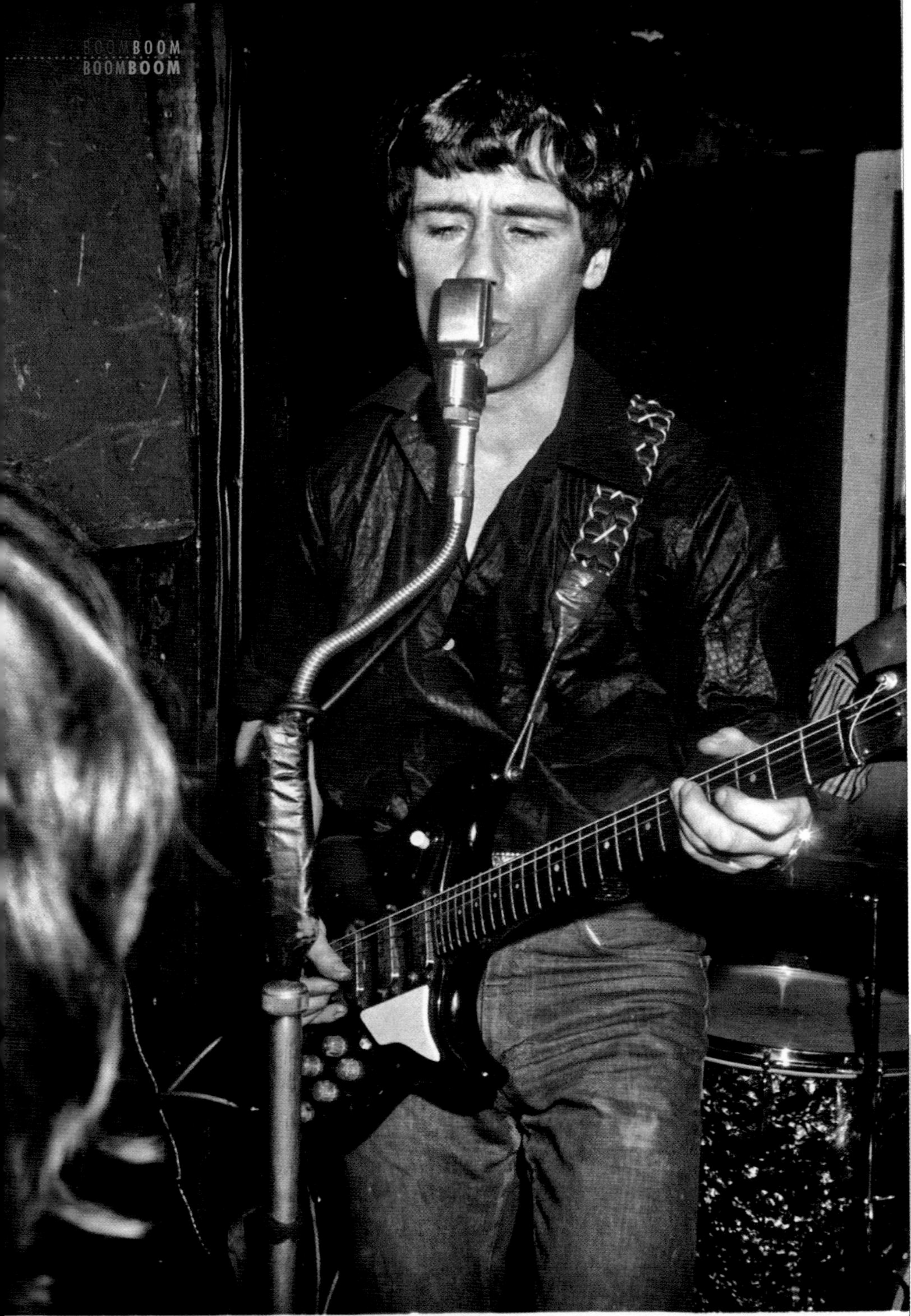

ALEX HARVEY

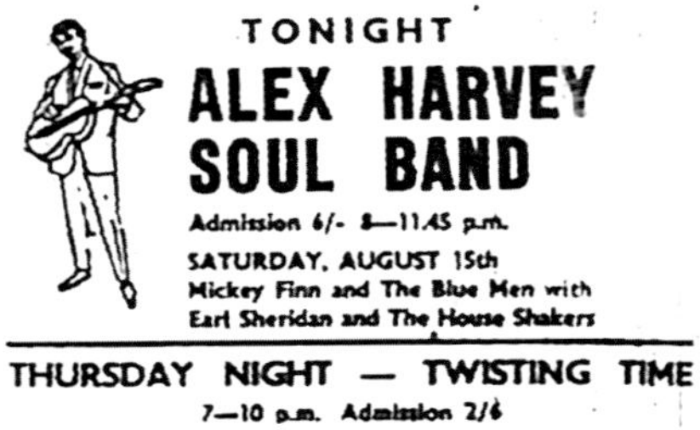

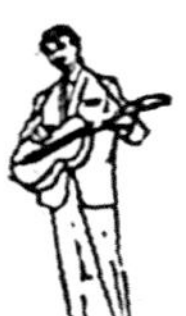

Hopefully remembered today for the brilliant Seventies rock outfit The Sensational Alex Harvey Band, Scottish singer Alex Harvey's early contributions to the blues and soul scene are certainly overlooked, but he toured Britain relentlessly in the early days.

At the time of this visit to The Twisted Wheel, he was fronting The Alex Harvey Soul Band, who issued two albums in 1964. I did wonder why just the one photo from this concert? Brian explained that he was on duty for the club that night, photographing the punters in the hopes of selling them prints on a later visit. *"I just snapped this shot as I was passing the stage, it was not a busy night! I may have taken some more later but they would have got mixed in with the crowd photos so I lost those. It's a miracle this one survived."*

However photos of Alex Harvey live at from this time are not exactly common so we decided to include it. A year later he would issue his first single *Agent 00 Soul* on Fontana (sounding remarkably like Tom Jones), which is today regarded as a Twisted Wheel classic and can fetch three figure sums from collectors.

📷 This negative has clearly taken a beating over the years but we kind of like the way the scratches blend with the general grottiness of the club's surroundings, with live wires everywhere and gaffa tape holding it all together. And we do wonder when Alex last had those jeans washed! The gig advert is contemporary but not from The Wheel. And don't forget, Thursday night is twisting time!

The OUTLAWS

B rian struggled at The Princess Club in Manchester as the lighting was low and his flash underpowered, but live photographs of The Outlaws are not common. The group would be a footnote in producer Joe Meek's biography except guitarist Ricky 'Bluebell' Blackmore (on the far right below) founded Deep Purple just five years after this was taken, drummer Mick Underwood went on to work with Ian Gillan and Roger Glover in Episode Six (while Chas Hodges later found fame with Chas'n Dave).

"I had a real liking for rock 'n roll instrumentals and, over here, I sort of looked at them as the British equivalent of The Fireballs," remembers Brian. The Outlaws, here in their trademark Western suits, were very proficient and got booked to back a number of visiting American rock and roll acts including here (September 29th 1963) Gene Vincent. They also did their own spot beforehand, fronted by Chas. The Outlaws had played The Top Ten club in the centre of Manchester two weeks before, but The Princess was in the suburb of Chorlton-cum-Hardy so attracted a different crowd. Opening act? Little and Large!

And if DJ John Peel is to be believed (and he was right about many things) they cut what he regarded as the first heavy rock single, a version of Little Richard's *Keep A Knockin'*. Brian is less sure: *"I never regarded them as heavy, or playing much part in any death-knell for the blues boom. Indeed, all the 'British Explosion' stuff went on alongside the blues and soul clubs for some years."*

The shot below with Gene Vincent was lost but Brian spotted it in a BBC4 documentary. *"I had sold a lot of my autographed prints around 1982, when fatherhood drained my resources! The BBC put me in touch with the new owner, a big Vincent collector, and he gave me scans."*

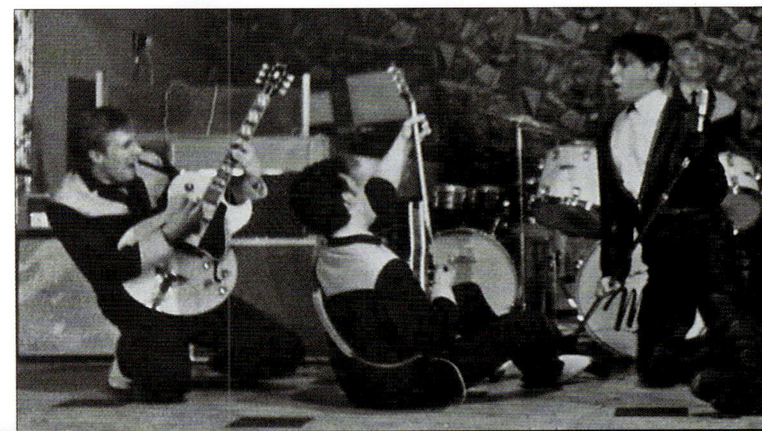

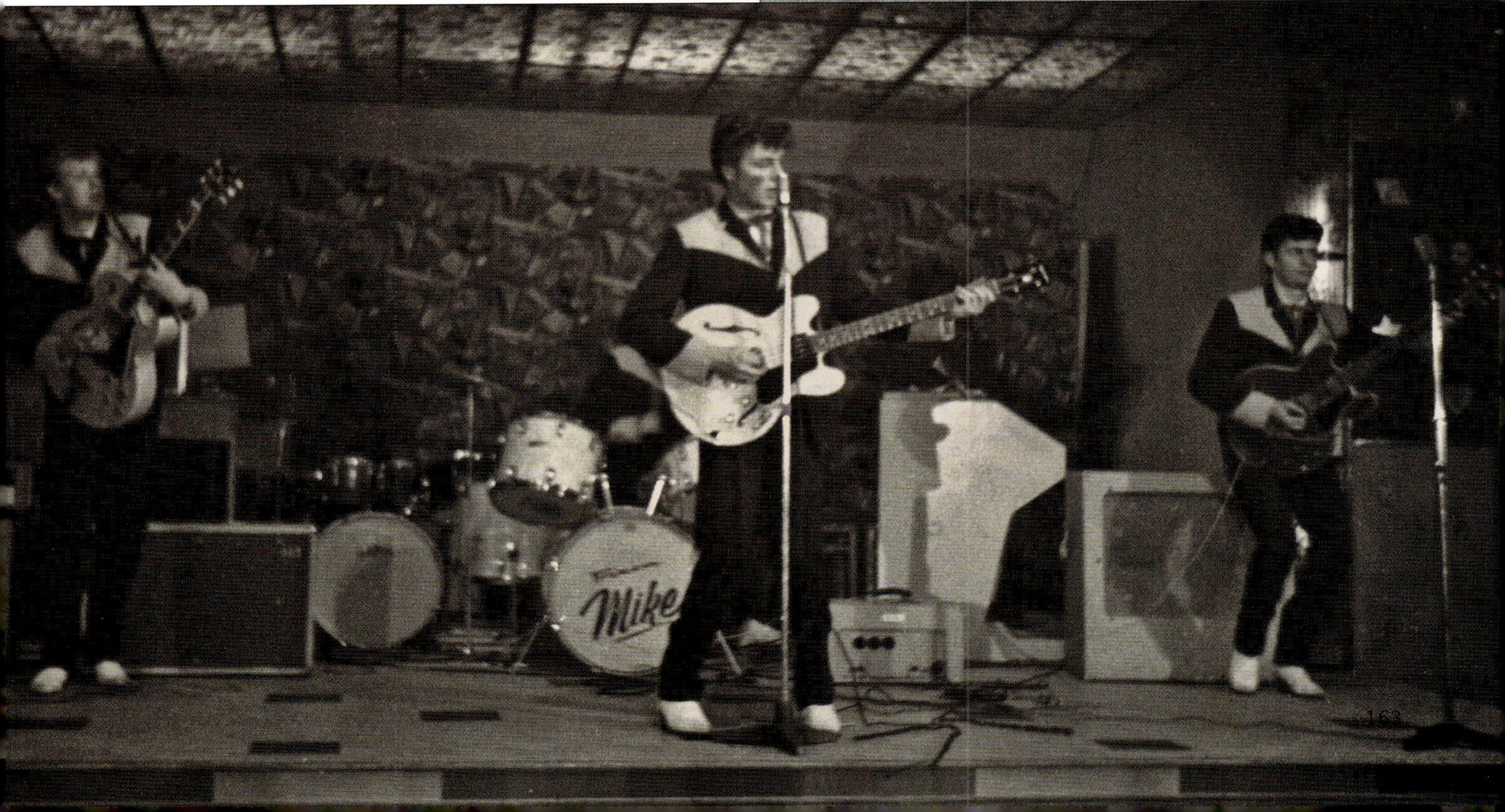

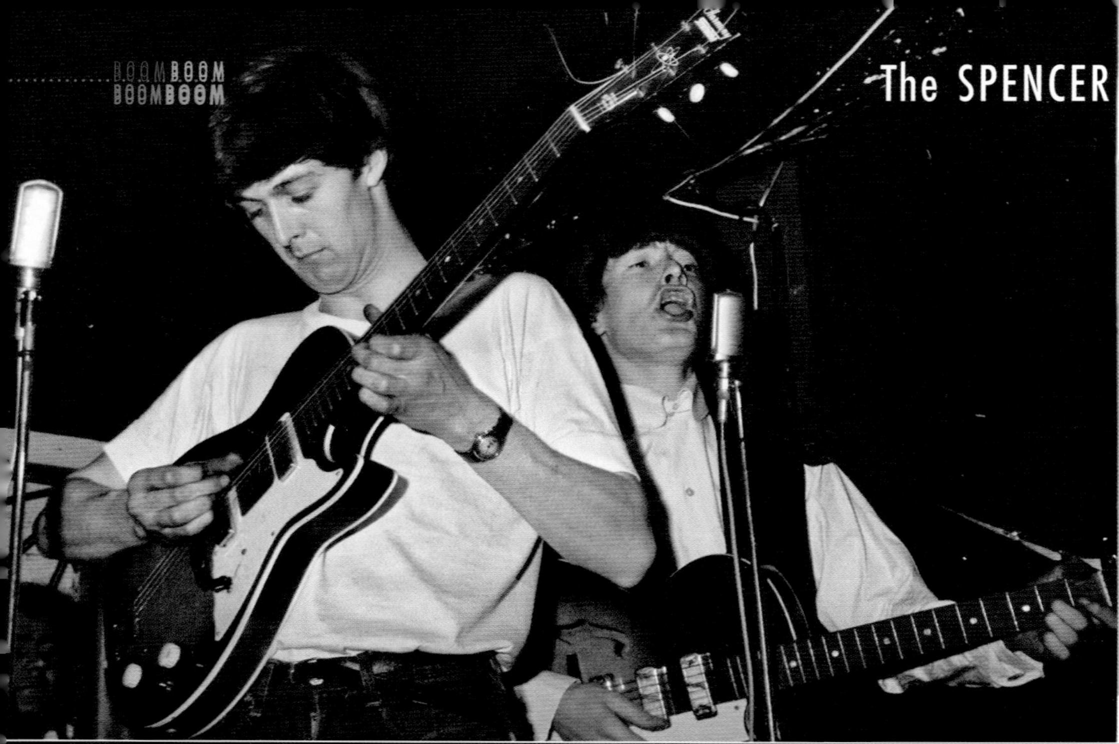

Booked to open the Wheel's first concert at their new site on Whitworth Street on September 18th 1965 (flyer next page), these photographs of Spencer Davis are usually attributed to that date. Brian says not: *"These were taken in 1963. Roger Eagle took me down there in the afternoon, when The Wheel was closed to the public, specifically to take them. I had thought they may have been taken at the first Twisted Wheel all-nighter at the old site, which Spencer Davis also headlined, but looking back I think that was too soon. I had only met Roger the week before that."*
The nearest date would be late October or early November '63, during a soundcheck, which is how Brian could take the shots without anyone in the way for once.

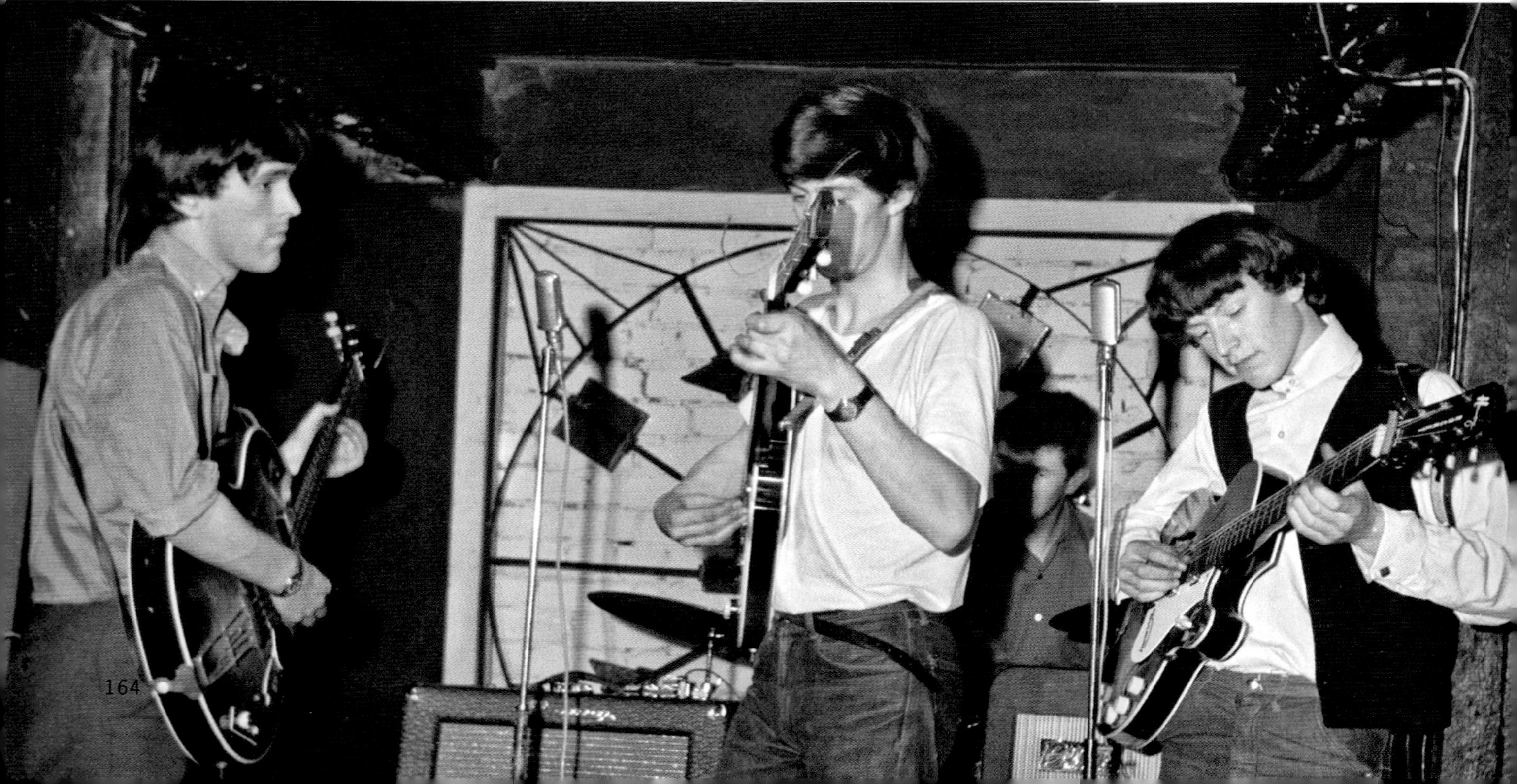

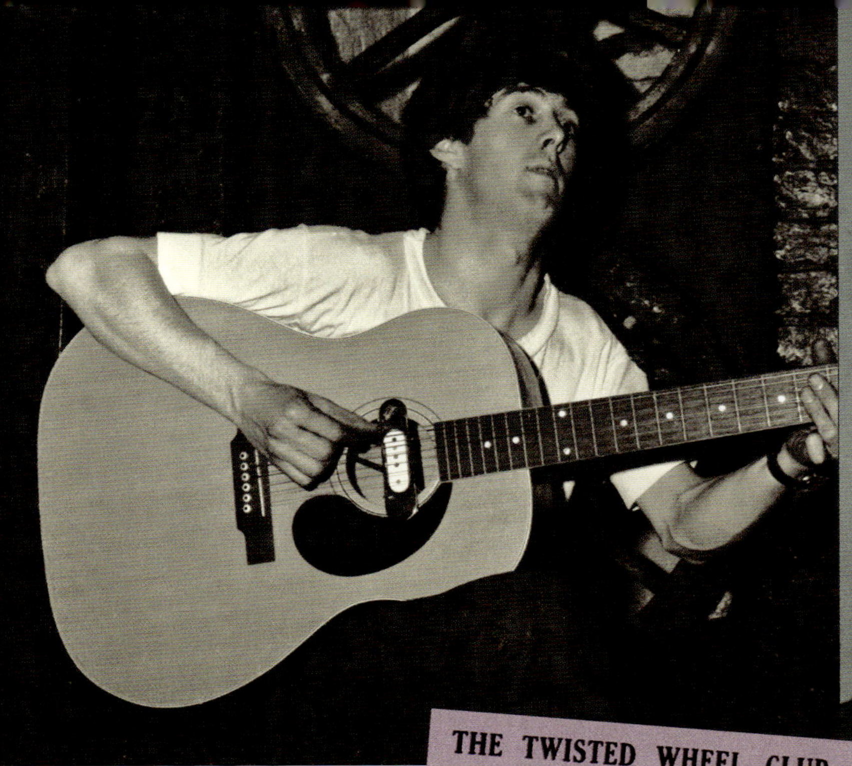

Seen here at The Twisted Wheel Club's first site, The Spencer Davis Group was formed in 1963 in Birmingham when Davis recruited vocalist and organist Steve Winwood (on the right playing guitar) and his bassist brother Muff Winwood (on the left in the smaller photograph), along with drummer Pete York (mostly hidden!).

THE TWISTED WHEEL CLUB
6 WHITWORTH STREET, MANCHESTER 1
Tel. CENtral 1179
(Opposite Fire Station)

★ **GRAND OPENING** ★
of New Twisted Wheel Club Premises on
SATURDAY, 18th SEPTEMBER, 1965
THE SPENCER DAVIS GROUP

The Club in Brazennose Street will Close on
SATURDAY, 11th SEPTEMBER, 1965

They played at The Wheel around two dozen times after their debut in August 1963 and were very popular thanks to their robust versions of Blues and R'n'B originals and great live performances, long before their first major chart hit with a brilliant reworking of *Keep On Running*. On DJ duties Roger Eagle often played the original versions of the tracks they covered or plugged the self composed 'B' sides, until they started releasing their own a-sides, but he was keen to see them do well and gave them plugs in R & B Scene magazine, and *ordered* Brian to come and see them at his inaugural all nighter.

"He had a lot of time for Spencer's lads, they were regulars to his Chorlton bedsit after all-nighters, listening to new imports. By then Roger was on the mailing list of US record companies (particularly Don Robey's Duke/Peacock labels in Houston) as were many who worked as a DJ at the Wheel; even my 10-minute 'coke and comfort-break' fill-in sessions meant I received Robey's generous promos for years. I remember Stevie discovering the Malibus' new 45 of 'Strong Love' on a visit in 1965. It was ME who first put it on but Stevie was still playing it when I left two hours later. They recorded it on their second Fontana album."

JOEY PAIGE

Joey Paige (above), bass player with Dickie Doo & The Don'ts, climbing out of a theatrical dressing box backstage at Manchester, October 16th 1963. As you do! Joey's band were based in New York and drew a lucky break when The Everly Brothers needed a backing group for their world tour and offered them the gig. Being with one of the biggest names in the music scene at the time they got decent accommodation and travel, but Joey remembers The Rolling Stones didn't have it so easy. *"This was before anyone outside of the U.K. knew who they were. The whole band lived out of a van. Bill [Wyman] came to me one day and said, 'Joey. Can you do me a favour? Could we use your bathroom to clean up?'"*

Joey went on to forge a solo vocal and songwriting career in America and Wyman didn't forget the favour, so he got to open for The Rolling Stones on some of their first American shows.

165

LONG JOHN BALDRY, ROD STEWART

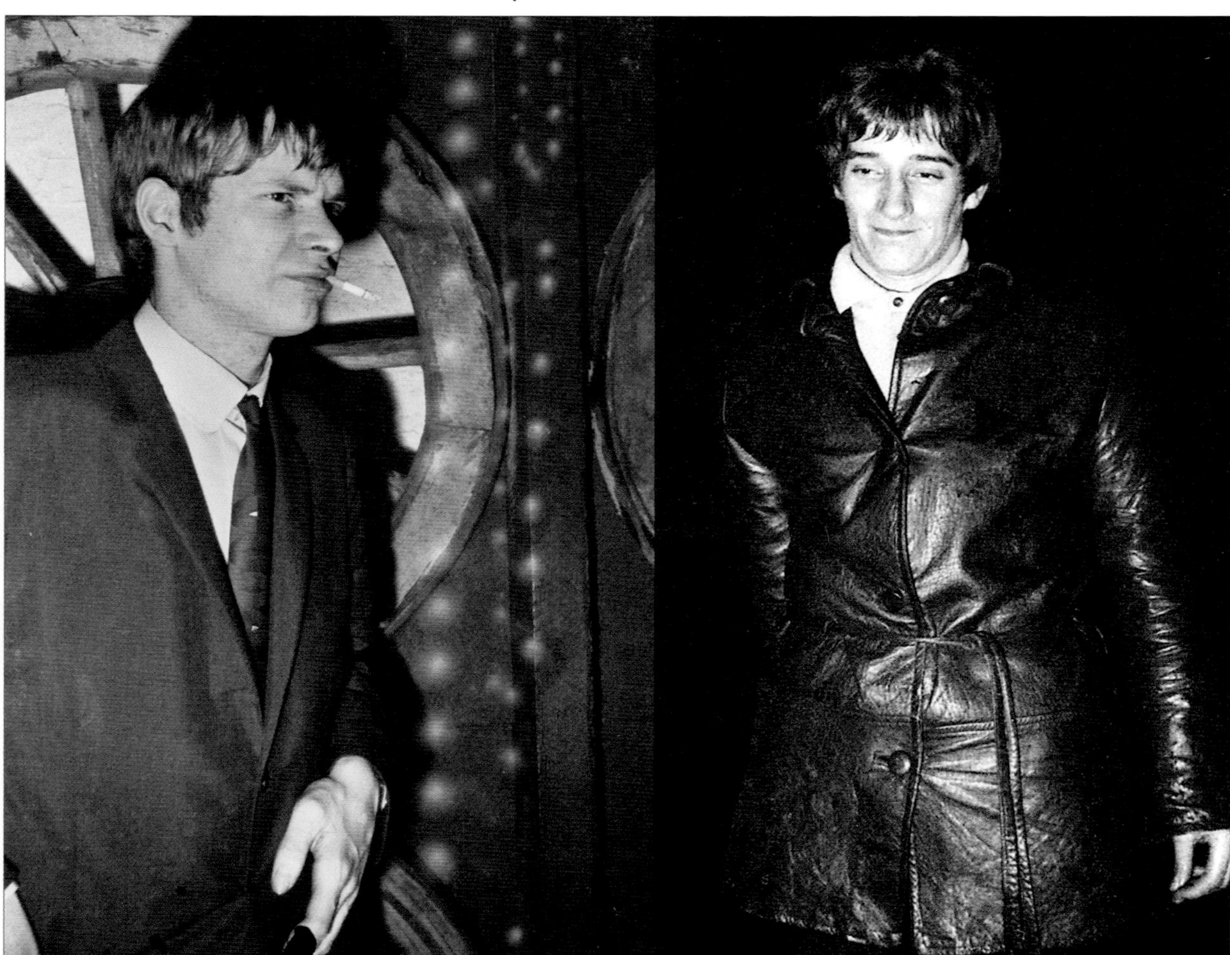

Brian has problems during the Baldry show as the club was totally packed and the humidity caused condensation to build up in his camera lens, so he was unable to take any photos during the show. He did manage to take just a couple of shots of Baldry before the show (including the one here), and then snapped one shot of Stewart outside the club in the dark; this grainy image is all that survives.

We might have left the shot of Rod Stewart out, except Brian had unwittingly caught him on the night of his professional debut. The Twisted Wheel's January 11th 1964 all-nighter had been booked for Cyril Davies' R & B Allstars, with Long John Baldry their featured vocalist. Cyril was 'the man' in UK blues with a couple of good-selling Pye singles, and it was sold-out. Sadly Cyril died on 7th January, many in the crowd arrived not having heard the news, so it was a very emotional occasion. Rather than disappoint people Baldry (who had been planning a new group with Rod Stewart) and the band went ahead as a tribute to Cyril with Stewart guesting.

It went well; scheduled to end at 5.15 am the group didn't come off stage until after 7.00 am, were rebooked at once for Feb 29th and after that appeared another half a dozen times during 1964 as Long John Baldry and the Hoochie Coochie Men. The crowd knew Rod from his brief amateur

166

spell with Jimmy Powell (and his sharp, back-combed look) and Brian recalls him playing some tight little guitar fills and riffs (*"the only time I ever saw him play a guitar"*) with minimal accompaniment. *"It was a memorable occasion. Many of my acquaintances, who never bought Rod's later records, still hold a soft-spot for his emotional, electric performance that night. A lot of it was off-the-cuff, and Baldry also lifted a fine little dwarf jazz harmonica player called Johnny Puleo onto a stool to play one or two swinging harp instrumentals."* According to Rod Stewart's fan club: *"Legend has it that he was pushed forward by Long John and asked to sing Night Time Is The Right Time, and he was asked to fill quite a big gap, and didn't know any other songs, so he made it last 45 minutes."* Stewart recalls having taken a pill to keep him going: *"It was a black pill, a black bomber. I didn't know anything about drugs, but I took it. It made the song last for almost an hour. I just kept singing the same verses, over and over."*

The BLUES GIANTS

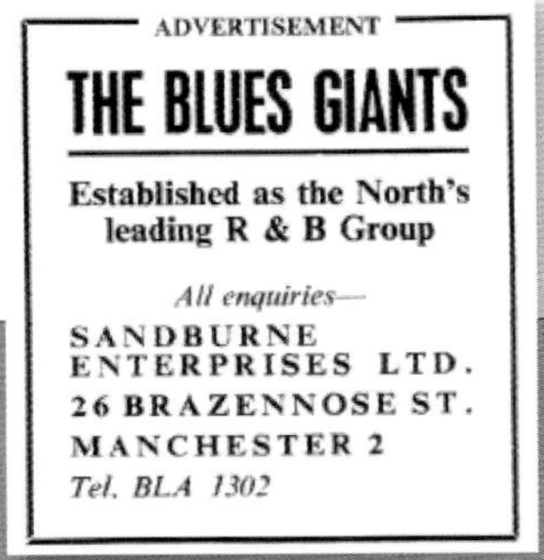

Little is known about The Blues Giants, who were managed by Twisted Wheel Club owners The Abadis (as Sandburne Enterprises). They preferred to concentrate on the club and never really pursued this side of the music business, even declining an offer to handle the Spencer Davis Group.

R & B Scene magazine gave The Blues Giants half a page in the February 1965 issue feature on the *'current best blues bands around'*, alongside Graham Bond, The Groundhogs and Rod Stuart (sic, readers were told he *"should do well, provided his backing band don't drown him"...*). Thanks to this article we can at least name them, l-r Dave Conrad, sax (and band leader), Hervey Jay, drums, Rod Dumford, trumpet, Big John McAttee, bass and vocals, Eileen Hampson, organ, and Rob Trick, guitar. Brian photographed the group at Manchester University (including a few accidental but arty double exposures!) and they were regulars at The Twisted Wheel Club (while their name certainly resonates with the subject of this book).

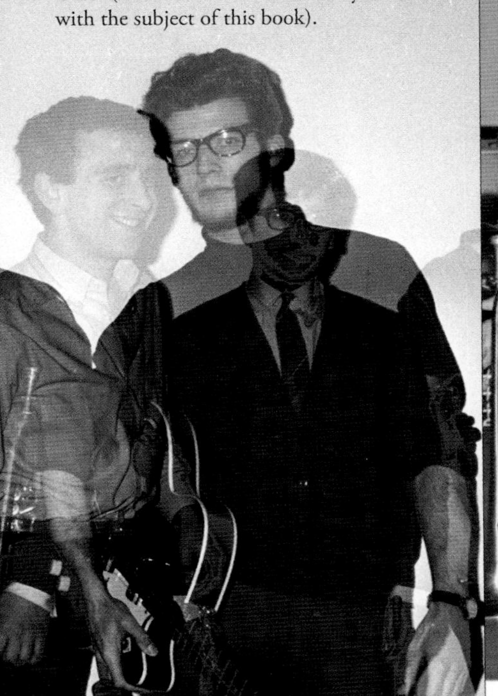

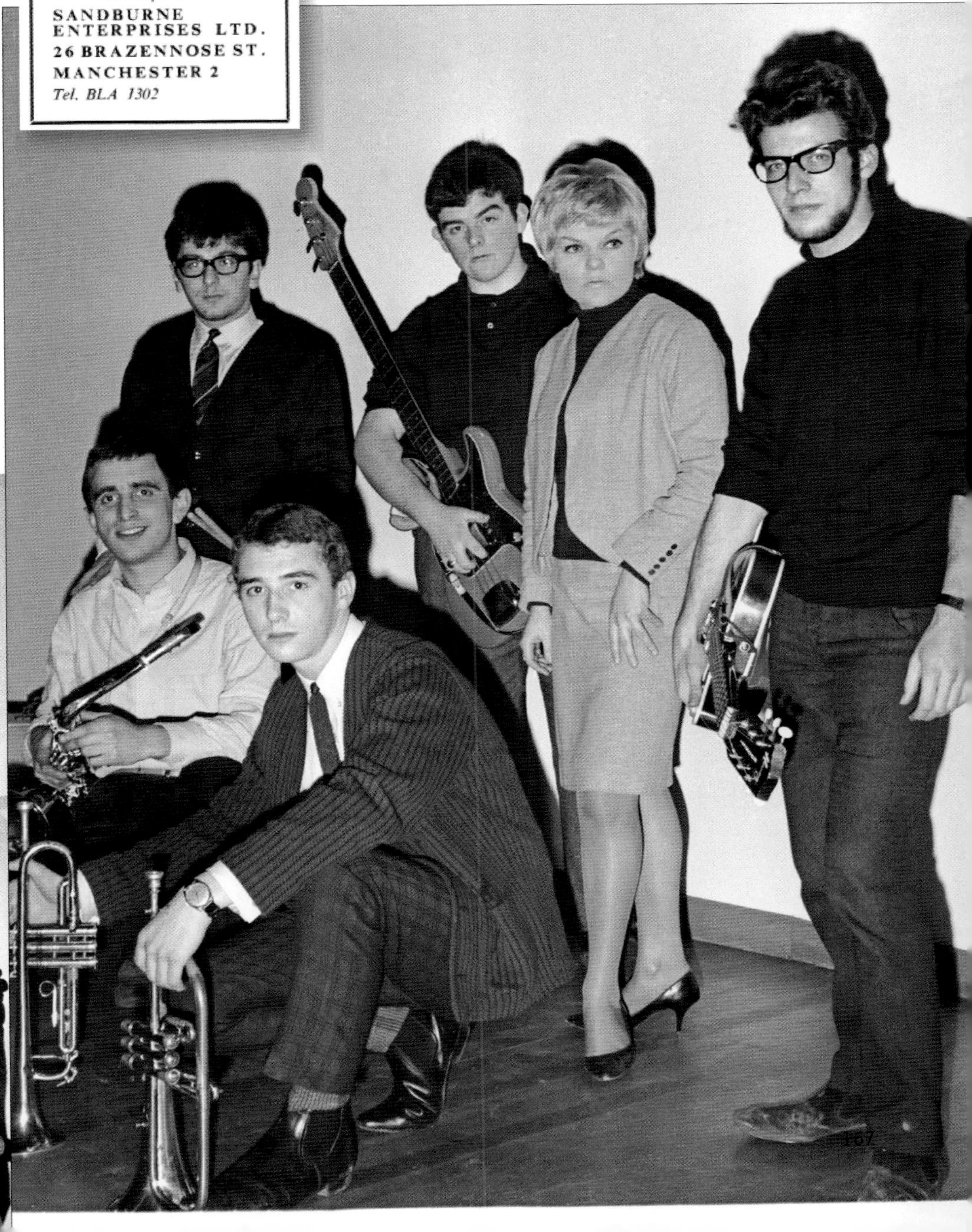

JIMMY POWELL and THE FIVE DIMENSIONS

According to rock historian Bruno Ceriotti, Jimmy Powell and The Five Dimensions were *"Undoubtedly one of the most underrated British rhythm and blues bands of the mid-60's.*

Carving out a career lasting over 15 years they had only been on the road about a year when they first played The Twisted Wheel at one of the Saturday all-nighters on October 12th 1963, with The Renegades (Brian was there but without his camera). Their music fitted the Wheel vibe perfectly, and after this debut they played more or less bi-monthly throughout 1964, then monthly during 1965 (as seen on the flyer here). Playing so often it's hard to date Brian's Twisted Wheel Club photographs of the group.

Although the rhythm guitarist is hidden on the cramped stage, Jimmy Powell himself is seated in the middle, Martin Shaw to his right with the guitar and Pete Hogman to his left, harmonica player (he can be heard on Millie's *My Boy Lollipop* 45) and second vocalist. Louis Cennamo is just visible. These four were together from November 30th 1963 to August 1964 and so Brian thinks they were probably taken on Saturday December 7th 1963.

As well as their own shows, the band were professional enough to be booked to back acts like Chuck Berry when he toured Britain (Brian met them again in that role in early 1965). They also took in Mod trends and even a touch of freakbeat as the Sixties progressed, and versions of the group carried on into the early 1970s before Powell left music.

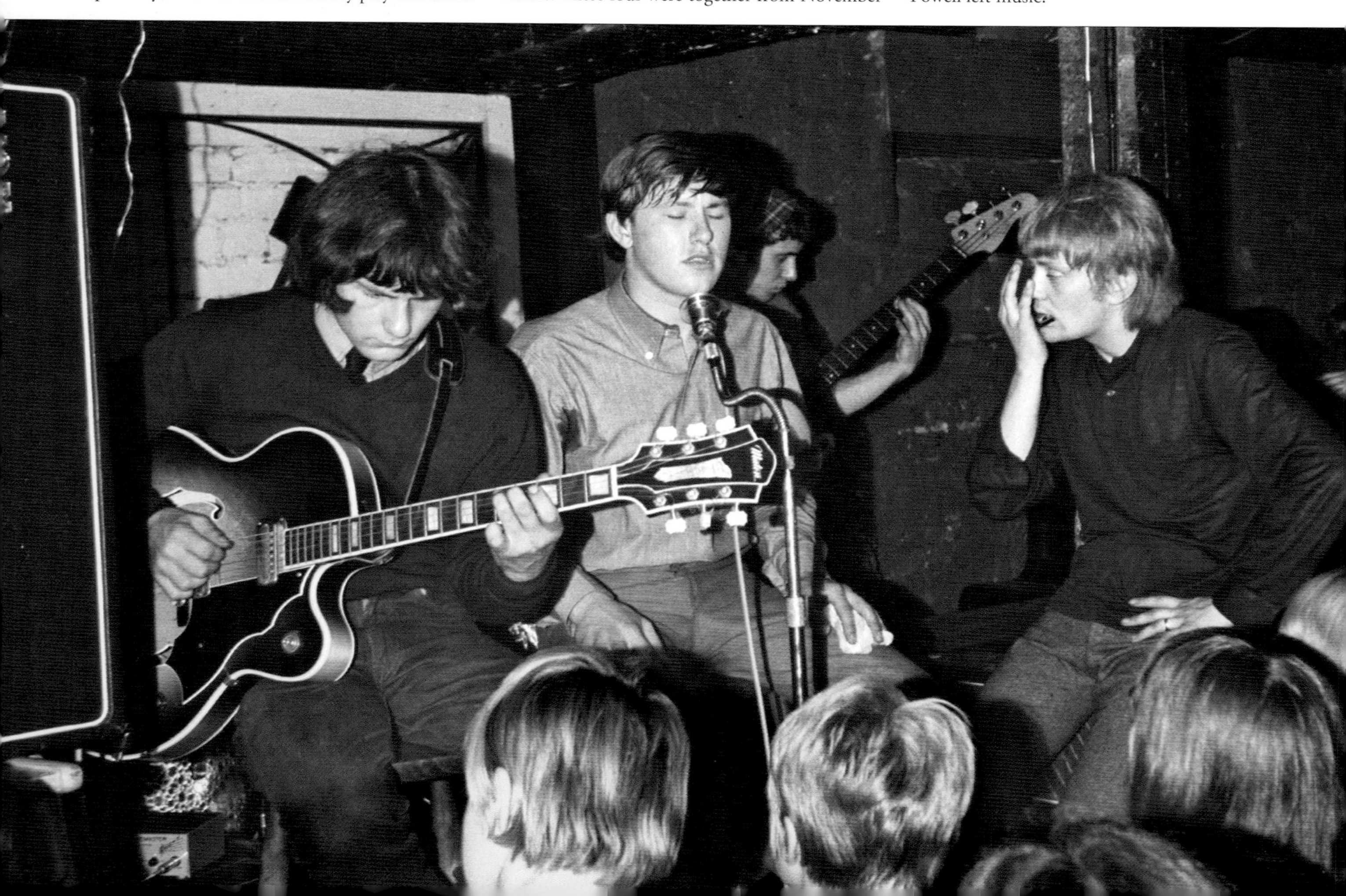

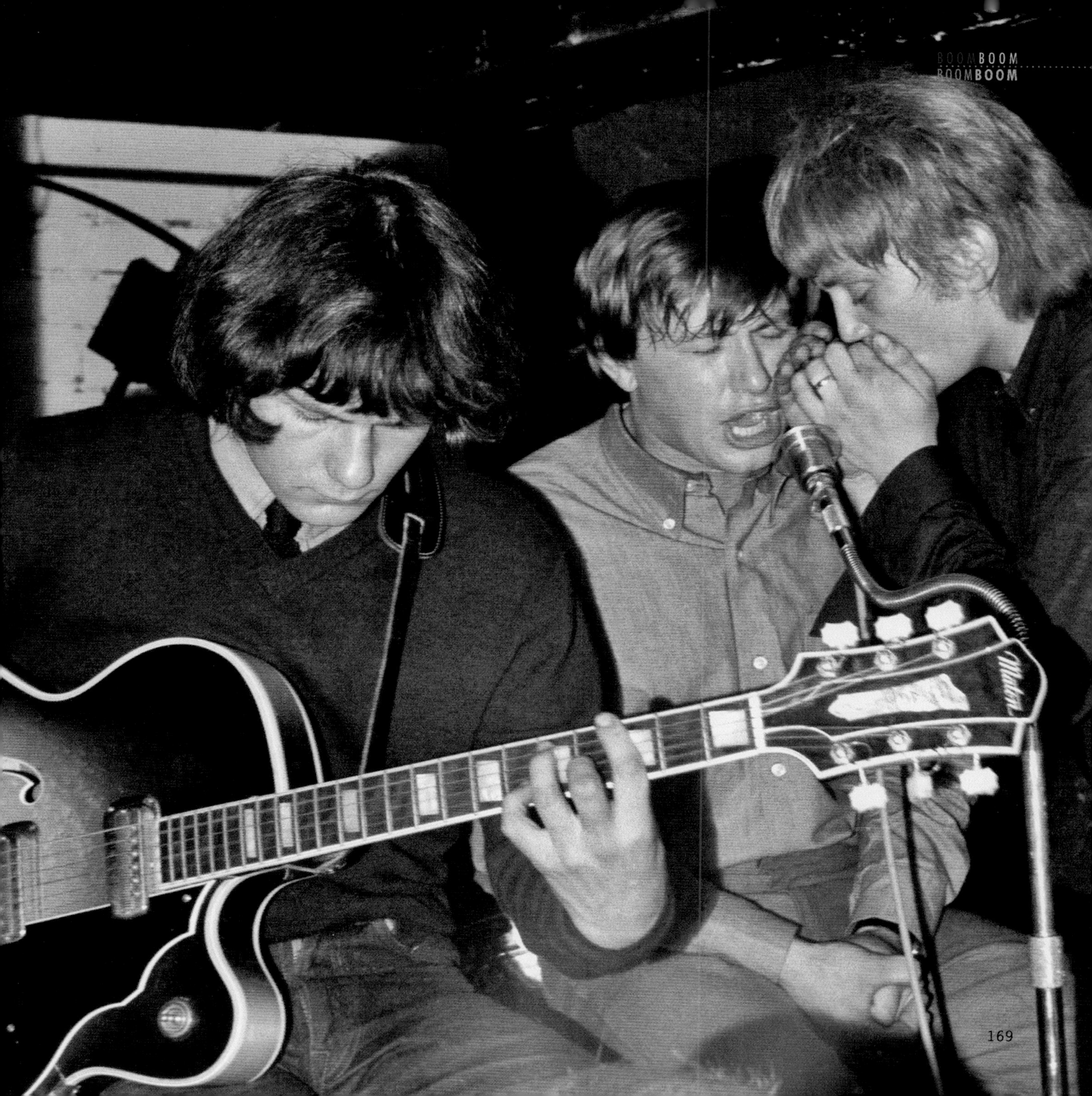

BOOMBOOM
ROOMBOOM

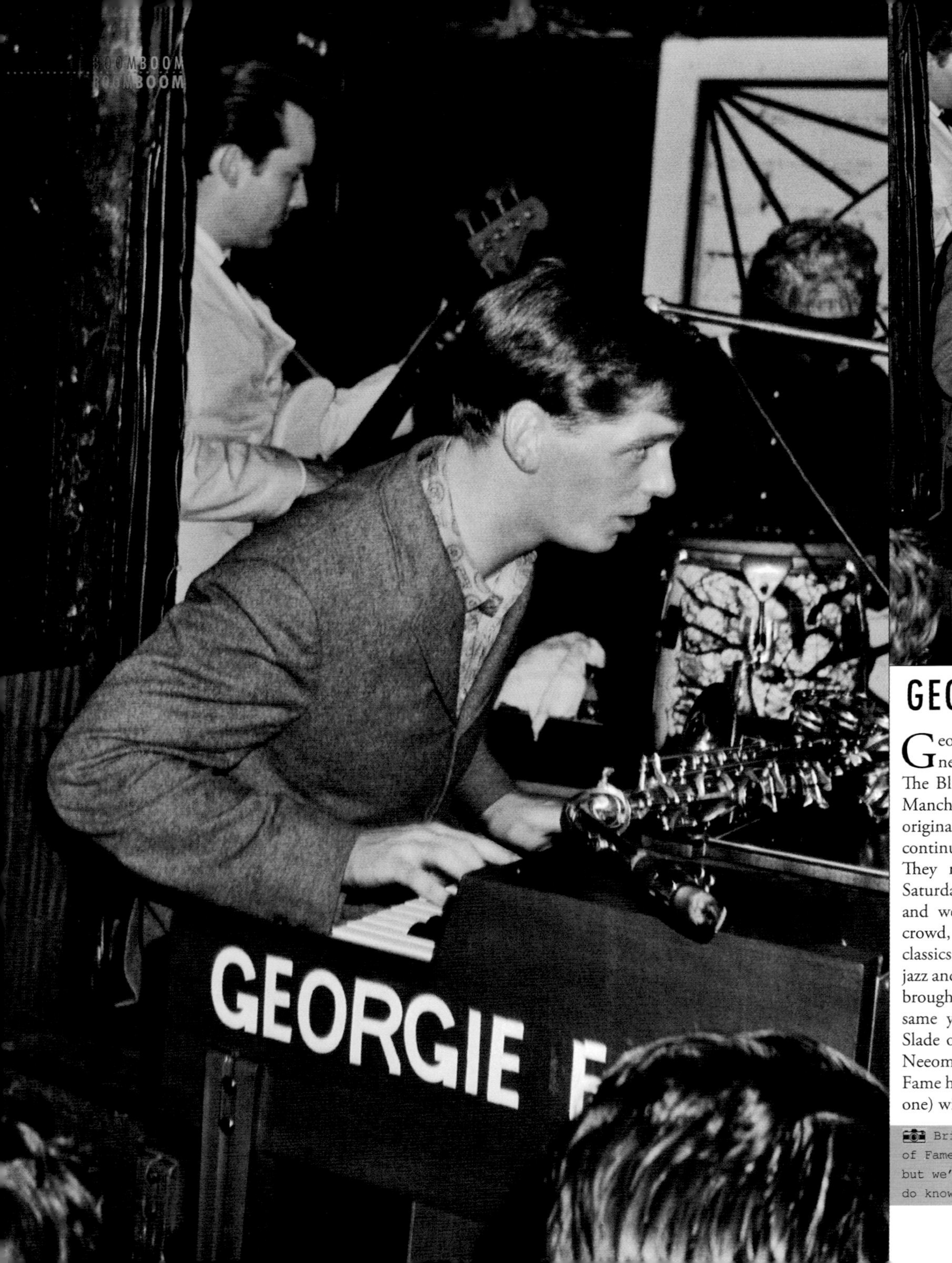

GEORGIE FAME

Georgie Fame was a local lad from nearby Leigh. So once he had formed The Blue Flames, he was a regular in the Manchester clubs and appeared at the original Twisted Wheel eight times (and continued to be booked at the new site). They made their debut at one of the Saturday all-nighters on May 30th 1964 and were very popular with the regular crowd, who appreciated his covers of soul classics mixed with the eclectic blend of jazz and r'n'b. A proficient band, they were brought in to back Memphis Slim later the same year. We think that's Rod 'Boots' Slade on bass and Ghanaian percussionist Neeomi 'Speedy' Acquaye on the tom tom. Fame had his first big hit (reaching number one) with a cover of *Yeh Yeh* in late 1964.

Brian grabbed just these two photos of Fame at the original Wheel in 1964, but we're not sure of the date. Still we do know who the keyboard belong to!

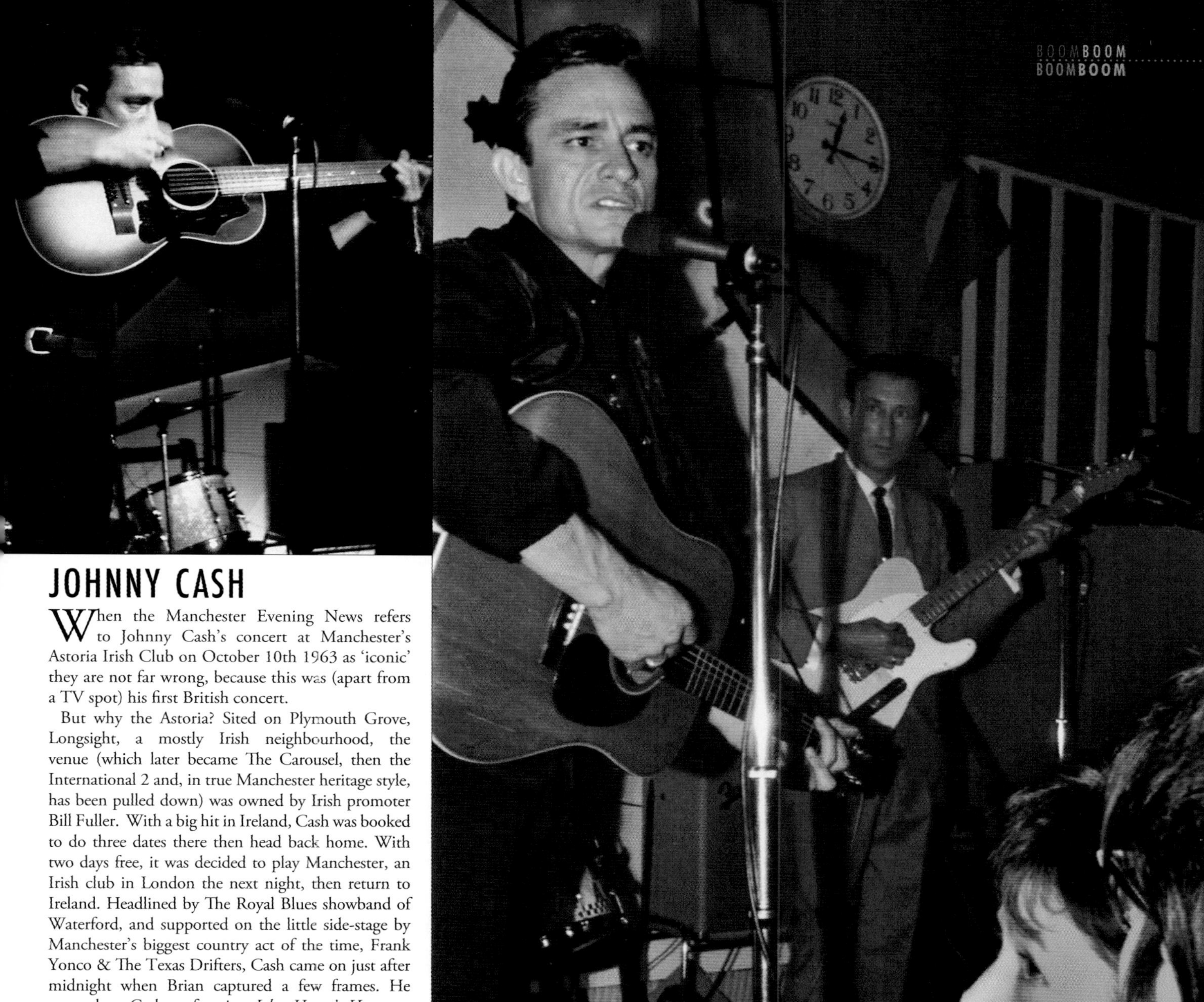

JOHNNY CASH

When the Manchester Evening News refers to Johnny Cash's concert at Manchester's Astoria Irish Club on October 10th 1963 as 'iconic' they are not far wrong, because this was (apart from a TV spot) his first British concert.

But why the Astoria? Sited on Plymouth Grove, Longsight, a mostly Irish neighbourhood, the venue (which later became The Carousel, then the International 2 and, in true Manchester heritage style, has been pulled down) was owned by Irish promoter Bill Fuller. With a big hit in Ireland, Cash was booked to do three dates there then head back home. With two days free, it was decided to play Manchester, an Irish club in London the next night, then return to Ireland. Headlined by The Royal Blues showband of Waterford, and supported on the little side-stage by Manchester's biggest country act of the time, Frank Yonco & The Texas Drifters, Cash came on just after midnight when Brian captured a few frames. He remembers Cash performing *John Henry's Hammer*, punctuating it with hammer-clunks from two iron bars and is pretty sure this was before he had committed it to vinyl.   In the background is Luther Perkins, Johnny Cash's legendary lead guitarist, idolised by Keith Richards amongst others.

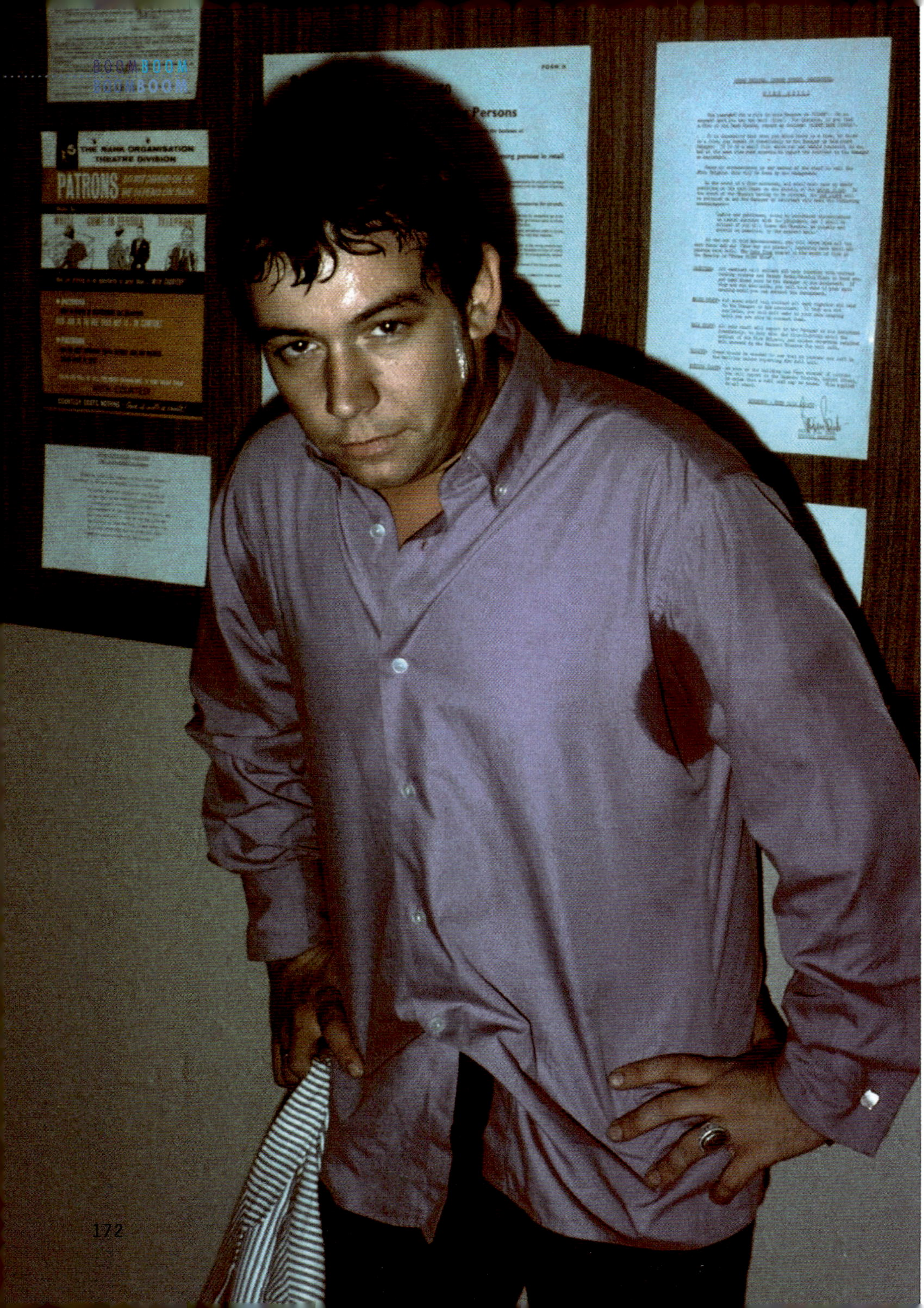

ERIC BURDON

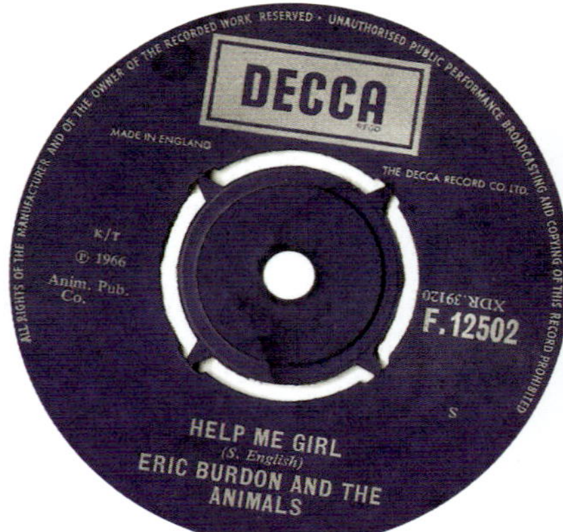

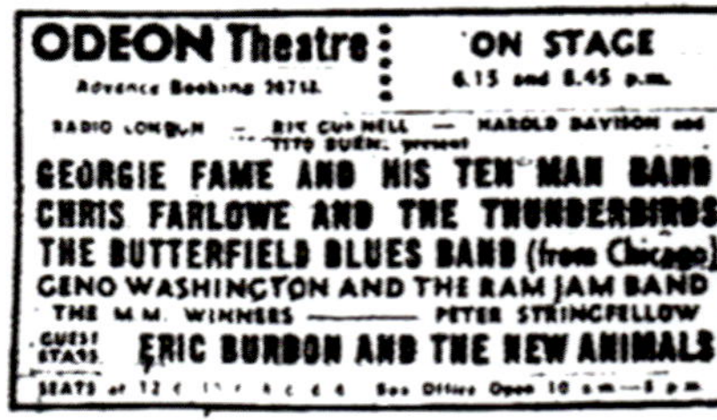

Brian got just this one photograph of Eric Burdon when his band, renamed The New Animals (to mark the departure of three of the previous musicians) appeared as Guest Stars at the Manchester Odeon on October 25th 1966, promoting *Help Me Girl*. Eric had just come off stage as is clear from the state of him and his shirt. This was a package tour but not the usual pop bill, instead bringing together an interesting array of groups, including Georgie Fame, Chris Farlowe & The Thunderbirds, The Butterfield Blues Band (*"from Chicago"* boasted the adverts) and Geno Washington's Ram Jam Band. Oh and Peter Stringfellow!

The tour was partly promoted by pirate station Radio London, all the bands had singles being aired on the station at the time

And the fabulous Odeon? Manchester council approved demolition of this fine 1930s building even as we were preparing this book. They'll have nothing left soon.

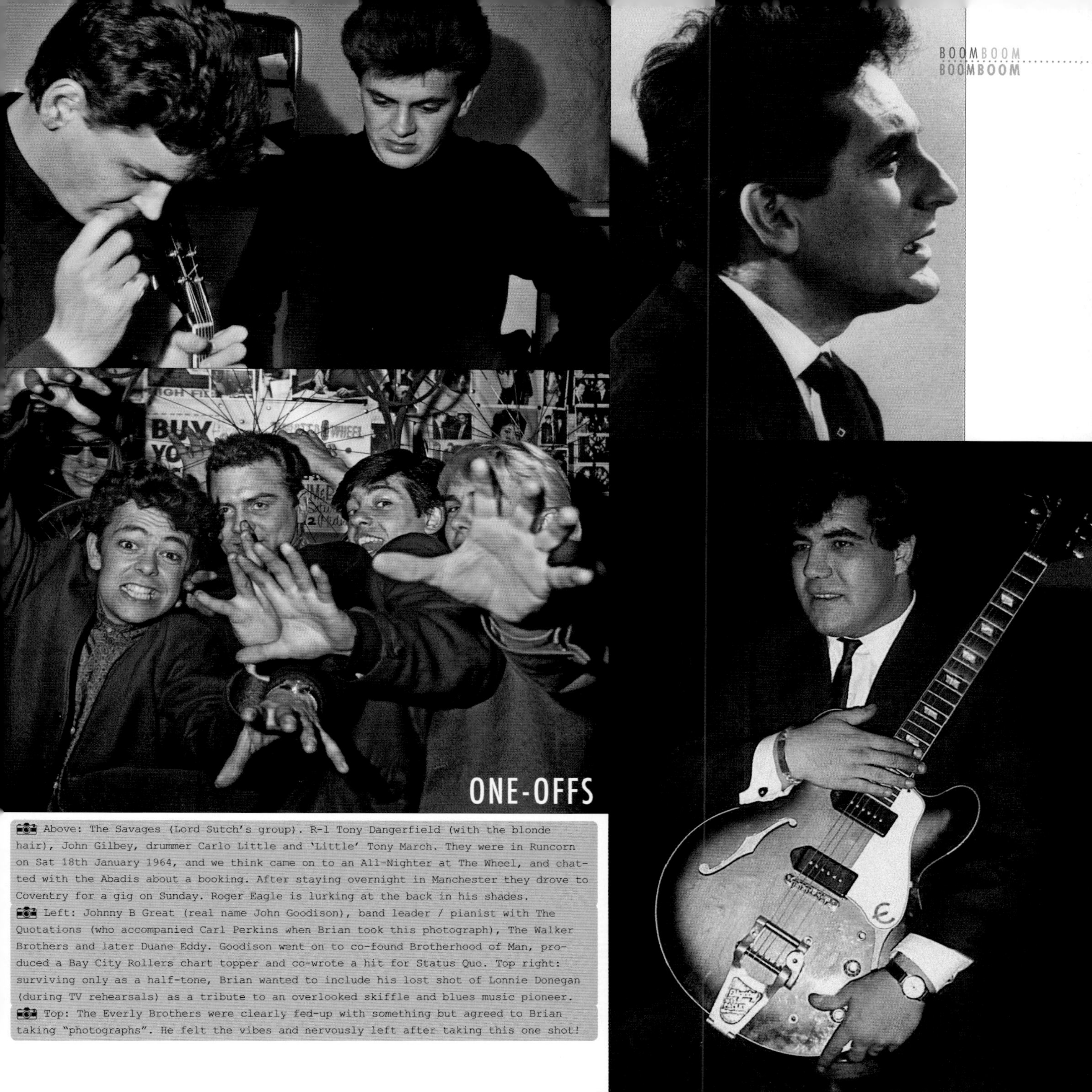

ONE-OFFS

Above: The Savages (Lord Sutch's group). R-l Tony Dangerfield (with the blonde hair), John Gilbey, drummer Carlo Little and 'Little' Tony March. They were in Runcorn on Sat 18th January 1964, and we think came on to an All-Nighter at The Wheel, and chatted with the Abadis about a booking. After staying overnight in Manchester they drove to Coventry for a gig on Sunday. Roger Eagle is lurking at the back in his shades.

Left: Johnny B Great (real name John Goodison), band leader / pianist with The Quotations (who accompanied Carl Perkins when Brian took this photograph), The Walker Brothers and later Duane Eddy. Goodison went on to co-found Brotherhood of Man, produced a Bay City Rollers chart topper and co-wrote a hit for Status Quo. Top right: surviving only as a half-tone, Brian wanted to include his lost shot of Lonnie Donegan (during TV rehearsals) as a tribute to an overlooked skiffle and blues music pioneer.

Top: The Everly Brothers were clearly fed-up with something but agreed to Brian taking "photographs". He felt the vibes and nervously left after taking this one shot!

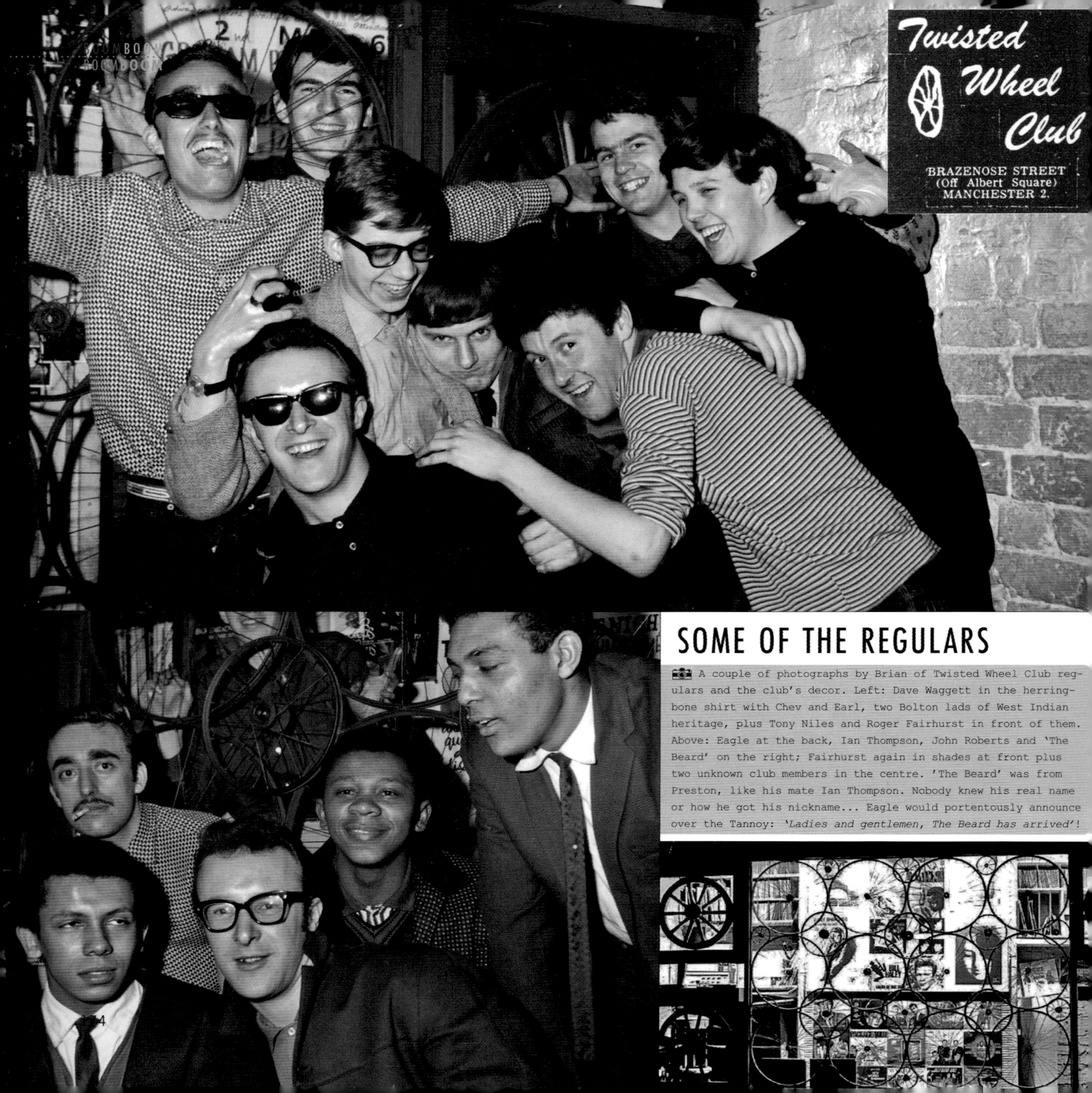

SOME OF THE REGULARS

A couple of photographs by Brian of Twisted Wheel Club regulars and the club's decor. Left: Dave Waggett in the herringbone shirt with Chev and Earl, two Bolton lads of West Indian heritage, plus Tony Niles and Roger Fairhurst in front of them. Above: Eagle at the back, Ian Thompson, John Roberts and 'The Beard' on the right; Fairhurst again in shades at front plus two unknown club members in the centre. 'The Beard' was from Preston, like his mate Ian Thompson. Nobody knew his real name or how he got his nickname... Eagle would portentously announce over the Tannoy: *'Ladies and gentlemen, The Beard has arrived'*!

... AND FRIENDS; BRIAN LOOKS BACK

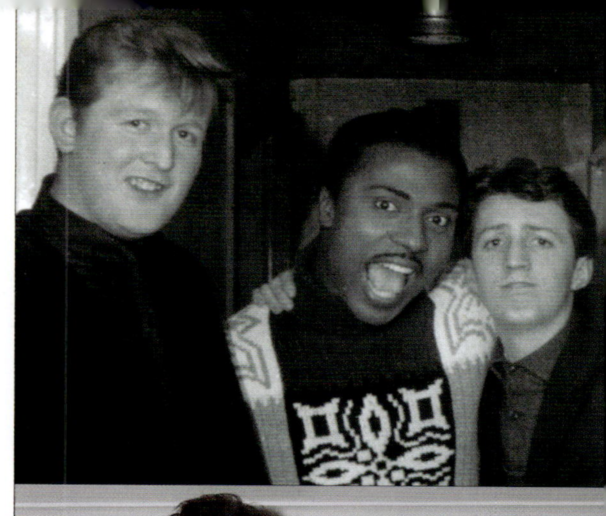

Nearly a lifetime later, it's hard to remember all the pioneering jazz and blues photographers whose work will have subliminally influenced me as a teenager (like, how an artist stands with a guitar or harmonica - and from which angle they look best when taking a photo - there is a difference!). Many photographs were uncredited at the time, but caught-up with later (*"Oh, he took that one, did he!"*) - like Alfred Wertheimer, the great Elvis Presley photographer; and Ernest Withers, who covered so many musicians working on Memphis' Beale Street. Others were later recognised in their own right, such as our own, glorious Val Wilmer and perhaps most of all, the great Ray Flerlage. All had a big impact. In 2001 I received a copy of Ray's own book via a photo editor we shared. I was unaware he knew I existed, but inside he had written: *"For Brian Smith, fellow photographer whose work I've admired for so long on jobs we shot together - although miles and years apart! Best Wishes, Ray."* It was the greatest, least expected and most moving acknowledgement I have ever had. Having processed few of my own photos once I'd left school, I was always reluctant even to call myself a 'photographer' - I take pictures, which to me is not the same thing (I've never lost the ability to "cock it up" - and have still never fully mastered digital!).

I would like to say thank-you to Mark Stratford who first put to me the idea of a collection of my photographs and his subsequent input. And to Simon Robinson, to whom Mark delegated the responsibility (or short straw!) of making it happen. And to everyone for their patience during the long period it has taken to get this finished.

I'd like to remember Roger Eagle for in effect giving me that break, and to all the people (a number of whom became long standing friends and appear in a some of the photographs here and throughout the book). Also everyone who was around back then at R 'n' B Scene magazine and the fondly remembered Twisted Wheel Club, and not forgetting The Wheel's proprietors, the Abadis.

For enabling me to get in to so many concerts, I must thank the great Johnnie Hamp for everything at Granada; Brian Bint at the Odeon; Barry Ancill for the Free Trade Hall; the formidable Peter Grant at Arden's and the City Hall gatekeeper at Sheffield Council. Not forgetting Neil Carter for ferrying me to many of the shows.

Above all, I want to thank my wife Shirley for putting up with me for so long, and her understanding on that first date so many years ago which you can read about in the preface.

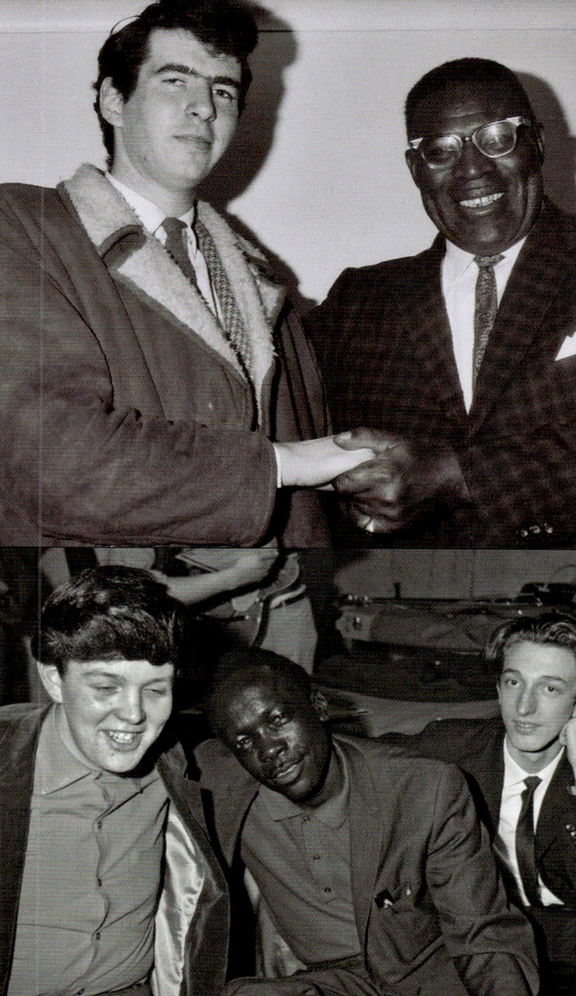

Preparing for this book inevitably sparked as much rummaging through my memories as it has endless bags and boxes of material. Despite my return to taking photographs at gigs and Blues festivals since the 1980s (for enjoyment and later for numerous magazines), it is the "museum pieces" in this book which still, for all their technical shortcomings, seem to fascinate music aficionados around the world. They continue to amaze me, turning up (sometimes even credited and every once in a while accompanied by a fee!) in magazines, biographies, CD booklets, films, television programmes, Mississippi Blues Trail Markers; even copied for street murals and as templates for tattoos and painters' portraits (and sometimes being surprised and unashamedly enjoying my own *"Oh, you took that one, did you!"* moment!). Perhaps not too bad then for a kid from a Manchester council estate - or a 'fan with a camera', as the longsuffering staff at some old Manchester venues used to call me.

Brian Smith.

Top: Little Richard with Stuart Robertson (right) and Malcolm Race (left) at Granada, November 1963 (they then snapped Brian with Richard, see page 6. Centre: Roger Eagle, his ubiquitous sheepskin jacket, and Howling Wolf. Right: John Roberts (left) and Neil Carter, R & B Scene staffers backstage with John Lee Hooker.

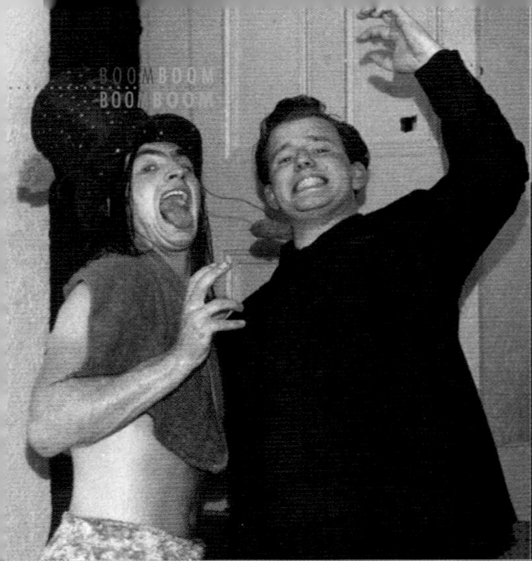

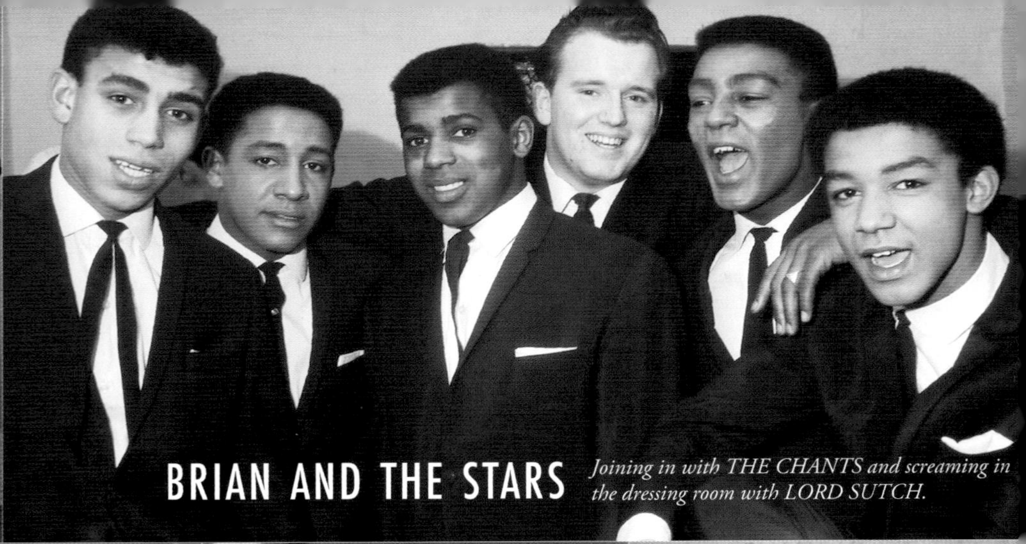

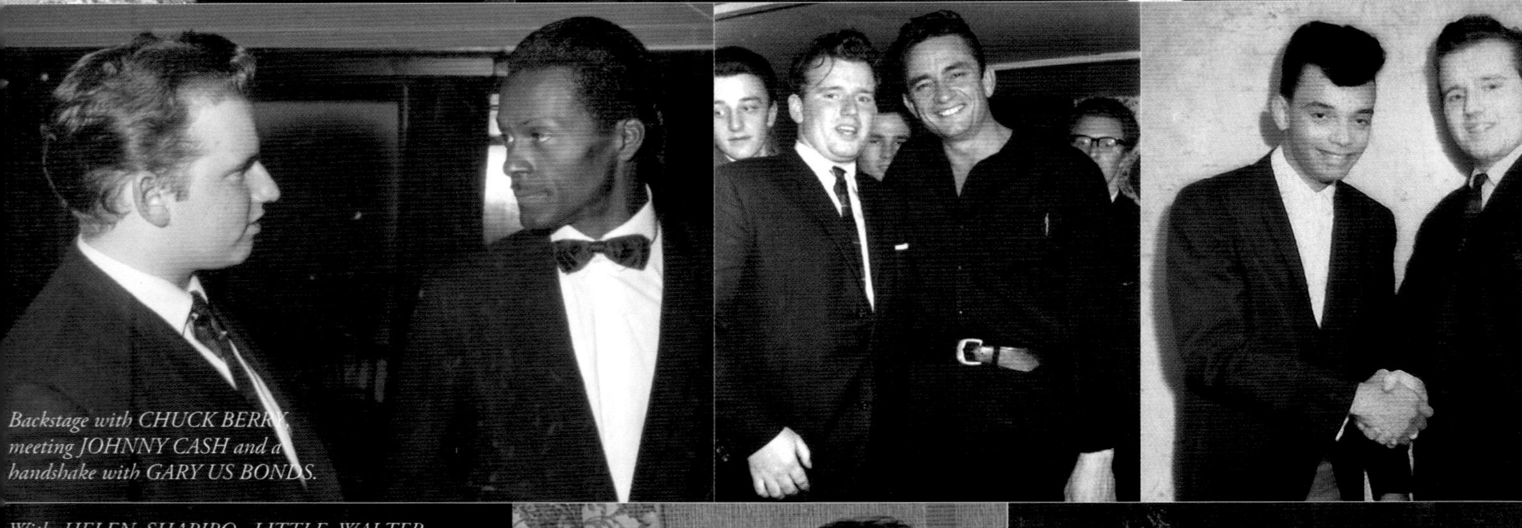

BRIAN AND THE STARS

Joining in with THE CHANTS and screaming in the dressing room with LORD SUTCH.

Backstage with CHUCK BERRY meeting JOHNNY CASH and a handshake with GARY US BONDS.

With HELEN SHAPIRO, LITTLE WALTER and CARL PERKINS.

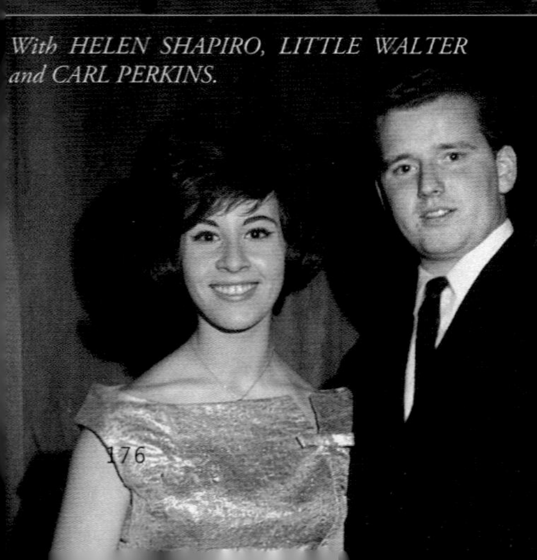

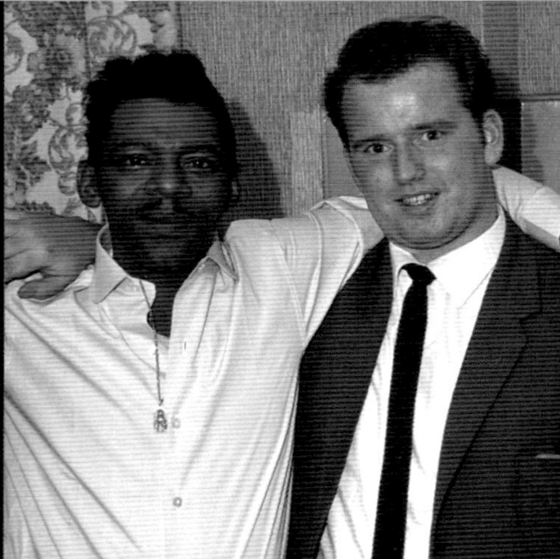

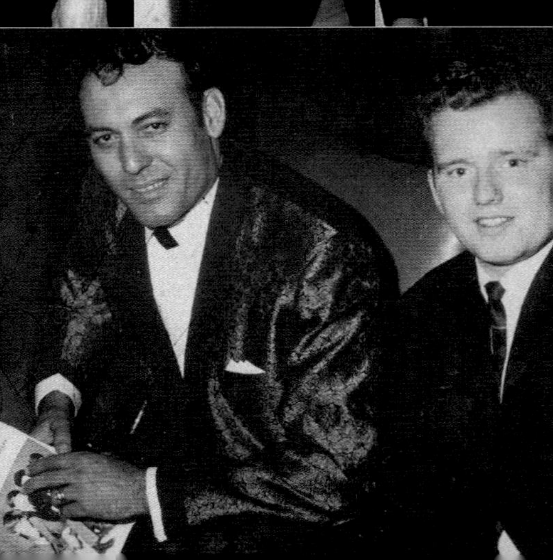

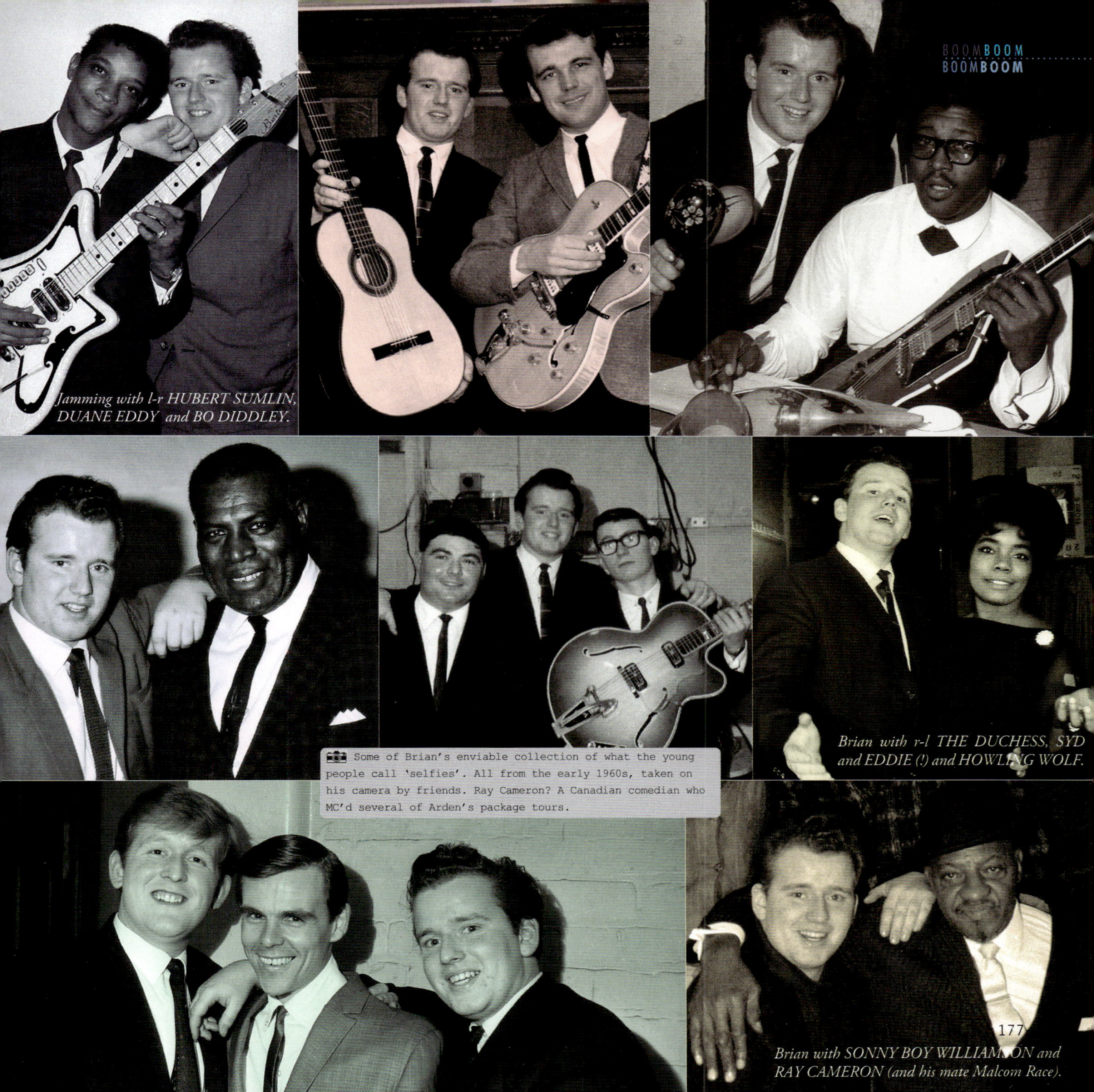

Jamming with l-r HUBERT SUMLIN,
DUANE EDDY and BO DIDDLEY.

Some of Brian's enviable collection of what the young
people call 'selfies'. All from the early 1960s, taken on
his camera by friends. Ray Cameron? A Canadian comedian who
MC'd several of Arden's package tours.

Brian with r-l THE DUCHESS, SYD
and EDDIE (!) and HOWLING WOLF.

177

Brian with SONNY BOY WILLIAMSON and
RAY CAMERON (and his mate Malcom Race).

INDEX • Text and *Photographs*

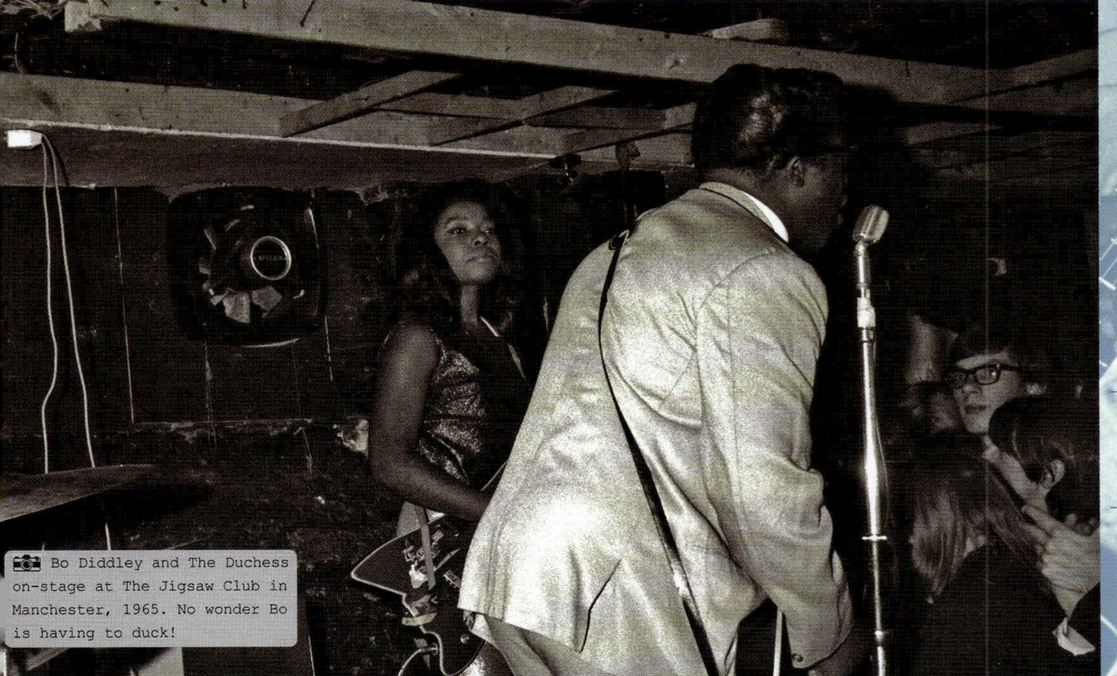

Bo Diddley and The Duchess on-stage at The Jigsaw Club in Manchester, 1965. No wonder Bo is having to duck!

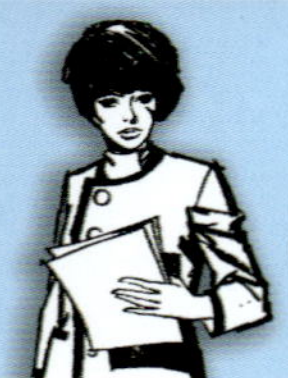

EASY ON THE EYE BOOKS • Design and artwork by Simon Robinson. Easy Books administration Ann Warburton.

Simon would like to first say thanks to *all* the staff at the Sheffield NHS Teaching Hospital who looked after him during a lengthy illness and without whom this book literally could not have been finished.

On top of that, we wish to thank Brian for his unstinting work answering hundreds of questions during the layout work. And everyone who has encouraged us over the years this book has taken to complete and for their patience. In particular to John Tucker for his eagle eyed proof reading; Steven Pollard for his continuing encouragement; Steve Harnell at Vintage Rock magazine for his numerous articles and support; Nick Robinson for his help with all things webular and the online Sheffield Music Archive; Dan at Star Books; all the helpful folk at Printworks in Sheffield. And of course Mark Stratford who kicked this all off but probably gave up waiting to see a finished copy long ago...

Finally we've lost a lot of great musicians in recent years but Simon would like to mention in particular Tony McPhee, who was kind enough to check over a proof and answer questions, and Bernie Marsden, who professed himself chuffed to see so many of the Blues greats he admired as a young kid (and some he later met) appear in the book.

MORE INFORMATION • There is a great book about the Twisted Wheel called *CENtral 1179* by Keith Rylatt and Phil Scott which tells the story of the club and the people behind it (and uses several of Brian's photographs). A BBC radio documentary on Roger Eagle's life and work as a DJ and promoter was aired in 2012 (Roger himself died aged just 56 in 1999). This is often available on the BBC Sounds site, use their search options.

Thanks to whoever ran the excellent Manchester Soul website too which was a big help. Enquiries there drew a blank and sadly the site has recently disappeared without us knowing who put it together. More about all the AFBF tours in Britain are on the Early Blues website : http://earlyblues.org/british-blues-articles-and-essays-american-blues-the-british-tours/

ONLINE • You can buy our titles direct from Easy On The Eye Books. Other recommended online retailers are Hive [https://www.hive.co.uk] and Bookshop [https://uk.bookshop.org] who both support bookshops through your purchases. Obligatory author's photograph below!

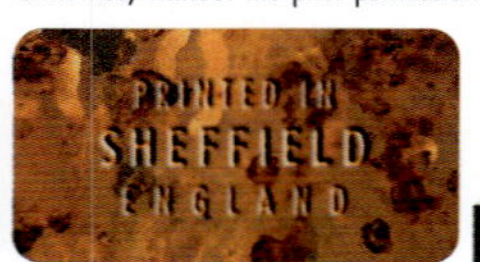

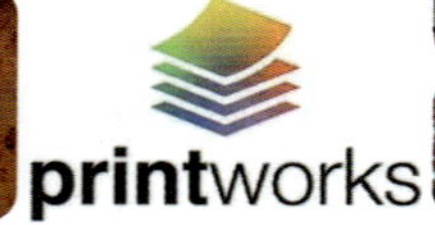

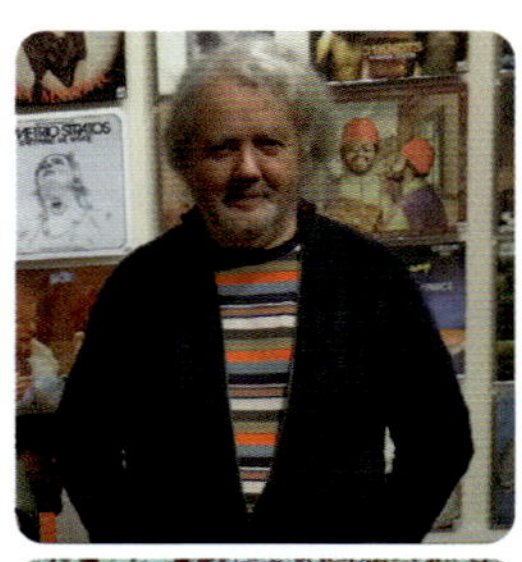

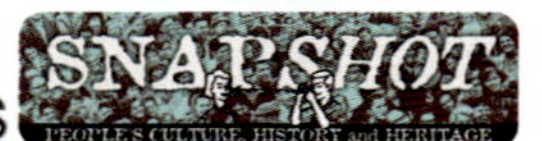

OUT NOW

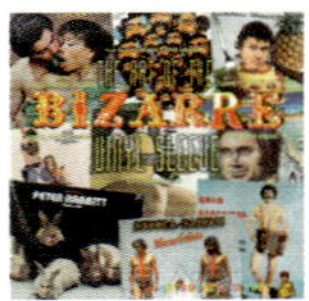

THE ART OF THE BIZARRE VINYL SLEEVE
THE WORST RECORD COVERS! • ISBN: 978-0-9955236-4-7
A brilliant look at over 300 of the strangest record sleeves of all from the Steve Goldman collection, as seen by visitors to his Worst Record Covers exhibitions across the UK, with the stories behind them and much more by Simon Robinson. A very funny book, but not for the wokerati! Forward by the great Stewart Lee.

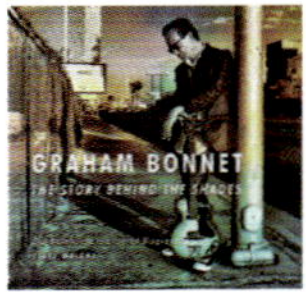

GRAHAM BONNET • THE AUTHORISED BIOGRAPHY
The Story Behind The Shades • ISBN: 978 0 9561439 7 6
Charting the career of one of rock's greatest singers, from the clubs of his hometown of Skegness, to his debut fronting Ritchie Blackmore's Rainbow on Top Of The Pops. Told by Steve Wright, who ran Graham's fanzine for many years, with loads of rare and unseen photos, gig diary, discography and more.

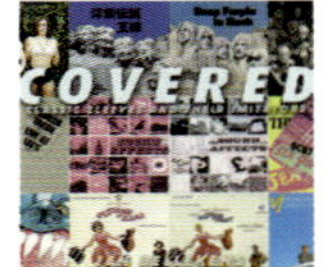

COVERED! Classic Sleeves And Their Imitators
ISBN: 978-0-9561439-2-1
The title says it all. 1,000 different sleeves shown and annotated; funny, sharp, and subversive versions of well known sleeves by bands from around the globe. Very entertaining, and very amusing!

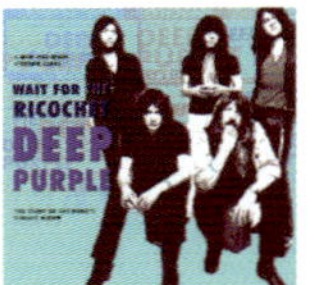

DEEP PURPLE • WAIT FOR THE RICOCHET
The Story of Deep Purple In Rock, 1969 - 1970
ISBN : 978-0-9561439-6-9
The matching title to Fire In The Sky. A detailed look at one of the most famous and hard hitting rock albums of all time, profusely illustrated, and very well reviewed by fans around the world. Second edition.

IN THE PIPELINE

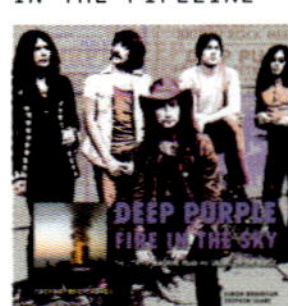

DEEP PURPLE • FIRE IN THE SKY
The Story of Machine Head and Smoke On The Water
ISBN : 978-0-9561439-9-0
Following our acclaimed first book, the story of one of the most successful rock albums and singles of all time. Beset by fire and police raids, the band ended up recording in an empty hotel corridor. Check the website for updates.

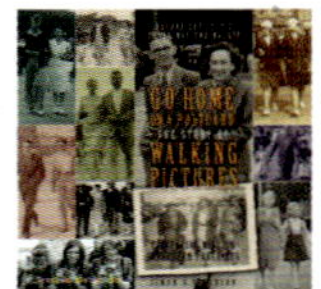

GO HOME ON A POSTCARD • The Story of Walking Pictures
ISBN : 978-0-9561439-5-2
Snapped on the promo at the seaside with your parents as a kid? These portraits began in the 1920s and now form a remarkable insight into British fashions and social history. The book has over 900 examples and also looks at the history of the trade.

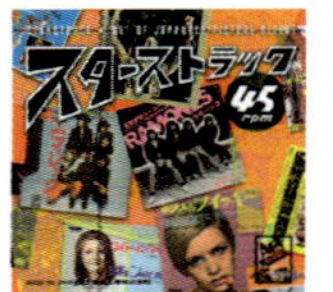

STARSTRUCK • Art of Japanese Single Sleeve
ISBN: 978-0-9561439-0-7
Japan was one of the first countries to issue vinyl singles in sleeves, and were free to do their own covers. This book presents a stunning selection of 7" covers from the 60s to the 80s, around a thousand sleeves in colour.